Medieval Russian Culture

California Slavic Studies
Series Editors

Nicholas V. Riasanovsky
Henrik Birnbaum
Robert O. Crummey
Hugh McLean
Ronald Vroon

CALIFORNIA SLAVIC STUDIES XIX

Medieval Russian Culture

VOLUME II

Edited by

Michael S. Flier and Daniel Rowland

UNIVERSITY OF CALIFORNIA PRESS

Berkeley   Los Angeles   London

University of California Press
Berkeley and Los Angeles, California

University of California Press, Ltd.
London, England

© 1994 by
The Regents of the University of California

Library of Congress Cataloging-in-Publication Data

(Revised for vol. 2)

Medieval Russian culture.

  (California Slavic studies; 12, 19)

  Vol. 2 edited by Michael S. Flier and Daniel Rowland; presents work of scholars who attended first Summer Workshop on Medieval East Slavic Culture, UCLA, 2–7 June 1990.

  Includes bibliographical references and index.

  1. Russian philology. 2. Russian S.F.S.R.—Civilization. I. Birnbaum, Henrik. II. Flier, Michael S. III. Rowland, Daniel B. (Daniel Bruce), 1941– IV. Summer Workshop on Medieval East Slavic Culture (1st : 1990 : University of California, Los Angeles) V. Series: California Slavic studies ; vol. 12, 19.

DK4.C33 no. 12 [PG2025]   306'.0947   82–23866

ISBN 0–520–08638–4

1 2 3 4 5 6 7 8 9

CONTENTS

Abbreviations   vii

Editors' Preface   ix

Acknowledgments   xi

From the Medieval Perspective
   Richard Pope   xiii

From the Modern Perspective
   James Cracraft   xvi

Textual Studies and Theories of Interpretation

Early East Slavic Literature as Sociocultural Fact
   Norman W. Ingham   3

Old Russia's "Intellectual Silence" Reconsidered
   William R. Veder   18

The *Life of Saint Filipp:* Tsar and Metropolitan in the Late Sixteenth Century
   Paul Bushkovitch   29

Fifteenth-Century Chronicles as a Source for the History of the Formation of the Muscovite State
   Jakov S. Luria   47

Determining the Authorship of the Trinity Chronicle
   Boris M. Kloss   57

Theory and Practice

Commerce and Pragmatic Literacy: The Evidence of Birchbark Documents (Mid-Eleventh to the First Quarter of Thirteenth Century) on the Early Urban Development of Novgorod
   Eduard Mühle   75

The Issue of a "Nonstandard" Translation of the Holy Scriptures in Muscovite Rus': Metropolitan Aleksij, Maksim Grek, Epifanij Slavineckij
   Olga Strakhov   93

Modeling the Genealogy of Maksim Grek's Collection Types: The "Plectogram" as Visual Aid in Reconstruction
    Hugh Olmsted   107

Early Russian Topoi of Deathbed and Testament
    Daniel E. Collins   134

Extending the Limits of the Text

Pilgrimage, Procession, and Symbolic Space in Sixteenth-Century Russian Politics
    Nancy S. Kollmann   163

Biblical Military Imagery in the Political Culture of Early Modern Russia: The Blessed Host of the Heavenly Tsar
    Daniel Rowland   182

Breaking the Code: The Image of the Tsar in the Muscovite Palm Sunday Ritual
    Michael S. Flier   213

Notes on Contributors   243

Workshop Participants   245

Name Index   247

ABBREVIATIONS

AE	*Arxeografičeskij ežegodnik*
AI	*Akty istoričeskie, sobrannye i izdannye Arxeografičeskoju kommissieju*
ASob	*Akty, sobrannye v bibliotekax i arxivax Rossijskoj Imperii Arxeografičeskoj èkspediciej Imperatorskoj Akademii nauk*
AN	Akademija nauk (Academy of Sciences)
BAN	Biblioteka Akademii nauk, St. Petersburg
ByzSl	*Byzantinoslavica*
BZ	*Byzantinische Zeitschrift*
CGADA	*Central'nyj Gosudarstvennyj Arxiv drevnix aktov*
ČNT	*Čudov New Testament*
ČOIDR	*Čtenija v Imperatorskom Obščestve istorii i drevnostej rossijskix pri Moskovskom universitete*
GBL	Gosudarstvennaja Biblioteka im. V. I. Lenina (State Lenin Library, now Rossijskaja Gosudarstvennaja Biblioteka), Moscow
GIM	Gosudarstvennyj istoričeskij muzej (State Historical Museum), Moscow
GPB	Gosudarstvennaja publičnaia biblioteka im. M. E. Saltykova-Ščedrina (State Saltykov-Ščedrin Public Library, now Rossijskaja Nacional'naja Biblioteka), St. Petersburg
IORJaS	*Izvestija Otdelenija russkogo jazyka i slovesnosti Imperatorskoj Akademii nauk*, St. Petersburg
IJSLP	*International Journal of Slavic Linguistics and Poetics*
Ioasaf	*Ioasafovskaja letopis'*, ed. A. A. Zimin (Moscow, 1957)
NPL	*Novgorodskaja pervaja letopis'*, ed. A. S. Nasonov (Moscow, 1950)
OIDR	Obščestvo istorii i drevnostej rossijskix (Society of Russian History and Antiquities), Moscow
ORRK	*Otdel rukopisej i redkix knig*
PL	*Patrologia Latina* (Migne)
PG	*Patrologia Graeca* (Migne)
PSRL	*Polnoe sobranie russkix letopisej*, 38 vols. (Moscow and St. Petersburg, 1841–)
RFV	*Russkij filologičeskii vestnik*
RK	*Razrjadnaja kniga 1475-1598 gg.*, ed. V. I. Buganov (Moscow, 1966)

RR	*Russian Review*
SbORJaS	*Sbornik Otdelenija russkogo jazyka i slovesnosti*
SEEJ	*Slavic and East European Journal*
SR	*Slavic Review*
TODRL	*Trudy Otdela drevnerusskoj literatury*
VJa	*Voprosy jazykoznanija*

EDITORS' PREFACE

This second volume of *Medieval Russian Culture* presents the work of scholars who attended the first Summer Workshop on Medieval East Slavic Culture. Held at UCLA, 2–7 June 1990, and supported by a grant from the Mellon Foundation, the workshop was sponsored by the Joint Committee on Soviet Studies of the Social Science Research Council and the American Council of Learned Societies, and by the UCLA Center for Medieval and Renaissance Studies. Its primary goals were to promote the interdisciplinary analysis of early East Slavic culture in its sociopolitical context and to encourage the involvement of younger scholars in the field. From the beginning the organizers stressed the coordination of traditionally discrete approaches to the medieval text: philological, art historical, musicological, critical-theoretical, historical.

The Program Committee comprised Michael Flier (Harvard), Gail Lenhoff (UCLA), Robert Mathiesen (Brown), Daniel Rowland (Kentucky), and Nancy Kollmann (Stanford), who devoted considerable time and energy to securing sponsorship for the workshop and served as committee chair. The committee sought to provide a broad field of inquiry while keeping the number of participants small. It solicited advice from senior scholars across the United States concerning those areas of medieval East Slavic scholarship in greatest need of attention and reevaluation. The strong response was an indication that an integrative conference like that envisioned for the workshop was long overdue.

Twenty senior scholars and specialists were invited to present papers or serve as discussion leaders. Eight younger scholars, some of whom presented papers as well, were selected through an international competition. The workshop participants were from Canada, Denmark, Germany, the Netherlands, the Soviet Union, and the United States. All distributed their papers in advance so that most of the conference could be devoted primarily to discussion. All authors had the opportunity to revise their contributions for the present volume.

The conference concluded with general remarks from the perspectives of Richard Pope (York), a medievalist, and James Cracraft (Illinois at Chicago), a modern Russian historian. Their particular views on the papers and discussion, included in the present volume, highlight those areas of medieval

East Slavic culture that appear amenable to reanalysis and integration and those that prove more intractable. The great strength of the workshop was its commitment to considering theory and practice, to expanding the traditional definitions of "texts," and to exercising judiciousness in the analysis of all materials. As a note of caution, there was universal recognition that East Slavic had been too often construed as Russian, and that the Belarusian and Ukrainian components of East Slavic culture were equally in need of reassessment and inclusion, if a more comprehensive understanding of that culture were to be achieved. Future workshops will be obliged to take this counsel seriously.

In 1984, a collection of articles by senior specialists entitled *Medieval Russian Culture* was published. Intended for a conference that unfortunately never took place, these articles were dedicated to Dmitrii Likhachev. Since a number of themes treated in that volume were continued and developed among the papers at the 1990 workshop, the organizers considered the present volume a fitting supplement to that worthy predecessor and submitted the manuscript to the University of California Press as *Medieval Russian Culture, II*. We are hopeful that the ideas presented here will contribute to the current revival of medieval Slavic studies, thereby bringing new talent, energy, and insight to our common enterprise.

Michael S. Flier
Cambridge, Massachusetts

Daniel Rowland
Lexington, Kentucky

ACKNOWLEDGMENTS

No undertaking as large as the Summer Workshop for Medieval East Slavic Culture would have been possible without the help and encouragement of many institutions and individuals. We are extremely grateful to the Mellon Foundation whose generous grant made the workshop a reality. The support of the Social Science Research Council was constant at every stage of planning and execution. We wish to single out Loren Graham, chair of the Joint Committee on Soviet Studies of the Social Science Research Council; Blair Ruble and Robert Huber, program officers; and Kathryn Becker, staff associate. All are from the Social Science Research Council.

We wish to acknowledge the enthusiastic support of the UCLA administration, particularly, Herbert Morris, dean of the Division of Humanities of the College of Letters and Science. Henrik Birnbaum, chair of the Department of Slavic Languages and Literatures, was most generous with his time and energy. The Center for Medieval and Renaissance Studies at UCLA was actively involved in all the local arrangements and deserves our utmost gratitude. We especially want to thank Michael Allen, director; Susanne Kahle, assistant to the director; and Pegeen Connolly, project assistant. All were tireless in their efforts to ensure that every plan involving rooms, food, transportation, finances, and entertainment was carried out to perfection. We also wish to express our appreciation to Slavic Department students Lori Ruth and Stephen Weissman, who helped to make the everyday operation of the workshop run more smoothly. We take this opportunity to thank all the scholars who provided their written opinions on what the workshop should be, and to all the participants, whose cooperation and energetic engagement made the workshop a lively and stimulating forum of ideas. Gail Lenhoff and Michael Flier shared responsibilities as co-directors of the workshop.

The labors of assembling and editing the collected papers from the workshop inevitably resulted in the transfer of the manuscript into the expert hands of our copyeditor and composer. Our thanks to G. Patton Wright of Cambridge Wordwright for his superlative job of copyediting an extremely difficult text with many unforeseen problems that required the utmost patience, diligence, and ingenuity every step of the way. We also salute Gareth Perkins for converting a heavily edited text into beautiful camera-ready copy in a short period of time.

We are indebted to Nancy Kollmann for first developing the idea of a workshop on medieval East Slavic culture and then devoting the requisite time and energy to stimulate interest among her colleagues and put together a written proposal that convinced a committee with many calls on its resources to offer support. Without her strong leadership, the workshop would not have occurred. Let us hope that it will be the first of many.

M.S.F.
D.R.

FROM THE MEDIEVAL PERSPECTIVE

RICHARD POPE

The purview of this volume is broad and includes aspects of medieval East Slavic culture ranging from birchbark documents and political rituals to biblical texts and icons. The aim of the volume as a whole is not just to focus attention on any one particular problem or area of culture but rather, in true medieval spirit, to be broad and eclectic, to open our focus on the period, to be synthetic; hence the presence of papers on such diverse subjects as language, literature, history, politics, the visual arts, and music. The interdisciplinary nature of this volume can be seen both in the breadth of its contents and in the coordination of traditionally discrete approaches reflected in many of the articles such as, for example, the two by Flier and Rowland, which rely heavily on visual art to illuminate pragmatic political reality. This volume illustrates how fruitful—and even necessary—the interdisciplinary approach is in studies of medieval East Slavic culture.

A number of papers in this volume tackle problems related to the interpretation of that culture's products—verbal, visual, and musical. The triad of closely related papers by Flier, Kollmann, and Rowland grapples with the problem of how to interpret medieval ritual and ritual art: what exactly *is* the relationship between ritual and reality? This is a key question when one studies a culture so ritualized as that of the early East Slavs. The paper by Bushkovitch is a theoretical, speculative one stressing the need to approach, read, and ultimately interpret texts without preconceptions. The paper by Luria underscores the need to question the authenticity, validity, and motivation of all texts before any interpretation is attempted.

Another group of papers focuses on the sociopolitical context of various aspects of East Slavic culture and strives to understand the interaction of culture with economics, politics, and other social realities of the times. Ingham's paper confronts the problem of whether literature or verbal art as such existed in the medieval period, and if it did, whether it was perceived as art by members of the society or was simply seen as fulfilling some pragmatic function. The papers by Collins and Mühle, which examine last testaments and birchbark documents respectively, attempt to make sense of and wrest meaning from the documents in light of social and commercial demands of the day.

A concern for method is reflected in many of the papers in the volume. Bushkovitch's paper offers a methodology of reading complete with rules. Concerned with the method behind their materials, both Ingham and Veder elaborate principles that allow one to make sense of the methods in question. Ingham argues for the principle of portability, whereas Veder discusses randomness. Olmsted describes a useful codicological tool for inserting some method into the madness of the almost inscrutable genealogy of so many East Slavic texts.

The papers reveal a number of strengths of the volume as a whole. Perhaps the foremost is the insistent stress on the fundamental importance of primary sources—particularly important in an area like early East Slavic culture where secondary sources can be few and unsatisfactory. The need to grapple with the sources and the advantages to be gained from so doing are clear in all the papers. The authority of Kloss's paper derives from the fact that he scrutinized manuscript sources and did his own work and thinking right from the start. The authority of Luria's and Veder's papers derives both from their return to the originals—chronicles and reading miscellanies, respectively—and their careful and exhaustive reading of the texts before making the leap to the speculative. Collins's paper reflects an exhaustive search of lesser-known saints' lives in his hunt for wills. Mühle's paper results from a return to the original documents and a fresh reading in an attempt to ascertain what the sources really say. One again thinks of Bushkovitch's paper with its stress on how to read sources. Thus in this volume as a whole we see the interest in sources reflected in the frequent return to originals, in the call for unprejudiced reading of primary sources, and in the cautions to approach such sources circumspectly, all of which represent a certain healthy iconoclasm in the refusal to rely merely on secondary sources and accepted wisdom.

A second strength of the papers in this volume viewed collectively is the painstaking and exhaustive care of the researchers. Kollmann obviously went over all the pertinent chronicles, culling from them examples of ritual. Looking at necrologies and wills, Collins inferred attitudes about hagiography. After examining all available secondary sources and accepted primary sources, Flier went on to search for new sources to help break the code of the Palm Sunday ritual. Olmsted's application of the plectogram to the genealogy of Maksim Grek manuscripts is an excellent example of how dramatic results can be wrung from perplexing material if only one is not deterred by time-consuming work that carries no guarantee of success.

A last notable characteristic of the volume is its attention to the Bible, the Church, and the medieval religious tradition as a whole. The pervasiveness of the Orthodox tradition in much of medieval East Slavic culture is, of course, something that must be reckoned with and appraised. Religion holds many of the keys to the semiotics of this culture, a fact that has not been overlooked in the present volume. Strakhov's paper, for example, deals with the Church Slavic Bible itself, examining hellenizing trends in Church Slavic biblical translation. Flier and Rowland study Orthodox visual art, seeking clues to myths and rituals of sociopolitical importance; Kollmann reads traditional sources in a new light to reveal political notions of time and space. Indeed the materials studied in nearly all the papers are of ecclesiastical or monastic provenance. It would seem that Bushkovitch's wish for more attention to church and religious history has been fulfilled here.

If among the strengths of this volume we include its orientation toward primary sources, the exhaustive care of the researchers, and the attention to the religious tradition, we could perhaps say that one area (leaving aside the folk-secular-prosaic tradition, which is the subject of a different kind of volume) that seems unrepresented is the contiguity of much of East Slavic culture with Byzantine Greek culture—a reality that perhaps figured too largely in the work of nineteenth-century philologists but is perhaps underestimated now. Although this situation is partly redressed by the papers of Flier and Strakhov, the examination of Greek archetypes and analogues of East Slavic verbal and visual sources would deepen and strengthen the conclusions of some of the other papers.

In concert with this volume's interest in sources, it is fitting to conclude these comments with an appeal to all scholars of the field to publish their sources whenever possible. Not to publish one's sources is, as William Veder puts it, contempt of criticism. Publication of sources is one of the most important directions for future work in this field. Long studies of unpublished materials are less acceptable now that technology has caught up with the demands of Cyrillic source publication. The obvious benefits of primary source study so clearly revealed in this volume force us to recognize our obligation to make available as much manuscript material as possible as quickly as possible.

FROM THE MODERN PERSPECTIVE

JAMES CRACRAFT

To attend the workshop that gave rise to this book was to experience the discourse of a sizable roomful of specialists from the United States, Europe, and the Soviet Union as they ranged unreservedly, not to say volubly, in both English and Russian, over the accumulated stock of East Slavic cultural history. It was a singular experience, one that lasted for several days, in the magical ambit of UCLA; and it was, to be sure, another instance of the unprecedented degree to which, thanks to developments in eastern Europe and the Soviet Union associated with the words *glasnost'* and *perestroika,* the Slavic past has been opened—or reopened—to free scholarly inquiry. Indeed our colleague from Leningrad suggested, in his final intervention, that in future such prolonged and concentrated exchange could only benefit the field as a whole. The point was reiterated by virtually all of the other participants, formally or informally, before the workshop was adjourned.

My own position in the workshop was that of a modern Russian historian whose more specialized work in the era of Peter the Great had mired me on occasion in the kind of textual problems familiar to specialists in earlier Russian or East Slavic literary culture. It was also the position of a general historian who has worked from time to time in the conventionally separate or parallel disciplines of literary, art, and architectural history. From this somewhat indeterminate perspective I was asked to comment at the workshop's conclusion on its daunting progression of papers, discussion, and debate.

I had thought, as the march proceeded, that the situation today of East Slavic specialists might resemble in significant respects that of scholars in some distant future who were attempting to interpret contemporary American culture on the basis of sundry movies, fragmentary though the evidence would be and frequently obscure in origin. No projector will have survived, to make the faded images come alive; sound tracks equally will have been lost, leaving specialists to speculate about the films' aural dimension; and most scholars, products themselves of a highly literate culture, will have concentrated their efforts on the films' credits, subtitles, and other written components, whence a few general yet enduringly controversial conclusions will have been drawn (e.g., that the subject culture was, in some measure, both literate and melodramatic). But I soon realized that my analogy, limping badly from the outset and induced, perhaps, by the enveloping aura of Los Angeles, was only the manifest content of an underlying, possibly occupational, unease.

I must come clean. To my mind the workshop's attention to questions concerning the authenticity, veracity, and meaning of selected literary monuments, stimulating and often enlightening as it was, appeared, at times, preemptive—and with two general results. Relatively technical matters of genre, prototype, convoy, textual interrelation and the like tended to extrude from discussion the larger problems of periodization, of cross-cultural or cross-temporal comparison, and of economic or social, even political, history. Similarly, the concentration on certain literary texts—typically chronicles or saints' lives—tended to exclude from consideration those aspects of the East Slavic past which may be more readily accessible from the evidence offered, say, by architectural or pictorial monuments. In this, it may well be, the workshop only faithfully reflected the overall state of the field. Yet equally regrettable was the absence of an archaeological perspective, which might have reminded the assembled "documentary historians" of the advances that have been made, both historiographical and substantive, by medieval (*medieval*, not prehistoric) archaeologists working in eastern as well as western Europe.[1]

Nevertheless, the workshop's lively discussion of participants' papers frequently raised points that seemed both fresh and worth recording. Several speakers agreed in insisting on the primarily religious meaning of expressly religious texts—whatever further interpretations scholars might wish to add to it. A call was made for the full-scale study of the history of the Bible in East Slavic culture. Other participants elaborated on the question of literacy in this historical context: how widespread was it in society, and among which classes? And more, what does the term really mean when applied to the old East Slavic scribes and their readers?[2] It was suggested that "ran-

---

[1] Cf. D. Austin and L. Alcock, eds., *From the Baltic to the Black Sea: Studies in Medieval Archaeology* (London and Boston, 1990).

[2] See, coincidentally, G. Marker, "Literacy and Literacy Tests in Muscovy: A Reconsideration," *SR* 49 (Spring 1990): 74-89, for further discussion of the problem, but limited here to printed books and later periods. By Marker's admittedly quite speculative calculations, even late seventeenth-century Muscovy seems to have been "a profoundly illiterate society [rudimentary literacy among no more than five percent of total population] in which reading was the privilege of a few [from one percent to two percent of the total population] and writing the domain of a tiny minority" (89).

domization" in the arrangement of texts with attendant incoherence was a basic principle of East Slavic book culture; that the (sacred) text functioned there much less as a conveyor of information (as in Roman Catholic Europe) than as a kind of mnemonic device, prompting the reader's own meditations; and that the (sacred) text or book itself, the physical object, was accorded iconic significance and "read" (revered) accordingly. One or two discussants, inspired tangentially by still other papers, pleaded the cause of the holy images: those thousands of surviving wall paintings and portable panel icons—more numerous, at times far more numerous than the contemporary written texts—which might be at least equally serviceable as sources of East Slavic theology, political ideology, or moral and aesthetic values. But this was not, to repeat, a popular cause. To the general indifference skeptics added problems of dating, attribution, provenance, and iconography that were at least as serious, they contended, as the parallel or similar problems facing students of the written texts.

In fact, an air of skepticism, no less pungent for being so familiar, haunted the workshop. Colleagues were gently admonished to beware of "idealizing" their sources, perhaps out of misplaced religious enthusiasm. Textual interpretation of almost any kind was equated with "speculation" and politely denounced. A kind of Cartesian doubt, universal in its scope and quest for mathematical certainty, was invoked. It began to seem that any firm understanding particularly of earlier East Slavic culture had to await the often tentative results of an apparently endless series of fontological exercises. At one moment, indeed, the purpose of the workshop itself seemed in doubt. Sensible reminders of the universal assumptions and methods of historical scholarship soon brought us back to earth.[3] Yet the basic point remained. Unblinking skepticism regarding the accumulated *dicta* and *data* of East Slavic cultural history is both necessary and appropriate, especially in this dawning new age of *glasnost'* and *perestroika*.

In still another matter, the workshop was enjoined by invited outside experts to profit as best its participants could from certain advances in computerized archaeography, and humanists generally were chided for their supposed "technophobia." With respect to this gathering, it may be reassuring to report, the reproof was largely groundless, the injunction unneeded. Several papers gave ample evidence of, or references to, a recent "revolution"

---

[3] Cf. K. R. Popper, *The Spell of Plato*, 5th ed., rev. (Princeton, 1971): ". . . the tests of an historical interpretation can never be as rigorous as those of an ordinary [scientific] hypothesis. The [historical] interpretation is mainly a *point of view*, whose value lies in its fertility, in its power to throw light upon the historical material, to lead us to find new material, and to help us to rationalize and to unify it" (171).

in source-study that reflects a number of new technological approaches. Indeed, it seemed to some participants that medievalists everywhere were succumbing, if anything, to a kind of technophilia, even technomania, in their search for solutions to hitherto intractable problems. In this view, the revolution in question appeared to imply two equal but opposite outcomes: first, that some good or better answers to important historical questions about the dating, composition, and actual texts of old East Slavic manuscripts would be forthcoming; second, that some further disintegration of the field into career-consuming specialties was in the making.

Questions concerning the health of our ruling paradigms (or "sets of assumptions," as one participant preferred to say) also surfaced in the workshop. Here the basic worry seemed to be that too much was still being borrowed from mainstream European (or western European, or Western) cultural history. How, it was asked, can we speak of earlier East Slavic written memorials as "literature"? What is "medieval" about these or other monuments of this culture? What can be meant by the terms "nation," "national," or "nationality" as applied to the East Slavic world of any period between the tenth and the seventeenth centuries? From a general historical perspective, it was asserted, that world looked decidedly different from the world of medieval (western) Europe or from that which ensued in Russia from the time of Peter the Great—a matter as much of the types and volume of sources available as of their literal, figurative, or functional content. It was suggested, further, that in approaching East Slavic history even of the later centuries we look for comparative models to the Carolingian as well as the Byzantine worlds, and to historical anthropology (e.g., the work of M. D. Sahlins). Yet no consensus emerged from the workshop in this area—so fixed, it seemed, were the paradigms of (western) European historiography. In this regard, it might be significant *ex silentio* that questions concerning the application of Marxist paradigms never arose.

In short, one came away from the workshop at once wary and refreshed: newly wary when looking down the trodden paths of East Slavic cultural history, yet refreshed by the prospect of new or better solutions to both old and new problems. I have concentrated in these brief remarks on some of the more general points made in the workshop. But the papers themselves were the main course—food for everyone's thought, grist for the skeptics' mill—just as they now make up, variously revised, the solid stuff of this book. I feel certain that readers, similarly wary and refreshed, will be grateful to its authors.

TEXTUAL STUDIES AND
THEORIES OF INTERPRETATION

EARLY EAST SLAVIC LITERATURE AS SOCIOCULTURAL FACT

NORMAN W. INGHAM

The ontological status of literature in Old Rus' has occasionally been questioned but seldom directly examined; discussions typically concentrate on the problem of determining which writings belong to literature and which do not.[1] Soviet and other literary historians usually take for granted that such a thing as literature existed in early East Slavic culture, that it is still more or less accessible to us, and that it can be discussed as a whole as well as in its individual parts (writings). We speak habitually of early East Slavic or "Old Russian" (Rusian) literature and of literary works, genres, and styles. Textbooks perpetuate this notion of a literature and effectively set up a canon. Indeed, for most purposes of modern readers, including scholars and students, there is no practical problem about regarding a certain core of early writings as literary. To many readers who accept the literature intuitively, a debate about the propriety of recognizing it must seem excessively academic.

Yet those of us who trouble ourselves with matters of fundamental principle have to take seriously the skepticism heard from time to time. If we wish to maintain the idea of literature in Old Rus', we must respond to those thoughtful scholars who claim that this was not truly *literature*—at least not in any sense of the word as we understand it today.[2] Unless the doubts on this score can be laid to rest, how is a "professor of medieval literature" to justify his calling? Am I really professing literature, or something else under

---

I am grateful to several colleagues whose astute comments have been helpful to me at various stages in developing this theoretical statement, and particularly to Gary Saul Morson, Edward Stankiewicz, and William R. Veder. My formulations in the article may, of course, differ from their views.

[1] Even the late Jan M. Meijer, in his relevant article, "The Limits of Literature in Old-Russian Literature" in *Poetyka i stylistyka słowiańska* (Wrocław, 1973), 137-44, was less concerned with the concept of literature as such than with finding criteria for telling literary texts from nonliterary ones.

[2] The present effort is in large measure motivated by and intended as a reply to the stated positions of my colleagues and friends Klaus-Dieter Seemann and Gail Lenhoff. See our collective work, "Forum: The Problem of Old Russian Genres," *SEEJ* 31 (1987): 234-79; hereafter cited as "Forum." I promised there (236) to defend the concept of literature at another time.

the guise of literature? Is this one of those old "paradigms" (conventional but anachronistic sets of assumptions) that ought to be discarded in favor of new ways of looking at premodern Rus'?

Any answer to the question about "literature" will depend not only on our perception of the writings in and of themselves but on how we conceive of their relationship to the cultural system and subsystems of the time. Some of my colleagues seem to think that the close ties of medieval East Slavic writings to pragmatic uses virtually disqualify them as literature. My own view is that literature is always, in all eras, in one degree or another a sociocultural fact and that literature could exist in medieval East Slavic culture, yet play the practical societal role that we all recognize for it. Indeed, the very literary nature of writing probably should not be regarded as secondary or external to its function in society but, on the contrary, it should be viewed as a qualification for it. I would argue that literature was itself an important sociocultural fact in Old Rus'.

What follows is an account of my current thinking about the central questions, along with a few preliminary theses. Proceeding from a functional definition of literature, I will offer arguments why some of early East Slavic writing should be regarded as literature, not only in our retrospective view but also in the practice of its contemporaries. Of necessity, I will touch upon questions of function-theory and literary canon, but these will need more detailed attention on another occasion.

At the outset I intentionally ask, "Was there literature in Old Rus'?" and not, "Was there *a* literature?" Certainly there was not *a* literature if by that we mean, as in our time, a body of creative writings conceived of by contemporaries as separate from practical writings and serving predominantly an aesthetic or entertainment function. It requires no particular proof that literate people in Rus' of the eleventh century through at least the fifteenth (and these centuries are the maximum limits of my discussion) lacked the conception of such an art-literature (*xudožestvennaja literatura*). For that matter, as K.-D. Seemann reminds us, the distinction was not fully accepted in Europe before the eighteenth.[3] One consequence is that if we are determined to speak of *a* medieval East Slavic literature, we will have the serious practical problem of establishing its canon—that is, of determining which compositions should be included. For the moment, however, my concern is

---

[3] Seemann, "Genres and the Alterity of Old Russian Literature," in "Forum" (see n. 2), 246.

with literature as a general concept and not with literature as a separate corpus or realm.

What is literature? That is probably the hardest question of all—and the answer must be carefully considered—because it will necessarily be crucial to all other considerations. Very possibly the whole debate about the existence of medieval literature can be traced to disagreements about what literature is in the first place. I cannot critically review here the entire scholarly dispute over the definition of literature, as that would require prefacing my article with a book; I must, however, state my own position succinctly.

I think we may brand inadequate those commonly seen definitions based wholly on style, aesthetic pleasure, fictionality, or the like. These are too narrow and/or too vague to delimit literature as a universal category, although they may be helpful for purely descriptive purposes. Many scholars and critics seem to think that fictionality is the essential criterion because they view creative imagination as a *sine qua non* of literature. This is no doubt a throwback to the Romantics' emphasis on creativity. Somewhat similarly, the Russian Formalists' concept of literariness (*literaturnost'*) puts a premium on inventiveness.[4] Soviet literary historians have pointed to a "belletristic" tendency in the early period, that is, the creative development of story (*sjužetnoe povestvovanie*), as one evidence of literature.[5]

While these suggestions may be helpful as partial *descriptions,* they cannot serve as *definitions* since none embraces everything which is conventionally considered literature. Neither fictionality nor *belletričnost'* has ever been a universal requirement of literature. In our time, some works of biography, historiography, and even journalism and private letters are by consensus included in the canon of literature. Although we may perhaps sympathize with Wellek and Warren in their wish to limit literature proper to "imaginative literature,"[6] this will not do as a universally valid and logical definition. We must keep in mind that describing and defining are different things. It is seldom if ever possible to arrive at a proper definition of a large conven-

---

[4] See Edward Stankiewicz's pertinent remarks on this and related matters in his "Poetics and Verbal Art," in *A Perfusion of Signs,* ed. T. A. Sebeok (Bloomington, 1977), 56.

[5] This approach is best represented by the book *Istoki russkoi belletristiki* (Leningrad, 1970). See also L. A. Dmitriev, *Žitijnye povesti russkogo severa kak pamjatniki literatury XIII-XVII vv.: Èvoljucija žanra legendarno-biografičeskix skazanij* (Leningrad, 1973). Valuable comments on *belletričnost'* were made by Richard W. F. Pope, "On the Comparative Literary Analysis of the Patericon Story (Translated and Original) in the Pre-Mongol Period," in *Canadian Contributions to the VIII International Congress of Slavists,* ed. Z. Folejewski (Ottawa, 1978), 1-23, esp. p. 4. My only disagreement with Pope is that literature need not be limited to imaginative (fictional) writing.

[6] René Wellek and Austin Warren, *Theory of Literature,* 3d ed. (New York, 1956), 22.

tional category like literature through description of the things that may make it up. Even if we were able to characterize exhaustively all variants that exist or might potentially exist (an obvious impossibility), we would end up with a vast number of individual descriptions and no definition of the category.

For a definition, I think we must in the end fall back on *function*. The best that I have seen is that of John Ellis, who defines literature as writing valued separately from any practical function it may have.[7] We regard as literature pieces of writing that are worth reading in themselves and not only for the sake of some routine purpose. Thus, for example, even an essay written for journalistic use may come to be regarded as literature if it is found to have value apart from its original function, that is, to be worth reading outside its original context. The same is true of historical and biographical compositions. Of course, the definition does not seek to tell us *why* certain compositions are valued in themselves; and here there is still ample scope for attempts to *describe* the kinds of qualities that may win writings some recognition as literature—even though such characterizations seem doomed to incompleteness. The fact is that we are dealing with a social convention: those works are literature which a consensus of readers regards as fulfilling the function of literature.[8]

In its separability from practical application, literature differs from ephemeral writing and from documents, which are normally not read except in their original function. Documents may be copied or quoted elsewhere, but usually for their *documentary value,* that is, for the information or legal act which they embody. We might turn to the East Slavic *Primary Chronicle* (*Povest' vremennyx let*) for examples. Its compilers no doubt chose and included entries mainly with the purpose of recording history. We modern

---

[7] John M. Ellis, *The Theory of Literary Criticism: A Logical Analysis* (Berkeley, 1974), 44: "... literary texts are defined as those that are used by the society in such a way that *the text is not taken as specifically relevant to the immediate context of its origin.*"

[8] There is no doubt that works recognized as literature all have some inherent qualities that motivate this perception; the problem is, rather, that potential literary qualities cannot be reduced to a simple formula. For example, Meijer's proposal that "a text belongs to literature if in it an aesthetic and a cognitive structure are in interference" ("The Limits" [see n. 1], 138) is too mechanical and is unlikely to provide a sure guide for predicting which works will meet the standards of literature and which will not. In 1958, I. P. Eremin listed various attempts to identify the "artistic" basis of the early literature and dismissed them as inadequate; see his "O xudožestvennoj specifike drevnerusskoj literatury," reprinted in his *Literatura drevnej Rusi (Ètjudy i xarakteristiki)* (Moscow and Leningrad, 1966), 245. See also a review of scholarship in Wolf-Heinrich Schmidt and Klaus-Dieter Seemann, "Einleitung: Die Gattungsforschung und die alteren slavischen Literaturen," in *Gattungsprobleme der älteren slavischen Literaturen,* ed. Wolf-Heinrich Schmidt (Berlin, 1984), 13-32.

readers, by contrast, may consider the etiological legends in the early parts of the chronicle as literature: things worth reading even if we seriously doubt their value as historical records. (It seems likely that contemporaries also enjoyed these passages for other than antiquarian interest, but it would be hard to prove.) Meanwhile, we probably regard the treaties with the Greeks as documents of historical interest only; and these we would not be inclined to anthologize as "literature."

Next, it is important to remember that works, in order to be literature, do not have to be completely free of any pragmatic function; they only have to be assigned a value in themselves beyond their pragmatic use. To put it another way, a literary work is not "exhausted" by the practical applications it may have.[9] We must also keep in mind that such functions are not necessarily inimical to literature and need not be branded "extraliterary."[10] For example, a frequent purpose of writings, including some entries in the *Primary Chronicle*, was didactic, and a moral message might be one element that would make the work valued by readers apart from the pragmatic (in this case annalistic) function. My concern will be precisely to show that early East Slavic writings—those which some of us boldly call literary—were not "exhausted" by any practical use that they were initially created to serve, and, moreover, that their original purposes did not disqualify them as literature.[11]

One important consequence of what has been said is that the identification of literary works can be retrospective. The author's intentions (the way he viewed his own writings at the time, and the function he assigned to it) is not decisive in whether his contemporaries or later generations consider it literature. Furthermore, each subsequent period may and does revise an earlier canon according to its own taste and judgment, in a process that goes on today even for literature of the nineteenth and earlier twentieth centuries.

The definition of literature that I have given is compatible with the con-

---

[9] I am indebted to Gary Saul Morson for this apt formulation in a private communication.

[10] The practical functions of written works can hardly be "extraliterary" or "nonliterary." This would be logical only if function or application were something imposed on an existing work from without and alien to its nature. Rather, for the Middle Ages we need to recognize that societal function was somehow inherent in the work from the time of its conception, that there was a juncture of literary form and practical use.

[11] Jan Meijer put it well and colorfully: "The religious or historical character of a text need not, in certain circumstances, exclude the possibility of its being literature. The selection and conscious reception of such texts as literature often takes place only much later, when differentiation within the culture has led to the acknowledgement of literature as a separate field. Up to that time the rose will smell as sweet by another name" ("The Limits" [see n. 1], 139). See also Pope, "On the Comparative Literary Analysis" (see n. 5), 4, 17.

cepts of *polyfunctionality* and *syncretism*, although I make little use of these terms. They both signal that medieval literature combined several functions which were not yet distinguished one from another, one of which was aesthetic ("literary" in the narrow sense).[12] Syncretism is perhaps the less appropriate term since it normally refers to a mingling of things that were previously discrete, as, for example, in "syncretic" Hellenistic cults that blended elements of disparate religions. Instead, we seem to be dealing here with distinctions that were to emerge only much later. The term *polyfunctionality* is more apt because it avoids the implication of historical convergence. It allows us to speak of an aesthetic function even as we admit that the aesthetic was not "dominant" in medieval art and that no sharp distinction was made between works with aesthetic purpose and those without. Yet the word *polyfunctionality*, like *syncretism*, has the disadvantage that it may seem to attribute to the literature certain inherent functions that in fact we are introducing retrospectively. It is useful only if we understand it to mean an amalgam of as yet *undifferentiated functions*.

Now to approach the literature itself. There is no doubt that the nature of written culture in Old Rus' was very different from that of our day. Most works that we know about were produced for immediate practical functions such as applied use in churches and monasteries. These writings were more closely tied to societal conditions and exigencies than are modern literary works, and whatever aesthetic function they possessed appears to have been secondary. It is also true that what has survived to our time is overwhelmingly religious in content and outlook, that it is almost wholly lacking in intellectual content (i.e., shows no interest in speculative thought), and that imaginative literature, as we understand it, is all but entirely missing before the seventeenth century. Moreover, originality and individual authorship were not prized; much was translated or imitated from the Greek, and texts often closely followed prior models and adhered to decorum (what D. S. Lixačev calls "literary etiquette"[13]). It is true as well that early East Slavic literature was severely limited in genres and means: verse and drama were totally lacking, as were most secular genres; indeed, there was no clear division between sacred and profane writing.

---

[12] Seemann includes polyfunctionality (*Funkstionspluralismus*) in his "Thesen zum mittelalterlichen Literaturtypus und zur Gattungssystematik am Beispiel der altrussischen Literatur," in *Gattungsprobleme der älteren slavischen Literaturen (Berliner Fachtagung 1981)* (Berlin, 1984), 283. For syncretism and polyfunctionality, see Schmidt and Seemann, "Die Gattungsforschung" (see n. 8), 23-24.

[13] D. S. Lixačev, *Poètika drevnerusskoj literatury*, 3d ed. rev. (Moscow, 1979), 80-102.

Yet nothing in the rather dismal picture I have sketched means there was no literature in Old Rus'. A comparison with painting and architecture will quickly suggest why. Old Russian painting, as far as we know it, is confined to icons and frescoes and has almost exclusively religious content. It served definite religious functions, including ritual ones, and was very limited in technique, subjects, and genres. Icons were made according to convention (post-Iconoclastic rules) and show only subtle differences of individual style. These distinctions, however, do not stop us today from viewing, say, Andrej Rublev's work as art, and even from considering it great art. Much the same can be said of medieval Russian church architecture; and architecture developed more daringly than did painting. What was at that time primarily *applied art (prikladnoe iskusstvo)* is now rightly regarded—at least in its better examples—as *art*. Of course, we ought never to forget that it is predominantly a religious art and fully comprehensible only in terms of the spirituality that motivated and informed it; but then much of Renaissance and Baroque art in the West is also Christian and requires that we know the traditional themes and the spiritual values.

Iconography and church architecture demonstrate that it is possible for a severely conventionalized art, created to meet practical requirements of a sociocultural subsystem, to be art. If anything, painting and architecture were even more circumscribed by pragmatic function than was literature. It would be paradoxical for us to designate them art while questioning that the somewhat freer *pis'mennost'* could be such.

I said that *we* view the icons and the architecture as art, and the writings as literature. Is that enough? We could, of course, content ourselves with the convictions that (1) art is, after all, a universal category, and (2) the canon of art is in large measure a retrospective category. But are these justifications satisfying, or will we require that contemporaries shared our understanding? Is it necessary that they had a consciousness of "art" and "literature"? In the absence of medieval treatises and works of criticism—indeed, of any documentary proof that contemporaries conceptualized art and literature as such—is it the case that these did not exist?

Here we must make the logical distinction between *practice* and *conceptualization,* two different activities not necessarily coexisting. Certainly it would be helpful if we had direct testimony that writers and readers in early Rus' at least were aware of the "literariness" of certain writings and valued them for that reason. But they need not have conceptualized or written about literature as such in order to be creators and consumers of literature. If the conception of literature as a separate category or phenomenon were required, then (to take Seemann's point to its extreme) no people had literature before the eighteenth century. In that event, presumably Homer, Virgil, Dante, Shakespeare, Cervantes, and Molière would not be literary figures. Furthermore, as already noted, even in our time the line between literature and other writing is not always clearly drawn.

Nonetheless, we would probably be uncomfortable conceiving of early East Slavic "literature" only retrospectively—on the subjective grounds that *we* like to read some of it from other than historical curiosity. And so we should look for clues that works were valued by contemporaries for the quality of the writing. Perhaps we could invoke a legal phrase here, *res ipsa loquitur* (the thing speaks for itself); that is, the creation and transmission of writings with literary qualities of form and technique, like the creation of masterly icons and church edifices, make it self-evident that contemporaries valued and sought artistic accomplishment.

For literature, one piece of concrete evidence might be the number of manuscripts of a particular work as a possible indication of the esteem in which it was held. However, the number of surviving copies of any given work may depend on accident or on some "extraliterary" factor such as official acceptance for institutional use. Many manuscripts got duplicated and preserved because they were prescribed reading in monasteries. Thus, even if we could know how many copies were around in the early period itself, this would be an ambiguous test of whether literary value was ascribed to the work. We surely would not wish to apply this criterion to the *Slovo o polku Igoreve*, which came down to modern times in a single copy.

Again, I do not concede that it is essential to prove that literature as art was conceived of or consciously practiced by contemporaries; art can rightly be thought of as a universal of human experience at least since the time of the cave painters of Lascaux. Nonetheless, in what follows I will endeavor to adduce arguments for the existence of early East Slavic literary practice in its own time, not only as a retrospective notion of ours.

Before proceeding, I must deal with the fundamental question of *work* and *text* (*proizvedenie i tekst*). By "text" I mean the verbal structure represented by a given set of written signs; by "work," the ideal creation behind all related texts and not necessarily identical with any one of them.[14] Do works

---

[14] Cf. D. S. Lixačev, *Tekstologija, na materiale russkoi literatury X-XVII vekov*, 2d ed. rev.

have to exist in order for there to be literature, and were there *proizvedenija* in Old Rus', or only *teksty?* My provisional answer to both questions is yes. In order for a writing to be treated as literature—i.e., used outside its initial pragmatic context and on account of its inherent value—it has to be treated as an entity that supersedes any particular text (single linguistic/graphic expression). D. S. Lixačev has pointed to evidence for *proizvedenija,* that is for written products with their own separate identity and redactional history.[15]

It is certainly true that the phenomenon of "works" was not as strict and pervasive as in modern literature. We are accustomed to expect the rather stable integrity of written works and to think of literature as a canon of such discrete products. The situation in the Orthodox Slavic Middle Ages was more fluid; an "open" type of text transmission predominated, and bookmen felt quite free both to alter writings in copying them and to appropriate material from existing writings when they composed or compiled new ones.[16] The result is that things we regard as works are often more variable in their textual tradition than modern literary products would be. Nonetheless, although this relative fluidity may cause us to qualify the concept of a work in the medieval context, it does not necessarily invalidate it.[17]

A related question could be raised in the light of William R. Veder's principle of the *segmentability* of early Slavic texts. It is a well-attested fact that pieces of texts, ranging from brief expressions to large sections, could be excerpted and compiled or reused elsewhere. In other words, smaller units than "works" were assigned a value, or at least usefulness, outside their original context. It might be possible to argue on this basis that works are not essential for proving the existence of literature. However, on the level of

---

(Leningrad, 1983), 127-130. In English-language criticism, and especially in classroom usage, this distinction is not regularly made; "text" is often made synonymous with "work," as even by Ellis (see n. 7).

[15] See Lixačev, 129: "priznakom otdel'nosti proizvedenija služit samostojatel'nost' izmenenij ego teksta otnositel'no drugix sosednix v rukopisnoj tradicii" ("a sign of the separateness of the work is that changes to its text occur independently of other neighboring texts in the manuscript tradition").

[16] On "openness," see Seemann, "Thesen" (see n. 12), 280; Riccardo Picchio, "Compilation and Composition: Two Levels of Authorship in the Orthodox Slavic Tradition," *Cyrillomethodianum* 5 (1981): 1-4; William R. Veder, "Old Russia's 'Intellectual Silence' Reconsidered" in this volume, pp. 18-27.

[17] William R. Veder, in reaction to the article by Meijer, offered a textologist's evidence that the "book" (codex) is the fundamental unit of early Slavic writing rather than the text or work. See Veder, "The Treatment of Texts in Early Slavic Literature," in *Miscellanea Slavica to Honour the Memory of Jan M. Meijer,* ed. B. J. Amsenga et al. (Amsterdam, 1983), 487-496. In my opinion, such arguments show only the comparative instability, or "openness," of text and work and not their absence.

small passages it would be harder to show that the material was accorded "literary" rather than merely utilitarian value. Veder's general concepts of segmentability and segmentation deserve more attention at another time.[18] For the present, I will emphasize the work as the basic literary unit because it has an identity in itself. If there are works, then the existence of literature certainly becomes possible.[19]

This leads to my main thesis, which centers on the principle of *portability* (*peresažaemost'*): writings could be and were moved from one functional context to another without losing their integrity as works. Portability seems to offer the strongest and most persuasive argument for the existence of works, and hence of literature. It goes to the heart of the question of whether writings are exclusively determined by and limited to their initial sociocultural function and context. I will add two secondary considerations that are dependent on the concept of portability: *functional flexibility* and the *diversity of genres*.

At least for now, I limit the notion of portability to whole texts (works) and do not apply it to passages compiled or reused elsewhere (Veder's "segments"). I do so because, in my understanding of the term, a "portable" item is an object with an identity of its own, a discrete whole with boundaries.[20] To establish portability, I need to show that works could be moved from one setting to another without losing their integrity. Indeed, there are sufficient examples of this occurrence. For the Kievan period we may take *The Life of Theodosius,* written (Nestor is very clear about this) for reading in the monastery, and later compiled in *minei* for regular reading on the saint's day. But the *Life* was also eventually added to the *Patericon* of the Caves Monastery for the quite natural reason that its subject was a former monk and abbot of that place. One of its purposes at that point was pre-

---

[18] The process Veder describes ("Old Russia's 'Intellectual Silence'" [see n. 16]) seems to be "selection" more than "segmentation." Rather than establish permanent subdivisions of the text (as, say, ancient scholars marked chapter and verse in books of the Bible), Slavic scribes excerpted passages that were useful to them elsewhere. The segments were by no means fixed; another bookman might choose pieces with different boundaries.

[19] The opposition work vs. text seems to be at the base of Seemann's objections to "literature." From the openness of tradition he infers that there was no integrity of works, and hence no literature in the proper sense; that there were only texts exploited for practical purposes and often readapted to current needs (*aktualisiert*); and that there were no genres but only *Textsorten*. In "Forum" Lenhoff's view appears to be similar (see n. 2).

[20] Further research is needed to show whether there could be kinds of segments with clear-cut identities so that they might be "ported" into new contexts. "Component parts," such as a eulogy or prayer, might possibly qualify.

sumably silent reading.²¹ Moreover, it was also included in the *Uspenskij sbornik* (late twelfth or early thirteenth century), an uncanonical collection of texts possibly compiled for a private patron.²² Carried from one context to another, the work did not lose its identity; it remained *The Life of Saint Theodosius* as the titles and the rather stable content and form show.

The fact of portability is my answer to Seemann's definition of the sermon, which he sees as a text integral to a social event: the performance of the sermon in church. He believes that a sermon has its identity only as part of the complex action.²³ I reply that a text, including that of a sermon, can possess integrity as a work (a product of writing) quite apart from its initial purpose or its role in an action (ritual). The evidence in this case is that sermons could be copied for silent reading or for possible future delivery, as were those preserved from the Kievan era. The sermons of Cyril of Turov were collected and frequently recopied in the *Toržestvennik* and *Zlatoust*.²⁴

It may be useful to note that the argument from portability is both less necessary and less applicable in the case of icons: less necessary, because these were and are very obviously "works"—that is, distinctively individual artifacts with a physical life of their own; less applicable, because icons seem to have been moved around little, except geographically. It would be unlikely for a church icon to end up in a private home. When today we put icons in museums, we are wrenching them out of their intended context and using them "improperly." Private collections of icons could not exist in medieval Rus'; but private *sborniki* of collected writings apparently did. On the basis of then contemporary norms, we might be justified in proclaiming that art-literature had a better claim to existence in the Middle Ages than did art-painting.

To meet the criterion of value apart from "documentary" use, a work does not have to lose *all* of its original functions when moved. In practice, the extent to which functions change with such moves can be inferred only imperfectly. In my "Genre-Theory and Old Russian Literature," I introduced

---

[21] Richard Pope, citing N. van Wijk, gave three expected applications of paterica: reading "at home" (in the cell), in church, and during the common monastic meal. See Pope, "O xaraktere i stepeni vlijanija vizantijskoj literatury na original'nuju literaturu južnyx i vostočnyx slavjan: diskussija i metodologija," in *American Contributions to the Seventh International Congress of Slavists, Warsaw, August 21-27, 1973,* 2; *Literature and Folklore,* ed. Victor Terras (The Hague, 1973), 484.

[22] *Uspenskij sbornik XII-XIII vv.,* ed. S. I. Kotkov (Moscow, 1971), 8-10; text, pp. 71-135.

[23] "Forum" (see n. 2), 249.

[24] I. P. Eremin, *Literaturnoe nasledie Kirilla Turovskogo* (Berkeley, 1989), 14 [*TODRL* 11(1955):342–367].

the term *implied function,* referring to the fact that in general the functions that we ascribe to medieval texts are ones that we infer from our analysis of the texts themselves.[25] I have commented on function-theory elsewhere.[26] Functions are of different kinds and pertain to different levels: a general ideological function (social purpose); the more specific goal or goals of the work; and the work's practical application (how, when, and where was it intended to be used?). In all considerations of function it is useful to make the logical distinction between "purpose" and (immediate) "function,"[27] as it were, between ultimate and proximate ends.

The Life of Saint Theodosius, for example, served the general purpose of furthering the Christian religion in Rus' and the narrower one of promoting his cult and the prestige of his monastery. It taught an ideal of the Christian life and its kenotic values, and more specifically provided a model for monks (as Nestor expressly stated). Its practical application, however, presumably was reading aloud in the monastery on his day and perhaps silent reading at other times. We can assume that some of these multilayered functions would be carried over even if the *Life* was copied for laymen and no longer had its original application in monastic routine, and that it might possibly acquire new functions in its new environment.

Gail Lenhoff has confirmed that the same *text* could be used in a new *functional slot,* but her assumption apparently is that a verbal structure is merely being borrowed for a new practical purpose. She argues that this disproves the existence of genres—and, for my purposes at present, it might also undermine the existence of works. The fact is, however, that this argument would eliminate genre only if the category were defined solely by immediate function, and works also defined merely by their immediate application. Contrary to this reasoning, if a whole "text" can be moved from one functional context and used in another, this points to its integrity as a work, thereby also supporting the argument for literary genre. Portability suggests that both the text and its structural model are *independent of any one functional slot.*[28] My working assumption is that, when an entire text is moved

---

[25] "Forum" (see n. 2), 242.

[26] See my "Genre Characteristics of the Kievan Lives of Princes in Slavic and European Perspective," in *American Contributions to the Ninth International Congress of Slavists, Kiev, September 1983,* v. 2: *Literature, Poetics, History,* ed. Paul Debreczeny (Columbus, 1983), 225-226.

[27] Ellis, *Theory* (see n. 6), 237.

[28] I changed my mind about a functional-slot definition of genre after making tentative use of it in my "Genre Characteristics" (see n. 26), 225. At that time I was trying to adapt my own understanding of literary genre to the function-theory of my colleagues. Ironically, it was Lenhoff who afterward demonstrated that the functional-slot definition will not work (e.g., in

essentially unchanged, that is prima facie evidence for the existence of work and makes literature possible.

This is not the place to take up again the debate about genres in the early literature. I consider the question to be still open; but I have argued for the existence of genres in at least some areas of writing, mainly conventional kinds of church compositions. If I am right, then the resulting *generic diversity*—while not actually decisive—would be one indicator of literature's existence in Old Rus'. Perhaps I can be accused of circular reasoning: I posit literature as proof of genres, and genres as proof of literature. Nonetheless, the two suppositions do reinforce one another; if we are convinced of the one, we will probably be convinced of the other. Of course, I do not wish to claim that literature was limited to those writings that most clearly employ genre.

At the same time, the generic argument in its elementary form cannot be decisive, because genres are not necessarily literary; documents, too, usually fall into sharply defined generic categories. We must still show that the genres in question were literary, and here the concept of portability may be helpful to my genre-theory. The unsatisfying alternative to what I have said would be to conceive of a partial system of quasi genres (Seemann's *Textsorten* or Lenhoff's protogenres) and a barren *knižnost'* confined to documents that no one would want to read outside of their original application.

To sum up succinctly, it seems to me that portability suggests works; typological similarities among works suggest a structural model (genre); and both work and genre give us the possibility to speak of literature. If it be objected that portability in and of itself (even supposing that I can demonstrate it) does not strictly prove that the values ascribed to written works in the Middle Ages were "literary," my answer is a reminder that most of the time, *all* functions we ascribe to medieval writing are inferential on our part. The aesthetic is not particularly exceptional in this respect. With pragmatic functions too, we often implicitly appeal to the principle that "the thing speaks for itself": the very fact that a writing had characteristics appropriate to a certain function is taken as grounds for inferring that it served that purpose (and was meant to).

"Forum" [see n. 2], 261) and thereby (unintentionally) restored my faith in the *literary* character of genre. Cf. my "Genre-Theory and Old Russian Literature" in "Forum" (see n. 2) 245, n. 14. See also Lenhoff's recent book *The Martyred Princes Boris and Gleb: A Socio-cultural Study of the Cult and the Texts* (Columbus, 1989), 20-23.

So far, I have emphasized the first half of my title—offering arguments for early East Slavic literature as a "fact." It is time now to comment more directly on the "sociocultural" significance of that fact. Literature per se has complex interrelations with society in every era, and it is not an intrusive concept for the premodern period—not one that in principle must be excluded from the model of a predominantly pragmatic sociocultural system. On the contrary, literature could and did play a role in the system itself. On the highest level where there existed sociocultural purposes, such as the propagation of the Christian faith and the inculcation of its values, these purposes were furthered by polished and memorable writings. To be effective precisely in its broadest function, a sermon, for example, was aided if it was well written in the literary sense, as is apparent in the sermons of Hilarion of Kiev and Cyril of Turov. Next, the same "literary" features that made it successful as a sermon read in church could lead to its being copied into a collection for private reading, whereby it might retain some of its general purpose (Christian edification) but without the immediate application. To fulfill a function, a piece of writing had to be adequate for the purpose; obviously, some writings qualified in part by what we call literary characteristics.

Literary factors were integral, too, on the level of production. Although it is true that a societal situation often *occasioned* the appearance of a text or work, that is, provided the need and motivation for it to be made, we must remember that the situation as such could not simply and directly generate or create it. The fact is that one or more human beings composed a text, presumably motivated by the perceived need. To the extent that what they created was a vehicle for sociocultural purposes and fulfilled functions of a cultural subsystem, the way they went about making it and the (literary) nature of their product are by no means extraneous considerations.

As I have argued elsewhere, writings were not and could not be composed in a literary vacuum; they appeared neither by spontaneous generation nor by creation *ex nihilo*.[29] Writers drew upon conventions of writing: existing models and standards, many of which can properly be called literary.[30] Daniel Rowland very aptly says that the text stands at the intersection of two contexts, the societal and the literary[31]. I would add only that the two contexts are not entirely separate to begin with.

---

[29] "Forum" (see n. 2), 243, 273.

[30] I hope that I will not be misunderstood if occasionally I employ "literary" in the sense of "using the means and materials of written culture" instead of more strictly to mean "qualifying for the canon of literature."

[31] "Biblical Military Imagery in the Political Culture of Early Modern Russia" (see pp. 184–202 in the present volume).

I fully recognize the pragmatic basis of written culture in Old Rus' and the obvious differences of what has survived from what we consider literature in our own time; and I value highly the contribution of sociological approaches to early East Slavic culture. The thrust of my argument has been to deny any claim of categorical "alterity"—the idea that medieval literature was something utterly "other." We are dealing here not with an absolute difference between literature and non-literature, but with differences of degree between kinds of literature. We have no right to say that literature did not exist in Old Rus' simply because it did not manifest itself in the same genres as in the modern period or even because it was not conceptualized as a special realm in the way it is today.

One danger is that if we deny literature we may lose sight of important dimensions of the problem just because they are usually thought of as "literary": genres, modes, and styles of writing; decorum ("literary etiquette"); and, perhaps most important, *intertextuality*, in the sense of the imitation or continuation of themes and ideas from within and without the written culture of Eastern Orthodoxy. Such factors are neither anachronistic for the Middle Ages nor somehow irrelevant to our concerns in reconstructing sociocultural reality. They are part of the very cultural system we are investigating, which cannot be fully understood without paying attention to them. New paradigms that exclude so-called literary factors are doomed to be incomplete and artificial. Literature existed in Old Rus', and it was an important sociocultural fact.

OLD RUSSIA'S "INTELLECTUAL SILENCE" RECONSIDERED

WILLIAM R. VEDER

Some thirty years ago Georges Florovsky, late professor of Eastern Church history at Harvard University, gathered from such eminent philologists and historians as Sergej Solov'ev, Fedor Buslaev, Alexander Pypin, Vatroslav Jagić, Evgenij Golubinskij, and George Fedotov the scattered doubts about the quality of the culture of Old Russia. In an essay that specifically addressed "The Problem of Old Russian Culture,"[1] he observed that Old Russia had produced great art and been highly creative in the social and political field, but had failed to produce anything outstanding in the realm of ideas. Discarding possible errors originating either from an incomplete assessment of the creative legacy of Old Russia or an all too biased interpretation of the "ways of Old Russia," he posed some disturbing questions, culminating in the most worrisome one: "What was the reason for what can be described as [Old Russia's] 'intellectual silence, or rather, dumbness'?"[2]

His query was answered, in the first instance, by Nikolaj Andreev and James Billington. The former pointed to the vigor and longevity of the pagan heritage at the foundation of Old Russia's culture, in conjunction with Russia's isolation from the West by the Mongols, as probable factors that effectively prevented the intellectual challenges of the Byzantine heritage from bearing fruit.[3] The latter, focusing exclusively on Muscovy, singled out the brutal subjugation of westward-looking Novgorod and Pskov, the harsh frontier conditions, the laxity of diocesan structures, the lack of a commonly accepted body of canon law, the lack of a clear distinction between law and morality, the lack of a classical heritage, and the Hesychast antischolastic bias as probable factors that stifled intellectual search.[4] In his reply to both Andreev and Billington, Florovsky showed himself unconvinced by their arguments. He suggested that Billington, notably, confused symptoms with

---

[1] SR 21 (1962): 1–15.
[2] Ibid., 12; idem, "Reply," SR 21 (1962): 39.
[3] N. Andreev, "Pagan and Christian Elements in Old Russia," SR 21 (1962): 19, 21.
[4] J. Billington, "Images of Muscovy," SR 21 (1962): 27–32.

causes. Moreover, he maintained that in Old Russian culture "the dynamism of search" had been "subdued to the static pattern of accomplishment."[5] Restating his initial requirement to consider separately culture as a function of society and as a complex of values, he recommended further research: "What we actually need most urgently is not a general discussion of certain basic topics, but rather a patient study of sources, critically evaluated and impartially assessed."[6]

This recommendation was taken to heart sixteen years later by one of Andreev's last disciples. At the Eighth International Congress of Slavists at Zagreb (1978), Francis Thomson presented a survey of the translations available in Russia from the tenth to fourteenth centuries, concluding that they formed "a typical monastic library similar to that in contemporary Byzantine monasteries," and concurring with Maximilian Braun in "that the comprehensibility of many translations is largely an illusion."[7] At the Ninth Congress (Kiev, 1983) and the Tenth (Sofia, 1988), he complemented the survey with a painstaking analysis of quotations from patristic Greek and Byzantine texts in original works from Kievan Rus', concluding that, with the sole exception of Metropolitan Hilarion's "Sermon on Law and Grace," they do "not enlarge the known corpus of translations or reveal any knowledge of Greek originals."[8] With these conclusions, he contended that Old Russia was heir not to "the intellectual world of Byzantine culture, but the obscurantist world of Byzantine monasticism, which was largely hostile to secular learning,"[9] and that it was "the Russian Church, mistakenly considering itself to be in possession of all the treasures of Orthodoxy," that "remained an obstacle to intellectual progress until its hold was broken by Peter the Great."[10] The true cause of Old Russia's intellectual silence he identified to be "the fact that a lack of a knowledge of Greek prevented direct access to the treasures of Byzantine thought and the limited range of translated material provided little intellectual stimulus."[11] This thesis was to include Latin and German as well in his survey of translations in Muscovite

---

[5] "Reply," (see n. 2), 39.
[6] Ibid., 42.
[7] "The Nature of the Reception of Christian Byzantine Culture in Russia in the Tenth to Thirteenth Centuries and Its Implications for Russian Culture," *Slavica Gandensia* 5 (1978): 117.
[8] Francis Thomson, "Quotations of Patristic and Byzantine Works by Early Russian Authors as an Indication of the Cultural Level of Kievan Russia," *Slavica Gandensia* 10 (1983): 73, and idem, "The Implications of the Absence of Quotations of Untranslated Greek Works in Original Early Russian Literature, Together with a Critique of a Distorted Picture of Early Bulgarian Culture," *Slavica Gandensia* 15 (1988): 68–69.
[9] Thomson, "Nature," (see n. 7), 118; cf. idem, "Quotations," (see n. 8), 65.
[10] Thomson, "Nature," (see n. 7), 118.
[11] Thomson, "Implications," (see n. 8), 70.

Russia, presented to the founding conference of the International Association for Ukrainian Studies (Naples, 1989), whereas "the use of Slavonic acted as a brake upon progress. It remained, if not entirely foreign, at least an artificial language and the lack of a recognized academy or university prevented the establishment of norms for its correct usage, so that it was all too often inadequately employed."[12]

Although Thomson's studies certainly meet Florovsky's recommendations of patient study of sources and critical evaluation, I think that his contentions are not unequivocally acceptable in view of either Florovsky's recommendation of impartial assessment or his call for separate investigation of culture as a system of values and as a function of society. Thomson asks, "Where is the Russian Peter Abelard? Where is the intellectual ferment similar to that caused by Berengar's teaching on the Eucharist in the eleventh century or Gilbert de la Porrée's on the Trinity in the twelfth?"[13] When he resignedly responds that "it is pointless to look for a Russian Abelard,"[14] he is, in fact, addressing the problem of Old Russian culture from a Western point of view and a Western set of values. Like Andreev, Billington, and Florovsky, Thomson takes a Muscovite point of view when he ascribes the breaking of the intellectual silence to Peter the Great. When he puts the blame for the intellectual silence on the translations and the Church, he is, I think, confusing symptom and cause just as Florovsky found Billington to have done and thereby unduly diverts attention from internal conditions of culture.

A study of a culture may well be occasioned by observations from a different culture, but it may not be conducted without the prior dispassionate description of its system in its own right. If it is, many more pertinent observations and generalizations than comparison can provide are bound to be missed. I shall attempt to prove this thesis with data gathered from the central component of any Christian culture: its books. I am unable to separate the data gathered from books produced in the East Slavic area from those produced elsewhere in medieval Slavia Orthodoxa (Moldavia, Bulgaria, Serbia, Mt. Athos, Sinai, and perhaps also Jerusalem).

The books of medieval Slavia Orthodoxa can be divided into two fundamental classes: (1) those with liturgical or other official ecclesiastical functions, and (2) the кънигы четии съборьнъіѧ or *Četii Sborniki*.[15] While the

---

[12] Thomson, "Nature," (see n. 7), 119.
[13] Ibid., 120.
[14] Thomson, "Implications," (see n. 8), 70.
[15] These two classes are, in fact, set apart by some of the compilers of the earliest Slavic library catalogues: M. V. Kukuškina, "Opisi knig XVI–XVII vv. biblioteki Antonievo-Sijskogo

former can best be envisaged not as separate books, but as parts of a complex score for the concert of divine worship (comprising distinct directions and texts for all occasions and all engaged in them, from the supreme hierarch to the lowliest parishioner), the *Četii Sborniki* lack any such functional relationship to each other. Each must be viewed not in a ceremonial function, but as a separate entity, serving individual epistemic, or more precisely, edificational ends. It is only in this class of books that we may expect to find data concerning the communication between the maker of the book and its addressee, the reader. In the case of the bookmakers, no such data may be sought, at least not on any level higher than that of incidental notes, for even though the books with a liturgical or paraliturgical function may be read, in addition to being performed, their texts are constituted by considerations largely beyond the control of their makers.

Both classes of books lack textual coherence. For the liturgical books, this is not surprising, since they each form only a part of a complex score, and the coherence of their texts is assured on the pragmatic level of the different cycles that govern the concert of divine worship (the annual, Easter, bimensual, hebdomadal, and diurnal cycles). For the *Četii Sborniki,* the lack of textual coherence is surprising, since they serve epistemic ends which would presuppose some observable internal organization of the contents. Let me give just five examples of the problems of textual coherence presented by these books:

1. The simplest case is that of Prince Svjatoslav's *Izbornik of 1073,* a copy of the *Izbornik of Tsar Simeon,* translated in Bulgaria between 914 and 919 from a contemporary Greek florilegium entitled *The Savior,* a unified collection of texts in defense of the dogma of the Holy Trinity. Either at the time of translation (in Glagolitic script) or of its transcription into Cyrillic (between 919 and 1073), excerpts were added in the middle from the Slavic translation of Gregory of Nazianzus's *Homily on the Sacrament of Baptism.* These additions disrupt the trinitarian context.[16]

2. The *Izbornik of 1076* is a copy of a Bulgarian compilation datable before 972, preserved also in two fragmentary South Slavic copies of the

---

monastyrja," *Materialy i soobščenija po fondam ORRK BAN SSSR* (Moscow-Leningrad, 1966), a fact ignored by the author of the recent first investigation of Old Russian literature as a system, R. W. Marti, *Handschrift — Text — Textgruppe — Literatur,* Slavistische Veröffentlichungen, no. 68 (Wiesbaden, 1989).

[16] This observation was first made by Mario Capaldo, who also identified the original title of the Greek florilegium, in his paper at the Symposium on Middle Greek and Slavic Literatures in Thessaloniki, 1979; cf. W. R. Veder, "Symposium on Middle Greek and Slavic Literatures," *Polata knigopisnaja* 3 (1980): 59.

fourteenth–sixteenth centuries.[17] Dietrich Freydank[18] and Francis Thomson[19] have presented divergent rationalizations of its text structure, obviously facilitated by a semblance of textual coherence on the generic level, the text being divided into short sections of comparable length which can be loosely classified as gnomes. Both rationalizations make sense, but neither of them accounts for the fact that the book has serious disturbances in textual coherence on the thematic level. The book was renovated at least twice in the fourteenth and fifteenth centuries.

3. The *Troickij Sbornik no. 12* was compiled in Kievan Russia between ca. 1175 and 1225.[20] It unites apophthegms, commentaries, epistles, erotapocrises, gnomes, and homilies without any discernible coherence on either the pragmatic, thematic, generic, or stylistic level. In its central part, forty-eight homilies from Antiochus Monachus's *Pandects*, the well-conceived topical structure of their original sequence[21] has been effectively disintegrated without being replaced by any alternative topical organization. This book, too, was renovated at least twice between the fourteenth and the sixteenth centuries.

4. The *Izbornik of the Thirteenth Century* was compiled in the Novgorod area between 1200 and 1250.[22] Its commentaries on biblical and other texts stem from both exegetic and nonexegetic sources; in the latter case, they are adapted to the format of exegesis (quotation, followed by commentary) and, whenever necessary, shortened. There is no discernible coherence of the text on either the pragmatic, thematic, or stylistic level. Moreover, two Hebrew-Slavic onomastica and a homiletic anti-Jewish treatise disrupt the pattern of symbolic exegesis. In the central part, which presents selections from Hesychius of Jerusalem's *Short Commentary on the Psalms*, the pragmatic ordering of the source text is effectively disintegrated without being replaced by any alternative form of organization.

5. The *Scaliger Paterikon* was compiled in the Galician-Volhynian area between 1250 and 1300.[23] It consists of what I have called the *Protopaterikon*

---

[17] B. S. Angelov, "Za tri săčinenija v Simeonovite sbornici," *Starobălgarska literatura* 5 (1979): 10–37; and W. R. Veder, "The 'Izbornik of John the Sinner': A Compilation from Compilations," *Polata knigopisnaja* 8 (1983): 15–37.

[18] "Der Izbornik von 1076 und die Apophthegmata Patrum," *Zeitschrift für Slawistik* 21 (1976): 358–359.

[19] Printed in Marti, *Handschrift* (see n. 15), 161.

[20] See J. Popovski et al., eds., *The Troickij Sbornik* (= *Polata knigopisnaja* 21–22 [1988]).

[21] The original from which this section was copied is preserved in Cod. Moskva, GIM, Voskr. 30p.

[22] See H. Wątróbska, ed., *The Izbornik of the XIIIth Century* (= *Polata knigopisnaja* 19–20 [1987]); also *Early Slavic Texts on Microfiche*, v. 3, 1).

[23] See W. R. Veder, ed., *The Scaliger Paterikon, I–III*. (Zug: IDC, 1976–1985).

Scaligeri (a Bulgarian compilation, datable before 972, of apophthegms culled from the translations of two Greek *paterika* and John Climacus's *Ladder to Paradise*) and a complement of chronographic texts, erotapocrises, eschatological and exegetic texts, gnomes, and homilies, or excerpts from them. There is no identifiable feature that unites the first part of the book with its additions, nor is there textual coherence on any level within the additions. The first part, the *Protopaterikon*, however, is homogenized at least on the generic level: all text selections, from whichever source they stem, have been adapted to the narrative format of apophthegms; yet the thematic ordering known to have existed in its sources is, once more, disintegrated without any new form of organization having been substituted for it.

I have found it quite pointless to search for a rationale underlying the text structure of *Četii Sborniki*, except on one single level: their compilation structure. It is only when it is known in which way a *Četii Sbornik* was compiled that the book makes sense as a whole. Let me add that only in this case does it become fully evident how many opportunities to make a coherent book were overlooked by the makers of *Četii Sborniki*. In this light, we can reexamine the five examples cited:

1. The *Izbornik of 1073*, like at least one of its Greek counterparts, originally consisted of two volumes, not one. The first volume had the customary blank folio (or, in this luxury edition, folios) at its end which, equally customarily, was filled with text (I am tempted to say, any text); this text was then mechanically copied into the equally luxurious manuscript of 1073.[24]

2. The *Izbornik of 1076*—or more precisely, its Bulgarian original—was compiled from an earlier Bulgarian compilation that I have named *Knjažij Izbornik*, essentially by reversing its order: the first entry was put at the end of the new book, the third and the last at the beginning, and the remainder in erratic order in between. Added were an introduction, compiled from the introductions to two earlier books,[25] and five excerpts from other sources. Four of these are associated with either the preceding or the following text; the last, on drunkenness, stands completely out of context.[26]

3. The *Troickij Sbornik no. 12* originated as the private work of one scribe. At a given point, it was taken over by six others, probably working in a scriptorium. All seven used more than ten secondary sources, which I leave

---

[24] Veder, "Symposium," (see n. 16), 59.
[25] W. R. Veder, "Three Old Slavic Discourses on Reading," in *Studia slavica mediaevalia et humanistica Riccardo Picchio dedicata*, 2 vols., ed. M. Colucci et al., (Rome, 1986), v. 1, 717–730.
[26] For the compilation structure, see Veder, "Izbornik," (see n. 17), 36.

out of consideration here, and two main sources, the *Zlatostruj* to frame the book and Antiochus Monachus's *Pandects* to form its central part. Homilies from the *Zlatostruj* were selected apparently at random from its extreme portions and most often conflated in pairs into a new homily with the seams of the compilation in full evidence. Homilies from the *Pandects* were selected equally at random in seven runs through the source, four of them progressive and three retrogressive, resulting in the total disintegration of its well-conceived topical structure.[27]

4. The *Izbornik of the Thirteenth Century* was compiled from at least ten different sources, three of which formed the framework of the new book: a thoroughly disorderly exegetic compilation of Bulgarian origin (copied in the Ukraine and in Muscovite Russia as late as the seventeenth century); the *Izbornik of Tsar Simeon* (or the *Izbornik of 1073*) to frame the book; and Hesychius of Jerusalem's *Brief Commentary on the Psalms* to form its central part. While the random selections from the first two sources have generally retained their original sequence (disrupted, of course, by entirely unrelated additions from other sources), the *Commentary on the Psalms* has been excerpted in two progressive runs of almost equal size, leading to a significant number of doublets. From no source was either the beginning or the end used. From *Commentary on the Psalms,* only randomly selected verses are given; the first and last verse are typically avoided.[28]

5. The *Scaliger Paterikon* is still so unclear as to its source structure as a book that I can give data only on the construction of its first part, the *Protopaterikon*. The three sources from which it was compiled were excerpted both progressively and retrogressively, so that the beginning of the compilation brings into contact selections from the extremes of the respective source, whereas it generally draws upon their middle portion towards its end.[29]

These five examples show, I think, that textual coherence in *Četii Sborniki* may well be fortuitous, subordinate to the mechanics of compilation. They also show that the disintegration of source structures may well be systematic and deliberate. It is hardly the case that these books were produced for private edification; rather, they were produced on large quantities of expensive vellum, most of them in well-appointed scriptoria, by teams and with the services of correctors and rubricators available. One of them was even

---

[27] Cf. Popovski et al., *Troickij Sbornik* (see n. 20).
[28] Cf. Wątróbska, *Izbornik* (see n. 22).
[29] W. R. Veder, "Elementary Compilation in Slavic," *Cyrillomethodianum* 5 (1981): 49–66.

produced as a prize object for a prince. Moreover, these books were well cared for and, with the possible exception of the fourth, copied to generate an independent tradition of their text structures.

These examples could easily be multiplied with cases of well-known books. The present structure of the *Codex Suprasliensis*, for example, may well be due to a binder's error: the sixteenth-century copy of this manuscript from the Melec'kyj Monastery presents two groups of entries in reverse: 26–48, followed by 1–25.[30] Furthermore, the *Uspenskij Sbornik*,[31] the *Ustjužskaja Kormčaja*,[32] the *Sinai Florilegium no. 34*,[33] and the Serbian *Mileševa Panegyricum*, (ca. 1275–1325),[34] can also be found in the transmission of Slavic book-length texts. For instance, the tradition of the *Zlatostruj* is such that "none of the extant collections reproduces entirely the original corpus,"[35] and the transmission of the alphabetico-anonymous collection of *Apophthegmata Patrum* can only be described in terms of "inversion," "reduction," "suppression of individuality," "dismemberment," "epitomation," and "free compilation."[36] Even individual works, component texts of books, exhibit the features of disintegration of source structures and lack of textual coherence of the resulting compilation. For instance, the *Conversation of the Three Hierarchs* is a textologist's nightmare: it has no retrievable original text. All manuscripts are different, and none of them is any more coherent than the others.[37] The versions of the *Zlatostruj* contain texts either mechanically divided into separate homilies[38] or so crudely conflated from excerpts of separate homilies that doubts arise as to the copyist's or compiler's competence[39] Finally, the crude construction

---

[30] J. Zaimov and M. Capaldo, *Supras"lski ili Retkov sbornik*, 2 vols. (Sofia, 1983). The manuscript is identified as Cod. Kiev, CBAN, Mel. m./p. 117.

[31] See O. A. Knjaževskaja et al., *Uspenskij sbornik XII–XIII vv.* (Moscow, 1971).

[32] See I. I. Sreznevskij, "Obozrenie drevnerusskix spiskov Kormčej knigi," *SborJaS* 65 (1879): 113–129.

[33] V. M. Zagrebin, "O proisxoždenii i sud'be nekotoryx slavjanskix palimpsestov Sinaja," in *Iz istorii rukopisnyx i staropečatnyx sobranij Otdela rukopisej i redkix knig GPB (Issledovanija, obzory, publikacii). Sbornik naučnyx trudov* (Leningrad, 1979), 61–80. The *Sinai Florilegium no. 34* was compiled on Mt. Sinai by one Russian and three Bulgarian scribes in the thirteenth century.

[34] M. Capaldo, "Contributi allo studio delle collezioni agiografico-omiletiche in area slava. [1] Struttura e preistoria del "Panegirico di Mileševa," *Europa orientalis* 8 (1989): 209–252.

[35] Francis Thomson, "*Chrysostomica Palaeoslavica:* A Preliminary Study of the Sources of the Chrysorrhoas (Zlatostruy) Collection," *Cyrillomethodianum* 6 (1982): 45.

[36] M. Capaldo, "L'Azbučno-Ierusalimskij Paterik (Collection alphabetico-anonyme slave des Apophthegmata Patrum)," *Polata knigopisnaja* 4 (1981): 39–40.

[37] Francis Thomson, "Apocrypha Slavica: II," *The Slavonic and East European Review* 61, no. 1 (1985): 91–96.

[38] Thomson, "*Chrysostomica Palaeoslavica*," (see n. 35), 10, 14, 28–29.

[39] Ibid., 14, 32, 35.

of autochthonous Slavic homiletic texts from bits and pieces of other texts has led me to question whether the early Russian *Slovo Daniila Zatočnika*, "which so ostentatiously excerpts and juxtaposes the incongruous," is not, "among other things, a parody."[40]

Disintegration of source structures and lack of textual coherence in the resulting compilation are phenomena so frequent and widespread in Slavia Orthodoxa, both geographically and chronologically, that they cannot be considered accidental. I propose to consider them as two manifestations of a single feature that distinguishes both classes of books of Slavia Orthodoxa from each other, specifically marking the *Četii Sborniki*. This feature obviously ensured the generation, by simple chaotization,[41] of an unlimited number of new textual structures on the basis of a limited number of available texts. To my mind, it is most aptly compared to the kaleidoscope, invented in 1816 by Sir David Brewster to ensure the creation, by simple rotation, of constantly changing patterns of reflection of a limited number of pieces of colored glass. It is the symmetry of the kaleidoscope's patterns that ensures their aesthetic value. In the case of the *Četii Sborniki*, it is the simple juxtaposition of previously distinct texts that appears to ensure the epistemic value of the new textual structures. I propose to consider this feature of chaotization, operative both on the level of the work (i.e. component text) and on the level of the book, to be one of the principles of the poetics of Slavia Orthodoxa.

Neither the generating power of this principle nor its epistemic effects provides sufficient explanation for its existence and its operation. A comparison of the different attitudes towards the reader as reflected by the products of Slavic bookmen and their Western counterparts, respectively, provides greater insight: there are very few, if any, medieval books for private reading in the Roman Catholic tradition, in which the maker does not try to convey to the reader at least some of the fruits of his own intellectual activity.[42] Conversely, most, if not all, of the medieval books for private reading of Slavia Orthodoxa are devoid of such pretense: they seem merely to convey to the reader raw material for fruitful intellectual activity.

---

[40] Veder, "Elementary Compilation" (see n. 29), 50.

[41] I am greatly indebted to Norman Ingham for pointing out that the term "randomization" I had used earlier ("Literature as a Kaleidoscope: The Structure of Slavic *Četii Sborniki,*" in *Semantic Analysis of Literary Texts*, ed. E. De Haard et al. [Amsterdam, 1990], 599–613) still reflects a definite structural principle and, therefore, should be avoided.

[42] Possible exceptions can be sought in the exceedingly tedious *Centos* and *Centuria* (series of gnomes), produced both in Greek and Latin, as well as the *Rapiaria* (edificational florilegia of the *Devotio moderna* in the fifteenth-century Low Countries, works which Nicolaas van Wijk

As the early Christian *Apophthegmata Patrum*, translated into Slavic presumably by Saint Methodius himself, put it:

> A certain brother, living in the desert, despairing in his study, asked his father, saying: "Why, father, do I labor over the Scriptures and understand naught of which I attend to?" He answered him, saying: "O child, the sheep, when they see the pasture, eat with great appetite and often swallow the food unchewed, striving which could swallow and take in the most food; and standing aside alone, they chew the food, throwing it up from within. Even so thou, child ...."[43]

To my mind, this evident difference in attitudes of bookmen towards communication with their readers points to an even more fundamental difference in the function and meaning of texts in the respective cultures. It would be worthwhile to consider this difference in the light of Jurij Mixajlovič Lotman's thought-provoking ideas set forth in his article "Canonic Art as an Information Paradox." Whereas in Western medieval culture, the graphically recorded text may "function as a source of information," in the culture of Slavia Orthodoxa it may function merely "as its catalyst," or as "a kind of reminder." The reader of the former "is first and foremost a listener, conditioned to extract information from the text"; the reader of the latter "is only brought into a favorable condition to listen to himself; he is not only a listener, he is a creator. Thus, in one case, the 'work' is equal to a graphically recorded text, it has fixed boundaries and a relatively stable information content; in the other, the text recorded graphically or otherwise is no more than the most noticeable, though not the most important part of the work. It requires additional interpretation, insertion into some much less organized context."[44]

It is tempting to speculate whether it was not a basically different type of communication that formed the culture of medieval Slavia Orthodoxa in general and Muscovite Russia in particular. But before we can undertake such an investigation, we must first determine whether the observations made fully support the generalizations I propose, a task that requires much source study and painstaking descriptive work. We must then investigate whether this specific type of communication between the maker of the book

---

so diligently studied as keeper of manuscripts at the Royal Library in The Hague). Even these works betray some inclination of their authors to organize their textual material in some systematic fashion.

[43] Apophthegm A:19 of the *Paterik Skitskij* (Greek), unpublished.

[44] "Kanoničeskoe iskusstvo kak informacionnyj paradoks," in *Problema kanona v drevnem i srednevekovom iskusstve Azii i Afriki. Sbornik statej* (Moscow, 1973), 18–20.

and its reader is, indeed, restricted to Slavia Orthodoxa. This investigation will require the reading of many unread Greek and Latin manuscript books. Finally, to examine the life span of this relationship, we must read many unread books of later Slavia Orthodoxa, varying by area from the early sixteenth century to the late twentieth. In conclusion, to quote Florovsky again: "What we really need most is monographic research. The time for a historical synthesis probably has not yet come."[45]

[45] "Reply," (see n. 2), 42.

THE LIFE OF SAINT FILIPP

TSAR AND METROPOLITAN
IN THE LATE SIXTEENTH CENTURY

PAUL BUSHKOVITCH

Introduction: Sources and Historiography

The traditional view of sixteenth-century Russia, inherited from prerevolutionary historians and maintained until recently, has been one that focused attention entirely on the supposedly all-powerful autocrat. Russian society was supposed to be passive and submissive, lacking any authentic life of its own. As this anachronistic conception, with its obvious identification of a sixteenth-century political institution with those of late Imperial and Stalinist Russia, begins to fade, the contours of Russian society begin to emerge from the shadows to which previous historians have consigned them. So far it is mainly the boyar elite that has emerged, but another major institution that needs fresh examination is the Church. The existing literature, both Western and Soviet, assumes that the sixteenth-century Church was a sort of Ministry of Propaganda for the monarch, especially after the victory of Josephism at the beginning of the century. Allegedly this situation remained unchanged until Nikon challenged the tsar's authority over the Church in the 1650s. The Church seems to follow the development of the state, "centralizing" as the state "centralizes," and glorifying the person and institution of the monarch. This view of the Church in the sixteenth century is not the result of careful research over the decades by many different scholars. Rather, it is one of those quasi-metaphysical assumptions about Russian history that arose in debates of the nineteenth-century intelligentsia and has become an accepted idea: the Church was always subordinate to the state in Russia. Parallel to this idea has been even greater neglect of religion (as opposed to the Church as an institution) in the same period.

Actual research on the Church and religion in the sixteenth century has been too specifically focused to illuminate these general issues. A few subjects have been the object of fairly intense scrutiny (the Judaizer heresy,

Josephism, the non-possessors, Maksim Grek), but whole areas—the liturgy, church administration, the parish clergy, monasticism (outside the well-known debates), and the entire period after about 1560—have remained virtually untouched. Moreover, research has been restricted because of the lack of basic source publications for the history of religion and the Church. The historian of medieval Western Europe can accomplish an enormous amount simply with the *Patrologia Latina,* the *Acta Sanctorum,* and the myriad series of source publications, Catholic and otherwise; but the historian of Russia must work with largely unpublished sources and spend great amounts of time merely to establish elementary facts.

In addition, most scholars have looked at the available texts searching for ideas other than the basic religious ideas and experiences recorded in those texts. The contemporary scholar must remember that for over a century historians and philologists alike in Russia and the West have mined the texts for political ideas, national ideas, stylistic conventions, anything imaginable, but not primarily for religious ideas. Furthermore, fundamental religious texts have received much less attention than secular texts, a situation that has distorted the picture of Old Russian culture. Philologists and historians have tended to avoid specifically religious subject matter as theological, and few historians of religion have filled the gap. Orthodoxy, even more in Russia than in Byzantium, is far less well-known than any of the Western forms of Christianity.

The study of the history of religion in Russia cannot be advanced merely by the subjective desire to do a better job, spend more time in BAN or TsGADA, or eschew themes whose interest is mainly publicistic. The tradition of reading religious texts to look for other ideas is now so entrenched that a much more self-conscious methodology is needed, one that keeps the interpreter of the text, historian or philologist, close to the basic meaning of the text in the world in which it arose. After all, the reading of sources is the primary act of the historian, for without it history becomes merely a publicistic debate about the past, a different type of activity. What is needed are some rules for reading religious texts, rules meant to redirect the attention of historians and philologists to the religious significance of the texts they study and to put other aspects in second place where they belong. The study of old Russian religious texts has not suffered from literalism, rather the reverse.

Some Rules of Reading

We should set forth the following rules to direct current research in Russian history, particularly the history of religion:

1. *A text is about what it says it is about.* Thus the *Zhitie* of Sergei of Radonezh is not about the development of national consciousness in Russia. It is the life of a monastic saint; it is about monasticism.

2. *A text conveys its content by the known devices of rhetoric and such simple matters as emphasis.* Thus the epistles of Filofei are not about the Third Rome. The epistle to Vasilii, for example, is an exhortation to piety and the avoidance of sin, particularly homosexuality. It is not devoted to apocalyptic, and the "theory of the Third Rome" is in fact the "subordinate clause of the Third Rome."

3. *The further implications of a text are to be considered only after its basic message has been read.* It is legitimate to find political implications in the *Life* of Sergei, but only after it is understood that these are merely implications derived from a text about another subject altogether. In addition, historians must differentiate between their own categories and those of the time they are studying. They need not abandon their own terminology, but if the words and categories do not exist in the time under scrutiny, they must admit that fact and justify their use of modern categories.

4. *A text or group of texts does not have to be consistent, especially to modern understanding.* Human beings do not have perfectly consistent worldviews. Therefore, we should not expect a single text or the works of one author to be consistent. In the case of Filofei, A. L. Gol'dberg noticed that the references to the Third Rome in Filofei's writings were not consistent, and therefore postulated two authors, setting off a largely pointless controversy.[1] No historian of the modern era, writing on Belinskii or Khomiakov, for example, would be bothered by contradictions in their writings and would merely note the contradictions with interest. Why should we assume differently about the sixteenth century?

A corollary is that we should not try to impose a false consistency on a particular era. The controversies over the Igor Tale are an example, for behind all the philological pyrotechnics of the skeptics is the belief that the Tale does not fit our conventional view of the Kievan era, filled as it is with pagan references long after 988. Indeed, the Tale does not fit our normal conception of the Kievan era, particularly our conception of its religious history. The conclusion should be not that the Tale was concocted by an unknown classicizing author of the eighteenth century, but that our idea of the

---

[1] A. L. Gol'dberg, "Tri 'poslaniia Filofeia' (Opyt tekstologicheskogo analiza)," *TODRL* 29 (1974), 68–97; Frank Kämpfer, "'Sendschreiben Filofejs' oder 'Filofej-Zyklus': Argumente gegen die Ergebnisse Alexander Goldbergs," *Canadian American Slavic Studies* 13, no. 1/2 (1979): 126–138; and on the religious message of the epistles, Nikolai Andreyev, "Filofei and His Epistle to Ivan Vasil'yevich'" *Slavonic and East European Review* 38, no. 90 (1959): 30–31.

Kievan era is wrong. The source has priority over the conception of the historian, not the other way around.

At the most general level, these rules demand that the interpreter of the text begin with a literal reading, as literal as can be achieved given that the interpreter lives in the late twentieth century. He or she should try to establish first what the author was trying to do, not an easy task, but an essential one. He or she should not start by trying to fit the text into modern historiographical controversies, as so many historians have done.

Metropolitan Filipp

The *Zhitie* of Metropolitan Filipp (1506/1507–1569) represents a case of the unjustly neglected text, one that contains a defense of the position of the Church rarely found in published sources. It was a relatively popular work in the seventeenth century, for over 150 manuscript copies of the Tulupov redaction of the text are known.[2] Filipp appeared for the first time in the printed service books in 1646, and his relics were brought back to Moscow by the future Patriarch Nikon in 1652, making him the object of a very official cult.[3] Of the two versions of his *Life*, one is a shorter version that provides many details on his activity as hegumen of the Solovetskii Monastery and fewer on his conflict with Ivan. This version is known in only one copy, named by Latysheva as the "Kolychev" redaction, found in a single seventeenth-century copy inscribed at the time by the owner, Mikhail

---

[2] Nikolai Barsukov, *Istochniki Russkoi agiografii* (St. Petersburg, 1882), 566–575. The copy used here is a late seventeenth-century copy of the Tulupov redaction from the Vatican Library, Vat. slav. 30, incipit *Elitsy ybo dukhom Bozhiim vodimi sut'*, synove Bozhii narekutsia, 'Those who are led by the spirit of God are called the sons of God'. That it contains the Tulupov redaction is established both by the incipit and the contents as compared to authors who used this version, quoting it extensively and paraphrasing it, Iakhontov and Bishop Leonid. See Harald Jaksche, "Slavische Handschriften in der Vatikanischen Bibliothek," *Römische historische Mitteilungen* 5 (1961/1962): 228. Barsukov knew of only fifty-two copies, three of them dated 1633, 1642, and 1644.

[3] See the *Sviattsy* (Moscow, 1646), ff. 116–117. Thus the correct date of his "canonization," that is, his proclamation as a saint throughout Russia, was 1646, not 1592, as Golubinskii asserted. Golubinskii emphasized local festivals in his work on canonization, giving a misleading picture of the Church's policy in the area of sainthood. E. E. Golubinskii, *Istoriia kanonizatsii sviatykh v russkoi tserkvi*, ČOIDR 1(1903): 118. Golubinskii's survey of printed liturgical books also establishes that after 1646 Filipp appeared under 23 December, the day of his death, and in such books in 1655 and 1656, after which he disappeared only to reappear under 9 January 1682: Ibid., pp. 239, 247. Latysheva asserts, following an earlier scholar, that Filipp's festival is found under 23 December in the 1636 *Mineia*. However, the Zernova catalogue describes the 1636 *Mineia* as listing festivals for September alone, a fact confirmed by Golubinskii. G. G. Latysheva, "Publitsisticheskii istochnik po istorii Oprichniny (K voprosu o datirovke)," *Voprosy istoriografii i istochnikovedeniia otechestvennoi istorii* (Moscow, 1974), 32; and A. S. Zernova, *Knigi kirillovskoi pechati, izdannye v Moskve v XVI–XVII vekakh: Svodnyi katalog* (Moscow, 1958), 43.

Dmitrievich Kolychev, and now in the Undol'skii Collection (GBL, f. 310, no. 380). The second version, she has named the "Tulupov" after the earliest dated (1633) version from the collection of the Trinity Monastery (now GBL).[4] Kliuchevskii, the first student of the history of the text, posited that the Tulupov (the "long" version, in his terminology) was the original text, composed in the 1590s after Filipp's body was returned to Solovki, whereas the Kolychev ("short") version came later. The basis of this conclusion is in the text where the account in the "long" redaction of the miracles worked at Filipp's shrine shortly after its return to Solovki includes the phrase "Shortly after the bringing of the blessed Filipp, Feodosii and Ermogen [var.: Feodosii the hieromonk] told me this" (51v). This seems quite straightforward and points to a date in the first or second decade after 1591. On the basis of rather intricate textual comparisons, Latysheva concluded that the Kolychev redaction was the primary one, composed in the Solovetskii Monastery in the years 1601–1610. This redaction lacks an account of the miracles and thus the phrase from which Kliuchevskii inferred the date of the Tulupov redaction. Latysheva's demonstration that the Kolychev redaction came first has some merit, but her insistence that it must come after 1601 is based only on a rather dubious account of fires in the monastery mills in the eighteenth-century version of the Solovetskii Chronicle. This conclusion is so questionable that the date of the Kolychev redaction must be based on that of the Tulupov redaction for which it was a source. Here the evidence of the text accepted by Kliuchevskii seems definitive.[5]

Latysheva, however, manages to find reasons to date the text later. She rejects the idea that the author himself could have been an eyewitness to Filipp's life and thus argues that the text need not be dated to the 1590s. She would have us believe that the author heard from Feodosii about the miracles shortly after 1591, but waited thirty years to write. At the same time she insists that the text is a useful source for the *Oprichnina* and tries to show that the author could have talked to eyewitnesses of the saint's life. Her impulses are contradictory. She presents no evidence why the text

---

[4] V. O. Kliuchevskii, *Drevnerusskie zhitiia sviatykh kak istoricheskii istochnik* (Moscow, 1871), 311–312. Latysheva, "Publitsisticheskii istochnik" (see n. 3), 30–62; R. P. Dmitrieva, "Zhitie Filippa mitropolita (Kolycheva)," *Slovar' knizhnikov i knizhnosti drevnei Rusi*, 2 vols. (Leningrad, 1988–1989), v. 2, pt. 1:342–344.

[5] M. V. Kukushkina, *Monastyrskie biblioteki Russkogo Severa* (Leningrad, 1977), 163, asserts that Nikol'skii believed that Gerasima Firsov was the author of the short version. She seems to have misunderstood the quotation from Firsov in Nikol'skii's work, which refers to the short version composed by Firsov for the *Prolog*. See N. Nikol'skii, *Sochineniia Solovetskogo inoka Gerasima Firsova po neizdannym tekstam* (St. Petersburg, 1916) (Pamiatniki drevnei pis'mennosti i iskusstva, no. 188), xxii. There is also a third version by Sergei Shelonin, also unpublished, from ca. 1630–1655 (Kukushkina, 98–99).

should be dated to the 1620s other than the shaky dating of the Kolychev redaction. She believes that a text so clearly asserting the metropolitan's authority was impossible for the sixteenth century, so a date closer to Nikon's time is needed. Offering no convincing refutation of Kliuchevskii's dating of the Tulupov redaction to the 1590s, she introduces contemporary interpretation as fact and rejects the authority of the source.[6] As I see it, both redactions probably date from the years 1590–1604 or from 1610, and served different audiences: the Kolychev redaction was intended for the monks of Solovki, whereas the Tulupov redaction was aimed at a wider audience. Both were products of the Solovetskii Monastery. Neither version is likely to be a reliable source for the events of the 1560s. The text of Filipp's *Life* is best taken only as a publicistic work of the 1590s or somewhat later.

The metropolitanate and death of Filipp were vivid episodes in the time of Ivan Grozny, and historians have commented on them frequently. Their main source was his *Life,* usually the Tulupov version, supplemented by the reports of Taube and Kruse and Heinrich von Staden.[7] Karamzin told the story as an example of Ivan's despotism and presented Filipp as a meek martyr humbly requesting the tsar to spare his victims. Solov'ev followed Karamzin's lead, asserting that Filipp's role was to beg for mercy (*pechalovat'sia*) for some of Ivan's victims. Later historians only added details to Karamzin's image of the event. Using the Kolychev version of the *Life,* Solov'ev merely quoted a short passage in which Filipp, ordered by Ivan to be silent, refused. The context of the dispute, it would appear from Solov'ev, was Filipp's desire to intercede for the innocent, nothing more. Kliuchevskii, although he had established the textual variants and dated them fairly suc-

---

[6] If contextual evidence is permissible, then a variety of conclusions could immediately be drawn. Why not take the context to be the deposition of Metropolitan Dionisii in late 1586, or more remotely the establishment of the patriarchate in 1589, imposed on Patriarch Jeremias by Boris Godunov? The former incident seems to present a clear parallel to the case of Filipp, and nothing like it occurs again until Nikon's time. If indeed it is accepted that the *Life* of Filipp was composed in the period 1591–1604 or thereabouts, then it may indeed be a reaction to Dionisii's deposition or the establishment of the patriarchate. These events, however, cannot be taken as evidence for the date of the *Life* without running the risk of using the modern historian's interpretation of the events as facts. On these episodes, see R. G. Skrynnikov. *Rossiia nakanune "Smutnogo vremeni"* (Moscow, 1980), 33; A. A. Zimin, *Kanun groznykh potriasenii* (Moscow, 1986), 134–136; and V. I. Buganov, M. P. Lukichev, and N. M. Rogozhin eds., *Posol'skaia kniga po sviaziam Rossii s Gretsiei (pravoslavnymi ierarkhami i monastyriami) 1588–1592 gg.* (Moscow, 1988).

[7] The most convenient editions are M. G. Roginskii, "Poslanie Ioganna Taube i Elerta Kruze," *Russkii istoricheskii zhurnal* 8 (1922): 10–59; and Heinrich von Staden, *Aufzeichnungen über den Moskauer Staat,* 2d ed., edited by Fritz T. Epstein (Hamburg, 1964). Universität Hamburg: Abhandlungen aus dem Gebiet der Auslandskunde, no. 34, ser. A, 5.

cessfully, did not use the texts in his famous course, preferring to quote from Karamzin and Solov'ev and, like them, to reduce Filipp's role to one of intercession for the victims of the tsar's wrath.[8]

The first of the church historians to turn to the subject of Filipp was Bishop Leonid of Dmitrov, whose 1849 biography of the metropolitan was not published until 1861. The great value of Leonid's work was the very detailed paraphrase of the *Zhitie* (Tulupov redaction) used by later historians. Leonid saw Filipp as a martyr to truth, murdered by Ivan because he opposed the *Oprichnina*. He emphasized Filipp's "gentry" origin and did not raise the larger issues of the rights of the metropolitan, omitting such parts from his paraphrase of the text. Metropolitan Makarii, using the same Tulupov redaction as his basic source, also emphasized in his account of Filipp the metropolitan's support of the boyars and opposition to Ivan. He thus politicized the text and did not mention the defense of the rights of the Church.[9] The church historians, following the lead of Karamzin and others, viewed the case of Filipp as essentially political, a matter of opposition to Ivan's policies.

Soviet historians have concentrated on placing Filipp in their schemas of the political alignments of Ivan's reign. The first Soviet historian to consider the story of Filipp was A. A. Zimin, in this case, as so many others, a pioneer. Zimin saw Makarii as a moderate centralizer in the spirit of Ivan's "reforms," whereas Filipp was a spokesman for Novgorodian interests with some ties to the boyar opposition. He based much of this on the *Zhitie* of Filipp, though aware it was composed no earlier than 1591, and used it as the basis of his chapter on the metropolitan's conflict with the tsar. However, he gave the actual speeches of Filipp from the *Zhitie* rather short shrift, devoting to them only two pages of a forty-seven page chapter on Filipp, most of it a consideration of the metropolitan's political alignments. R. G. Skrynnikov sees the political alignments differently, making Filipp a spokesman of the Staritskii interests and the boyars. Skrynnikov asserts that Filipp

---

[8] N. M. Karamzin, *Istoriia gosudarstva rossiiskogo* (St. Petersburg, 12 vols., 1851–1853), v. 9, 96–101, 105–111, Notes, v. 9, 57–59, 67–73. Karamzin's sources were the Tulupov redaction of the *Life*, the eighteenth-century Solovetskii Chronicle, and Taube and Kruse. He was also the first to assert that Filipp came from a boyar family (ibid., 96). S. M. Solov'ev, *Istoriia Rossii s drevneishikh vremen*, 15 vols. (Moscow, 1960–1966), v. 3, 556–557; V. O. Kliuchevskii, *Kurs russkoi istorii*, 5 vols., in *Sochineniia* (Moscow, 1957), v. 2, 191–192, 430, n. 8; S. F. Platonov, *Ivan Groznyi* (Petrograd, 1923), 137, mentions only the fact of Filipp's death.

[9] Leonid, Bishop of Dmitrov, *Zhizn' sviatogo Filippa mitropolita Moskovskogo i vseia Rossii* (Moscow, 1861); Makarii [Bulgakov], *Istoriia russkoi tserkvi*, v. 6 (St. Petersburg, 1887), 300–312. Iakhontov concentrated on Filipp's life as a monk in Iv. Iakhontov, *Zhitiia sv. severnorusskikh podvizhnikov Pomorskogo kraia kak istoricheskii istochnik* (Kazan', 1881), 135–154.

"came from a very noble old-Moscow boyar clan" and describes his reproof of Ivan as a defense of boyar interests. He, too, used the Tulupov version of the *Life* as well as Taube and Kruse and chronicle sources. Both historians view the Church as simply a spokesman for other interests with no point of view of its own, and Filipp as merely the mouthpiece of either the Novgorodians or the boyars. Skrynnikov evaluates Filipp's position as highly unusual, since he states that "In the course of the whole sixteenth century the Church unwaveringly remains a most important support of the monarchy." Thus by definition Filipp could only have been a spokesman for other than Church interests, for the Church as such allegedly wholly identified with the monarchy.[10]

In the West historians of the era of Grozny have not devoted much attention to Filipp. The exception was the émigré historian G. P. Fedotov, who wrote a short book on Filipp and was perhaps the only historian to take seriously the notion of a real conflict of Church and state in the events. Fedotov's work went largely unnoticed, in part perhaps because it did not fit the overall assumptions of the field. but also such a revolutionary idea could not make much headway without the original text. Fedotov relied on A. N. Murav'ev's paraphrase of the text, not the text itself. More recently, Ihor Ševčenko looked at the content of Filipp's speeches in the *Life* primarily to show that they are a recasting of the Byzantine tract of Archdeacon Agapetus, a recasting that turned a defense of monarchical authority into its opposite.[11]

The analysis of the *Life of Filipp* has been hampered by the discussion of the text as a source for the period of the *Oprichnina*, though Kliuchevskii long ago noted that it could not have been composed before 1592. From the start, it should be made clear that it is a very problematic source for the events of 1568–1569. Although biographical details such as the names of the saint's parents, his time at the Solovetskii Monastery, and general facts about the metropolitanate may be relied upon (within the limits of the hagiographical genre), it is hard to imagine that the long speeches in the text have much reliability. Ševčenko's analysis of the speeches' relation to Agapetus is helpful, for it shows their sophisticated literary sources. This

---

[10] A. A. Zimin, *Oprichnina Ivana Groznogo* (Moscow, 1964), 212–259, esp. 221–223; R. G. Skrynnikov, *Nachalo Oprichniny,* Leningradskii gosudarstvennyi pedagicheskii institut im. A. I. Gertsena, Uchenye zapiski, no. 294 (1966): 339–342, 345–347, 381–386 (quotation taken from p. 381), 396–409.

[11] G. P. Fedotov, *Sv. Filipp, mitropolit Moskovskii* (Paris, 1928); Ihor Ševčenko, "A Neglected Byzantine Source of Muscovite Political Ideology" in Michael Cherniavsky, ed., *The Structure of Russian History* (New York, 1970), 80–107; and D. M. Bulanin, "'Pouchenie' Agapita" in *Slovar'* (see n. 4), v. 2, pt. 2, 300–303.

analysis may tell nothing whatever about the disputes of 1568 but a great deal about the worldview of an author of the 1590s.[12] The *Life of Filipp* is to be studied not primarily as a source for the *Oprichnina*, for which it has only marginal value, but as a source of the worldview of the monks of the Solovetskii Monastery and their audience in the 1590s.

The text opens with an introduction setting the tone as the story of a man of truth and a great monk (ff. 1–3). The *Life* itself begins with an account of his parents and childhood, in accord with the topoi of a monastic saint. He was born in Moscow and named Fyodor in 7015 (1506/1507), the son of Stefan and Varvara Kolychev. Stefan is described as having attained favor and rank (*vysota sanovnaia*) and being originally from Novgorod.[13] Fyodor loved divine learning, not play, even as a boy (3–6). The next section (6–18v) covers the period 1533–1568, and describes Filipp's youth, his decision to enter a monastery, and his career as a monk, ending on the eve of his appointment as metropolitan. According to the *Life*, Fyodor Kolychev began to serve the boy prince Ivan IV on Vasilii's death, and the young ruler loved him for his piety. He had an experience at this time, when he was about thirty years old (ca. 1537). He went to the church at the time of his maturity and heard the Gospel words about serving two masters (Matthew 6:24). They seemed to be spoken to him personally. This made him think of the monastery of Zosima and Savvatii on Solovki. Because the Solovetskii Monastery was too far, he settled at first at Lake Onega, on Kizhi, apparently as a hermit (6–8v). After some time he went on to the Solovetskii Monastery, where hegumen Aleksii accepted him as a novice. The text briefly describes his labors, his humility, chastity, and his likeness to Christ in his manner of life (8v–9v). Rejoicing in his virtue, Aleksii and the brothers tonsured him a monk with the name Filipp. He was given for training in obedience to Iona, formerly an associate of Aleksandr Svirskii (died 1533). Iona prophesied that Filipp would be hegumen himself some day. Filipp became a hermit for a while, practicing harsh asceticism, but eventually returned to the monastery and helped Aleksii for nine years (9v–12v). When Aleksii grew old, the brothers turned to Filipp to replace him as hegumen,

---

[12] Latysheva attempts to show that the *Zhitie* must be based on contemporary reports because of some coincidences in the speeches of Filipp to Ivan as reported by Taube and Kruse. These coincidences, however, are between passages so general in content as to be of little value: Latysheva, "Publitsisticheskii istochnik" (see n. 3), 56–60. Ševčenko also notes a coincidence of one phrase borrowed from Agapetus in both the *Zhitie* and Taube and Kruse, but this again is a very slender reed. Ševčenko, "A Neglected Byzantine Source" (see n. 11), 96–97.

[13] What this rank was (if it existed) is unknown, though a nineteenth-century genealogist asserted that Stefan was the *diad'ka* of Prince Iurii Vasil'evich. Zimin found no evidence of this fact, nor any other office. Zimin, *Oprichnina* (see n. 10), 224.

but he naturally refused: the monks convinced him to go with a delegation to Feodosii, archbishop of Novgorod (1542–1563), who ultimately convinced him to accept the office (ca. 1548). Filipp later abandoned the hegumenate to return to his hermitage, turning over the office again to Aleksii. Aleksii lived only one year after this event, and Filipp had to resume the office, which he held until 1566 (12v–16). During his hegumenate Filipp was extremely active in building up the monastery, both expanding the economic base by seeing to fishing, farming and various buildings, and improving the churches (Dormition, Transfiguration, Saint John the Baptist) and the refectory. Finally, in the time of Tsar Ivan's victories over the infidels (*supostaty:* presumably Russia's enemies in the Livonian War), the tsar tried to find a good candidate for metropolitan, at first settling on Afanasii (16–18v).

The next section (18v–44v) describes Filipp's metropolitanate up to his deposition and imprisonment. This is the core of the *Life*. It begins with Ivan's invitation to Filipp to come to Moscow for a council and his journey by way of Novgorod where the people begged him to intercede with the tsar on behalf of the city. At the council Ivan convinced Filipp to accept the dignity of metropolitan despite his plea of inadequacy. Filipp exhorted the tsar to be meek, good, and just, and to oppose heresy.[14] At first things went well: Filipp followed in the path of his predecessor Makarii, and piety and love reigned (18v–23). Satan then entered into the hearts of men; hostility grew among the great and the simple, and the tsar grew angry at his innocent servants. He called together a council, of the boyars and clergy bringing together Pimin of Novgorod, Pafnutii of Suzdal', and others. At the council Ivan established the *Oprichnina* and asked the bishops to bless his innovations. Out of fear they complied, except for Filipp, who asked the tsar to leave off the idea and return to the ways of his father Vasilii III. Filipp spoke of the need of love and of his own authority over all Christians. Pimin, German of Kazan', and the priest Evstafii of the Kremlin Annunciation Cathedral supported Ivan, and the tsar divided the boyars between the *Oprichnina* and *Zemshchina*. The executions began (23–27v). Filipp then remonstrated with the tsar, telling him that since he was like God, he must be just and good like God; he must follow the customs of

---

[14] This speech (21–22) is Agapetus 5, 8, 2, 22, 15, 20, 28: cf. Ševčenko, "A Neglected Byzantine Source" (see n. 11), 93–94, and Agapetus, "Expositio capitum admonitorium," *PG* 86.1, 1163–1186. The quotations from Agapetus form an unbroken Old Russian text in this speech. The text in the original *Zhitie* is notably closer to the Greek than the paraphrase of Filipp's speech by Fedotov used by Ševčenko (e.g., Agapetus 20 on f. 21v). The last comment of Filipp about heresy is not from Agapetus.

his ancestors.[15] Ivan became angry and asked him what authority he had to interfere in the tsar's affairs. Filipp replied that as metropolitan he had authority over all Christians, together with the tsar. Ivan ordered him to be silent and bless him, but Filipp replied that his silence would put sin in the heart of the tsar. If the ship's pilot should fall into temptation, then the ship would perish.[16] He spoke of the need for love. Ivan accused him of rebellion like that of those close to King David.[17] Filipp answered that as tsar, Ivan must listen to good counsellors and be merciful to the obedient, for he must think of eternal life.[18] Ivan told him not to oppose his power or to leave his office. Filipp told him to depose him if he dared, as it would violate the canons of the Church (28–30v).

After consulting with Vasilii Griaznoi and Maliuta Skuratov, Ivan decided to continue the *Oprichnina*. Much bloodshed and suffering followed, and a group of laymen came to Filipp for his aid. On Sunday at the service the tsar came with his followers all dressed in black "like Chaldeans." Ivan came up to Filipp three times for a blessing, but each time Filipp refused. Then Filipp spoke reproving the tsar quoting the "God-voiced writer of songs," *bogoglasnyi pesnopisets* (33), that is, Agapetus. He told the tsar that he should avoid flatterers, for innocent blood was being spilled, that he should remember that though in image he was like God, he was connected to earth by dust, that he should forgive those who sinned against him, and as Saint John the Theologian reminds us, show love for man.[19] Ivan answered that it was Filipp's business to agree with the tsar. When Filipp asserted his duty to care for the faithful, Ivan threatened him and reproved him for opposing the tsar's power. Still, Filipp refused to obey and said that he was prepared for suffering (30v–35).[20]

Then Filipp's enemies began to plot to depose him. Led by Pimin of Novgorod, the bishops reproached Filipp, and the reader (*anagnost*) in church

---

[15] This speech (28–28v), except for the final admonition to follow the customs of the ancestors is Agapetus 1, 7, 10, 18: Cf. Ševčenko, "A Neglected Byzantine Source" (see n. 11), 95. The chronology here is inaccurate, for the *Oprichnina* was established before Filipp's appointment. The text also omits Filipp's agreement with Ivan not to interfere in it: Zimin, *Oprichnina* (see n. 10), 246–247.

[16] This speech (29–29v) is Agapetus 10: Cf. Ševčenko, "A Neglected Byzantine Source" (see n. 11), 95.

[17] Cf. Ia. S. Lur'e and Iu. D. Rykov, *Perepiska Ivan Groznogo s Andreem Kurbskim* (Leningrad, 1979), 19, referring to 2 Samuel 5, 6–8.

[18] This speech (30) repeats Agapetus 22 and 20, adding 15: Cf. Ševčenko, "A Neglected Byzantine Source" (see n. 11), 96.

[19] This speech (33–33v) is Agapetus 12, 21. Cf. ibid., p. 96. Fedotov's epithet for Agapetus was quite different; thus Ševčenko was misled.

[20] This appears to be the incident mentioned in the Novgorod Second Chronicle: *PSRL* 3:162, and dated 22 March 7076 (1568). Such was the opinion of Bishop Leonid: *Zhizn'* (see n. 9), 91.

publicly slandered the metropolitan. Filipp told Pimin that he too would lose his episcopal seat, but he forgave the reader after he confessed that he had acted under pressure. The Christian people and the pious monks were not swayed in their loyalty to the metropolitan.

On the day of Saints Prokhor, Nikanor, and Parmen (28 July), the tsar appeared in the Church of the Mother of God in the Novodevichii Monastery with his *oprichniki,* one of whom wore a small cap (*tafia*) that attracted Filipp's wrath. The guilty party concealed his action, but this incident only further inflamed both the tsar and his court. A commission—consisting of Pafnutii, bishop of Suzdal', Archimandrite Feodosii, and Prince Vasilii Temkin-Rostovskii, an *oprichnik* of the tsar—was sent to the Solovetskii Monastery to investigate Filipp's alleged misdeeds.[21] They had difficulty getting the monks to slander Filipp, but eventually Pafnutii persuaded the hegumen Paisii to do so by promising him a bishopric. Back in Moscow, Ivan could now call together the boyars to hear the evidence and depose Filipp. The author of the *Zhitie* points out that Ivan's action was illegal since only bishops could judge the metropolitan, not the tsar or his boyars.[22] The next day as Filipp conducted service in the Uspenskii Cathedral, Aleksei Basmanov appeared and forcibly removed his robes. Filipp predicted that the Church would be widowed and that he would not be buried in the cathedral with his predecessors. Basmanov and his men then put Filipp in a patched and torn monastic habit and set him in a cart, mocking him and taking him to be imprisoned in the Bogoiavlenskii Monastery in the Kitaigorod.[23] The people followed him weeping. Filipp blessed the people, exhorting them to imitate Christ and to love their enemies. The tsar then ordered Filipp brought to the *episkopiiu* (the episcopal, perhaps meaning metropolitan's, residence) to hear Paisii repeat his slanders, but Filipp reminded the tsar of the better ways of his ancestors. The tsar gave him over to his soldiers, who said among themselves that Filipp must be removed, for he

---

[21] Temkin-Rostovskii, who had been a prisoner in Lithuania, was released in 1567 and became a boyar of the *Oprichnina*. After his involvement in 1568 with the case of Filipp, he was executed in 1571: A. A. Zimin, *Oprichnina* (see n. 10), 144, n. 2.

[22] "*Tsarem ne podobaet sviatitel'skie viny ispytovati, no episkopi po pravilam sudiat. I ashche viny dostoiny budet, i tsar' vlast' svoiu na nem pokazuet*" [It is not proper for tsars to investigate the crimes of a bishop, but bishops judge by the rules. And if he is guilty, then the tsar will show his power upon him.] Andrei Kurbskii (*Kurbsky's History of Ivan IV*, ed. J. L. I. Fennell [Oxford, 1965], 234, 236), makes the same charge, that Ivan violated the canons of the Church in judging Filipp at a council that included laymen. The *Zhitie*, however, does not use the word "council."

[23] Apparently as a result Filipp's relative Grigorii Ivanovich Kolychev was buried there in 1570: Nikodim, "Opisanie Moskovskogo Bogoiavlenskogo Monastyria," *ČOIDR*, 1876, bk. 4: 166–167. I have not been able to identify this particular Kolychev.

alone denounced the misdeeds of the tsar and his soldiers. The soldiers put him in a barn in chains and starved him. The chains fell miraculously from Filipp, and after a while Ivan ordered him brought to the Monastery of Saint Nicholas the Elder. Soon after, the tsar ordered the metropolitan's cousin (*brata ot rodnykh*), Mikhail Ivanovich Kolychev, executed and the head sent to Filipp.[24] He took the head, blessed it, and kissed it (35–44v).

The rest of the text concerns Filipp's transfer to the Tver' Otroch' Monastery (where he perished in December 1569) and his subsequent translation and miracles. Maliuta Skuratov strangled him when he accompanied the tsar to Novgorod for the famous destruction of Novgorod of 1570. In 1590 the pious monks of the Solovetskii Monastery decided to return Filipp's remains to Solovki, and led by hegumen Iakov they received permission to do so.[25] In 1591 the remains of Filipp were taken to the Solovetskii Monastery, and shortly after three miracles occurred at the shrine (44v–56v).

An Application of the Rules

This account should already suggest the insufficiency of previous readings of the text. As noted above, for the pre-Revolutionary Russian historians the main idea was the intercession of Filipp for Ivan's victims, only one of several episodes of conflict in the text. For Zimin and Skrynnikov, Filipp was the spokesman for boyar interests, though the text nowhere describes the conflict in these terms. It is mentioned briefly that the Novgorodians asked Filipp to intercede with the tsar, but this was not the basis of the metropolitan's conflict with Ivan in the text.[26] Ševčenko also saw the story in political terms, as an imperfect ideology of political resistance to the tsar. The text, however, goes beyond the political issue of resistance, and at the same time concerns only the Church, not laymen. The Agapetus texts that were the core of Ševčenko's analysis appear only when Filipp is reproving the behavior of the tsar. When he defends his position as metropolitan,

---

[24] According to Zimin, this was Filipp's second cousin, Mikhail Ivanovich Kolychev-Khromoi, not his uncle the *okol'nichii:* Zimin, *Oprichnina* (see n. 10), 218–219. In contrast Skrynnikov believes him to be the uncle: R. G. Skrynnikov, *Oprichnyi Terror,* Leningradskii gosudarstvennyi pedagogicheskii institut im. A. I. Gertsena, Uchenye zapiski, no. 374 (1969), p. 8.

[25] R. P. Dmitrieva, "Iakov," *Slovar'* (see n. 4), v. 1, pt. 2, 368. Iakov was hegumen of the Solovetskii Monastery from 1582 to 1597.

[26] The Novgorodian chronicles were clearly sympathetic to Filipp: Novgorod Second Chronicle, *sub anno* 7076, and Novgorod Third Chronicle, *sub anno* 7077 (1568/1569, mentioning Filipp's death on Ivan's order): *PSRL* 3:162, 253. Even if we accept them as the expression of point of view of "Novgorodians" at the time, they still only prove that Novgorodians supported Filipp, not that he was their spokesman.

asserting the illegality of his deposition, for example, then the author does not use Agapetus, who does not discuss such subjects. Fedotov alone took the story as a religious work coming from a religious world. His interpretation was that the story glorified an ideal of an autonomous role for the Church in society, one that rejected the notion of necessary subservience to the monarch. He did not, however, clearly spell out what this role was to be, perhaps because he tangled himself up in the issue of the relation of the text to the facts of Filipp's life. Most of Fedotov's little book is written as if the life is a reliable source for Ivan's reign, but then he tells us (178-179) that in fact Filipp's speeches cannot be used to characterize his ideal of the Church's role, as they are too late to be authentic speeches of Filipp. Only Ševčenko saw this last issue clearly, noting correctly that the text reflects not the reality of the 1560s but the ideas of the 1590s, when the text was composed.[27]

The task then is to examine a publicistic work of the 1590s that presents a historical narrative of the life of a holy man and puts into his mouth the ideas of the author, presumably a Solovetskii monk of the 1590s. Such an examination reveals a much more complex conception of the role of the metropolitan (and, by implication, that of the bishops, though not necessarily the clergy as a whole, in spite of Fedotov). Taking the history of the conflict between Ivan and Filipp episode by episode makes this assertion clear. The first episode is the installation of Filipp and the establishment of the *Oprichnina*. Here, using the text of Agapetus, Filipp exhorts the tsar to be just, meek, and good, and to follow the ways of his father Vasilii. This conception of the good tsar is basic to the text, presenting a moral ideal of harmony of tsar and people but not specifically mentioning boyars.[28] Later, Ivan asks the bishops to approve the establishment of the *Oprichnina*, but only Filipp has the courage to refuse. He opposes it as an innovation and contrary to the need for love among men. He based his refusal on his authority over the souls of Christians, an authority shared with the tsar. Again, this part of the text is a garbled variant of the actual events. The text presents the situation as if it were entirely natural for Ivan to consult the Church on political issues, but only Filipp had the courage to object to the tsar's policy. Clearly, the author of Filipp's *Life* believed that the Church (meaning here the bishops and greater abbots, the *osviashchennyi sobor*)

---

[27] Fedotov, *Sv. Filipp* (see n. 11), 178-179; Ševčenko, "A Neglected Byzantine Source" (see n. 11), 96-97, admitting only a few echoes of 1568 in the metropolitan's speeches.

[28] This is the passage in which the author altered the text of Agapetus so that Filipp describes the good tsar as meek (*krotok*) rather than "accessible" (*euporistos*) as in the original of Agapetus: Ševčenko, "A Neglected Byzantine Source" (see n. 11), 93.

should be consulted about major political decisions. This is a greater role for the Church than we assume to have existed in either reality or thought in this period.

The next two episodes are quite different in a literary sense, for one is a dialogue between tsar and metropolitan, whereas the other is a narrative of an incident, but both have the same ideological message. In both episodes Ivan demands obedience from Filipp, and in both cases he refuses. His explanation is that he too has responsibility for Christians and that his silence would put sin in the heart of the tsar. In both incidents Filipp refuses to bless the tsar and preaches the need for love of one's fellow man. Ivan accuses him of opposing his power (*derzhava*). Ivan's threat to depose Filipp meets the reply that such an action would violate the canons of the Church. The question at hand is no longer Filipp's right to be consulted on political matters, but his right to disagree with the tsar and oppose his will.

The final episode, the fabrication of a case against Filipp and his deposition, raises still other issues. Here both bishops and boyars agree to do the tsar's bidding and find false witnesses against the metropolitan in the Solovetskii Monastery. But Filipp is not tried. Ivan attempts to assemble a council to depose Filipp, but as the author points out, only bishops could depose Filipp, and the tsar wanted to include himself and the boyars at the council. This assertion follows on the earlier remark of Filipp that his deposition by the tsar would violate the canons of the Church. Here is another issue of principle, that the secular authorities may not judge the Church. This is surely the first time that such a principle was asserted in the Russian church, and it looks forward to the conflict between Tsar Aleksei and Nikon.

It is important to stress that the *Life of Filipp* does not present its hero as the spokesman for the boyars or any other group of society. It does not connect his decision to enter a monastery around 1537 with the case of Prince Andrei Staritskii. as did Bishop Leonid and Zimin. Twice laymen ask him to intercede with the tsar, first in Novgorod and later in Moscow, but the text does not state who they are. Given the landholding structure of the Novgorod area, the supplicants are unlikely to have been boyars. Further, the text seems to blame the boyars for the events, as it states that the *Oprichnina* was the result of hatred in hearts of men that affected the tsar. Ivan was not then the sole originator of the policy. The idea that Filipp should be a boyar spokesman seems to come from two sources, one the claim in Kurbskii's *History* that Filipp's clan perished with him. This assertion, however, has long been known to be false and reflects a level of inaccuracy unusual even for Kurbskii. The identity of the relative of Filipp executed after his deposition is open to some question. Furthermore, Filipp did not come from a boyar family; he was born into a lesser branch of the Kolychev clan that was part of the Novgorod gentry, not into the elder branch active in Moscow politics, a complication that may have confused Kurbskii.[29] The actual history of Filipp's family and clan, however, is to a large extent irrelevant to our text, which has frequent errors of fact (the sequence of events in the *Oprichnina*, for example). The second basis for this assertion may be the description of Filipp in later texts such as the 1646 *Sviattsy* (*rodom Moskovitin, slavnykh boiar imenovaniem Kolychevykh*, 'by family a Muscovite, of the glorious boyars named Kolychev'), a rhetorical flourish (or simple mistake) that may have led later historians astray.[30] Whatever the reality of the 1560s may have been, the crucial point is that the *text* presents Filipp as a spokesman neither for the boyars nor the Novgorod gentry, but for the Church. It also presents a quite detailed and specific justification for Filipp's actions, asserting his right both to be consulted in political matters and to have autonomy from the state (the metropolitan cannot be judged by the tsar).

The text does not reflect the sort of thinking that can properly be called political theory. The view of the actions of the tsar that Filipp voices in the text is basically moral. He must be just, good, loving, meek, in all respects like the God of whom he is the image. The only "secular" element is the remark (made twice) that Ivan should follow the ways of his father Vasilii, but this is not really secular since Vasilii corresponded (in the view of the text) to the moral ideal. That ideal is in turn set into an entirely religious conception of the world, not into a secular political theory. The only evidence of legalism is the reference to the canons of the Church that supposedly should prevent the tsar from deposing the metropolitan.

The *Life of Filipp* was the life of a holy metropolitan, one that presented in the narrative and the dialogues a certain view of the church. This conclusion is in accord with the rules for reading that I set out at the beginning. First, the text is not the life of a monk or a political tract, for it advertises itself from the beginning as the life of a metropolitan, a holy man and a

---

[29] On the 1537 incident, see Leonid, *Zhizn'* (see n. 9), p. 20; and Zimin, *Oprichnina* (see n. 10), p. 225. Fennell, *Kurbsky's History* (see n. 22), 214–216. Zimin in his *Oprichnina*, 214–217, stresses that though basically Novgorod *pomeshchiki*, the immediate family of Filipp had boyar ties. In *Formirovanie boiarskoi aristokratii v Rossii vo vtoroi polovine XV – pervoi treti XVI v.* (Moscow, 1988), 176, 180, A. A. Zimin seems to stress more the divisions among the various branches, an argument which is more in accord with that of Nancy Shields Kollmann, *Kinship and Politics: The Making of the Muscovite Political System 1345–1547* (Stanford, 1987), 211–213. Skrynnikov insists on the boyar connections: Skrynnikov, *Nachalo* (see n. 10), 340.

[30] *Sviattsy* (see n. 3), f. 116. Firsov, in contrast, stressed that Filipp's "brightness" came not from his family but from his establishment of piety: Nikol'skii' *Sochineniia* (see n. 5), 61.

martyr. Second, it makes its points about Filipp in a very clear manner. Most of the text concerns his metropolitanate, not his life as monk. The monastic period in his life is presented schematically; his metropolitanate, in detail. The dialogues of Filipp with the tsar are the centerpieces of the text, and they carry the message, that of the rights of the Church. Third, we cannot draw any conclusions about the relation of Church opposition to Ivan to lay opposition from this text. It does not tell us that Filipp "allied" with the boyars or that he was their spokesman. Historians may argue that other evidence suggests such relations, but they cannot use this text as evidence. The speeches of Filipp and the incidents of narrative simply do not back up such conclusions although they equally do not disprove such an interpretation of the real actions of Filipp as determined by other sources. Fourth, it is improper, as Latysheva has tried, to remove the text from the context of the 1590s simply because it does not fit the current historiography on the Church. The current scholarly literature has a great many ideological and historiographic assumptions that are not strongly grounded in research, and they must be continually tested by the discovery and use of new or neglected sources, especially manuscript sources that have hitherto escaped attention.

The *Life of Filipp* tells us that its author, a monk of one of Russia's three most important monasteries, thought that the Church was to be consulted on important secular policy decisions, that it had the right to act contrary to the will of the monarch, and that Ivan and his *Oprichniki* had committed an evil and sinful act not only in executing Filipp but in refusing to listen to his reproaches. The author thought that the tsar could not depose a metropolitan at will, for the head of the Church could only be tried by churchmen.

How important was the *Zhitie* of Filipp? It was a relatively popular text in the seventeenth century, being among the more frequently copied hagiographic texts. That fact alone, however, does not show that its point of view gained universal or even widespread acceptance.[31] Nikon certainly shared its

---

[31] There is some evidence that Filipp had opponents in the Solovetskii Monastery as well: the (probably) very early seventeenth-century version of the Solovetskii Chronicle is friendly to Archbishop Pimin, Filipp's enemy, barely mentions his appointment as metropolitan and his hegumenate, and omits his death entirely. It also omits any mention of Hegumen Iakov, so heavily praised in the *Zhitie*. See M. N. Tikhomirov, "Maloizvestnye letopisnye pamiatniki," *Istoricheskii arkhiv* 7(1951): 207–253. The Solovetskii Chronicle, which breaks off in 1598, is a curious document, containing the "Tale of the Two Embassies," on which see M. D. Kagan, "'Povest' o dvukh posol'stvakh': legendarno-politicheskoe proizvedenie nachala XVII veka," *TODRL* 11 (1955): 218–253, and Daniel Clarke Waugh, *The Great Turkes Defiance* (Columbus, 1978), 175–183. Gerasim Firsov's account of Filipp's life in the 1650s presented a much simpler picture than that in the Tulupov redaction. Firsov made Filipp simply an opponent of the *Oprichnina* and a victim of the tsar's wrath, omitting the defense of the metropolitan's rights against the tsar: Nikol'skii, *Sochineniia* (see n. 5), 19–64.

worldview, but between the 1590s and the 1650s we have at present no evidence one way or the other. We cannot assert that the text represented the mainstream conception of the Church before Nikon. This does not imply, however, that we should immediately try to trivialize the text and declare it marginal; instead, we should recognize that there is evidence that the view of the Church accepted in modern scholarly literature was subject to challenge at least in some parts of the Orthodox Church of Old Russia. Mainly we should begin more seriously to explore the large body of unknown manuscripts and archival holdings that survive from this period.[32] Only then can we assert whether the views of the author of the *Life of Filipp* were those of an isolated forerunner of Nikon or of a distinct tendency of thought in the Church.

---

[32] A start might be the publication of the whole complex of texts about Filipp, the Tulupov and Kolychev redactions, as well as the work of Shelonin and the republication of Firsov, so as to arrive at a sense of the evolution and variety of accounts of his life.

FIFTEENTH-CENTURY CHRONICLES AS A SOURCE FOR THE HISTORY OF THE FORMATION OF THE MUSCOVITE STATE

JAKOV S. LURIA

In 1940, summing up years of research in his *History of Russian Chronicle Writing from the Eleventh to the Fifteenth Century*, Priselkov wrote,

> If the historian who does not delve deeply into the study of chronicle texts picks the entries he needs from the chronicle *svody* (compilations) of various epochs, as if from a stock prepared especially for him, that is without paying attention to the questions of when, how, and why a particular entry about this or that fact was composed, he thereby restricts the number of possible observations on the particular source in two ways. On the one hand, a determination of the original form of the entry and a study of its subsequent changes in the chronicle tradition might give the researcher new points of view about the fact and explain its reflection in the chronicles. On the other hand, the historian can in such cases often find himself in the awkward position of accepting a fact incorrectly, of seeing it through the lens of Muscovite political bias whose influence is seen in many of the compilations which have come down to us.[1]

Comparing an analytical approach to the chronicles with the historian's arbitrary choice of entries as needed (i.e., with what he himself and his fellow researchers called "the consumer approach,"[2]) Priselkov at the same time touched on the broader question of two research problems that might be posed in investigating any source: first, texts as evidence that can serve as the basis for establishing concrete facts, and second, texts as monuments of a particular epoch—as "relics of the past."

The second of these problems was rarely considered in the work of eighteenth- and nineteenth-century scholars, inclined as they were toward a

Translated from the Russian by Michael S. Flier and Karen Freund.

[1] M. D. Priselkov, *Istoriia russkogo letopisaniia XI–XV vv.* (Leningrad, 1940):6.
[2] *Izvestiia Gosudarstvennoi Akademii istorii material'noi kul'tury*, no. 86 (Moscow and Leningrad, 1934), 111–112 (the speech of S. N. Chernov; cf. Ia. S. Lur'e, "Mikhail Dmitrievich Priselkov—istochnikoved," *TODRL* 13 (1962): 468–471; idem, "Problems of Source Criticism (with Reference to Medieval Russian Documents)," *SR* 27 (March, 1968): 6.

somewhat mechanical separation of sources into "true" and "false," but historians began thereafter to resort more and more to the use of a source as "a relic of the past." The inaccuracy or unreliability of the source constitutes an important fact since it characterizes the text itself, its tendencies, ideology, etc.

The approach to a text as a "relic of the past," however, does not mean indifference to it as a direct source of information or a refusal to try to clarify "how it really was," in Ranke's famous phrase.[3] Unlike works of art, as Collingwood wrote, "a historian's picture is meant to be true."[4]

A basic and quite detailed presentation of the political history of fifteenth-century Muscovite Rus' is contained in the chronicles. But the chronicles that reflect the history of the fifteenth century vary and often contradict one another. In turning our attention to them, we must determine their value as transmitters of information about concrete facts and as "relics of the past"— that is, as publicistic works.

In speaking of the history of the creation of the Muscovite state, historians have relied constantly on the Nikon and Resurrection (*Voskresenskaia*) Chronicles of the sixteenth century. The prominent eighteenth-century Russian historian Tatishchev based his exposition on these two chronicles. Karamzin sharply criticized the Nikon Chronicle and Tatishchev's part in developing its traditions, but in presenting events after 1408, where the text of the Trinity Chronicle ends, Karamzin himself was forced to use the Nikon text and refrained from any criticism in his notes.[5] Relying on the same set of narrative sources as Karamzin, Solov'ev returned to an even greater degree to the tradition of the Nikon Chronicle and Tatishchev. Shakhmatov was the first to discover and to analyze chronicles reflecting the tradition of the fifteenth century— the Simeonov, Nikanor, Vologda-Perm', and Ermolin Chronicles, the late fifteenth-century Moscow *svod*, and several others. He also determined the "basic *svody*" of the late fourteenth and fifteenth centuries, indirect sources (protographs) of the later chronicles.[6] Unfortunately, however, Shakhmatov's constructs, although based on the comparison of real chronicle texts and very well (often irrefutably) substantiated, did not exert enough influence on subsequent historiography. There still exist no

---

[3] L. V. Ranke, *Sämtliche Werke*, vols. 33–34 (Leipzig, 1876), p. ii.
[4] R. G. Collingwood, *The Idea of History* (New York and Oxford, 1946), 246.
[5] N. M. Karamzin, *Istoriia gosudarstva Rossiiskogo*, 12 vols. in 4 (St. Petersburg, 1842), v. 1, notes 293, 419, 424, 483; v. 2, notes 244, 260, 277, 390, 400, 410; v. 3, notes 28, 167; v. 4, notes 179, 229, 232; v. 5, notes 65, 74, 76, 93. Cf. the reference to the observations of Karamzin about Tatishchev in my "Problems of Source Criticism," 2, n. 2 (see n. 2 above).
[6] See especially A. A. Shakhmatov, *Obozrenie russkikh letopisnykh svodov XIV–XVI vv.* (Moscow and Leningrad, 1938).

established rules for the use of chronicles. They are selected arbitrarily according to the "consumer approach"; official grand-princely chronicles of the late fifteenth century and chronicles of the sixteenth century, above all the Nikon Chronicle, have been the most important to historians. The result is *that* perception of facts as seen through the "Muscovite political bias" that Priselkov warned us against.

Meanwhile, research into the chronicles of the fifteenth century has progressed significantly since the time of Shakhmatov. Relying on the work of my predecessors (Priselkov, Nasonov, and others) and on my own monograph of 1976,[7] I would like to outline the basic facts of the political history of fifteenth-century Muscovite Rus' in the light of chronicle sources nearer to them in time and therefore more reliable.

The stemma of chronicle *svody* of the fifteenth century can be viewed in basic outline (see fig. 1). The earliest of the fifteenth-century chronicles can be considered the Trinity Chronicle, brought up to 1408 and available to us not in complete form (it burned in 1812), but in extensive excerpts in Karamzin and in its reflections in later chronicles. Up to 1390, the texts of the Rogozhskii Chronicle (*letopisets*) and the Simeonov Chronicle basically coincide with that of the Trinity Chronicle; in the sections for 1390–1412, both of these chronicles reflect a particular version of the Russian *svod* written in Tver'. Parallel with the Muscovite chronicle tradition were local chronicles, reflected for the most part in the Novgorod I and Pskov Chronicles. Various sources—Muscovite, Novgorodian, and others—formed the basis for a *svod* that brings the narrative all the way up to 1418; this *svod* was reflected in two chronicles, Sophia I and Novgorod IV. The continuation of this *svod*, done in the first half of the fifteenth century, is preserved, apparently, in the second redaction of the Sophia I Chronicle. The Sophia I Chronicle in turn served as the basic source for the chronicle tradition of the Muscovite grand princes. It is reflected in various redactions of the Nikanor Chronicle; the Vologda-Perm' Chronicle, reflecting the *svod* of 1472; the Chronicle of the 72 Tribes (*Letopisets ot 72 iazyk*), reflecting a fragment of the *svod* of 1477; the Moscow *svod;* the *svod* of 1479; the *svody* of the 1490s; and other chronicles. Along with the chronicles of the grand princes, there also existed in the fifteenth century more independent chronicles, represented in the Ermolin, Printing Office (*Tipografskaia*), Sophia II, L'vov, and other chronicles (see fig. 1).

In historical works, the account of the Battle of Kulikovo Field in 1380

[7] M. D. Priselkov, *Istoriia* (see no. 1); A. N. Nasonov, *Istoriia russkogo letopisaniia XI-nachala XVIII v.* (Moscow, 1969); Ia. S. Lur'e, *Obshcherusskie letopisi XIV–XV vv.* (Leningrad, 1976).

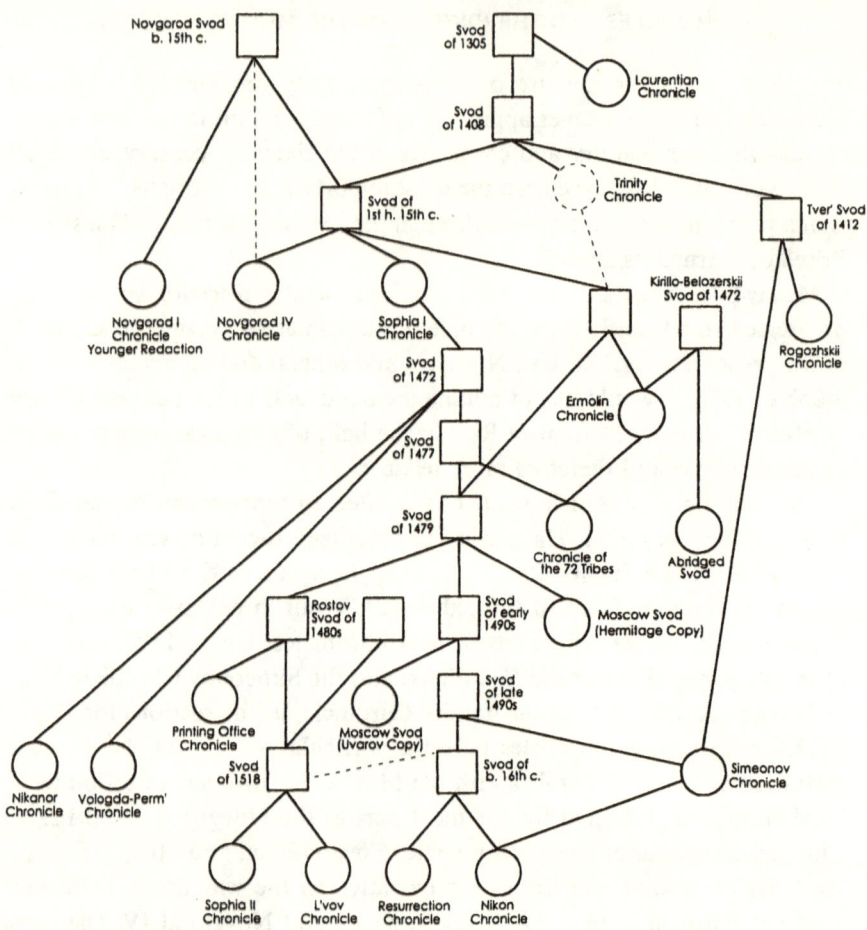

Figure 1. Stemma of Russian Chronicles and Compilations

is usually based on the Nikon Chronicle and sources like it.⁸ Sources close to the battle—the Trinity Chronicle and the similar *svod* of 1412 (reflected in the Rogozhskii Chronicle and the Simeonov Chronicle)—state that it was "a great victory," but give it little attention.⁹ Later accounts ascribe an ever greater significance to the "great victory." In the Russian *svod* of the first half of the fifteenth century (Sophia I, Novgorod IV), information appears about Sergii Radonezhskii's participation in preparing for the campaign.¹⁰ Other details, introduced into the chronicles of the sixteenth century, go back only as far as the historical narratives of the late fifteenth and the early sixteenth centuries ("The Tale of Mamai's Battle").¹¹

In their accounts of the times of Vasilii I (1389–1425), the Trinity Chronicle and the *svod* of 1412 differ from one another; they tell different stories about the annexation of Nizhnii Novgorod in 1392 and about Edigei's invasion in 1408. The distinctive feature of the account in the *svod* of 1412 is its sharp condemnation of Vasilii I for his maneuvering between the Horde and Lithuania and his concessions to the Horde; the compiler considers Edigei's sudden attack a direct result of this policy. The account in the *svod* of 1412 is not only a valuable source, but also an outstanding example of public opinion. Compiled, apparently, by a Muscovite chronicler who had fled from Edigei's attack to Tver', the account reflects not a Muscovite or a Tverian point of view, but a Russian one—a realization of the necessity for unity in the face of universal danger.¹²

The struggle of Vasilii II against his uncle Iurii and his cousin Dmitrii Shemiaka for the throne (1425–1453) is depicted in later grand-princely chronicles as the struggle of a lawful Russian prince against usurpers. Unfortunately, the earliest Muscovite account of these events has not been preserved. The Russian *svod* of the first half of the of the fifteenth century stops abruptly at the beginning of the conflict in the chronicles available to

---

⁸ George Vernadsky, *A History of Russia*, v. 3 *The Mongols and Russia* (New Haven and London, 1953), 260–262; M. N. Tikhomirov, "Kulikovskaia bitva 1380 g.," *Voprosy istorii*, 1955, no. 8: 11–25, reprinted in *Povesti o Kulikovskoi bitve* (Moscow, 1959), 335–376.

⁹ *PSRL*, v. 15, pt. 1, cols. 139–141; ibid., 18, 129–130; cf. M. D. Priselkov, *Troitskaia letopis'. Rekonstruktsiia teksta* (Moscow and Leningrad, 1950), 419–421.

¹⁰ *PSRL*, v. 4, pt.1, no. 1 (2d. ed.), 311–320; no. 2, 321–325; ibid., 6, 90–111.

¹¹ *PSRL*, v. 2, 46–68; ibid., v. 26, 328–342; *Povesti o Kulikovskoi bitve* (see n.7), 41–76. The dating of the "Skazanie" to the end of the fifteenth or the beginning of the sixteenth century is more convincing than dating it a century earlier. (For the later date, see V. A. Kuchkin, "Pobeda na Kulikovom pole," *Voprosy istorii*, 1980, no. 8, 7; for the earlier date, see Charles J. Halperin, *The Tatar Yoke* (Bloomington, Indiana, 1985), 107–108, 205, notes 56–59.) See also Ia. S. Lur'e, "O putiakh dokazatel'stva pri analize istochnikov," *Voprosy istorii*, 1985, no.5: 64–65.

¹² *PSRL*, v. 15, cols. 177–185; ibid., v. 18, 155–159. Cf. Ia. S. Lur'e, "Iz nabliudenii nad letopisaniem pervoi poloviny XV v.," *TODRL* 39 (1985), 285–304.

us; further presentations have come down to us only in small excerpts in the Sophia I Chronicle.[13] The information in the Novgorod and Pskov chronicles is very important for elucidating this subject.[14] Historians have already noted that Vasilii II, in his struggle for the throne, relied to a considerable extent on the help of the Tatar khan[15] and not the support of the urban population. Likewise, in my opinion, Iurii Galitskii and Dmitrii Shemiaka can scarcely be considered representatives of the national idea and the struggle for centralization.[16]

We discover the idea of the centralization of Rus' not in the programs of rival princes, but in the previously mentioned Russian *svod* of the first half of the fifteenth century, compiled in the years of feudal war. This *svod*, compiled apparently in the metropolitan's court (which at that time used to move from Moscow to Smolensk, Novgorod, and Pskov) developed the Russian idea of the *svod* of 1412. It urgently called on "brother" princes to unite; this is where detailed accounts of the attack of Batu, the Battle of Kulikovo, and Dmitrii Donskoi first appeared. The idea of unifying the Russian lands while preserving their autonomy (in particular, the self-government of Novgorod—its right to drive away undesirable princes) was not realized in subsequent years, but the *svod* of the first half of the fifteenth century had a considerable influence on subsequent chronicles.[17]

From the middle of the fifteenth century, the Russian Church was independent from the Constantinopolitan patriarchate—the metropolitan was appointed without the blessing of the patriarch. Later Muscovite chronicles depicted Iona, who became metropolitan in 1448, as the lawful successor to Metropolitan Fotii, who died in 1430. These chronicles, and historians after them,[18] confirm that Iona traveled to Constantinople and received the condi-

---

[13] *PSRL*, v. 5 (1851 edition), 262–274 (left column).

[14] *Novgorodskaia pervaia letopis' starshego i mladshego izvodov* (Moscow and Leningrad, 1950), 416–426; *PSRL*, v. 4 (1915–1925 edition), pt.1, no. 2, 433–444; *Pskovskie letopisi* (Moscow and Leningrad, 1941, 1955), v. 1, 39–48, v. 2, 126–137.

[15] Vernadsky, *The Mongols and Russia* (see n. 8), 318–322. The suggestion by Vernadsky that Vasilii II's nickname, *temnyi* ("the dark"), was linked not with his blinding but with the word temnik ("prince captain of the myriad") was justly refuted by Zimin, who pointed out that the nickname itself appeared only in the historiography of the eighteenth century; see Halperin, *The Tatar Yoke* (see n. 11), 144–147.

[16] This question is examined in more detail in Zimin's monograph, *Vitiaz' na rasput'e. Feodal'naia voina v Rossii XV v.* (Moscow, 1991), 200–201. Cf. A. A. Zimin, "V bor'be za Moskvu (vtoraia chertvert' XV stoletiia)," *Voprosy istorii*, 1982, no. 12, 87.

[17] Ia. S. Lur'e, *Obshcherusskie letopisi* (see n. 7), 67–121; idem, "O politicheskikh ideiakh obshcherusskogo svoda 1448 g.," *Festschrift für Fairy von Lilienfeld zum 65. Geburstag* (Erlangen, 1982), 135–152.

[18] *PSRL*, v. 25, 270; ibid., v. 12, 74; E. E. Golubinskii, *Istoriia russkoi tserkvi*, 2 vols. (Moscow, 1900–1911), v. 2, 414–416, 418–428, 471–478, 481–483; A. V. Kartashev, *Ocherki po istorii russkoi tserkvi*, 2 vols. (Paris, 1959), v. 1: 346, 360–361.

tional consent of the patriarch to take on the duties of the metropolitan see. Earlier chronicles, however, say nothing of Iona's trip and the patriarch's promise; documents on Iona's trip appear in the manuscript tradition considerably later, contradict each other, and, in my opinion, show signs of later falsification. Iona's recently discovered testament says not one word about the trip.[19]

The Novgorod and Pskov Chronicles do not mention Iona either before or after his appointment as metropolitan. In 1432 the metropolitan was Gerasim, who directed the metropolitanate from Smolensk; and in 1437–1441, the see was held by the Greek Isidor, who in 1439 took part in the Council of Florence. Isidor's activities as metropolitan in Rus' are mentioned in fifteenth-century chronicles and documents: after the Union of Florence, Isidor acted as intermediary in the Moscow–Tver' agreement.[20]

The earliest mention that the Union was rejected and that Isidor left Rus' is in the Novgorod I Chronicle,[21] not in the Muscovite chronicles. Ivan's inconsistency on this issue is shown by the fact that at the beginning of the 1470s he decided to marry an obvious Catholic (and ward of the Pope), Zoe-Sofiia Paleologa.

Iona, a supporter of Dmitrii Shemiaka who helped him seize the children of Vasilii II, was ordained as metropolitan by Shemiaka, and was officially confirmed by Vasilii only after he had moved to the latter's side.[22] The selection of Iona did not elicit a quick reaction from the patriarch, for Constantinople was seized by the Turks in 1453. But at the end of the 50s, the metropolitan of Kiev was declared to be the lawful "Metropolitan of All Rus'" not only by the Uniate patriarch in Rome but also by the patriarch who had rejected the Union and resided in Turkish Istanbul while the metropolitan of Moscow was excommunicated.[23] Only after that did Ivan III declare Greek Orthodoxy "collapsed," paving the way for a radical restructuring of the Russian Church in the future.

---

[19] "Novonaidennaia dukhovnaia grammota mitropolita Iony," in A. I. Pliguzov, G. V. Semenchenko, L. F. Kuz'mina, eds., *Russkii feodal'nyi arkhiv XIV-pervoi treti XVI v.*, v. 3 (Moscow, 1986–88), 640–654; Ia. S. Lur'e, "Iona," *Slovar' knizhnikov i knizhnosti drevnei Rusi. Vtoraia polovina XIV–XVI v.*, v. 1 (Moscow, 1988), 420–426.

[20] *Novgorodskaia pervaia letopis'* (see n. 14), 419, 421; *Pskovskie letopisi* (see n. 14), v. 1, 44–46; no. 2, 46–47; *PSRL,* v. 6, 152; L. V. Cherepnin, ed., *Dukhovnye i dogovornye gramoty velikikh i udel'nykh kniazei XIV–XVI vv.* (Moscow and Leningrad, 1950), no. 37.

[21] *Novgorodskaia pervaia letopis'* (see n. 14), 421–422. There is no mention of the rejection of the Union and the exile of Isidor in the Sophia I Chronicle: *PSRL,* v. 5 (1851), 267 (left column).

[22] Zimin, "V bor'be za Moskvu," (see n. 16), 89; Lur'e, "Iz nabliudenii . . . ," (see n. 12), 302.

[23] Ia. N. Shchapov, *Vostochnoslavianskie i iuzhnoslavianskie knigi v sobraniiakh Pol'skoi narodnoi respubliki* (Moscow, 1976), v. 2, 145–147 (Appendix 52).

In the historiography, the account of the annexation of Novgorod is usually based on the grand-princely chronicles of the 1470s (the Nikanor Chronicle, the Vologda-Perm' Chronicle, and the Moscow *svod*),[24] on a particular composition apparently created in the metropolitan's chancellery before the campaign against Novgorod (the Selected Discourses [*Slovesa izbranny*]),[25] and on official chronicles of the sixteenth century. According to these accounts, the campaign of 1471 was explained by the fact that the people of Novgorod had sunk into "Latinity" (i.e., Catholicism), wanted to accept the Kievan metropolitan, and invited the Kievan prince Mikhail Olel'kovich to the city. The chronicles written outside Moscow in the fifteenth century, however, do not confirm this version. The Kievan princes Semen and Mikhail Olel'kovich were vassals of the Polish-Lithuanian king, but they were also cousins of Ivan III, sons of Vasilii II's sister and active associate, and adherents of Orthodoxy.[26] Semen Olel'kovich traveled to Moscow in 1451. In Lithuania, Mikhail Olel'kovich was considered a supporter of Moscow, for which reason the Polish king refused to declare him governor in Kiev; later Mikhail was executed in Lithuania for taking part in a pro-Muscovite conspiracy.[27] Mikhail was invited to Novgorod, according to the Pskov Chronicle, before disagreements began there about which metropolitan, Muscovite or Kievan, the local archbishop should be subordinate to; he left Novgorod before Ivan III's campaign against the city.[28] One might conclude, therefore, that the invitation to Mikhail was not against the will of the Muscovite prince and that only later was it called a pretext for war.

Marfa Boretskaia, glorified in the historiography, is mentioned as the main opponent of Moscow only in the obviously legendary "Selected Discourses" and, more briefly, in the grand-princely chronicles; in the Nikon Chronicle, this motif is supported by a reference to the "prophecy . . . of Zosima Solovetskii."[29] The northern Russian (apparently Kirillo-Belozerskii) *Svod*, reflected in the Ermolin Chronicle and the Abridged *(Sokrashchennyi)* Compilation, ignores the explanation of the campaign against Novgorod given by the grand-princely chronicles; according to this chronicle, Isak Boretskii, Marfa's husband, was a supporter of Vasilii II and helped him

---

[24] *PSRL*, v. 26, 229–242; v. 25, 284–293; v. 12, 125–146.
[25] *PSRL*, v. 6, 1–15, 194; v. 20, pt.1, 283–296.
[26] *PSRL*, v. 26, 210; v. 32, 210; J. Długosz, *Opera omnia*, v. 6 (Cracow, 1870), 515, 657–658; v. 14 (Cracow, 1878), 547, 657–658. Cf. K. V. Bazilevich, *Vneshniaia politika Russkogo tsentralizovannogo gosudarstva. Vtoraia polovina XV v.* (Moscow, 1952), 94–95.
[27] *PSRL*, v. 6, 233; v. 20, 348.
[28] *Pskovskie letopisi* (see n. 14), v. 1, 73–74; v. 2, 54–55, 172–185.
[29] *PSRL*, v. 6, 5; cf. v. 26, 231; v. 12, 126, 129, 137–138.

to assassinate Shemiaka.[30] The Novgorod chronicle, unlike the Muscovite chronicles, gives a fully realistic and convincing explanation of Moscow's victory in 1471. It says nothing about any opposition by Ivan III to Mikhail's invitation. The reason for the defeat was an internal crisis in the republic: a clash between the "lesser" and the "greater," who were accused of conspiring with the grand prince.

The justification for the final annexation of Novgorod in 1477 in the grand-princely chronicles (the Novgorod Chronicle of the time has not been preserved) seems even less convincing than the explanation of the campaign of 1471. Only in the Moscow *Svod* of 1479 do we find information that in March 1477 Novgorod envoys declared Ivan III their sovereign (*gosudar'*), but later repudiated this. A comparison of the *Svod* of 1479 with the fragment of the grand-princely *svod* that has come down to us in the "Chronicle of the 72 Tribes" (*Letopisets ot 72 iazyk*), brought up to June 1477, reveals that the account of the alleged Novgorod mission is an interpolation in the former, done after Muscovite troops were victorious and the republic was destroyed.[31]

In discussing the final liberation from the Tatar Yoke as a result of Akhmad's unsuccessful campaign and the "stand on the Ugra" of 1480, the chronicles—both the official chronicles of the princes and the unofficial chronicles—state that the grand prince hesitated upon entering into battle and that his entourage included supporters of compromise with the khan. Historians, however, have believed that this account belongs to a tradition hostile to Ivan III and that the true version of the grand-princely chronicles has for some reason not survived.[32] The history of the chronicles of the 1480s and 1490s requires further research,[33] but it seems that all versions of the grand-princely chronicles that have come down to us from the end of the century reflect an unofficial account of the Ugra events, an account close to, but not identical with, that which can be read in the Printing Office Chronicle. The grand-princely chronicles brought changes to the Printing Office version intended to vindicate Ivan III and to put the blame for the hesitation

---

[30] *PSRL*, v. 23, 155; cf. 159.

[31] *PSRL*, v. 25, 309; v. 12, 169–170; cf. v. 28, 140, 311. See also Ia. S. Lur'e, "K istorii prisoedineniia Novgoroda v 1427–1474 gg.," *Issledovaniia po sotsial'no-politicheskoi istorii Rossii. Sbornik pamiati B. A. Romanova* (Leningrad, 1971), 89–95.

[32] A. E. Presniakov, "Ivan III na Ugre," *Sergeiu Fedorovichu Platonovu ucheniki, druz'ia i pochitateli* (St. Petersburg, 1911), 284–289; Bazilevich, *Vneshniaia politika* (see n. 26), 134–137; P. N. Pavlov, "Deistvitel'naia rol' arkhiepiskopa Vassiana v sobytiiakh 1480 g.," *Uchenye zapiski Krasnoiarskogo pedagogicheskogo instituta* 4, no. 1 (1955): 202–212.

[33] B. M. Kloss and V. D. Nazarov, "Rasskazy o likvidatsii ordynskogo iga na Rusi v letopisanii kontsa XV v.," *Drevnerusskoe iskusstvo. Iskusstvo i kul'tura epokhi Kulikovskoi bitvy* (Moscow, 1981), 283–313.

on "bloodsucking" advisers.[34] The message from Archbishop Vassian of Rostov to the Ugra, a text included only later in the chronicles,[35] reflects not only disagreements on the significance of the oath to the khan, but also the new political idea of Russian sovereignty, expressed in Ivan III's assuming the title "Grand Prince of All Rus'" in 1485.

At the end of the 1480s, unofficial all-Russian chronicle writing comes to an end; only the chronicles of the grand princes and the local chronicles in Pskov and partially in Novgorod continue. This circumstance makes the study of the history of ideological struggle in the late fifteenth and early sixteenth centuries extremely difficult. The grand-princely chronicles mention almost nothing about the role of heresy at the end of the fifteenth century. The inclusion of material from outside the chronicles gives the impression of a broad flow of ideas lasting a quarter of a century. The break with the patriarch had paved the way for ideological inquiry. Apparently, Ivan III originally contemplated something similar to a "princely reformation," but later consented to reprisals against the heretics. Nevertheless, the ideas that developed among circles of free-thinkers ("Moscow as the new city of Constantine") influenced the ideology of the Russian state.[36]

---

[34] Ia. S. Lur'e, "Konets zolotoordynskogo iga ('Ugorshchina') v istorii i literature," *Russkaia literatura* 1982, no. 2, 52–66.

[35] *PSRL* v. 26, 266–273; v. 6, 255–260.

[36] For details, see Ia. S. Lur'e, *Ideologicheskaia bor'ba v russkoi publitsistike kontsa XV–nachala XVI v.* (Moscow and Leningrad, 1960).

DETERMINING THE AUTHORSHIP OF THE TRINITY CHRONICLE

BORIS M. KLOSS

The Trinity Chronicle is an extraordinarily important monument of Muscovite chronicle-writing at the beginning of the fifteenth century. Most unfortunately it perished in the fire of 1812, but before that date the chronicle was used by Karamzin, who left numerous excerpts from it in the footnotes to his *History of the Russian State*. The beginning part of the text, down to the article for the year 907, is found in variant readings to the (unfinished) 1804 edition of the Laurentian Chronicle. According to the testimony of Karamzin, the Trinity Chronicle was written on parchment and carried its account down to the year 1408, ending with a description of the invasion of Edigei.[1] In the eighteenth century, the manuscript was preserved in the Trinity-Saint Sergius Monastery, where the following description was made of it in 1768: "A Russian chronicle [*letopisets*], in quarto [*v maloi list*], written on parchment in the oldest type of uncial hand. It begins with Riurik and continues to the reign of Grand Prince Vasilii Dmitrievich, on 371 folios."[2]

Shakhmatov suggested the possibility of reconstructing the Trinity Chronicle by observing that from its beginning 1177 to the year 1390 the Simeonov Chronicle was similar to the Trinity Chronicle, judging by the citations of Karamzin.[3] Priselkov carried out the basic job of reconstructing the Trinity Chronicle.[4]

The ultimate reconstruction cannot, however, be accepted as reliable in every instance. Shakhmatov had already noted that the Simeonov Chronicle entries for 1235–1237, 1239–1249, and 1361–1365 represent insertions from the Moscow Compilation (*svod*) of 1479. To this we should add that entries for 1402–1408, omitted in the Rogozhskii Chronicle, were provided in the

---

Translated from the Russian by Daniel Rowland.

[1] N. M. Karamzin, *Istoriia gosudarstva Rossiiskogo*, 12 vols. in 3, 5th ed. (St. Petersburg, 1842–1843), bk. 2 (1842), notes to v. 5, col. 78, note 207.

[2] S. N. Kochetkov, "Troitskii pergamennyi spisok letopisi 1408 goda," *Arkheograficheskii ezhegodnik za 1961 god* (Moscow, 1962), 23.

[3] A. A. Shakhmatov, *Simeonovskaia letopis' XVI v. i Troitskaia nachala XV v.* (St. Petersburg, 1910).

[4] M. D. Priselkov, *Troitskaia letopis'. Rekonstruktsiia teksta* (Moscow and Leningrad, 1950).

Simeonov text of the Moscow Compilation. (The Rogozhskii Chronicle and the Simeonov Chronicle both reflect a reworking of the Trinity Chronicle carried out in Tver'.[5]) Priselkov, therefore, should have turned his attention to such supplementary sources as the Laurentian Chronicle, the Rogozhskii Chronicle, and the Resurrection (*Voskresenskaia*) Chronicle.

At the present time the chances for resolving the problem of reconstructing the Trinity Chronicle have significantly increased. A copy of the 1767 edition of the Radziwill Chronicle, corrected by Miller according to the Trinity Chronicle, has become available to scholars. (Priselkov took into account Miller's corrections according to Obolenskii's edition.[6]) Additionally, "a copy of the first three folios of the Trinity Chronicle was found among Miller's papers."[7] Tikhomirov brought the Vladimir Chronicle to the attention of scholars, the text of which he believed was similar to the Trinity Chronicle to the end of the 1380s. In my opinion, the Vladimir Chronicle represents in part the text of the Tverian reworking of the Trinity Chronicle, but other sources were used as well.[8] In reconstructing the Trinity Chronicle, we should consult directly the Compilation of 1479 itself, which is known in several copies, instead of using the Resurrection Chronicle, which is a compiled work based on the Moscow Compilation of 1479 and other sources. (Several readings of the Moscow Compilation, moreover, are preferable to readings of the Simeonov Chronicle.)

Even in the form in which it was reconstructed by Priselkov, the text of the Trinity Chronicle permits us to make judgments about both its ideological direction and its author. I will show that the author of the Trinity Chronicle clearly belonged to the brethren of the Trinity-Saint Sergius Monastery. For that reason, it is natural to compare the text of the Chronicle with the works of the greatest writer of medieval Rus', the pupil of the famous Sergius of Radonezh, Epiphanius the Wise, who lived in the second half of the fourteenth and the beginning of the fifteenth centuries, roughly at the time when the Trinity Chronicle was compiled.

Three works may be confidently attributed to Epiphanius the Wise: the *Life of Stephen of Perm'*, the *Life of Sergius of Radonezh*, and the *Encomium of Sergius*. The earliest known copies of the *Life of Stephen of Perm'* go back no earlier than the sixteenth century, but recently Tuzov found a manuscript of the *Life* dated 1480 (GPB, Viazemskii Collection, no. 10). For

---

[5] B. M. Kloss, *Nikonovskii svod i russkie letopisi XVI–XVII vv.* (Moscow, 1980), 26.
[6] Priselkov, *Troitskaia letopis'* (see n. 4), 8–9.
[7] G. N. Moiseeva, "Otryvok Troitskoi pergamennoi letopisi, perepisannyi G. F. Millerom," *TODRL* 26 (1971): 93–99.
[8] Kloss, *Nikonovskii svod* (see n. 5), 135–140.

my part, I can point to a still earlier copy, from the 1470s: LOII, *fond* 238 (the N. P. Likhachev Collection), op. 1, no. 161. In principle, all copies reflect one redaction. In the scholarly literature there is a widespread opinion that the *Life of Stephen* was written soon after 1396, the year of Stephen's death. Nevertheless, the text of the *Life* contains a phrase that is significant for dating the work. In particular, the author at the end of the work addresses the Saint:

> князю великому в благоверстве многолетство даруй и благоденьство
> и тишину мирну, и долготу дни устрой; *митрополита* же, правяща
> слово твоея истины, святительством честно устроена и благочестием
> преукрашена, в мире долгоденьствующа, *даруй*.⁹

Here the text speaks of the "granting" of a metropolitan to Rus', a request that, during the period from the end of the fourteenth to the beginning of the fifteenth centuries, was only possible from 1406 to 1410: Metropolitan Cyprian died in September 1406, and the new metropolitan, Photius, arrived in Moscow in April 1410. Thus it follows that we should date the composition of the *Life of Stephen of Perm'* to 1406–1410.

The *Encomium of Sergius of Radonezh* was written by Epiphanius between 1406 and 1418, after the death of Metropolitan Cyprian, about whom it is said "togda zhe be (then he was)," and before the composition of the *Life of Sergius*, as we can judge by the remark "prochaia ego dobrodeteli inde skazhem i mnogaia ego ispravleniia inde povem."¹⁰ The doubts of several researchers that the *Encomium* contains later layers are without foundation: from a stylistic point of view, the text is homogeneous.

It is harder to resolve issues of attributing the texts and dating the various redactions of the *Life of Sergius of Radonezh*. Epiphanius's *Life of Sergius* was later reworked several times by the South Slavic hagiographer Pachomius the Serb, and the texts that come down to us combine the texts of both authors. In order to separate the texts of Epiphanius, one must carry out a detailed classification of manuscripts and ascertain the relationships among them. This work, involving the textological comparison of about 400 manuscripts, has been done. In addition, an inventory has been compiled of the handwriting of scribes working in the Trinity-Saint Sergius Monastery and

---

⁹ Grant to the Grand Prince many years in piety, prosperity, and peaceful calm, and provide him with a long life [lit., length of day]; *grant [us] a Metropolitan*, overseeing the word of thy truth, honorably confirmed in high rank and clothed in piety, and living long in peace. *Zhitie sv. Stefana, episkopa Permskogo, napisannoe Epifaniem Premudrym*, ed. V. G. Druzhinin (St. Petersburg, 1897), 100; LOII, Likhachev Collection, no. 161, ff. 283v.–284. The same reading is found in other copies. Italics in this and subsequent citations are mine.

¹⁰ Another time I will tell of his other virtues and another time recount his many attainments.

of watermarks found on paper from dated Trinity manuscripts. In this way it has been possible to localize the copies and to date with great precision the various redactions of the *Life of Sergius*. While not enumerating all of the results here, I shall indicate only what is relevant to the present argument: the text of Epiphanius is preserved in its pure form within the structure of the Long Redaction of the *Life* of the 1520s, beginning with the chapter "*O izvedenii istochnika*" (On the Bringing Forth of the Spring) and leaving out an insertion about Sergius's age (twenty-three years) when he was tonsured. In the introduction to the *Life*, Epiphanius writes that he began to collect material for the biography of Sergius a year or two after the elder's death and after twenty years wrote "glavizny ezhe o zhitii startseve pamiati radi" (the chapters for the *Life* for the sake of the elder's memory), chapters which he kept in rolls and notebooks but not "po riadu" (in order). The writer undertook the final finishing touches on the work in 1418, twenty-six years after the death of Sergius on 25 September 1392.

It is important to specify the years of Epiphanius's life. The able compilers of a list of those buried in the Trinity-Saint Sergius Monastery wrote that Epiphanius the Wise died "around 1420."[11] The basis for this date is not clear since there are no direct references to the sources, but we can verify it with the aid of a 1575 parchment memorial book (*sinodik*) from the Trinity Monastery. In the first part of the memorial book the name Epiphanius is recorded three times, but it is in a significant reference to the names of princesses located further on that we can deduce the year of Epiphanius's death: "Princess Anastasiia" (above is written "of Prince Konstantin"), "Kseniia," and "Princess Anastasiia" (above is written "of Prince Iurii").[12] According to the Moscow Academy Chronicle, Princess Anastasiia, wife of Prince Konstantin Dmitrievich, died in October 6927. If we assume a year which starts in March, we calculate the year 1419, but the last entries of the chronicle seem to use a system of year numeration based on a year that starts in September. The death of Anastasiia should, therefore, be dated to October 1418. Judging from the preface to the *Life of Sergius of Radonezh*, we determine that Epiphanius was still alive in September 1418. Although we do not know exactly when the name of Anastasiia was entered in the memorial book, we can surmise that it was no later than the end of 1418–1419. This, then, is the period to which we should date the death of Epiphanius, especially since we can confirm the approximate date of his

---

[11] *Spisok pogrebennykh v Troitskoi Sergievoi lavre ot osnovaniia onoi do 1880 goda* (Moscow, 1880), 11–12.

[12] GBL, *fond* 304/II, no. 25, f.12v.

death given by the compilers of the list of those buried at the Trinity-Saint Sergius Monastery.

An epistle—"from the Hieromonk Epiphanius, written to Cyril, a certain friend of his"—in 1415 can be assigned to Epiphanius the Wise. The letter is preserved in a single copy from the second half of the seventeenth century.[13] The letter testifies that Epiphanius had a wide-ranging library of manuscripts and therefore that he was a person of considerable erudition, a quality confirmed by the works he wrote. In the letter to Cyril, Epiphanius recalls that at the end of 1408 he arrived in Tver' while escaping the invasion of Edigei and showed Cyril his books, "elitsy ot raseianiia i ot rastocheniia ostashasia" (as many as remained after dispersion and dissipation), among them a Gospel with drawings of Hagia Sophia in Constantinople that Epiphanius had copied from images made by the famous painter Theophanes the Greek.[14]

Several manuscripts of Epiphanius the Wise, so it seems, have survived to the present. A sticherarion of 1380 (GBL, *fond* 304/1, [the Collection of the Trinity-Saint Sergius Monastery] no. 22) can be conditionally ascribed to Epiphanius. In fact, his name can be uncovered in the cinnabar *viaz'* on the lower margin of the verso of folio 1: "Mnogogreshnyi rab bozhii Epifan v nedostoian'i svoem napisa si" (the very sinful servant of God, Epiphanius wrote these things in his unworthiness), and in the cinnabar inscription on folio 98 under the stichera for 12 May, dedicated to Saint Epiphanius of Cyprus: "Gospodine sviatyi Epifan Kiprskii, s"imenniche moi, eleison mi" (O Lord Saint Epiphanius of Cyprus, my namesake, have mercy on me). The writer reveals a knowledge of the Greek language in numerous inscriptions; this fact can be placed alongside the constant use of Greek words in the works of Epiphanius the Wise: *arkuda, didaskal, devtoronomia, tetravasilios, epistolia, posmaga, eklisiarkh, ponomanarkh,* etc. On the margins of the sticherarion, the writer has made a number of remarkable notations of a chronological and mundane nature.

In order to be sure that the sticherarion belongs to Epiphanius the Wise, we need also to analyze other manuscripts in the same handwriting. A parchment *Prologue* for the September half of the year is written in the same uncial hand found in the sticherarion of 1380. (This manuscript is now divided into two halves: GBL, *fond* 304/1 [The Trinity-Saint Sergius Monastery Collection] no. 33 [September–November] and BAN 17.11.4 [December–February].) The notes and corrections are done in the same small semi-uncial

---

[13] GPB, Solovetskii Collection no. 1474-15, ff. 130–132.
[14] I. E. Grabar', *O drevnerusskom iskusstve* (Moscow, 1966), 31–32.

writing as are the notations in the sticherarion. The *Prologue*, to judge by its more developed handwriting, was written later than the sticherarion and can be dated to the 1380s or 1390s.

The handwriting of Epiphanius and two of his pupils can be found in a parchment miscellany (*sbornik*) from the Trinity Monastery (no. 34) dating from the beginning of the fifteenth century.[15] The handwriting of Epiphanius is semi-uncial and is similar to the hand in which the additions to Trinity Mss. 22 and 33 were made. The central part of the miscellany (folios 69v.–144v.) contains the *Life of Epiphanius of Cyprus*, the patron saint of Epiphanius, as we will remember from the inscription on f. 99 of the sticherarion. As in the sticherarion, but in greater quantities, Greek texts are written in the margins of the miscellany. There is a chronicle-like notation on folio 153: "4 chas noshchi pogremel" (after 3:00 a.m. it thundered a while). But the most remarkable addition was made on folio 157: "Kir'e voifi ton Epifanu . . . iushchiuumu" (Lord, help Epiphanius, who is . . .). The writer again mentions his own name, Epiphanius. It must be noted that the addition was placed in the margin opposite the beginning ten lines of the *Life of Mary of Egypt*, copied in the hand of Epiphanius (further on, the text was copied by a disciple). It is precisely this notation that enables us to make a connection to a known composition of Epiphanius the Wise—the *Encomium of Sergius of Radonezh*. The point is that the beginning fragment of the *Life of Mary of Egypt* is used to open the *Encomium of Sergius:*

> Таину цареву добро есть хранити, а дела божия проповедати преславъно есть.... Еже не хранити царевы таины, пагубно есть и блазньно, а еже молчати дела божья преславная, беду души наносить. Тем же и азъ боюся молчати дела божия, воспоминая муку раба оного, приимшаго господень талантъ и в земли скрывшаго, а прикупа ими не створивша.[16]

The data in Trinity Ms. no. 34 already allow us with considerable justification to regard Epiphanius the Wise himself as the copyist (and compiler) of the miscellany, inasmuch as the *Encomium of Sergius of Radonezh* is inscribed in all copies with the name of Epiphanius the Wise. In fact, the addition on folio 157 may be regarded as signaling that moment when the writer began work on the *Encomium of Sergius*.

[15] GBL, *fond* 304/1, no. 34. Epiphanius's hand is found on ff. 1–2, 5–7v., 69v.–157, 183.

[16] It is good to keep the secrets of the king, but it is glorious to preach the affairs of God . . . . For not to keep the king's secrets is ruinous and shameful, but to keep silent about the glorious affairs of God brings misfortune to the soul. Therefore I am afraid to keep silent about the affairs of God remembering the torment of that servant who, having accepted a talent from the Lord and buried it in the ground, made no profit with it [corrupt text: instrumental plural *imi* instead of instrumental singular *im"*, eds.].

Thus in the judgment of contemporary scholars, we now have several autographs of Epiphanius the Wise (Trinity Mss. 22, 33, 34 and BAN 17.11.4) which enable us to present his activities as a book copyist and to sketch more fully his creative portrait.

Let us return now to an examination of the literary style of Epiphanius the Wise. After discovering the texts of Epiphanius among the surviving redactions of the *Life of Sergius of Radonezh,* we can now connect them with those works written earlier—the *Life of Stephen of Perm'* and the *Encomium of Sergius*—and work out a fuller assessment of the literary style and worldview of Epiphanius.

In the *Life of Sergius of Radonezh,* Epiphanius painted a portrait of an ideal according to the values of that time. In his description, Sergius received the love and respect of all people, from princes and grandees to simple working people; his glory spread even to Constantinople. Moreover, in Epiphanius's depiction, the holy elder was distinguished by his extraordinary humility; he did not strive for power as his contemporaries did, and he even refused the metropolitan's throne. Sergius dressed in rags and wore them for many years, not scorning the simple work of uncouth village peasants. He was close to the people and interceded on their behalf. These democratic traits in his character, his sharp attacks against "lovers of rank" (*sanoliubivykh*) and those who craved the wealth of churchmen, and other critical passages were gradually erased in the alterations by Pachomius the Serb. Those elements of social justice which Epiphanius attributed to Sergius in his text were taken out.

Let us now compare the text of the Trinity Chronicle with the works of Epiphanius the Wise. Considering the text of the chronicle as represented in the Rogozhskii Chronicle and in the Simeonov Chronicle, and in Priselkov's reconstruction we immediately notice the heightened interest of the compiler of the Trinity Chronicle in the history of the monastery, particularly its founder—Sergius of Radonezh. One might say that the history of the Trinity-Saint Sergius Monastery was inscribed in the history of all Rus'.

The Trinity Chronicle contains much biographical information about Sergius and his brothers-in-arms, as well as about the history of the monastery. For example, the entry for 6882 tells of Sergius's founding a monastery in Serpukhov at the request of Prince Vladimir Andreevich. Especially noteworthy are the expressions used to characterize Sergius and his monastery:

> Живяше же в его области и стране в нарицаемеи в Радонеже, в его пределе, в его отчине, некто по истине раб божии, мужь свят старець преподобен именем Сергии, игумен мнозеи братии, отець многым мо-

настырем, о нем же суть многа сведетельства. Сего чюднаго старца умолив, подвиже и понуди потружатися, дабы своима рукама трудоположныма церкви основу положил и монастырь назнаменал. Да якоже князь въсхоте мыслию, сице честныи старець делом сътвори, умолен быв. Исшед *от великиа своея обители, честнаго монастыря,* и пришед в Серпохов, изглядав место подобно и пригоже монастырю и молитву сотворив и основание церкви положи своима рукама и тако чюдно есть.[17]

Further on, the founding of the monastery is discussed in detail, a discussion in which the "obshchee zhitie" (common life) is stressed. The text tells of the fate of Sergius's pupil Athanasius Vysotskii and his departure to one of the monasteries in Constantinople where he lived "v molchanii" (in silence), the hesychastic ideal of Epiphanius. Under the same year, the birth to the Grand Prince of a son Iurii is related: "i kresti ego prepodobnyi igumen Sergii, *sviatyi starets*" (and the Abbot Saint Sergius, *the holy elder,* baptized him). Under the year 6883, the compiler feels it necessary to report on the illness of "prepodobnogo igumena Sergiia, *sviatogo startsa*" (the Abbot Saint Sergius, *the holy elder*). Under the year 6887, we find described the foundation by "igumenom Sergiem, prepodobnym startsem" (Abbot Sergius, the saintly elder) of a monastery on the Dubenka River by order of the grand prince. Sergius installed as abbot his pupil Leontius, whom "izved ot bolshago monastyria, *ot velikyia lavry* (he brought from the great monastery, *from the great lavra*). The entry for 6889 mentions the baptism of the son of Prince Vladimir Andreevich of Serpukhov by Sergius and Metropolitan Cyprian. Under the year 6890, while he is discussing the departure of Metropolitan Cyprian for Kiev, the compiler observes that Athanasius Vysotskii, Sergius's pupil, left with the metropolitan. The entry for 6892 discusses the death of Elias, the cellarer of the Trinity Monastery, and describes him as "dobryi, poslushlivyi, zhivyi sviatym zhitiem v poslushanii *u sviatogo startsa,* byv poslushliv i do smerti" (good, obedient, living a holy life in obedience *with the holy elder,* he was obedient even unto death). The en-

---

[17] "In his [Prince Vladimir Andreevich's] territory and land, called Radonezh, within his boundaries and his patrimony, there lived a certain man who was in truth a servant of God, a holy man, a saintly elder by the name of Sergius, abbot of many brethren, father to many monasteries, about whom there is much testimony. After [the prince] had implored this marvelous elder, the latter acted and made [everyone] work, that he might found a church with his exemplary hands and establish a monastery. And as the prince wished in his mind, so the honorable elder did in deed, having been implored. Having left *his great residence, the honorable [Trinity-Sergius] Monastery,* he arrived in Serpukhov and, having sought out a place suitable and fitting for a monastery and having prayed, he laid the foundations for a church with his own hands, and thus it is marvelous." *PSRL,* v. 15, pt. 1, col. 107. Hereafter, passages are cited according to the Rogozhskii Chronicle.

try for 6893 mentions the christening by Sergius of the grand prince's son Peter and Sergius's trip to Riazan' on a diplomatic mission to Prince Oleg:

> преже бо того мнози ездили к нему не возможе утолити его, преподобныи же старець кроткыми словесы и тихими речми и благоуветливыми глаголы, благодатию вданою ему, много беседова с ним о ползе души и о мире и о любви. Князь же Олег преложи сверепьство свое на кротость и покорися, и укротися, и умилися душею, устыдеся толь *свята мужа* и взя со князем с великым мир вечныи.[18]

As he discusses the diplomatic mission of Sergius, the author creates a panegyric to the elder. The entry for 6895 contains news of the death of Isaac, "uchenika *velikago otsa igumena Sergiia,* prepodobnago startsa" (the pupil of *the great father and abbot Sergius,* the saintly elder) and enumerates the virtues of Sergius's pupil, all in the style of Epiphanius:

> послушание, чистота, смирение, млъчание, братолюбие, воздержание, нищета, нестяжание, рукоделие, любовь, пост, кротость, безлобие и иныя многы добродетели его, яже не могу по единому и сказати; паче же безмлъвие любляше и млъчанию прилежаше, от того и млъчалником прозван бысть, да по истине таковыи свят и божии угодник.[19]

The entry for 6897 notes the presence of Sergius, "prepodobnogo startsa" (the saintly elder), at the funeral of Grand Prince Dimitrii Ivanovich.

Under 6900 we find a passage about the death of Sergius, his portrait being given in the style of previous stories in the Trinity Chronicle:

> преставися преподобныи игумен Сергии, *святыи старець,* чюдныи, добрыи, тихии, кроткыи, смиреныи, просто рещи и не умею его житиа сказати, ни написати. Но токмо вемы, преже его в нашеи земли такова не бывало, иже бысть богу угоден, царьми и князи честен, от патриарх прославлен, и невърныя цари и князи чюдишася житию его и дары к нему слаша, всеми человекы любим бысть честнаго ради житиа его, иже бысть пастух не тъкмо своему стаду, но *всеи Русскои земли нашеи учитель и наставник.*[20]

---

[18] Before this, many came to him and were not able to tame him. Through the grace with which he was endowed, however, the saintly elder talked with him at length using humble words, quiet statements, and affable expressions, about the benefit to his soul and about peace and love. Prince Oleg transformed his rage into meekness and submitted himself, humbled himself, was touched by his very soul, became ashamed before such a *holy man,* and made eternal peace with the grand prince.

[19] Obedience, purity, humility, silence, brotherly love, temperance, poverty, nonpossession, handiwork, love, fasting, meekness, kindliness, and his many other virtues which I simply cannot enumerate one by one; moreover, he loved quiet and adhered to silence, so that he was called "the silent one." Yes, in truth, such a man is holy and a servant of God.

[20] The saintly abbot and holy elder Sergius died, marvelous, good, quiet, meek, humble— to speak plainly, I am unable either to relate his life or to write it down. But I only know that

In the Trinity Chronicle itself, according to Karamzin, the entry for 6900 contained a eulogy to Sergius "listakh na 20" (twenty folios in length). There can be no doubt that this eulogy was precisely the *Encomium of Sergius* that is attributed in all copies to the name of Epiphanius the Wise and that is approximately the same length (for manuscripts in quarto) as that indicated by Karamzin. Let us compare the length of the *Encomium* in its oldest copies: Trinity Ms. no. 755, 22ff.; Trinity Ms. no. 763, 20ff.; Tikhonravov Ms. no. 705, 18ff.; Trinity Ms. no. 643, 22ff.; Volokolamsk Ms. no. 644, 18ff.; Eparchy Ms. no. 387, 24ff.; and so forth. The *Short Encomium* of Sergius that is known in the manuscript tradition is considerably shorter in length than Epiphanius's version. We were unable to discover any other encomia in the manuscripts.

There is also a textological link between the reports of the death of Sergius in the Rogozhskii Chronicle and the *Encomium* by Epiphanius:

Rogozhskii Chronicle	*Encomium of Sergius*
Сергии, святыи старець, чудныи, добрыи, тихии, кроткыи, смиреныи, просто рещи и не умею его жития сказати, ни написати.	Сергие святыи старець, чюдныи, добродетелми всякыми украшен, тихыи и кроткыи нрав имея, и смереныи, не могыи по достоянию написати жития... по подобию нарещи или похвалити достоино...
и невернныя цари и князи чудишася житию его всеи Русскои земли нашеи учитель и наставник.[21]	но и невернии мнози удивишася правыи учитель, нелестныи наставник князем великымь русскым учитель[22]

In the enumerated passages of the Trinity Chronicle, the character of Epiphanius clearly emerges as that of someone interested in glorifying the "Great Lavra," the Trinity-Sergius Monastery, and its founder, the "holy elder" Sergius, before whom "v nashei zemli takova ne byvalo" (there had

---

there was never such a man in our land before him. He was pleasing to God, honored by tsars and princes, glorified by the patriarch; unbelieving tsars and princes marveled at his life as well and sent him gifts. He was loved by all men because of his honorable life and was not only a pastor of his own flock but also *the teacher and mentor of our whole Rus' land*.

[21] Sergius, the holy elder, marvelous, good, quiet, meek, humble—to speak plainly I am unable either to relate his life or to write it down . . . . [U]nbelieving tsars and princes marveled at his life as well . . . the teacher and mentor of our whole Rus' land.

[22] O Sergius, the holy elder, marvelous, adorned with all kinds of virtues, having a quiet and meek disposition, and humble—[I am one] incapable in merit to write down the life . . . or to speak or praise [thee] properly as is befitting . . . but even many unbelievers marveled . . . our just teacher and mentor who did not flatter . . . , the teacher of the grand princes of Rus'. N. S. Tikhonravov, *Drevnie zhitiia prepodobnogo Sergiia Radonezhskogo* (Moscow, 1892), 134, 137.

never been such a person in our land). Also glorified are the outstanding monks of the Trinity Monastery. We should note here that no other monastery receives the same amount of attention in the chronicle as the Trinity Monastery. The author, who placed monastic virtues above all else, must himself have been a monk, and, judging by his bias toward the "Great" Trinity-Saint Sergius Monastery, we infer that he was a monk of that very monastery. This evidence narrows the circle of possible authors of the Trinity Chronicle. Considering that Epiphanius's *Encomium of Sergius* is inserted into the article for 6900, that biographical material about Sergius and his fellow hermits is placed in the chronicle, and that no one else compiled a biography of Sergius except Epiphanius (see the prologue to the *Life of Sergius*), we conclude that Epiphanius the Wise himself was the author of the Trinity Chronicle.

This inference is further supported by stylistic comparisons between the Trinity Chronicle and the texts assigned to Epiphanius. The phrase in the chronicle that Sergius was "ot patriarkh proslavlen" (glorified by the patriarch) finds a parallel in the *Life of Sergius,* which tells about the sending of a document of benediction from the patriarch to Sergius. Moreover, a factual detail about the metropolitan's emissaries Paul and Gerasimus, mentioned in the Trinity Chronicle under the year 6871, finds a parallel in the *Life of Sergius,* where, in the chapter about the founding of the Kerzhak Monastery, the very same envoys of the metropolitan are mentioned. The same chronological inaccuracy is present in both the *Life of Sergius* and the Trinity Chronicle: that the reigns of the Byzantine Emperor Andronicus II and Patriarch Callistus were contemporaneous. Andronicus II Paleologus ruled from 1282 to 1328, whereas Patriarch Callistus took the throne in 1350. From evidence in the *Life*, we deduce that Sergius was born in 1322:

> в лета благочестиваго преславнаго дръжавнаго царя Андроника, самодръжца гречьскаго, иже в Цариграде царьствовавшаго, при архиепископе Коньстянтина града Калисте, патриарсе вселеньском... егда рать Ахмулова,[23]

An analogous mistake in the Trinity Chronicle is contained in the article for 6886 where it is reported that Princess Vasilisa was born "v leto 6839, v tsarstvo Andronika Tsaregradskago, a patriarkha Kalista" (in the year 6839, in the reign of Andronicus of Constantinople and Patriarch Callistus).

Let us turn our attention to the fondness of the compiler of the Trinity

---

[23] In the years of the pious most glorious powerful emperor, Andronicus, Greek autocrat who ruled in Constantinople, and in the reign of the archbishop of Constantinople, Callistus, the ecumenical patriarch ... at the time of the campaign of Akhmulov ....

Chronicle for enumerating secular and ecclesiastical rulers under whom one or another important event occurred. In the news about the birth of the Princess Vasilisa, the author enumerates, in addition to the Byzantine Emperor and the Patriarch of Constantinople, "a v Orde togda tsar' byl Ozbiak v Sarae, a na Rusi v kniazhenie velikoe Ivanovo Danilovicha Kalitino, pri arkhiepiskope Fegnaste, metropolite" (and in the Horde at that time the tsar was Ozbiak in Sarai and in Rus' during the reign of Grand Prince Ivan Danilovich Kalita, under Archbishop Theognost, metropolitan). The same device is also characteristic of Epiphanius the Wise. In the *Life,* Epiphanius includes the following political and religious references on a par with those of the Byzantine emperor Andronicus and Patriarch Callistus: "v zemli zhe Russtei v kniazhenie velikoe Tfer'skoe pri velikom kniazi Dimitrii Mikhailoviche, pri arkhiepiskope presviashchennem' Petre, mitropolite vseia Rusi" (in the Rus' land, during the great reign of Tver', under Grand Prince Dimitrii Mikhailovich, under the most holy Archbishop Peter, metropolitan of all Rus'). An analogous device can be found in the *Life of Stephen of Perm'*. Epiphanius writes that Stephen put together the Permian alphabet

> в лето 6883, в царство Иоанна царя греческаго, в Цареграде царствовавшего, при архиепископе Филофеи, патриарсе Костянтина града, в Орде же и в Сараи над татары тогда Мамаи царствует, но не вечнует абие, на Руси же при велицем князи Дмитрей Ивановичи, архиепископу же митрополиту не сущу на Руси в ты дни никому же, но ожидающим митрополича пришествиа от Царяграда, его же бог дасть.[24]

And here is how Epiphanius designates the date of the death of Stephen of Perm' (26 April 6904):

> в царство правовернаго греческаго царя Мануила, иже в Цареграде царствовавша, при патриарсе Антонии, архиепископе Костянтинополи, при патриарсе Иерусалимьстем Дорофеи, при патриарсе Александриистем Марке, при патриарсе Антиохиистем Ниле, при благоверном князи великом Василии Дмитриевичи, в седмое лето княжениа его, при архиепископе Киприане митрополите всея Руси, тогда бо в ты дни сущу ему в Киеве, при прочих князех благочестивых и христолюбивых: князе Владимере, Юрии, Андреи, Петре, Костянтине, Юрьи, Иоанне, Симеоне, Афонасии, Андреи, Василии, Литовьскою же всею землею обладающу в ты дни князю великому Витофту Кестутиевичю, во дни

---

[24] In the year 6883, in the reign of the Greek emperor John, who ruled in Constantinople, under Archbishop Philotheus, patriarch of Constantinople, whereas among the Horde at that time in Sarai, Mamai ruled over the Tatars but inconsistently at first, whereas in Rus' it was during the reign of Grand Prince Dimitrii Ivanovich, there being in those days no archbishop and metropolitan in Rus', the people awaiting the arrival of a metropolitan from Constantinople, whomever God might grant.

христолюбца князя великого Михаила Александровича Тверскаго, и Ольга Рязаньскаго, и Андрея Ростовьскаго, и Иоанна Ярославскаго, в шестое на десять лето владычества Тактамыша царя, и обладающу ему Мамаевою Ордою, Заволжьское царство обдержащу второму царю именем Темирь Кутлую, иже тою страною обладающу ему.[25]

From this enumeration we can, by the way, discern interesting facts about the distribution of political forces in eastern Europe at the beginning of the fifteenth century and their hierarchy in the mind of Epiphanius, who presented the structure of the Grand Principality of Vladimir in the form of a union (*soiuz*) of sovereign principalities with the grand prince of Vladimir at its head.

From this follows the critique by Epiphanius of the Muscovite regime's activities aimed at restraining the independence of the individual principalities. An example of this attitude in the *Life of Sergius of Radonezh* is the characterization of the reign of Ivan Kalita as one of "aggression" (*nasilovanie*) and the description of "persecutions" (*goneniia*) and "great coercion" (*velikaia nuzha*) against the "city of Rostov" (*grad Rostov*) on the part of the representatives of the grand-princely administration. The "oppressive measures" (*tiazhesti*) and the "oppressive tributes and violations" (*dani tiazhkie i nasil'stva*) of the Muscovites in the land of Perm' are phrases found in the *Life of Stephen of Perm'*. Similar expressions of such a critical attitude are evident in the Trinity Chronicle. A condemnatory tone characterizes the words of the article for 6876 describing how

князь великии Дмитрии Ивановичь да Алексеи митрополит зазваша князя Михаила Александровичя Тферскаго любовью на Москву..., а в правде, да его изымали, а что было бояре его около его, тех всех поимали, розно разведоша, и быша вси в нятьи, и дръжаша их в истоме.[26]

We should remember that in the *Life of Stephen*, Epiphanius set apart the name of Mikhail Aleksandrovich by the epithet "khristoliubets" (Christ-lover).

---

[25] In the reign of the right-believing Greek emperor Manuel, who ruled in Constantinople; under Patriarch Antonius, archbishop of Constantinople; under Dorotheus, patriarch of Jerusalem, Mark, patriarch of Alexandria, and Nilus, patriarch of Antioch; under the pious Grand Prince Vasilii Dmitrievich, in the seventh year of his reign; under archbishop Cyprian, metropolitan of all Rus', who was in Kiev in those days; and under the remaining pious and Christ-loving princes Vladimir, Iurii, Andrei, Peter, Konstantin, Iurii, Ivan, Simeon, Afanasii, [and] Vasilii; in those days Vitovt Keistutievich controlled the entire Lithuanian land; in the days of the Christ-loving grand prince Mikhail Aleksandrovich of Tver', and Oleg of Riazan', and Ivan of Yaroslavl'; in the sixteenth year of the rule of Khan Tokhtamysh, who ruled the Horde of Mamai with the second khan named Temir Kutlui holding the [Tatar] kingdom beyond the Volga and controlling that land.

[26] Grand Prince Dimitrii Ivanovich and Metropolitan Alexius called Prince Mikhail Aleksandrovich of Tver' with love to Moscow ... but in truth they took him prisoner, and those of his boyars who were around him, they seized them all, interrogated them separately, and they all were in prison and they were left to languish.

Other passages in the Trinity Chronicle have parallels in the works of Epiphanius the Wise. For example, the expression under the year 6848 "napolnishasia velikyia pechali i placha" (was filled with great sorrow and weeping) corresponds to the phrase in the *Encomium of Sergius* "mnoga plachia i pechali napolnishasia" (was filled with great weeping and sorrow). In the Trinity Chronicle *sub anno* 6879, and in the *Life of Stephen,* we find "novgorodtsi ushkuinitsi razboinitsi" (the marauding thieves of Novgorod). Furthermore, the Trinity Chronicle reports that "Riazantsi zhe surovi sushche . . . viazati moskvich', ponezhe sut' slabi i strashlivi" (the Riazanians being rough . . . took the Muscovites prisoner, since they are weak and cowardly); likewise, the *Life of Stephen* describes them as "suroveishii muzhi nevernii cheloveky," "slabi zhe i grubi zelo i strashivi" (very rough men and unbelievers, truly weak and very coarse and fearful). Analogously in the Trinity Chronicle under the year 6900, the Novgorodians are described as "chelovetsy surovy, nepokorivi" (rough, unsubdued men), and under 6901 as "surovi chelovetsi, sverepii liudie" (rough men, fierce people).

The reference to the Trinity-Saint Sergius Monastery as the "velikaia lavra" (great lavra) finds a full correspondence in the texts of Epiphanius: the *Encomium of Sergius* refers to "preslovushchei lavre i velitsei ograde i v slavnei obiteli" (the most glorious lavra and great garden and in the glorious monastery), and the *Life of Stephen* mentions "sii velikyi monastyr' iako lavra" (this great monastery or lavra).

The glorification by Epiphanius of the Trinity Monastery as a cenobitic house finds a parallel in passages of the Trinity Chronicle where the cenobitic character of the monasteries founded by Sergius is stressed; particular attention is generally paid to this principle of structuring the monastic life. Compare under the year 6882: "Dionisia . . . obshchemu zhitiiu nachalnika" (Dionysius . . . the head of the community); under 6885: "Chudov obchii monastyr'," (the cenobitic Chudov Monastery) that "byti obshchemu zhitiiu" (was a cenobitic community) and, describing Ivan Petrovskii: "se byst' pr"vyi obshchemu zhitiiu nachalnik na Moskve" (he was the first head of the cenobitic community in Moscow), "iasha i posadisha v zheleza Ivana Petrovskogo arkhimandrita, moskovskogo kinoviarkha, nachalnika obshchemu zhitiiu" (Archimandrite Ivan Petrovskii, the Muscovite cenobitic abbot, the head of the community, was seized and put in irons); and under 6886: Princess Vasilisa "i vsi obshchee zhit'e zhiviakhu" (and all of them lived a cenobitic life).

Other coincidences can be found. Under the year 6885, it is asserted that Ol'gerd "piva i medu ne piiashe" (did not drink beer or mead); under 6886, Vasilisa "piva i medu ne piiashe." These phrases correspond to passages in the

Life of Stephen of Perm', "piva ne piiashe" (did not drink beer), and in the *Life of Sergius*, "piva zhe i medu nikogda ni vkushaiushchii" (never drinking beer or mead). Under 6882, the Trinity Chronicle reports that "promyshliaiushchim podast' velikuiu voliu i oslabu i mnoguiu lgotu" (to those planning he gave great liberty and freedom and many privileges). In the *Life of Sergius*, we read: "i lgotu liudem mnogu darova i oslabu veliku" (and he granted many privileges and great freedom to the people).

We should also point out the parallels found by G. M. Prokhorov between the entries for 6882 and 6885 in the Trinity Chronicle and passages in the *Life of Stephen of Perm'*.[27]

It is interesting that even the well-known phrase "i ashche khoshcheshi raspytovati, razgni knigu Letopisets velikii rus'skii i prochti" (and if you wish to question, open wide the Great Russian Chronicle and read) in the Trinity Chronicle under 6900 finds parallels in the *Life of Sergius:* "i kuiuzhdo razgnet knigu" (and whatever book he might open wide) and in the *Life of Stephen:* "elika v pis'mena sia prinitsaiushchikh i razgybaiushchikh i pochitaiushchikh" (however many of those investigating, opening wide and reading these letters).

In the light of what we have set forth, the conclusion that Epiphanius the Wise was the author of the Trinity Chronicle seems to us sufficiently proven. Furthermore, the Trinity Chronicle appears to be Muscovite in the full sense of the word. In all the conflicts described in the Chronicle (between Moscow and Riazan', Moscow and Tver', Moscow and Novgorod, Moscow and Lithuania), the Muscovite side is always declared to be right and the opposing side is condemned. This pro-Muscovite bias appears to be the basis for the thesis about the patrimonial ownership by the Muscovite princes of the Grand Principality of Vladimir. On these grounds it is stipulated under the year 6868 that Dimitrii Konstantinovich of Suzdal' received the grand principality "ne po otchine, ne po dedine" (not as a patrimony or as a grandfather's inheritance), whereas under 6870 it is asserted that Dimitrii Ivanovich took possession of the Vladimir principality "po otchine i po dedine" (as patrimony and as a grandfather's inheritance). Along the same lines, it is reported (*sub anno* 6870) that Dimitrii Ivanovich "sede na velikom kniazhenii, na stole otsa svoego i deda i pradeda" (ruled the grand principality, the throne of his father, grandfather, and great-grandfather), whereas in the article for 6871, Dimitrii Ivanovich drove out Dimitrii Konstantinovich "s velikago kniazhenia s Volodimiria, s svoee otchiny v ego grad Suzdal'" (from the Grand Principality of Vladimir, from the former's patrimony into the latter's town of Suzdal').

---

[27] *Pamiatniki perevodnoi i russkoi literatury XIV–XV vekov* (Leningrad, 1987), 116–117.

In addition to compiling the Trinity Chronicle, Epiphanius created still other works: several letters under the name of Metropolitan Photius, the *Tale about Temir Aksak*, several articles in the *Prologue*, the *Tale about the Capture of Moscow by Toktamysh*, the *Tale about the Battle of Kulikovo Field*, the *Oration about the Life of Grand Prince Demetrius Ivanovich*, the *Oration about the Life of Michael Alexandrovich, Prince of Tver*, and the *Encomium of Arsenius, Bishop of Tver'* all of which are found in the body of the Sophia First and Novgorod Fourth Chronicles. These works not only mark the level of Russian literature at the beginning of the fifteenth century but are also monuments of ideology, of political thought. They permit us more fully to bring to light the activity of the outstanding writer of medieval Rus', Epiphanius the Wise.

THEORY AND PRACTICE

COMMERCE AND PRAGMATIC LITERACY

THE EVIDENCE OF BIRCHBARK DOCUMENTS (FROM THE MID-ELEVENTH TO THE FIRST QUARTER OF THE THIRTEENTH CENTURY) ON THE EARLY URBAN DEVELOPMENT OF NOVGOROD

EDUARD MÜHLE

In 1951, when Soviet archaeologists unearthed the first piece of birchbark with carved Cyrillic letters on it, their discovery immediately attracted much interest among scholars studying early East Slavic Culture. The specimens of carved birchbark, found not only in the waterlogged deposits at Novgorod but also in some other places, did indeed become a valuable kind of written source for the rather poorly documented early history of Rus'. The documents on birchbark caused heated debates and led to a new branch of study, "birchbark science" or *berestologija,* which, having produced hundreds of specialized studies, now merits its own bibliography.[1]

By the end of 1989, the number of birchbark documents had increased to 764, while their locations had risen to ten with the new discoveries from Moscow and Zvenigorod in the summer of 1988. Seven hundred and ten of these texts come from Novgorod.[2] Twenty-five documents are known from

---

[1] See *Arxeologija Novgoroda. Ukazatel' literatury 1917–1980,* ed P. G. Gajdukov (Moscow, 1983), 211–212 (index). For summaries on the results of *berestologija* in Western languages, see W. Vodoff, "Les documents sur écorce de bouleau de Novgorod," *Journal des savants,* 1966, no. 4:193–233; K. -D. Grothusen, "Das altrussische Birkenrindenschrifttum," in *Frühe Schriftzeugnisse der Menschheit* (Göttingen 1969), 21–240; V. Janin, "Nowgoroder Schriftstücke auf Birkenrinde," *Gesellschaftswissenschaften,* 1977, no. 4:144–158; W. Vodoff, "Les documents sur écorce de bouleau de Novgorod. Découvertes et travaux récents," *Journal des savants,* 1981, no. 3:229–281.

[2] A. V. Arcixovskij and M. N. Tixomirov, *Novgorodskie gramoty na bereste (iz raskopok 1951 g.),* (Moscow, 1953), documents 1–10; A. V. Arcixovskij, *Novgorodskie gramoty na bereste (iz raskopok 1952 g.),* (Moscow, 1954), documents 11–83; A. V. Arcixovskij and V. I. Borkovskij, *Novgorodskie gramoty na bereste (iz raskopok 1953–1954 gg.),* (Moscow, 1958), documents 84–136; idem, *Novgorodskie gramoty na bereste (iz raskopok 1955 g.),* (Moscow, 1958), documents 137–194; idem, *Novgorodskie gramoty na bereste (iz raskopok 1956–1957 gg.),* (Moscow, 1963), documents 195–318; A. V. Arcixovskij, *Novgorodskie gramoty na bereste (iz raskopok 1958–1961 gg.),* (Moscow, 1963), documents 319–405; A. V. Arcixovskij and V. L. Janin, *Novgorodskie gramoty na bereste (iz raskopok 1962–1976 gg.),* (Moscow, 1978),

Stara Russa,³ fifteen from Smolensk,⁴ six from Pskov,⁵ two from Zvenigorod,⁶ and Tver',⁷ one each from Mstislavl',⁸ Toržok,⁹ Vitebsk,¹⁰ and Moscow.¹¹ Chronologically these documents belong to the period from the mid-eleventh to mid-fifteenth century.¹² Nearly thirty-five percent (248) of the 710 Novgorodian documents, eighty percent (20) of those from Stara Russa,

---

documents 406–539; V. L. Janin and A. A. Zaliznjak, *Novgorodskie gramoty na bereste (iz raskopok 1977–1983 gg.)*. *Kommentarii i slovoukazatel' k berestjanym gramotam (iz raskopok 1951–1983gg)*, (Moscow, 1986), documents 540–614; with the important corrections of the reading of documents 1–539. Documents nos. 615–710 are still unpublished; some information, however, is to be found in *Arxeologičeskie otkrytija 1984–1986 gg.*, (Moscow, 1986–1988); A. A. Zaliznjak, "O jazykovoj situacii v Drevnem Novgorode," *Russian Linguistics* 11 (1987): 115–132; E. A. Rybina, "Svedenija o torgovle v berestjanyx gramotax," in *Istorija i kul'tura drevnerusskogo goroda* (Moscow, 1989) 74–81. In the summers of 1988 and 1989, I studied the unpublished *gramoty* in Novgorod. For this opportunity and the help rendered I am deeply indebted to Valentin Janin and Andrej Zaliznajk; for further assistance I wish to thank Elena Rybina. In the following the *gramoty* are cited only by their numbers.
³ Documents 1–13 published in Arcixovskij and Janin, *Novgorodskie gramoty (1978)*, (see n. 2), 143–153; 14 in Janin and Zaliznjak, *Novgorodskie gramoty (1986)*, (see n. 2), 77; documents 15–23 in V. G. Mironova, Berestjanye gramoty iz Staroj Russy (naxodki 1985g.), *Sovetskaja arxeologija*, 1990, no. 2: 216–225.
⁴ Documents 1–11 are published in D. A. Avdusin and E. A. Mel'nikova, "Smolenskie gramoty na bereste (iz raskopok 1952–1968 gg.)," in *Drevnejšie gosudarstva na territorii SSSR 1984 g.* (Moscow, 1985), 199–211. Documents 12–15 were discovered in 1988 and are still unpublished; I was able to study document 12, the only legible one of these last discoveries, in Novgorod in the summer of 1988; for further information I wish to thank Natal'ja Astašova.
⁵ For documents 1–4, see G. P. Grozdilov, "Raskopki drevnego Pskova (1956, 1958–1960 gg.)," *Soobščenija Gosudarstvennogo Èrmitaža* 23 (1962):65–66; V. D. Beleckij, "Drevnij Pskov po materialam arxeologičeskix raskopok èkspedicii Gosud. Èrmitaža," *Soobščenija Gosudarstvennogo Èrmitaža* 29 (1968); I. K. Labutina and I. Ja Kostjučuk, "Pskovskie berestjanye gramoty No. 3 i 4," *Sovetskaja arxeologija*, 1981, no.1: 66–78; documents 5 and 6 were found in the summer of 1988 and are still unpublished. I examined these in August 1988 in Pskov; for her help I am indebted to Inga Labutina.
⁶ The documents from Zvenigorod (western Ukraine) are still unpublished; only no. 2 seems to be legible, but until the spring of 1990 its reading was unknown, even to the Soviet berestologists Janin and Zaliznjak. These documents have now been published by Ihor Svešnykov; see "Zvenyhorods'ki hramoty na beresti," *Dzvin* 6 (1990): 127–131.
⁷ N. V. Žilina, "Tverskaja berestjanaja gramota No. 1." *Sovetskaja arxeologija*, 1987, no. 1: 203–216; L. A. Popova, "Issledovanija v Tveri," *Arxeologičeskie otkrytija 1985 g.* (Moscow, 1987), 92–93 [*Gramota no.*2].
⁸ L. V. Alekseev, "Berestjanaja gramota iz drevnego Mstislavlja," *Sovetskaja arxeologija*, 1983, no. 1: 204–212.
⁹ P. D. Malygin, "Raboty v Toržke i ego okruge," *Arxeologičeskie otkrytija 1985 g.* (Moscow, 1987), 80–81.
¹⁰ N. N. Dročenina and B. A. Rybakov, "Berestjanaja gramota iz Vitebska," *Sovetskaja arxeologija*, 1960, no. 1: 282–283.
¹¹ *Pravda*, 31 August 1988.
¹² The rather difficult problem of dating the uncovered birchbark scrolls could be solved fairly reliably on the basis of a stratigraphical and dendrochronological analysis of the archaeological complex to which each find is directly connected. Thus every birchbark document, except those few random finds, that cannot be related to an archaeological complex, has its dating at least within a century and often even within one or two decades.

seventy-three percent (11) of those from Smolensk, and five of the six from Pskov, and those documents from Zvenigorod, Toržok, and one out of the two from Tver' date from the mid-eleventh to the first quarter of the thirteenth century. Thus a considerable number of the known birchbark texts may throw some light on the early development of Old Russian towns. This paper will endeavor to show what sort of information birchbark documents actually reveal to the historian interested in urban developments of early northwestern Rus'.

Shortly after the first birchbark scrolls were found, A. V. Arcixovskij, then head of the archaeological expeditions at Novgorod, argued that most of these documents were private letters reflecting the customs of a "society of craftsmen." Refuting the traditional view of Novgorod as primarily a commercial town,[13] Arcixovskij's interpretation was soon confronted with the argument that birchbark literacy was probably more concomitant with Novgorod's function as "a major commercial and political center of Old Rus'."[14] This view indeed seemed to be confirmed in 1966 when A. A. Konovalov analyzed the content of the first 405 Novgorodian documents and concluded that the birchbark texts of eleventh–thirteenth centuries deal predominantly with matters of commerce and trade.[15] The majority of Soviet berestologists, however, continued to regard the early *gramoty* also as the legacy of feudal landlords and trading craftsmen. Thus, for example, L. V. Čerepnin identified only three early documents among the 415 known to him in 1969 as referring to the sector "commerce."[16] In the studies by E. A. Rybina, the leading expert on Novgorod's commercial history, one can find only a few other examples. In 1978 she counted only eleven *gramoty* connected to commerce, whereas in 1989 she referred to nineteen documents regarding commercial activities.[17] And even where we find the explicit conclusion that the *gramoty* of the eleventh to first quarter of the thirteenth century provide us primarily with information on money matters, as in V. L. Janin's works, birchbark literacy nevertheless appears mainly as a result of the requirements of landholding boyars and their *votčina* econ-

[13] A. V. Arcixovskij, "Nouvelle découvertes à Novgorod," *Riassunti delle comunicazioni*, 7, ed. G. C. Sansoni, (Florence 1955), 95–97.

[14] L. P. Žukovskaja, *Novgorodskie berestjanye gramoty* (Moscow, 1959), 13.

[15] A. A. Konovalov, "Periodizacija novgorodskix berestjanyx gramot i èvoljucija ix soderžanija," *Sovetskaja arxeologija*, 1966, no. 2:61–74.

[16] L. V. Čerepnin, *Novgorodskie berestjanye gramoty kak istoričeskij istočnik* (Moscow, 1969), 267–298 (documents 165, 223, 381).

[17] E. A. Rybina, *Arxeologičeskie očerki istorii novgorodskoj X–XIV vv.* (Moscow, 1978), 85–102 (documents 105, 107, 109, 160, 163, 165, 335, 381, 437, 439, 524); Rybina, "Svedenija," (see n. 2), 74–81 (in addition to those mentioned in 1978, nos. 153, 222, 245, 438, 456 and the newly discovered nos. 548, 624 and 675).

omy.[18] Thus, Soviet historiography rather neglects the sector "commerce" as a potential factor in generating the kind of pragmatic literacy to which birchbark documents attest.

But would it not have been the merchants in conducting commercial transactions, money transfers, and credit who would have had the greatest interest in the use of written notices, testimony, and epistolary communication? The precedents of pragmatic literacy in the mercantile milieu of the major commercial centers of Flanders and northern Germany or—in this case using carved rune-stokes—in Scandinavia, which we find from the end of the twelfth century,[19] allow the hypothesis that in Rus' too nonparchment or lay literacy outside the monasteries and princely courts originated primarily among the merchants. How does this hypothesis—by no means entirely new[20]—correspond to the evidence provided by the 248 early Novgorodian documents and 53 others from the various locations? To answer this question we have to take a closer look at the content of our birchbark texts.

Since we are interested only in the subject to which the texts refer, there is no need to describe here in detail the physical shape, size, and state of preservation of the *gramoty,* nor do we have to discuss their paleographic and linguistic peculiarities. We have to bear in mind, however, that only a few birchbark documents contain complete texts and that the majority are fragments. Moreover, the texts that are regarded with certainty as complete are also extremely short and laconic in most cases. The matter they communicate with an almost telegraphic brevity is, as a rule, taken out of its original context and thus to a high degree inaccessible to posterity. The temptation, therefore, to supplement the missing elements by conjecture and overinterpret the texts is great. To avoid this danger in our analysis, we have

---

[18] See, for example, V. L. Janin, "K 30-letiju otkrytija novgorodskix berestjanyx gramot (metodologičeskie aspekty issledovanija)," in *Arxeografičeskij ežegodnik za 1982 g.* (Moscow, 1983), 82.

[19] Cf. F. Rörig, "Mittelalter und Schriftlichkeit," *Die Welt als Geschichte* 13 (1953): 29–41; A. Wendehorst, "Wer konnte im Mittelalter lesen und schreiben," in *Schulen und Studium im sozialen Wandel des hohen und späten Mittelalters,* ed. J. Fried (Sigmaringen, 1986), 9–23; I. S. Johnsen, "Die Runenschriften über Handel und Verkehr aus Bergen (Norwegen)," in *Untersuchungen zu Handel und Verkehr der vor- und frühgeschichtlichen Zeit in Mittel- und Nordeuropa,* pt. 4. *Der Handel der Karolinger- und Wikingerzeit,* ed. K. Düwel (Göttingen, 1987), 716–744.

[20] See S. Franklin, "Literacy and Documentation in Early Medieval Russia," *Speculum* 60 (1985):1–38; T. V. Roždestvenskaja, "Pis'mennaja tradicija Severnoj Rusi po èpigrafičeskim dannym," in *Drevnerusskij literaturnyj jazyk v ego otnošenii k staroslavjanskomu* (Moscow, 1987), 36–44. The latter article traces the usage of pragmatic literacy to the ninth and tenth centuries connecting it with the milieu of early long-distance traders. See also Eve Levin, "Novgorod Birchbark Documents: Medieval Russia," in *Medieval Archeology,* ed. Charles L. Redman (Binghampton, 1989), 127–137.

Table 1: *Contents of the Early Novgorodian Birchbark Documents (Mid-Eleventh–First Quarter of Thirteenth Century)*[21]

Rubric	Field of Content	no.	% of all documents	% of interpretable documents
1	Sums of money	18	7.3	
2	Money lending/credits	38	15.3	
3	Merchandise/purchasing	26	10.5	
	Subtotal (1–3)		*33.1*	*49.1*
4	Transfers of undefined property	8	3.2	
5	Arrangements for appointments or journeys	5	2.0	
6	Labels	3	1.2	
	Subtotal (1–6)		*39.5*	*58.7*
7	Judicial/hereditary matters	9	3.6	
8	Agriculture/hunting	3	1.2	
9	Tributes from countryside	4	1.6	
10	Crafts	8	3.2	
11	Political/military affairs	6	2.4	
12	Ecclesiastical/religious affairs	23	9.4	
13	Single names	5	2.0	
14	Alphabets	3	1.2	
15	Private affairs	8	3.2	
16	Noninterpretable	81	32.8	
	TOTAL	248	100.0	

kept strictly to a close reading of the documents and tried to establish, without any conjecture, what sort of information they reveal. For this purpose we first scrutinized the contents of the 248 Novgorodian documents by differentiating between sixteen "fields" or "sectors" of content (see Table 1). Almost a third (81 or 32.8 percent) of the relevant birchbark pieces appear to be illegible or too fragmented to allow assignment to any one of the specified fields of content. Of the legible texts only a surprisingly small number of documents are equivocal in referring to more than one sector of content. In seventeen of eighteen cases, however, these *gramoty* refer only to two different thematic sectors, and only in one case (no. 605) does a *gramota* actually mention three fields of content (merchandise, ecclesiastical affairs, and private affairs). All in all, the "doublings" thus do not seriously contaminate our classification (see Table 2).

[21] See Appendix for a listing of these *gramoty* by rubric.

Table 2: *"Doublings" of Fields of Content in the Early Novgorodian Birchbark Documents*

Field of Content	"Doubled" in Sector	Gramota no.
Sums of money	Family affairs	672
Money lending	Judicial matters Agriculture Crafts	235, 238, 246 219 638
Merchandise	Money lending Judicial matters	163, lead-gramota, 422, 675 109
Private affairs	Merchandise	605
Transfers	Agriculture	103, 232
Judicial matters	Money lending Agriculture	222, 531 562
Agriculture	Judicial matters	8, 108

As the table shows, the "doublings" appear in several cases in closely related sectors, such as merchandise and money lending, or money lending and judicial matters. In these *gramoty* the subjects are related to credit law. The sixteen *gramoty* with such equivocal readings were classified according to the thematic sector that appears to be the dominating one.

Turning to the different fields of content, we find that documents categorized under the first heading in Table 1, "Sums of money," are almost all very short and fragmentary. Often they have only a single legible word: "vekša," the smallest unit of the Rus'ian monetary system, "kuna," "nogata," or "grivna." In some cases, apart from the unit itself, a certain amount also appears, e.g. seven, ten or thirty "grivn." The absence of context of the eighteen *gramoty* in the first category (7.2 percent of all or 10.8 percent respectively of the legible documents) prohibits any inferences about the nature of these monetary transactions.

We get some certainty with items in the second comprising thirty-eight documents (15.3 percent of all, or 22.7 percent of the legible documents). Here we find not only short but also extended fragments and even several complete texts. The sphere of money lending and credit business is reflected in different ways and varying degrees of lucidity. A number of fragments simply state that someone gives, will give or gave (*vdati/vdajati*), or takes, will take, or took (*vzjati*) a certain amount of money to or from somebody (nos.

119, 231, 525, 664, 667, 710). These monetary transactions are not necessarily connected with loans; they could also have been a result of some sort of transaction or service for which the recipient or sender of the *gramota* still had to pay. Even if so, belated payment actually meant a form of credit.

More explicit evidence shows a number of *gramoty* preserving financial terms from the sphere of borrowing such as "capital" (*isty, istina* in nos. 114, 449, 509, 526), "debt" (*dolgъ* in nos. 235, 676), "debtor" (*dolož'nica* in no.449) and "interest" (*natъ* in nos. 227, pencilled document 526, 665). Other possible examples occur in the expressions *zajato v tret* and *v druguju tret* (nos. 75, 170). In no. 227, a son requests his mother to send him two *grivna;* if she does not have the money at hand, she should take a loan:

> ...аняние ко матьри. Водае семоу 2 гривьне. Не могы же ми, матоко, согре... оу себе не боуд... заемоши. Моги же водати *от* тога ти нама хоце болого... оти зем... оти 6 гр... лоуце... ашя е...[22]

The procedure of taking a loan is well demonstrated in *gramota* no. 336, which also provides details about the interest rate of two *soroček* out of five. Because the document gives no details about the period of validity and the amount of the loan taken is partly illegible, we can say nothing about the actual amount of interest rate:

> *От* Петра грамота къ Влътькови. То еси ты повѣдалъ къ Рожьнѣтови на Нустуе емати 2 срочька. Ни векшею не длъжнъ. А ныне оу Даньши заялъ есмь 2..2 срочька въ 5ть срочькъ. А емли на немь Даньша.[23]

Another group of documents in the second category refers to periods when the recipient or sender had to pay back a given loan or be reminded of the deadline (nos. 105, 113, 380, 389, 524, 676). A fine example of a reminder, which at the same time threatens to take judicial measures if the outstanding amount is not sent, is provided by *gramota* no. 246:

> *От* Жировита къ Стоянови. Како ты оу мене и чьстьное дрѣво въздъмъ и веверицъ ми не присълещи, то девятое лето. А не присълещи ми полоупяты гривьны, а хоцоу ти выроути въ тя лоуцьшаго новъгоржянина. Посъли же добръмъ.[24]

---

[22] [Gree]tings to mother. Give him [the one who brought the letter] two grivnas. Do not [be devious with] me, mother, if you don't have [it], you can borrow [it]. Give from that [loan. If] he wants high interest of us ... from the lan[d] ... from 6 gr[ivnas] ... better ... .

[23] Letter from Peter to Vlot'ko. You told Rožnet to take two soročki from Nustuj. Nustuj doesn't owe a penny [vekša]. Now I have taken a loan of two [with an interest rate of] two soročki out of five from Dan'ša. Take it from Dan'ša.

[24] From Žirovit to Stojan. It is already the ninth year since you kissed the cross before me and you still have not sent the money. If you do not send me four and a half grivnas, I intend to confiscate the goods from the most distinguished Novgorodian in your stead. Send me the money of your own free will.

Such reminders were perhaps not always fully justified as we learn from *gramota* no. 238:

> ...Несъдицеви полъ пятѣ рѣза[нѣ, а] (м)нѣ еси | въдале дъвѣ коунѣ; цьто же за[с] — [о] твориши, | [за] мъною осмь коунъ и гривьна? поид[и] же въ горо | (дъ, м)[о]гоу ся съ тобою яти на водоу.²⁵

The largest group in the second category is comprised of debtors. Such a list might simply state a number of names and a certain amounts of money, as for example, *gramota* no. 228:

> Оу Доброжира полоуторе. Оу Яръшековее дявяте. Оу Завида семе векоше i резана. Оу Олисея резана. Оу то....²⁶

In other cases the lists also name the places where the debtors lived, thus indicating the extent of the Novgorodian credit business. *Gramota* no. 526 gives an excellent example:

> На Бояне въ Роусе гривна, на Житоб(о)уде въ Роусе 13 коуне и гр(и)вна истине. На Лоуге на Негораде 3 коупе и гр(и)вна съ намы. На Добровите съ людьми 13 коуне и гр(и)вна. На Нежьке на Пръжневици полъгр(и)вне. На Сироме без дъвоу ногатоу гр(и)вна. На Шелоне на Добромысле 10 коуно. На Животтъке 2 гр(и)вне кроунемъ. Серегери на Хъмоуне и на Дрозьде 5 гр(и)внъ бес коупе. На Азъгоуте и на Погощахъ 9 коунъ семее гр(и)вне. Доубровьне на Хрипане 19 третьее гр(и)вне.²⁷

According to this list, debtors of a Novgorodian creditor lived in Stara Russa, by the rivers Luga and Šelon, by Lake Seliger and in a village called Dubrovno.

The fact that such lists indeed were lists of debtors rather than lists of outstanding tributes is demonstrated by *gramota* no. 509 where we explicitly find the terms for "capital" and "interest." How the lists were used by a creditor is shown by *gramota* no. 662, once again providing names and amounts of money owed. This time, however, some of the names are crossed out. It is

---

²⁵ To Nesdič you gave four and a half rezanas and to me two kunas. Why do you claim that I owe you eight kunas and one grivna? Go on to town . . . you should take the water route.

²⁶ From Dobrožir one and a half; from Jaroškov, nine; from Zavid, seven vekša and one rezana, from Olisej, one rezana, from To . . . .

²⁷ From Bojan in Rusa one grivna; from Žitobud in Rusa 13 kunas, one grivna capital; from Negorad in the River Luga area, three kunas and one grivna with interest; from Dobrovit with [his] people, 13 kunas and a grivna; from Nežek Prožnevič, one and a half grivna; from Sirom, 45 kunas [one grivna less two nogatas]; from Dobromysl in the River Selon area, ten kunas; from Životek two grivnas in small coins; from Xomun and Drozd of the Seliger region five grivnas less one kuna; from Asgut and the Pogoščani six grivnas and nine kunas [nine kunas of the seventh grivna]; from Xripan in Dubrovno two grivnas and 19 kunas [19 kunas of the third grivna].

possible to observe the places where an attempt was made to smooth out the surface of the bark, probably after the debtors had paid their debts.

Debtors did not only pay their obligations in cash, however. Besides amounts of money, some lists specify certain kinds and quantities of products demanded by an authorized representative of the creditor. For example, *gramota* no. 219 states that a certain Ivan owes nine *grivna*, of which the representative of the creditor should take half a quarter of a *grivna* (*polučetvert' grivni*) and fifteen buckets (*dežka*) of oats. From a certain Danešinica he should take corn for three *grivna;* from Jareševic, who lived down the river Sjas', two *berkovec* of some product (salt? wax? honey?); and from Tušueviv salt for a *grivna* and two *nogata*. Similar lists of debtors who had to pay back their debts partly in cash, partly in kind, are to be found in *gramoty* nos. 630, 665, and probably also in the very fragmentary no. 223, where the product was fur.

It has been argued that such birchbark documents listing amounts of money and products were not in fact registers of debtors but of tax or tribute payments.[28] In a few cases this argument cannot be wholly excluded. Tax or tribute payment on a larger scale to private people outside the princely administrations, however, presupposes an already fully developed manorial system, which in fact only began in the twelfth century. Thus *votčina*-landholdings could not have constituted the predominant form of economic relations between town and countryside as early as the eleventh–beginning of the thirteenth century.[29] This is also confirmed by the four *gramoty* that can actually be linked with tax paying, since their texts contain terms from this sphere: *poljudie* (no. 226); *pos'liščenycho kuno* '*kuna* per settlement [*poselenie*]' (no. 550); *pogost'* 'tax district' (no. 640) and *ralo* 'plough tax' (no. 663). Three of them date from the end of the twelfth or the beginnings of the thirteenth century; only one can be dated to the second half of the twelfth century. Most of the early money and product lists on birchbark thus undoubtedly are to be assigned to the sphere of lending and borrowing. The combination of money and products in these debt-registers points to the close connection between money lending and merchandise that characterized the economic relations between town and country from the eleventh century to the beginning of the thirteenth century. For what reason should people in the country

---

[28] Cf. V. L. Janin, "Arxeologičeskij kommentarij k Russkoj Pravde," in *Novgorodskij sbornik. 50 let raskopok Novgoroda* (Moscow, 1982), 153–154.

[29] For a detailed argumentation see E. Mühle, *Die städtischen Handelszentren der nordwestlichen Rus'. Anfänge and frühe Entwicklung altrussisches Städte (bis gegen Ende des 12. Jahrhunderts)* (Stuttgart, 1991), 133–153.

take loans, if not to buy basic consumer or luxury goods manufactured in or imported by the town and distributed by Novgorodian merchants? It is true that in some regions tax and tribute payments already had to be delivered in cash. This alone, however, does not provide sufficient explanation for the scope of the Novgorodian credit business. Rather it seems that money lending was a covert form of purchasing natural products. The profit margin of the Novgorodian merchants—who, after having refined a purchased product, resold it either within the town or within the long-distance trade network—must have been considerable. Not only could they gain from the additional charge every commercial agent demands for merchandise but also from the interest rates which must have been rather high. The gramoty give us no certain details about this practice. Only a prescription of the *Voprošanie Kirikova* (first half of the twelfth century), which demands a general reduction in interest rates to 60–80 percent, gives us an idea of their exorbitance.[30]

If the birchbark documents related to money lending and credits (Rubric 2 in Table 1) already reflect commercial activities, the twenty-six *gramoty* that we find in the third category (10.5 percent of all, or 15.6 percent of the legible documents) explicitly speak of merchandise and purchases, small trade with groceries (nos. 605, 682, 700) as well as commerce with serfs (nos. 109, 155), horses (nos. 109, 160, 163, 437, 442), salt (no. 624), wax (no. 439), honey (no. 671), craft items (e.g., leather goods), different sorts of metal, rivets, jewelry (nos. 335, 438, 439) and luxury goods, such as Byzantine cloth and furs (nos. 7, 586, 675). A number of documents refer to the sphere of commerce, or in some cases, only to its terminology. So we find the word *tovar* 'goods' or 'wares' (nos. 107, 165, 624), *kriti* (=kupit')[31] 'to buy' (no. 153, lead-*gramota*, 160, 456, 685) and *prodati* 'to sell' (nos. 160, 163, 165, 439, 679). Two *gramoty* also contain lists of prices (nos. 437, 438). These latter examples were discovered together with no. 439, in which the author writes to a certain Spirok that he and Prus should buy a certain amount of *pi* 'wax' for him, if Matejka has not already taken it. The writer reports that he has sold all the tin, lead, and rivets, so that he has decided to cancel his journey to Suzdal'; he has also bought three *pi*. Furthermore the recipient, whom he asked to come to him, should buy four *bezmen*, about 4 kg., of tin:

---

[30] *Kirchenrechtliche und kulturgeschichtliche Denkmäler Altrusslands nebst Geschichte des russischen Kirchenrechts,* ed L. K. Goetz, (Stuttgart, 1905), 217, §54: "...budite miloserdi, v-zmete lьgko; ašče po 5 kun dal iesi, a 3 kuny v-zmi ili 4."

[31] See A. A. Zaliznjak, "Novgorodskie berestjanye gramoty s lingvističeskoj točki zrenija," in Janin and Zaliznjak, *Novgorodskie gramoty* (1986) §78, (see n.2), 174–175.

...ко Спирокоу. Оже ти не возяло Матеека пи, воложи ю со Проусомо ко мне. Язо ти олово попродале, и свинеце, и клепание вьхо. Оуже мне не ехати во Соужедале. Воскоу коуплены 3 пи. А тобе поити соуда. Воложи олова со цетыри безмене, полотенеца со дова цереленая. А коуны прави сопроста.³²

This text not only gives a good example of how several merchants worked together in a sort of company, but also shows that their businesses were indeed far-reaching. In addition to Suzdal' we find mention of Kiev, Perejaslavl', Pskov, and Velikie Luki as places where Novgorodian merchants traveled. Of special interest is *gramota* no. 675, which recounts a rather complicated commercial transaction: in Kiev a Novgorodian merchant had business dealings with another merchant—probably Kievan—about valuable Byzantine cloth (*fofud'i*). Both partners in business were joint creditors of a loan for six *grivna*, which they had given to somebody living in Velikie Luki. We learn, moreover, that one of them or a third person should travel to Suzdal'. Though this is all that the very fragmentary *gramota* reveals, it nevertheless offers proof of the merchant's impressively large commercial radius.

If we take the three categories discussed so far together, regarding them in a wider sense as one "field" of content referring to commercial activities, we see that they constitute a third of all *gramoty* analyzed, or 39.5 percent of all legible documents. This percentage could be enlarged although with declining degree of certainty. Thus it is highly probable that a number of the eight *gramoty* classified as "Transfers of Property" (category 4) might have been connected with commerce. The same may be true for at least one of the labels, classified in category 6. *Gramota* no. 458 has only one word and a number, *Voloce* 4, and the birchbark has two holes at its left preserved edge. It very well could have been sent with four objects to a certain Voloca.

Looking at the nine *gramoty* dealing with judicial affairs (category 7 / 3.6 percent of all, or 5.4 percent of the legible documents), we see that some of them may actually have been connected with the sector "commerce," since some of the court proceedings to which they refer resulted from quarrels about business dealings. Thus, *gramota* no. 222 tells us of litigation between a Novgorodian (merchant) and a group of *kolbjagi*, i.e. Scandinavian merchants:

От М[а]тья къ Гюргю: топьрьво е[с]мо пришль тога д[ьля] н[ь шль] | оустяцю мя н-...-си. ожь [л]и право запираютьс | а я даю княжю дьцьскамоу гривноу сьрьвра. едоу с нимо. ожь мя тать | мо [по]ставили.

---

³² ... to Spirok. If Mat[v]ejka has not yet taken the balls of wax, send them together with Prus to me. I sold the tin, the lead, and all the rivets. I do not have to go to Suzdal' any longer. I bought three balls of wax. And you should come here. Send some four bezmen of red tin, in other words, about two pieces. And collect the money immediately.

ожь ти нь бьжяли колобягъ оу тьбь жрьбье | скоть по людьмо. ни тоу тобь тощины вькшь одоное.³³

Gramota no. 531 provides evidence about litigation that was connected to a commercial transaction, namely money lending:

От Ане покло ко Климяте. Брате господине, попецалоуи и моемо ороудье Коснятиноу. А ныне извета емоу людеми. Како еси возложило пороукоу на мою сестроу и на доцере еи, назовало еси сьтроу мою коровою и доцере блядею. А нынеца Федо прьехаво, оуслышаво то слово и выгонало сетроу мою и хотело потяти. А нынеца, господине брате, согадаво со Воелавомо, молови емоу тако. Еси возложило то слово, тако доведи. Аже ти возомолови Коснятино. Дала роукоу за зяте. Ты же, браце господине, молови емо тако. Оже боудоу люди на мою сьтроу, оже боудоу люди, при комо боудоу дала роукоу за зяте, то те я во вине. Ты пако, брате, испытаво, которое слово звело на мя и пороукоу. А боудоу люди на томо, тобе не сетра, а моужеви не жена. Ты же мя и потени, не зеря на Федора. И даяла моя доци коуны людеми с ызветомо, а заклада просила. И позовало мене во погосто. И язо прехала, оже онь поехало проце, а река тако: Азо солю 4 дворяно по гривене сьбра.³⁴

Thus, with a rather high degree of certainty, we can conclude that well over 40 percent of all and at least about 50 percent of the legible documents of those from the eleventh to the first quarter of the thirteenth century originate from a commercial milieu. In comparison, the other main sections of economic life—agriculture, crafts, and tax or tribute—are very poorly represented. They account for no more than 1.2 percent to 3.2 percent of all, or 1.8 percent to 4.8 percent of the legible *gramoty*. Besides the commercial sector, only the ecclesiastical sphere (rubric 12 / 9.4 percent of all, or 13.8

---

³³ From Mat[v]ej to Jurij. Now I have come. That is why I did not come [before]. You will be met [or I will meet you]. If they in fact do not agree, I will give a silver grivna to the prince's man and will come with him, since they have made me out to be a thief. If the Kolbjagi have not run off, you have the lots, the amounts [owed] per person. You won't lose a single penny.

³⁴ Greetings from Anna to Klimjata. My lord brother, take care of my case with Kosnjatin. Inform him now in front of witnesses [of his injustice]. "For what reason have you leveled a charge of surety against my sister and her daughter, and called my sister a cow and her daughter a whore? After Fedor arrived and heard that charge, he drove my sister out and wanted to kill her." And now, my lord brother, after consulting with Vojeslav, tell him [Kosnjatin] thus: "Since you have raised the charge, prove it." And if Kosnjatin replies to you: "She had vouched for [her] son-in-law," tell him thus, my lord brother: "If there are witnesses [people] against my sister, if there are witnesses before whom I [= she] will have vouched for [my] son-in-law, then I am [= she is] at fault." And for your part, my lord brother, should you discover upon investigation the surety of which he is charging me, if there are witnesses for this charge, then I am no longer your sister and my husband's wife; kill me then regardless of Fedor! As a matter of fact, my daughter had given the money with a declaration in front of witnesses and had asked for surety. And he [Kosnjatin] had summoned me to the district office. And when I arrived there, he rode off, saying: "I am sending four bailiffs [to collect] one silver grivna each [from all of you = Anna, her son-in-law, her daughter, and her husband Fedor]."

Table 3: Contents of the Early Birchbark Texts from Places Other than Novgorod (Mid-Eleventh–First Quarter of the Thirteenth Century)[35]

Category	Stara Russa	Smolensk	Pskov	Zvenigorod	Tver'	Toržok	no.	% of all documents / % of interpretable documents
1. Sums of money	1	1					2	59
2. Money lending	12	2			1		15	
3. Merchandise	3	1	2				6	74
4. Journey arrangements	1						1	
5. Administration	2						2	
6. Ecclesiastical affairs		3					3	
7. Single names	1						1	
8. Alphabets						1	1	
9. Noninterpretable		5	3				8	
							39=	100

percent of the legible documents) finds a more significant representation. This is mainly due to a rather large group of *gramoty* (16), found in the courtyard of a priest, which can be interpreted as lists of names used for commemorating the dead in church service.

Our examination of the 248 early Novgorodian birchbark documents shows that although providing evidence of pragmatic literacy in different professional and social milieux, they were indeed primarily a legacy of Novgorodian merchants. This conclusion is confirmed by an analysis of the birchbark texts we know from other places. As shown in Table 3, the 39 *gramoty* of Stara Russa, Smolensk, Pskov, and Toržok, which can be dated from the eleventh to the first quarter of the thirteenth century, constitute only a relatively small number. Nevertheless an analysis of their content shows the same trend as our examination of the Novgorodian *gramoty*. About 59 percent of all, or 74.2 percent of the legible *gramoty* are to be assigned to the commerce sector (categories 1–3). Again only the ecclesiastical sphere (three text fragments) has significant representation.

If we conclude that birchbark literacy was mainly used in dealing with commercial matters, we may perhaps not be totally wrong in assuming that

---

[35] See Appendix.

Table 4: Contents of the Novgorodian Birchbark Texts (Mid-Eleventh– Mid-Twelfth Centuries)[36]

Rubric	Field of Content	no.	% of all documents	% of interpretable documents
1	Sums of money	7	9.5	
2	Money lending/credits	13	17.6	
3	Merchandise/purchases	8	10.8	
	Subtotal 1–3		37.9	43.2
4	Transfers of undefined property	1	1.3	
5	Arrangements for an appointment or journey	2	2.7	
6	Labels	1	1.3	
	Subtotal 1–6		59.6	68
7	Judicial matters	3	4.2	
8	Agriculture/hunting	–	–	
9	Tributes from countryside	–	–	
10	Crafts	1	1.3	
11	Political/military affairs	4	5.4	
12	Ecclesiastical/religious affairs	–	–	
13	Single names	2	2.7	
14	Alphabets	1	1.3	
15	Private affairs	4	5.4	
16	Noninterpretable	27	36.5	
TOTAL		74	100.0	

its very origins as well ultimately go back to the requirements of the daily business among Novgorod's merchant class. If this was indeed so, the use of birchbark for written messages and communication would have spread increasingly from this milieu to other social spheres such as the private sector or the sectors of crafts and agriculture, whereas birchbark literacy within ecclesiastical circles had its roots in the tradition of parchment literacy. To test this hypothesis, we have divided the early Novgorodian birchbark texts into two groups: the first comprises the *gramoty* of the mid-eleventh to the mid-twelfth century; the second, the documents of the latter half of the twelfth and the first quarter of the thirteenth century. We should expect a higher percentage of the commerce sector within the first group when we analyze their contents, as shown in Table 4.

A comparison of amounts in Tables 1 and 4 shows that in the earlier

---

[36] See Appendix.

period a greater number of *gramoty* are connected with commerce. The difference is especially remarkable when we look just at the legible documents and compare how many of them deal with commerce: 59.6 percent of the legible birchbark texts from the earlier period as opposed to only 39.5 percent in the later period. Here we have a glimpse of the dynamism in the unfolding of birchbark literacy for which commerce was obviously crucial.

So far we have looked only at the evidence of the *gramoty* themselves. But of course, as V. L. Janin has rightly pointed out,[37] the birchbark documents found in medieval courtyards, beneath street pavements, or under log buildings are an inseparable part of a special archaeological complex. Thus they are always directly connected with other material testimonies of the past.

Turning to the archaeological complexes in which the Novgorodian birchbark documents were found, we should first take a look at the topography of the excavation sites.[38] It appears that our *gramoty* are found throughout Novgorod without recognizable concentration in any special quarter. Having observed this wide, though by no means wholly even topographical distribution,[39] we may ask whether this picture is also true with respect to the content of the *gramoty*. Do we find significant topographical concentrations of documents related to commerce in only one or two of the excavated areas? Table 5 shows that this is not the case. In every excavation site with a countable quantity of legible *gramoty*, we find the greatest number of *gramoty* concerned with commerce, though we can also observe a difference in percentages: in the Nerevskij excavation it reaches 71 percent whereas in Troickij it is only 49.2 percent. This is obviously due to the ecclesiastical element that we find in one of the courtyards of the latter excavation site. The courtyard, which as we may conclude from some of the *gramoty* found there, (cf. nos. 502, 546, 549, 558) was occupied by a certain Olisej Grečin, gives an excellent example of how the birchbark documents are connected with the archaeological complex in which they are found. The twenty-nine birchbark documents from the courtyard of Olisej Grečin may be categorized as follows:[40]

---

[37] Janin, "Nowgoroder Schriftstücke" (see n.1); idem, "K 30-letiju" (see n. 18), 83.
[38] Several sites were already excavated before 1951. That these diggings in the 1930s and 1940s have not yielded a single birchbark document can be explained by the fact that the expeditions not only were not professionally led, but also were not attentive to fragments of birchbark. Only with the discovery of the first *gramota* did the archaeologists henceforth examine every piece of birchbark with special care.
[39] Cf. the statistics given in Janin and Zaliznjak, *Novgorodskie gramoty* (1986), (see n.2), 9 where the index of one *gramota* per one excavated square meter lies between 17.2 and 140.
[40] Cf. B. A. Kolčin, A. S. Xorošev, and V. L. Janin, *Usad'ba novgorodskogo xudožnika XII v.* (Moscow, 1981), 43–58.

Ecclesiastical affairs 16
Crafts (icon painting) 6
Commerce 3
Labels 1
Judiciary 1

The picture derived from Table 5 of the contents of the *gramoty* corresponds to the impression conveyed by the other archaeological material uncovered on the site. Since we cannot go into details here, it may suffice to state that several half-finished icons, remnants of colors, special tools, raw and waste materials, and half-finished and finished metal accessories give sufficient evidence on the craftsmanship (icon-painting, jewelry) of the people who lived on this site. Obviously a priest also, Olisej Grečin not only received orders for painting icons (*gramoty* nos. 549, 552, 553, 558, 559) but also handled lists with names of deceased people whom he should commemorate in his prayers to God at church service (nos. 508, 522, 541, 542, 544, 545, 546, 551, 554, 555, 557, 560, 561).

Table 5: Distribution of Legible Gramoty *According to Contents and Excavation Sites*

Excavation site	Sector of content	no.	%	TOTAL
Nerevskij	Commerce Judiciary Crafts, agriculture, tribute Others		71.0 5.0 7.0 17.0	57=100%
Troickij	Commerce Judicial matters Crafts, agriculture, tribute Ecclesiastical affairs Others		49.2 5.9 11.8 25.9 7.2	85=100%
Bujanyj	Commerce Others	4 1		
Tixvinskij	Commerce Others	5 2		
Il'inskij	Commerce Others	2 2		

In a similar way we can trace all the other *gramoty* in their archaeological context. The texts from the eleventh to the first quarter of thirteenth century taken as a whole do confirm the picture obtained by analyzing the content of the early birchbark documents from these same archaeological complexes. Commerce was, indeed, the main branch of economic life in Novgorod during the early stages of its development. The rich import goods connected with long-distance trade and artifacts connected with regional or local small trade that we find among the archaeological materials from the very beginning of the town's existence give ample evidence of this.[41] Moreover, other written sources—chronicles, Scandinavian runic inscriptions, saga literature, the *Pravda Russkaja* and princely charters, especially the treaty on trade between Novgorod and the German towns of the Baltic—show Novgorod as a major commercial center of the Rus'. To be sure, we do not find very convincing evidence about a dominance of crafts and agriculture in early Novgorod in these archaeological and written sources.[41]

The early birchbark literacy of Novgorod was, therefore, not at all a reflection of the customs of a "society of craftsmen," as Arcixovskij has put it, but as Žukovskaja has rightly pointed out, concomitant with the town's function as the major commercial center of northwestern Rus'. This was probably true also for the other places with documented birchbark literacy. Here the evidence is much slimmer, but the tendency appears to be the same: the requirements of commerce were crucial for the early unfolding of pragmatic literacy in the birchbark documents.

Appendix

Table 1. Numbers of the Gramoty by Rubric

1. 76, 84, 120, 164, 338, 440, 459, 547, 613, 617, 621, 650, 654, 672, 677, 678, 683, 686
2. 75, 105, 113, 114, 119, 168, 170, 219, 223, 227, 228, 231, 235, 238, 240, 246, 296, 336, 380, 389, 430, 449, 509, 516, 524, 525, 526, 630, 631, 638, 649, 657, 662, 664, 665, 667, 676, 684, 710
3. 7, 78, 107, 109, lead-gramota, 153, 155, 160, 163, 165, 335, 381, 422, 437, 438, 439, 456, 548, 586, 624, 671, 675, 679, 682, 685, 700
4. 79, 103, 232, 430, 454, 627, 651, 655
5. 82, 233, 566, 656, 673
6. 429, 458, 546
7. 115, 222, 247, 421, 502, 531, 562, 600, 603

[41] For a detailed argumentation see Mühle, *Die Städtischen Handelszentren* (see n. 29).

8. 8, 108, 174
9. 226, 550, 640, 663
10. 522, 549, 552, 553, 558, 559, 602, 644
11. 225, 241, 527, 590, 607, 633
12. 462, 504, 506, 507, 508, 541, 542, 544, 545, 551, 554, 555, 557, 560, 561, 571, 595, 648, 652, 660, 674, 681, 688
13. 86, 116, 158, 194, 523
14. 444, 460, 591
15. 9, 87, 156, 400, 424, 487, 605, 705
16. 74, 77, 80, 81, 83, 88, 89, 90, 117, 118, 121, 123, 150, 152, 159, 175, 176, 181, 230, 234, 236, 237, 239, 245, 341, 379, 399, 405, 423, 425, 426, 427, 428, 431, 432, 433, 434, 435, 443, 450, 451, 452, 453, 455, 457, 461, 486, 493, 505, 5-11, 512, 513, 515, 517, 518, 556, 593, 604, 606, 608, 620, 625, 626, 628, 629, 632, 635, 637, 639, 641, 642, 643, 647, 653, 658, 659, 661, 666, 668, 669, 680

Table 3. Numbers of the Gramoty *by Rubric*

1. Stara Russa 17; Smolensk 8
2. Stara Russa 5, 6, 13, 14, 15, 16, 18, 19, 20, 21, 22, 23; Smolensk 9, 12; Tver', 1
3. Stara Russa 4, 8, 11; Smolensk 11; Pskov 5, 6
4. Stara Russa 7
5. Stara Russa 10, 12
6. Smolensk 5, 7, 10
7. Stara Russa 9
8. Toržok 1
9. Smolensk 1, 6, 13, 14, 15; Pskov 1, 2, 3

Table 4: Numbers of the Gramoty *by Rubric*

1. 84, 120, 338, 613, 677, 678, 164
2. 105, 119, 168, 235, 238, 246, 336, 380, 524, 525, 526, 630, 631
3. 109, 160, 335, lead-gramota, 381, 422, 586, 679
4. 232
5. 566, 673
6. 429
7. 247, 421, 562
8. —
9. —
10. 644
11. 241, 527, 607, 633
12. —
13. 158, 194
14. 591
15. 156, 424, 487, 605
16. 83, 88, 89, 90, 117, 121, 127, 175, 176, 181, 234, 245, 341, 423, 425, 426, 427, 428, 433, 434, 435, 517, 518, 593, 608, 635, 680

THE ISSUE OF A "NONSTANDARD" TRANSLATION OF THE HOLY SCRIPTURES IN MUSCOVITE RUS'

METROPOLITAN ALEKSIJ, MAKSIM GREK, EPIFANIJ SLAVINECKIJ

OLGA STRAKHOV

Without doubt one of the most important tasks facing scholars of Russian culture is to establish and characterize the redactions of the Slavonic Bible in manuscript. Gorskij and Nevostruev formulated this program fully and clearly some 150 years ago:

> While annotating the differences in New Testament translation among the various copies, we were governed incidentally by this thought as well: when we have gathered more observations like these on the text of New Testament copies by examining a greater number of old manuscripts, we will be in a better position to determine the characteristic features of the copies from a particular place and time and to elaborate a concept of families or categories of copies . . . . Then we will be able to reach plausible conclusions about when and where the devout Zealots of Piety labored over the collation of the old translation with the Greek manuscripts, or, by restricting themselves solely to an individual understanding of the translation that had come down to them, tried to clarify it by replacing old, outmoded foreign words with new, more familiar ones.[1]

The present study attempts to analyze a group of texts that, although somewhat peripheral in the history of Slavic New Testament translation, provide a clear idea of "when and where the devout Zealots of Piety labored over the collation of the old translation with the Greek manuscripts."

The Manuscript Division of the Lenin State Library in Moscow houses a unique manuscript (fond 310, № 1291), the four Gospels translated from

---

Translated from the Russian by Michael S. Flier

[1] A. Gorskij and K. Nevostruev, *Opisanie slavjanskix rukopisej Moskovskoj Sinodal'noj biblioteki*, sec. 1: *Svjaščennoe pisanie* (Moscow, 1855), xi.

Greek into Church Slavonic by Epifanij Slavineckij (? – 1675). The original has not been preserved. The manuscript is a carefully executed copy of the text done in the first half of the eighteenth century (watermark № 137 [Dianova and Kostiukhina], indicating the years 1716, 1723, or 1740). The manuscript is written in small semi-uncial on 272 sheets and measures 19.7 cm. x 15.7 cm. It is covered in leather-bound boards, stamped in gold. The manuscript is well documented in the literature,[2] but has yet to be the subject of a special study. Furthermore the manuscript is of enormous interest to textologists of the Slavonic version of the New Testament. There is scarcely a single line of the Gospel text left unchanged.

The Preface to the manuscript proves to be invaluable for reconstructing the creation of this text and, moreover, provides essential aid in clarifying the issue of a "nonstandard" translation of the Church Slavonic Gospel text.[3] The Preface indicates that as a result of the lengthy history of the Gospel text's presence on East Slavic territory, and because of the poor knowledge of Church Slavonic and Greek, numerous errors were introduced into the biblical text:

---

[2] Cf. A. I. Sobolevskij, *Perevodnaja literatura Moskovskoj Rusi* (St. Petersburg, 1903), 22.

[3] The Preface has long attracted the attention of investigators. See, for example, I. Rotar, *Epifanij Slavineckij, literaturnyj dejatel' XVII v.* (Kiev, 1901) [= *Kievskaja Starina*, 1900, no. 10, 1–38; no. 11, 189–217; no. 12, 344–400]; V. S. Siromaxa, "'Knižnaja sprava' i voprosy normalizacii knižno-literaturnogo jazyka Moskovskoj Rusi vo 2-oj polovine XVII v.," unpublished candidate's dissertation, Moscow State University; T. A. Lisovaja, "Leksika kormčix knig vtoroj poloviny XVII v.," unpublished candidate's dissertation, Russian Language Institute, USSR Academy of Sciences, Moscow, 1986. Sobolevskij, and Siromaxa and Lisovaja after him, assumed that the author of the Preface was Evfimij Čudovskij, named for his place of residence, the Čudov Monastery. For more on Evfimij, see S. Brailovskij, "Otnošenie Čudovskogo inoka Evfimija k Simeonu Polockomu i Sil'vestru Medvedevu," *RFV,* 1889, sec. 22, pt. 4, 263–290; idem *Očerki iz istorii prosveščenija v Moskovskoj Rusi v XVII v. Čtenija v Obščestve ljubitelej duxovnogo prosveščenija,* 1890, no. 3, sec. 1, 225–250; no. 9, sec. 1, 361–405; A. Florovskij, "Čudovskij inok Evfimij," *Slavia* 19, nos. 1–2 (1949): 100–152. For Evfimij's poetic legacy, see the article by L. L. Sazonova, "Poètičeskoe tvorčestvo Evfimija Čudovskogo," *Slavia* 56, no. 3 (1987): 243–252; on his linguistic views, see my article "Iz istorii cerkovnoslavjanskoj okkazional'noj leksiki konca XVII v.," *Ètimologija, 1985* (Moscow, 1988), 57–62.

I assume that Sobolevskij's attribution should be accepted. Evfimij's authorship is manifested not only in the specifics of linguistic features that distinguish the Preface. It is interesting that certain passages in the Preface coincide with similar ones found in the text of *The Orthodox Creed* (GIM, Sinod. sobr., № 473), translated by Evfimij in 1695. Cf. the Preface of Epifanij's translation in (a) and the Preface of *The Orthodox Creed* in (b):

a. Не две ли птице ценитеся ассарию единому? Не слично съчинение сие в преведении и неправильно. Греческое же евангелие (яко писаша святии евангелисти) и иных диалектов, и преведение святаго Алексия чудотворца, и Златоуста святаго в беседе девятой на Матфеа, лист 98, глаголет чинно сице: не два ли врабия продаются на ассарии (f. viii).

(Не две ли птице ценитеся ассарию единому? [Are not two birds worth a single farthing?] This phrasing is not equivalent in the translation and [therefore] incorrect. The Greek Gospel [as the Holy Evangelists wrote it] and that in other dialects, and the [Gospel] translation by

Но времене растоянием, ово от преписующих, ово же и от невежно правящих многа погрешения во многих писаниих явишася, паче же ветхаго и новаго завета богостроеный храм премнога повреждения пострада от недобре той назидающих, ибо в разуме, в речениях и в сочинении зело отстоит от греческаго (ff. IIv–III).[4]

Living in Moscow at the behest of Tsar Aleksej Mixajlovič, Epifanij Slavineckij set himself the task of translating anew the text of the New Testament—a remarkable undertaking, given the fact that like the Psalter and the Apostol, the Gospel in Old Rus' was learned "by ear"—it was read in church, and everyone knew it nearly by heart. A scholar of acute linguistic awareness, Epifanij Slavineckij approached the authorities of the Church with this proposal and received the blessing of Patriarch Pitirim and the council of bishops especially convened for this purpose in September 1671. For assistants Epifanij selected from among the intellectual elite of Muscovite Rus', the professional editors and scribes of the Moscow Printing Office, and commenced work on his translation. Because of his death on 19 November 1675 and that of his patron Paul, metropolitan of Sara and the Don, on 9 September of the same year, a full translation was never completed. The translators, however, did produce the tetraevangelion, the text of which is analyzed here.

Saint Aleksij the Miracleworker, and that of Saint Chrysostom in the Ninth Commentary on Matthew, folio 98, thus state properly: не два ли врабия продаются на ассарии? [Are not two sparrows sold for a farthing?])

b. В святых преведениих погрешенно написано: Не две ли птице ценится единому ассарию и паки Не пять ли птиц ценятся пенязема двема? Ниже убо речение зде истинно, ниже съчинение благочинное имуще. В нынешних же правопреведениих... право и истинно преведеся: Не два ли врабия на ассарии продаются и в другом: Не пять ли врабиев на ассариях двух продаются? (f. 22v).

(In the holy translations we see incorrectly written: Не две ли птице ценится единому ассарию? [Are not two birds worth a single farthing?] and yet again Не пять ли птиц ценятся пенязема двема? [Are not five birds worth two coins?] Neither is the locution here correct, nor the composition proper. In the current correct translations . . . it is translated correctly and properly: Не два ли врабия на ассарии продаются? [Are not two sparrows sold for a farthing?] and in the other, Не пять ли врабиев на ассариях двух продаются? [Are not five sparrows sold for two farthings?])

That portion of the Preface concerning the history of the Gospel translation and the last years of the life of Epifanij Slavineckij was published by Metropolitan Evgenij (Bolxovitinov) in his *Slovar' istoričeskij o byvšix v Rossii pisateljax duxovnogo čina greko-rossijskoj cerkvi*, pt. 1 (St. Petersburg, 1818), s.v. Epifanij. The Preface as a whole was never published. Some three-fourths of the entire text of the Preface is devoted to substantiating the changes made by Epifanij. Hereafter I will use Roman numerals when indicating pages in the Preface and Arabic numerals for pagination in the text proper.

[4] But over the long course of time, whether by those copying or those revising in ignorance, a great many errors appeared in many [sacred] writings; furthermore, the temple of the Old and New Testaments built by God suffered considerable damage from those erecting it, because in sense, in locutions, and in composition it departs considerably from the Greek.

The author of the Preface, Evfimij Čudovskij (see n. 3), in relating the history of the creation of the text and the circumstances of the last years of Epifanij Slavineckij's life, recalls a number of texts and manuscripts utilized in Epifanij's work:

> У преведения сего... быша книги рукописныя греческия и славенския. О них же всех подробну повествовати много будет, о единей или двох славенских древлних поведати доволно будет. Первая славенская бе у преведения сего преводу и рукописания Алексиа митрополита всея России, чудотворца, писаная в лето 6863 до смерти его за 23 лета, яже и до днесь обретается в обители его в Чудове монастыре в книгоположнице блюдома и прочитаема бывает над болящими. Вторая славенская книга бе у исправления сего преводу цареградского, в лето 6890, прежде Флоренского съседалища за 56 лет писаная. Третия книга Беседы святаго Иоанна Златоустаго на священное евангелие, преводу святогорца мужа премудра монаха Максима Грека в лето 7032 (f. V).[5]

We are justified in asking several questions: Which manuscripts are being described here? Why were these specifically selected? Did the translators really use these manuscripts as a base? I shall attempt to provide answers to these questions below.

Čudov New Testament

The first manuscript noted by Epifanij is none other than the Čudov New Testament, which was kept in the Kremlin's Čudov Monastery and apparently disappeared during the first years of Soviet rule. According to G. Voskresenskij, who studied it at the end of the nineteenth century,[6] the manuscript was written in small, precise fourteenth-century semi-uncial on thin, high-quality parchment (the first folio was paper) in small octavo, with two columns of 38–41 lines each per folio, 170 folios in all. There are cinnabar notations in the margins: ecclesiastical incipits, beginnings of readings, and the days for which they are intended. The ornamental headings in the

---

[5] Greek and Slavonic manuscripts were used ... for this translation. To discuss all of them in detail would be excessive; it will suffice to mention one or two of the early Slavonic ones. The first Slavonic book used in the reworking of this translation and in the hand of Aleksij, metropolitan of all Russia, the Miracleworker, was written in 6863 [1355], 23 years before his death, and to this very day is found in his own Čudov Monastery, looked after in the library and read aloud over the infirm. The second Slavonic book, the [so-called] Constantinopolitan redaction, written in the year 6890 [1382], 56 years before the Council of Florence, was used in this correction. The third book, the *Commentaries of Saint John Chrysostom on the Holy Gospel*, is from a translation by a man of the Holy Mountain [Athos], the most wise monk Maksim Grek, in the year 7032 [1524].

[6] "Xarakterističeskie čerty četyrex redakcij slavjanskogo perevoda Evangelija ot Marka po sta dvenadcati rukopisjam Evangelija XI–XIV vekov," *ČOIDR* (1896), bk. 1, 176.

beginning of the Gospels and the Epistles are not large and are simple in design. The orthography is Russian with the rendering of ъ and ь as o and e, the distinction of e and ѣ, the writing of ю instead of оу after palatal obstruents, the abridgement of u to ь before vowels, the reflex of *dj as ж.[7] The most vivid feature of the Čudov New Testament (hereafter ČNT) is the consistent placement of accent marks (the Greek supralinear marks ' ' ' ` and the hook ˆ are used).[8] The manuscript was stitched into boards entirely studded with pearls and decorated with emeralds, jacinths, and uncut diamonds. The first numbered page bears the inscription of Metropolitan Platon, who notes that he decorated the manuscript in 1798.

It is assumed that the attribution of the manuscript to Aleksij, metropolitan of Moscow, is only a legend of the end of the seventeenth century. The manuscript is written in several hands, but the four Gospels are written in only one, which tradition has apparently linked with Aleksij.[9] The likely source of this legend is Evfimij Čudovskij, judging from data from Epifanij Slavineckij's Preface to the Gospels. Being a monk in the Čudov Monastery (founded, as is well known, by Metropolitan Aleksij), Evfimij was especially zealous in revering the memory of the prelate Aleksij. He dedicated a special *vita* and sermon in his honor. Both of these texts, written by Evfimij after 1690, were included in the printed Prolog (eighth edition, Moscow Printing Office, 1696).[10] From the literary perspective, V. O. Ključevskij viewed Evfimij's version of the *Life of Aleksij* as "one of the best Rusian monuments of its kind in terms of literacy of exposition, artistry of the tale, and striving to avoid the conventional forms and commonplaces of the *vita*."[11] In the *Life of Aleksij*, Evfimij Čudovskij places special emphasis on the metropolitan of Moscow's philological activities, developing in great detail the idea of the prelate's authorship of ČNT. This redaction of the *Life*,

---

[7] On the scribes and also the language of the monument, see M. Korneeva-Petrulan, "K istorii russkogo jazyka. Osobennosti pis'ma i jazyka piscov moskovskix vladyk XIV v.," *Slavia* 15(1937-1938): 1-23.

[8] For more details on the supralinear marks and the character of accentuation, see V. A. Dybo, "K voprosu o dialektnoj prinadležnosti Čudovskogo Novogo zaveta," *Filologija. Issledovanija po drevnim i novym jazykam. Perevody s drevnix jazykov* (Moscow, 1961), 29-42; idem, "Zakon Vasil'eva-Dolobko v drevnerusskom (na materiale Čudovskogo Novogo zaveta)," *IJSLP* 18 (1975): 7-81; V. E. Ušakov, "Drevnerusskie akcentuirovannye pamjatniki serediny XIV v.," *VJa*, no. 5 (1971): 91-104.

[9] For more details in general about the different hands of the manuscript and the possible similarity of Metropolitan Aleksij's handwriting to that of one of the ČNT scribes, see W. Lehfeldt, ed., *Neues Testament des Čudov-Klosters. Bausteine zur Geschichte der Literatur bei den Slaven*, v. 28 (Cologne and Vienna, 1989), 1-41.

[10] See Gorskij and Nevostruev, *Opisanie* (see n. 1), sec. 2, pt. 3, pp. 257, 814; Sobolevskij, *Perevodnaja literatura* (see n. 2), 31.

[11] *Drevnerusskie žitija svjatyx kak istoričeskij istočnik* (Moscow, 1871), 355-356.

rewritten in Evfimij's own hand, was included in the "rough" (i.e., galley proof) copy of the eighth edition of the Prolog (CGADA, *fond* 1182, № 846, September half), with the manuscript interpolated between folios 709 and 710.[12] Evfimij's explicit statements about Metropolitan Aleksij's authorship of ČNT are found in others of his works—translations done by him after 1690. These are *The Orthodox Creed*[13] and *Works of Nilus of Salonika*[14] (translated after 1693).

ČNT has been published photomechanically three times: by Archimandrite Amfiloxij in 1887, by Metropolitan Leontij in 1892, and by Werner Lehfeldt, who republished the 1892 edition in 1989.[15]

The most important characteristic feature of the manuscript is its extreme literalness: the structure of the Greek phrase is usually preserved, while all preceding and subsequent copies follow the norms of Church Slavonic syntax. Transmission of grammatical forms shows complete adherence to the Greek original; thus, for example, *praesens historicum* is translated with the present tense, whereas previous and current texts use aorist forms. The manuscript shows a tendency towards a consistent, one-for-one transmission of Greek prepositions and prefixes. The Greek personal pronouns are conveyed by corresponding personal pronouns, and not the possessive *svoj* 'one's own' as occurs in previous copies. The Greek article (in predicative constructions) is consistently rendered by the pronoun иже. For the first time, single rather than double negation is introduced. The tendency towards the literal reaches an extreme in the partial preservation of Greek letters: (cf. варѳоломáια [Mark 3:18, 12:18]; саδδουκάιοι [Mark 12:18];

---

[12] See L. A. Černaja, "Kavyčnye Prologi konca XVII–načala XVIII vv. i xarakter ix pravki (6, 8, 9, 10, 11-e izdanija Prologa)," *Russkaja staropečatnaja literatura XVI–pervaja četvert' XVIII vv. Literaturnyj sbornik XVII veka. Prolog* (Moscow, 1978), 132–141; on Evfimij, see esp. pp. 136–137.

[13] GIM, Sinod. sobr., № 473, ff. 19, 28, 29–29v, 31–31v.

[14] GIM, Sinod. sobr. № 198, f. 169.

[15] Arxm. Amfiloxij, *Novyj Zavet Gospoda Našego I. Xrista* (Moscow, 1887); mtr. Leontij, *Novyj Zavet Gospoda našego Iisusa Xrista. Trud svjatitelja Aleksija* (Moscow, 1892); W. Lehfeldt, *Neues Testament* (see n. 9). The basic literature includes G. Voskresenskij, *Drevnij slavjanskij perevod Apostola i ego sud'by do XV v.* (Moscow, 1879); idem, "Xarakterističeskie čerty," (see n. 6); idem, *Pogodinskij № 27 Apostol i Čudovskaja, usvojaemaja sv. Aleksiju, rukopis' Novogo Zaveta* (St. Petersburg, 1904) [= *Sbornik po slavjanovedeniju*, v. 1]; idem, *Drevne-slavjanskij Apostol*, no. 2: *Poslanie k Korinfjanam 1-e* (Sergiev Posad, 1906); idem, *Drevne-slavjanskij Apostol*, nos. 3,4,5: *Poslanie k Korinfjanam 2-e, k Galatam i k Efesjanam* (Sergiev Posad, 1908); I. Dujčev, "Centry vizantijsko-slavjanskogo obščenija i sotrudničestva," *TODRL* 19 (1963): 107–129; V. A. Dybo, "K voprosu" (see n. 8); M. Muretov, "Cerkovno-praktičeskoe i naučno-bogoslovskoe značenie slavjanskogo perevoda Novogo Zaveta v trude svjatitelja Aleksija," *Bogoslovskij vestnik*, 1897, no. 11, 177–199; no. 12, 375–414; M. Korneeva-Petrulan, "K istorii" (see n. 7); M. N. Rižskij, *Istorija perevodov biblii v Rossii* (Novosibirsk, 1978).

φαρισѣοι [Mark 3:6]; cf. also на Го́лгофан [ἐπὶ τὸν Γολγοθᾶν: Mark 15:22]; Κοδράнтис [Matt. 5:26], γαλιλέος [Mark 14:70] and many others).[16]

Tetraevangelion of 1383

The second manuscript mentioned by Evfimij is a tetraevangelion written on parchment, single-column format, in quarto, in small semi-uncial on 282 folios.[17] According to a notation on folio 281, it was written in 1383: "Написах святое благовестие в лет<о> 6891 (se͠ωчаι [sic]) месяца маиа, в богоспасаемем граде царстем Констянтинополи."[18] The orthography is Russian: о and е stand in place of the reduced vowels ъ and ь, double а is common. The marks ˝ or ˜ or a dot are placed over vowels, but accentuation is not consistent. In contradistinction to all previous copies, the spelling ы and not ъı is strictly maintained. The so-called "anchor е"—є—is used instead of the letter ѥ. The comma is the other mark of punctuation used besides the period; syllabification is strictly observed.

The 1383 manuscript is essentially different from other early East Slavic New Testament texts. It does not coincide with previous copies, randomly selected, from the eleventh to the thirteenth centuries in the readings: Matt. 5:9, 9:7, 24:51, 27:49; Mark 2:12, 14:30,68,72; Luke 1:3, 6:9, 8:26,29,37, 12:21, 21:1,4, 22:34, 24:27; John 1:28, 5:4, 7:39, 11:50, 13:38, 15:25, 28:27.

As a general statement, the 1383 Gospel coincides with previous copies of the Gospel *only* in those readings that most exactly follow the Greek source, and it differs in readings that treat the Greek original liberally or imprecisely. Without being literal in the full sense of the word, the translation of this Gospel is noted for its thoroughness and accuracy in comparing the Church Slavonic text to the Greek source.

---

[16] The tradition of ČNT is reflected in at least two other monuments from the second half of the fourteenth century: the 1399 Tetraevangelion of Nikon of Radonež (GBL, *fond* 304, 111, № 6 [m. 8652]) and the Tetraevangelion from the F. A. Tolstoj Collection (GPB, O. P. I, № 1). Cf. G. Voskresenskij, "Xarakterističeskie čerty" (see n. 6), 54–56; V. E. Ušakov, "Drevnerusskie akcentuirovannye pamjatniki" (see n. 8); idem, "Akcentologičeskij slovar' drevnerusskogo jazyka serediny XIV veka," *Slavjanskoe i balkanskoe jazykoznanie. Problemy interferencii i jazykovyx kontaktov* (Moscow, 1975), 263–321.

[17] GIM, Sinod. sobr., № 742.

[18] I finished writing [this version of] the Holy Gospel in the year 6891 [1383] (6891–10 [sic], possibly on the 10th day?) in the month of May in the God-spared imperial city of Constantinople.

For a description of the manuscript, see Gorskij and Nevostruev, *Opisanie* (see n. 1), pt. 1, 224–227; I. I. Sreznevskij, *Drevnie pamjatniki russkogo pis'ma i jazyka (X–XIV vekov)*, 2d ed. (St. Petersburg, 1882), 249–250; G. Voskresenskij, "Xarakterističeskie čerty" (see n. 6), 56, 292–297. Individual folios from the manuscript are reproduced in Bishop Savva, *Paleografičeskie snimki s grečeskix i slavjanskix rukopisej Moskovskoj Sinodal'noj biblioteki, VI–XVII veka* (Moscow, 1863), 32.

Readings maintained in subsequent copies of the Gospel and read in the contemporary Church Slavonic variant were introduced into the text for the first time: Matt. 5:9, 10:48, 14:50–51; Mark 9:17, 14:30, 68; Luke 1:3, 6:10, 7:12, 9:14, 10:16, 21:4, 22:34; John 1:1,28, 7:39, 11:50, 13:38, 14:18, 18:27.

According to Gorskij and Nevostruev, the copy of 1383 was probably made from a corrected manuscript, and precisely because of that fact, one can explain its ambivalence in the choice of new and old readings of the Gospel verses.[19]

Commentaries of John Chrysostom on the Gospels of Matthew and John

The *Commentaries of John Chrysostom on the Gospels of Matthew and John* existed throughout Muscovite Rus' in an enormous number of copies.[20] The dating of the *Commentaries on Matthew* (1524) is derived from the preface to this monument written by Selivan, a disciple of Maxim Grek.[21] This date is also included in an epistle of Maksim Grek discovered by N. B. Tixomirov, in which the author characterizes the contents of the translated book and the merits of Selivan as a translator.[22] The date for the translation of the *Commentaries on the Gospel of John* is not completely clear. A notation in one of the copies[23] with the date 1524–1525 is contradictory and cannot be accepted as completely reliable.[24]

Epifanij Slavineckij used a printed edition of the *Commentaries* (Moscow Printing Office, 1664–1665). This fact is established by the folio numeration noted by Evfimij in the Preface that coincides with the pagination of the Moscow editions. The preface to the Moscow Printing Office editions states the following:

> Преведена же бысть от еллинскаго премудрейшаго языка в славяно-российскии язык монахом Максимом Греком и учеником его монахом Селиваном... в лето от создания мира 7032. В настоящее же сие время... свидетельствовася и исправися с российских писменных и с греческих печатных преводов и напечатася первое в царствующем

---

[19] There is one other manuscript quite similar to the 1383 Gospel, a manuscript from the Moscow Church Academy (presently in the Manuscript Division of the Lenin Library), № 138. For a description of the manuscript, see Sreznevskij, *Drevnie pamjatniki* (see n. 18), 198; G. Voskresenskij, "Xarakterističeskie čerty" (see n. 6), 56–57.

[20] S. A. Belokurov cites a random list of these texts (about 40 manuscripts): *O biblioteke moskovskix gosudarej v XVI stoletii* (Moscow, 1898).

[21] I. V. Jagić published this preface in his work *Rassuždenie južnoslavjanskoj i russkoj stariny o cerkovnoslavjanskom jazyke* (St. Petersburg, 1895), 626–631 [338–343].

[22] GBL, Egor. 920.

[23] GIM, Voskr. 82-bum.

[24] For more on this question, see N. V. Sinicyna, *Maksim Grek v Rossii* (Moscow, 1977), 66, n. 21; see also 1–15, 65–67.

великом граде Москве...в лето от создания мира 7173, от воплощения же Бога Слова 1665. Совершися и издася от печатнаго тиснения месяца иуния в 9 день.²⁵

According to the Preface the text was edited and corrected by the editor Dionisij Ivirit "елико мощно и время достигло" (as much as time allowed). But four commentaries—44, 45, 46, and 47—which, according to the Preface, were translated by Andrej Kurbskij, were not corrected against the Greek original because of lack of time; thus the text of these commentaries was checked only against the Slavonic sources. Compare this Preface to that for the *Commentaries on the Gospel of Matthew:*

> Преведена же бысть от еллинскаго премудрейшаго языка сия душеполезная книга в славянороссийский язык иноком Селиваном...учеником бывшем Максима Грека в лето 7032 в матере градовом...граде Москве....В настоящее сие время...изследовася и исправися с триех переводов и напечатася первое в царствующем граде Москве... в лето от создания мира 7172, от воплощения же Бога Слова 1664.²⁶

The translation of the Gospel verses in these editions literally corresponds to the Greek original, often not coinciding with the contemporary (sixteenth-century) reading. This literalness apparently dates back to the time of Maksim Grek, whose early period of translation activity is marked by faithfulness to the Greek source.²⁷

Such is the short description of the three texts mentioned by Evfimij in the Preface to Epifanij Slavineckij's Gospel. What unites these three texts in the eyes of seventeenth-century editors? The answer to that question is rather obvious: all three texts are translations, directly and immediately tied to the Greek original. All three texts are reflections of a fully concrete goal set by the translators, complete correspondence with the original. From this perspective all three texts demonstrate literalness in transmitting Greek linguistic features.

---

²⁵ [This book] was translated from the most wise Greek language into Russo-Slavonic by monk Maksim Grek and his disciple, monk Selivan . . . in the year 7032 [1524] from Creation. And at the present time, it has been examined and corrected against written Russian and printed Greek redactions and has been printed for the first time in the great imperial city of Moscow . . . in the year 7173 from Creation, or 1665 from the Incarnation of the Word of God. It was completed and published by printing press on 9 June.
See *Besedy Ioanna Zlatoustago . . . na Evangelie ot Ioanna* (Moscow, 1665), ff. 1–1v.
²⁶ This edifying book was translated from the most wise Greek language into Russo-Slavonic by monk Selivan . . . a former disciple of Maksim Grek in the year 7032 in the mother of cities, the city of Moscow. At the present time . . . it has been examined and corrected against three redactions and has been printed for the first time in the imperial city of Moscow . . . in the year 7172 from Creation, or 1664 from the Incarnation of the Word of God.
²⁷ On the literalness of Maksim Grek's translations, especially from his early period, see E. Kravec, *Knižnaja sprava i perevody Maksima Greka kak opyt normalizacii cerkovnoslavjanskogo jazyka XVI veka* (unpublished manuscript).

These three factors lead us to a fourth: Epifanij Slavineckij, translating the text of the New Testament anew, maximally strove to approximate the original and in doing so used the methods and principles of literal translation. We shall analyze several of his suggested alternatives.

The most important component of the Preface to the Gospel is the explanation of innovations Epifanij Slavineckij introduced by means of references to a prestigious literary source, most commonly the Greek original, then ČNT or the 1383 Gospel and the *Commentaries of John Chrysostom*. As a rule, the Preface cites the "standard" reading of the verse, then states that Epifanij replaced this reading, as demanded by the Greek text and the relevant Slavonic texts. For the sake of exposition, I have somewhat altered the structure of the Preface: I cite Epifanij's variants in full, followed by references to the Slavic texts as represented in the Preface. I have provided the pagination of ČNT; the folios of the *Commentaries* are indicated by Evfimij himself. Unfortunately without direct access to the text of the 1383 Gospel, we must trust Evfimij's integrity.

1. Matt. 3:12 — є҆гѡ́же лопа́та в' рꙋцѣ̀ є҆гѡ̀, и҆ ѡ҆чн́ститъ гꙋмно̀ своѐ и҆ соберетъ пшенн́цꙋ [свою] в' влага́лнще, пле́вꙋ же пожже́тъ ѻ҆гне́мъ неꙋга́снными (f. 23).

Luke 3:17 — є҆го́же лопа́та в' рꙋцѣ̀ є҆гѡ̀, и҆ разчи́ститъ гꙋмно̀ своѐ и҆ соберетъ пшенн́цꙋ [свою] во влага́лнще своѐ, пле́вꙋ же пожже́тъ ѻ҆гне́мъ нега́сными (f. 144). Cf. reference: "яко и преведение святаго Алексиа митрополита всея России чудотворца показуюущо глаголет" (f. VIIv–VIII).[28]

2. Matt. 10:29 — Не два̀ ли врабі̑а а҆сса́рїемъ продаю́тсѧ? (f. 39v).

Luke 12:6 — Не пѧ́ть ли враби̑и продаю́тсѧ на а҆сса́рїахъ двохъ? (f. 174). Cf. the reference to ČNT and Maksim Grek: Преведение святаго Алекса чудотворца (ff. 6,33) и Златоуста святаго в Беседе девятой на Матфеа, лист 98, глаголет чинно сице: Не два ли врабия продаются на ассарии (f. VIIIv).[29]

3. Matt. 11:5 — Слѣпі́и прозира́ютъ, и҆ хромі́и ѡ҆бхо́дѧтъ, прокаже́нїи чи́стѧтсѧ, и҆ глꙋсі́и слы́шатъ, ме́ртвїи воста́ютъ, и҆ ни́щїи блговѣ́ствꙋютсѧ

---

[28] As the indicative translation of Saint Aleksij the Miracleworker and metropolitan of all Russia says as well.

[29] The translation by Saint Aleksij the Miracleworker and [the translation] of Saint Chrysostom in the Ninth Commentary on Matthew, folio 98, thus state correctly: Не два ли врабия продаются на ассарии.

(f. 40v). Cf. the reference to John Chrysostom, Commentary 36, folio 444: Яко святый Златоуст толкуя глаголет: И нищии благовествуеми бываютъ (f. VIIIv).[30]

4. Luke 6:44 — Коѥ́ждо бо дрє́во ѿ своѥгѡ́ плода̀ познава́ѥтсѧ, нѐ бо̀ ѿ те́рнїѧ собира́ютъ смо́квы, нижѐ ѿ кѹпины̀ ѡб'е́млютъ [the gloss гре́знатъ is in the margin] гро́здѧ (f. 154). Cf. the reference to ČNT: В преведении святаго Алексиа (f. 29) чудотворца глаголет: Не бо от терния събираютъ смоквы, ниже от купины об'емлют" (f. IX).[31]

5. Luke 8:46 — І҃ис жѐ речѐ: прикоснѹ́сѧ мнѣ̀ нѣ́кто. а́зъ бо позна́хъ мо́щь изшє́дшѹю ѿ менѐ (f. 161v.). Cf. the extensive reference: В святем евангелии сие место по еллински ἔγνων, по славенски же претолкуется познах или разумех, яко и в преведении святаго Алексиа митрополита написано (f. 31) разумех (f. IX).[32]

6. Luke 11:53 — Глю́щѹ же ѥмѹ̀ сїѧ̀ къ ни́мъ, нача́ша пи́смєнницы ѝ фарисе́є лю́тѣ гнѣ́ватисѧ ѝ заѹста́ти ѥго̀ [the gloss заѹша́ти is in the margin] ѿ мно́жа́йшихъ (f. 173). Cf. the reference to ČNT: Подобне и Алексиа святаго преведение глаголет (f. 32v): И заграждати усто ему о мнозе (f. IXv).[33]

7. John 4:14 — И́же а́ще же пїе́тъ ѿ воды̀, ю́же а́зъ да́мъ ѥмѹ̀, не в' жа́ждетъ во вѣ́къ, но вода̀, ю́же да́мъ ѥмѹ̀, бѹ́детъ в' нѣмъ исто́чни"ъ воды̀

---

[30] As Saint Chrysostom says in his interpretation: И нищии благовествуеми бываютъ.

[31] The translation by Saint Aleksij the Miracleworker says: Не бо от терния събираютъ смоквы, ниже от купины об'емлют.

[32] In the Holy Gospel this place in Greek is ἔγνων, whereas in Slavonic it is rendered *познах* or *разумех*, just as *разумех* is written in the translation by Saint Aleksij, the metropolitan. The impression of the noncoincidence of readings of this verse from the Gospel of Luke (*познах* in the Gospel, *разумех* in ČNT) is only apparent. Epifanij protests here against the "standard" translation of the verb form (found in earlier monuments, for example, in the Ostrog Bible of 1581 and the Moscow Bible of 1663). The "standard" Church Slavonic translation here used the aorist of the verb *чути:* чух. The semantics of the Church Slavonic form *чух* and the Greek ἔγνων in no way coincide. In Church Slavonic translation practice the Greek verb γιγνώσκω (from which the form ἔγνων derives) was assigned the meaning 'know, understand, sense'. Cf. the *Ostromir Gospel:* Matt. 1:25, Luke 12:2, John 7:26, John 14:8,; cf. also the *Efremov Kormčaja* (twelfth c.): V. I. Beneševič, *Drevneslavjanskaja Kormčaja XIV titulov bez tolkovanija,* v. 1 (St. Petersburg, 1906), 246, 263, 352, 407, 410, 417, 426, 490, 491; and a considerable number of other monuments from this period such as *The Pandects of Antiochus, The XIII Commentaries of Gregory of Nazianzus.* In this light the reference to ČNT that Evfimij relies on should be understood as an argument in favor of the substitution proposed by Epifanij Slavineckij.

[33] Similarly Saint Aleksij's translation also says: И заграждати усто ему о мнозе.

скач8ціа в' жи́знь вѣ́чн8ю (f. 220v). Cf. the reference to Maksim Grek: Такожде . . . в печатаных на Москве Беседах святаго Иоанна Златоуста, беседа 39, преводу Максима Грека, в сущем и в толковании, лист 236, 238 (f. XIIIv).[34]

8. John 5:28 — Ꙗ́кѡ грѧде́тъ ча́съ, в' не́мже вси с8щіи во гробѣ́хъ ѹ҆слы́шатъ гла́съ е҆гѡ̀ (f. 224v). Cf. the reference to ČNT and the 1383 Gospel: В греческих бо и Алексиа святаго (f. 44) и в цареградском преведении . . . сице читается: Услышат глас его (f. XIIv).[35]

9. John 6:23 — И҆ни́и же прїидо́ша кораблци ѿ тїверїа́ды бли́з мѣ́ста, и҆дѣ́же ꙗ҆до́ша хлѣ́бъ, блгодари́вшу г҃ду (f. 227v). Cf. the reference to ČNT and the 1383 Gospel: И в преведении цареградском, наипаче же достовернее в потруждении преславнаго . . . Алексиа (ff. 44v–45) глаголет: Ядоша хлеб, благодаривше Господу (f. X).[36]

10. John 7:22 — Ра́ди сегѡ̀ мѡѷсе́й дадѐ ва́мъ ѡ҆брѣ́занїе (не ꙗ҆́кѡ ѿ мѡѷсе́а е҆́сть, но ѿ ѻ҆ц҃е́въ.) и҆ в' субботѣ́ ѡ҆брѣ́зѧете чл҃ка (f. 231v). Cf. the reference ČNT and the 1383 Gospel: В греческом бо и святаго Алексиа чудотворца (f. 46v) и в цареградском преведении . . . сице глаголет: Сего ради Мосис даде вам обрезание (f. XII–XIIv).[37]

11. John 7:26 — И҆ се дерзнове́ннѡ гл҃етъ, и҆ ничто́ же е҆му̀ глю́тъ, е҆да̀ ка́кѡ и҆́стиннѡ позна́ша нача́лницы, ꙗ҆́кѡ се́й е҆́сть и҆́стиннѡ х҃с (f. 231v). Cf. the reference to ČNT and Maksim Grek: В преведении святаго Алексиа митрополита (f. 46v) и святаго Златоустаго в беседе 50 на святаго Иоанна Богослова и Евангелиста...сице лежит: Еда како истинно познаша началници, яко сей есть истинно Христос (f. Xv).[38]

12. John 8:40 — Н҃нѣ же и҆́щете менѐ бы́ти чл҃ка, и҆́же и҆́стинну ва́мъ гла́хъ, ю҆́же слы́шахъ ѿ бг҃а, сегѡ̀ а҆враа́мъ не сотворѝ (f. 235v). Cf. the reference to ČNT, the 1383 Gospel, and Maksim Grek: Истинно глаголетъ греческое,

---

[34] So also . . . in the *Commentaries of Saint John Chrysostom*, printed in Moscow, Commentary 39, translated by Maksim Grek, in essence and exegesis, ff. 236, 238.
[35] For in the Greek texts, and Saint Aleksij's [translation], and in the Constantinopolitan redaction, it reads thus: Услышат глас его.
[36] And in the Constantinopolitan redaction, and most trustworthy of all, in the work of the most glorious . . . Aleksij, it says: Ядоша хлеб, благодаривше Господу.
[37] For in the Greek text and in [the translation by] Saint Aleksij the Miracleworker, and in the Constantinopolitan redaction . . . it says thus: Сего ради Мосис даде вам обрезание.
[38] In the translation by Saint Aleksij the metropolitan and [the translation] of Saint Chrysostom in his Fiftieth Commentary on Saint John the Theologian and Evangelist . . . it occurs thus: Еда како истинно познаша началници, яко сей есть истинно Христос.

цареградское и Алексиа святаго преведение (f. 47v), и Златоустаго Святаго беседа 54 на Иоанна Евангелиста, лист 398: Иже истинну вам глаголах, юже слышах от Бога (f. XIIv).³⁹

13. John 13:37 — Глетъ ему Петръ: Гди почто не могу тебѣ послѣдовати нн҃ѣ? Дш҃у мою за тѧ положу (f. 250v). Cf. the reference to ČNT: В гречестем и алксиа [sic] чудо (f. 54v) . . . сице лежит: Чесо ради не могу тебе последовати ныне? душу мою за тя положу (ff. XI–XIv).⁴⁰

14. John 14:3 — И аще поиду, и уготовлю вамъ мѣсто, паки приду и поиму вы ко мнѣ самому, да идѣже есмь азъ и вы будете (f. 251). Cf. the reference to ČNT: В потруждении святаго Алексиа митрополита (f. 55) . . . : И аще поиду и уготовлю вам место (f. XI).⁴¹

15. John 14:17 — Дха истинны, его же мiръ не можетъ прiѧти, ꙗко не видитъ его ниже знаетъ его. Вы же знаете его, ꙗкѡ в' васъ [the gloss у васъ is in the margin] пребываетъ, и в' васъ будетъ (f. 252). Cf. the reference to ČNT: В Алексии святаго митрополита (f. 55) зде лежит не прилагателное имя мужескаго рода истинный, но лежит имя нарицателное существителное истинна (f. XIIv).⁴²

16. John 16:6 — Но ꙗкѡ сиѧ глахъ вамъ, печаль исполни [the gloss на<полни> is in the margin] ваше срце (f. 255). Cf. the reference to ČNT: В преведении свяаго Алексиа митрополита (f. 57v) глаголет сице: Печаль исполни [the gloss напол<ни> is in the margin] сердце ваше (f. XIv).⁴³

17. John 18:40 — Воскликнуша убѡ паки вси глюще: не сего, но варавву. Бѣ же варавва разбойникъ (f. 261). Cf. the reference to ČNT: В Алексиа митрополита (f. 60) глаголет евангелист: Возопиша же паки вси, глаголюще (f. XIv).⁴⁴

---

³⁹ The Greek, Constantinopolitan, and Saint Aleksij redactions as well as Commentary 54 of Saint Chrysostom on John the Evangelist, folio 398, say properly: Иже истинну вам глаголах, юже слышах от Бога.
⁴⁰ In the Greek text and [the translation] by Aleksij the Miracleworker . . . it occurs thus: Чесо ради не могу тебе последовати ныне? душу мою за тя положу.
⁴¹ In the work of Saint Aleksij, the metropolitan, . . . : И аще поиду и уготовлю вам место.
⁴² It is not the masculine adjective истинный that occurs here in [the translation] by Saint Aleksij, the metropolitan, but the common noun истинна.
⁴³ The translation by Saint Aleksij, the metropolitan, reads thus: Печаль исполни [the gloss напол<ни> is in the margin] сердце ваше.
⁴⁴ In [the translation by] Aleksij, the metropolitan, the Evangelist says: Возопиша же паки вси, глаголюще.

I conclude this study with a few generalizations. By following "the letter of the Greek," introducing into the canonical text of the Holy Scriptures "strange locutions" quite alien to his contemporaries, Epifanij raises the "legitimate" status of his innovations by referring to a prestigious source (quite possibly prestigious in his eyes only). Epifanij Slavineckij thus creates the *fact of precedent,* and consequently establishes cultural preeminence across boundaries: ČNT, the 1383 Gospel, the translations of Maksim Grek. Epifanij's activity in the new translation of the Gospels bears witness to a consciously cultivated tradition at odds with the mainstream tradition that preceded it. Epifanij's Gospel possibly places the final period on the more than three-hundred-year history of the coexistence between the "standard" and the "hellenized" texts of the Slavonic New Testament.

The present study without doubt must be viewed as raising the issue, not solving it. The task at hand is to produce a comparative analysis of all the Gospel verses of the texts indicated, with the aim of clarifying the actual relationships among them. Only then will we be in a position to know what in these texts is the product of textual interference and what is the result of textual convergence.

I have attempted to show that the writers of the seventeenth century in the hellenizing camp did not feel themselves isolated from the highly specific earlier tradition. Epifanij's activity on the whole falls fully within the bounds of the prevailing grecophile orientation of Patriarch Nikon's time, and a careful comparison of the Church Slavonic text with the Greek is not surprising.[45] Rather what is important here is that this seventeenth-century philologist has selected unique and original texts from the enormous corpus of Church Slavonic copies. The relative chronological age of the monument ceases to be the crucial factor; for Epifanij it is not the temporal distance of the texts, but the linguistic principles found in them that are decisive. Epifanij's work on the Holy Scriptures reveals a linguistic consciousness concerned with more than simple hellenization of Church Slavonic on all levels. It reflects his resolute rejection of the principles of the Nikonian editors, that is, his rejection of any balance between Greek and Church Slavonic norms with priority given to the latter.[46] For Epifanij, the Greek norm always carried the higher authority.

---

[45] On the comparison of Church Slavonic and Greek texts by Nikonian editors and the priority of the Greek with respect to the Church Slavonic monuments from the early period, see my article "Attitudes to Greek Language and Culture in Seventeenth-Century Muscovy," *Modern Greek Studies Yearbook* 6 (1990): 123–155.

[46] These same principles were embraced by the editors of the 1751 reworking of the Church Slavonic Bible, the so-called Elizabethan Bible.

MODELING THE GENEALOGY OF MAKSIM GREK'S COLLECTION TYPES

THE "PLECTOGRAM" AS VISUAL AID IN RECONSTRUCTION

HUGH OLMSTED

...писана бо [сия книга] с триех преже писанных книг от различных писарей.... аз же писах, что в первой книге обретох, и потом из вторыя преписовах, такожде и с третие и сице во едино совокупих.[1]

The closer we look, the more striking is the admiration and interest inspired by Maksim Grek among generation after generation of Orthodox Eastern Slavs. His numerous works were studiously collected, copied, disseminated, read, excerpted, and referred to for hundreds of years. Substantial manuscript compendia of hundreds of folios each have descended to us, over 200 codexes containing Maksim's compositions in sets ranging from dozens of chapters to over a hundred and fifty.[2] Maksim's other works were also preserved and disseminated in profusion: scores of manuscripts of his major translations have survived,[3] dozens more containing his grammatical and

---

[1] "This book has been written from three books which had been written earlier by various scribes.... I wrote what I found in the first book, and then transcribed from the second and likewise from the third, and thus united them into one." From the manuscript GPB Solov 495/310 (for abbreviations in addition to those used for this volume of essays, see the separate list at the end of this article) as cited in I. I. Porfir'ev, A. V. Vadkovskii, and N. F. Krasnosel'tsev, *Opisanie rukopisei Solovetskogo monastyria nakhodiashchikhsia v biblioteke Kazanskoi dukhovnoi akademii*, 3 vols. (Kazan', 1881–1898) v. 1, 488.

[2] The most detailed register of the manuscripts containing Maksim's compositions remains the one published in S. A. Belokurov's *O biblioteke moskovskikh gosudarei v XVI stoletii* (Moscow, 1898); also issued in *Sbornik MGA MID* 6[1899]–7[1900], ccxxxvi–cccxiv, nos. 1–243 [App. 3]. In this article, numbers with the prefix BMS will be used to refer to Belokurov's listing; BMS — will signify a manuscript not listed by Belokurov. For other manuscript registers, and for the major families into which these manuscripts fall, see the monographs by N. V. Sinitsyna, *Maksim Grek v Rossii* (Moscow, 1977), 223–279, and D. M. Bulanin, *Perevody i poslaniia Maksima Greka: Neizdannye teksty* (Leningrad, 1984), 220–251. Broader introductions to the study of Maksim Grek can also be found in V. S. Ikonnikov, *Maksim Grek i ego vremia*, 2d ed. (Kiev, 1915), and J. V. Haney, *From Italy to Muscovy: The Life and Works of Maxim the Greek*, Humanistische Bibliothek, ser. I: Abhandlungen, v. 19 (Munich, 1973).

[3] Foremost among these translations are the Psalter with Commentary, Chrysostom's Commentaries on the Acts, the Commented Apostol, and Chrysostom's Homilies on the Gospels

lexicographic works,[4] and hundreds of others encompassing various smaller groups of his compositions and minor translations.[5] Numerous other manuscripts are known to have existed once but through time have perished or have otherwise been lost from view. All in all, if we discount the later lexicographic and grammatical compendia that drew from Maksim's tradition, the work of *spravshchiki* with his translated texts, and the endless *chet'i sborniki* containing allusions to or excerpts from his corpus or occasional stray copies of entire compositions, the total number of manuscripts devoted entirely or in significant measure to the works of Maksim Grek is certainly well over 600.

Numbers of this sort are seldom interesting by themselves, but such quantities reflect an extraordinary amount of personal involvement, years of dedicated editing and copying on the part of Maksim's devoted public, in places widely scattered throughout many parts of East Slavic territory: in the heartland of Muscovy, in Orthodox Ruthenian lands, and, beginning in the eighteenth century, radiating out through the centers of the Old Belief. The phenomenon of Maksim Grek—his corpus of compositions and translations, his example, his authority, and even his cult—was a major factor in the book culture of the lands where he was known. There were stronger centers on the map to be sure, and peaks and valleys in his popularity over time, but from Maksim's own sixteenth century (the traditional date of his death is 1556), scarcely a decade passed without active study and dissemination of his works

---

of John and Matthew (the latter two done under Maksim's direction by his disciple, Selivan). On Maksim's translation activity see Sinitsyna, *Maksim Grek v Rossii* (see n. 2), 61–74; for basic bibliography concerning these particular works see also the entries in A. I. Ivanov's master list of the works and translations of Maksim: *Literaturnoe nasledie Maksima Greka.* (Leningrad, 1969), where they are listed as nos. 1, 4–7, pp. 39–49. Although there are many problems with this book (see a sampling in my review article, H. M. Olmsted, "A. [I.] Ivanov on Maksim Grek: Problems of attribution and manuscript study [review article]," *Kritika* 7, no. 1 [Fall, 1971]: 1–27), it provides the closest thing to a standard listing that is available. Hereafter, numbers given according to this list cited with prefixed Ivc- (plural Ivcc-), will be used as shorthand references to the compositions, with published loci and secondary literature listed there taken as implicit. Thus, these translations are, respectively, Ivc 1 and Ivcc 4–7.

[4] V. Jagić, *Rassuzhdeniia iuzhnoslavianskoi i russkoi stariny o tserkovno-slavianskom iazyke.* (Berlin, 1896: issued also as pt. 3, pp. 289–1070 of *Issledovaniia po russkomu iazyku,* v. 1, *ORIaS* Imp. AN, 1885–1895; also reprinted with added title: *Codex slovenicus rerum grammaticarum,* Slavische Propyläen, 25 [Munich, 1968]); L. S. Kovtun, *Leksikografiia v Moskovskoi Rusi XVI–nachala XVII v.* (Leningrad, 1975); L. S. Kovtun, *Azbukovniki XVI–XVII vv: starshaia raznovidnost'* (Leningrad, 1989); particularly in her most recent work, Kovtun has demonstrated the great and continuing influence Maksim's philological work had upon his followers and upon succeeding lexicographic endeavors.

[5] These have yet to be properly studied, but for a helpful basic discussion of Maksim's early compositions see Sinitsyna, *Maksim Grek v Rossii* (see n. 2), 75–90.

until the eclipse of the traditional scribal culture in the nineteenth century.

However traditional this manuscript culture, the production of new copies of Maksim's compositions did not mean simple passive transmission of inherited collections. Maksim's followers, respectful though they were of his memory and intent upon preserving his heritage, also culled and selected in response to their own needs, introduced radical revisions of arrangement, pulled together the contents of multiple protographs, and performed detailed textual comparisons to establish the most authoritative and useful versions of his works.

By late in the sixteenth century there existed already a number of types or families of manuscripts of Maksim's compositions—in which the various manuscripts of a single type share the same collection of works in the same arrangement (with some slight variations in individual cases or variant subtypes), and presumed genealogical proximity.

The author himself had set the roots of some of these divergent types. Beginning late in the 1530s and continuing well into the 1540s at least, Maksim actively assembled and disseminated various versions of a sort of "showpiece" collection of his compositions. Interested readers were requesting his works, and this provided some opportunity for the jailed, excommunicated, and humiliated writer to attempt to clear his name by demonstrating his innocence, orthodoxy, and authority. The resulting variants of the collection became fixed as the nuclei of the earliest family types, each containing anywhere from forty to seventy or more of his selected compositions.[6]

Once in circulation, they continued to develop and give rise to new types after his death. Not all of Maksim's compositions had been gathered in the major collected assemblages: many were scattered elsewhere in manuscript miscellanies, and others were evidently kept in what must in effect have been his personal archive in the Troitse–Sergiev Monastery where he spent his final years. There were bookmen in Muscovy who actively kept his tradition alive not only by copying and disseminating the works and types already known, but also by seeking out the less accessible material. Comparing, selecting, and collating from the available large collections, and adding from the small, they assembled ever larger, more extensive assemblages. Through

---

[6] See Sinitsyna, *Maksim Grek v Rossii* (see n. 2), 161–186; H. M. Olmsted, "Studies in the Early Manuscript Tradition of Maksim Grek's Collected Works," 2 vols. (unpublished doctoral dissertation, Harvard University, 1977); H. M. Olmsted, "A Learned Greek Monk in Muscovite Exile: Maksim Grek and the Old Testament Prophets," *Modern Greek Studies Yearbook* 3 (1987): 1–73.

the centuries these collection types multiplied and diversified. Altogether, not counting variant subversions, some twenty or more major families have now been identified.[7]

Each step in the developing reception of Maksim deserves careful investigation in its own terms. If much has been achieved, the problems are objectively daunting in their complexity; progress seems disappointingly slow. With the hundreds of works and translations ascribed to Maksim, the variety of the manuscripts in which they are contained, and the subtlety and complexity of their interrelationships, the work has still only begun.

In charting the work to be done on the historical development of Maksim's heritage, description and classification are the first steps, and they are well along. More evaluative, synthetic work lags far behind; historical explanation is sadly thin. To this day we have no overall genealogical reconstruction of the development of the types, not to mention the textual traditions of their individual contents or proper historical understanding of contexts, causes, motivations that prompted the various new stages in the process. Significant progress has been made in reconstructing the origins of some types, but the roots and affiliations of many others remain completely unstudied. Moreover, we have no clear canon of Maksim's works, no acceptable edition, and not even agreement about the principles according to which we should work towards one.[8]

Not all of these problems can be tackled at once. In the present article, it is my aim to propose some reconstructions for and interconnections among the major family types, to suggest some further directions for study, and to introduce a visual research aid designed to make this sort of work easier.

The complexities of interrelationship among the types, their varying degrees of similarity, the riddles of their descent all have intrigued researchers for some time.[9] The typical method for adducing comparisons involves citing chapter numbers in order from other types as orientation points, using sim-

---

[7] Though many researchers have contributed to this work, chief honors are due to N. V. Sinitsyna; see her first setting forth of the basic types in "Rukopisnaia traditsiia XVI–XVII vv. sobranii sochinenii Maksima Greka (k postanovke voprosa)," *TODRL* 26 (1971): 259–266; and the more complete survey in her monograph, *Maksim Grek v Rossii* (see n. 2), especially pp. 161–186, 223–279 (Prilozheniia I–X). Major addenda and corrections were added by D. M. Bulanin, *Perevody i Poslaniia* (see n. 2), 220–251.

[8] The problems of canon and edition have been clearly seen as a central problem for generations: cf. discussion by E. Denissoff, "Les editions de Maxime le Grec," *Revue des Etudes Slaves* 21 (1944), 112–120, and S. A. Shcheglova, "K istorii izucheniia sochinenii prep. Maksima greka," *Russkii filologicheskii vestnik* 66 (1911): 22–36. Currently discussion of such issues is again active among researchers concerned with Maksim; it is much to be hoped that some consensus can emerge and useful results can be achieved soon.

[9] E. E. Golubinskii, *Istoriia russkoi tserkvi*, 2 vols. (Moscow, 1900–1917), v. 2, pts. 1–2; V. N. Peretts (review of Ikonnikov, *Maksim Grek i ego vremia* [see n. 2]), *Bibliograficheskaia*

ple lists of numbers. N. V. Sinitsyna frequently refers to chapter numbers of the Khludov/Bol'shakov and the Ioasaf collection–types,[10] as orientation points in describing the contents of subsequent collections—for example:

The "Khludov" type, basic variant is described (pp. 242–247) through reference to chapter numbers in the "Ioasaf" type (described earlier in Sinitsyna's book), as follows: (numbers to the left, prefixed with *c* [plural, *cc*] refer to chapter numbers:

cc 1–18 coincide with the Ioasaf collection
c 19   (corresponds to c 45 of the Ioasaf collection)
c 20   (corresponds to c 19 of the Ioasaf collection)
c 21   (corresponds to c 20 of the Ioasaf collection)
. . .   . . .

If the work in question is lacking from the Ioasaf collection, a reference number to Ivanov's master list is provided, together with an indication of where and whether the text is published.

The "Archive type" (Arkhivnoe sobranie) is described (p. 276) with a list of numbers referring to chapters in the Khludov type: Archive collection cc 1–30 = Khludov chapters 27 to 40, 43, 45, 46, 56, 59, 63, 54, 55, 72, 73, 41, 10–12, 61, 50.

The "Khludov/Synod type" (Khludov/Sinodal'noe sobranie) is related (p. 277) to both the Khludov type (cc. 1–59 = Khludov cc 26–73, 10–12, 18, 19) and the Synod type (cc 60–101 = Synod collection in ascending order, but with the omission of those already included among cc 1–59).

A. T. Shashkov gives a similar comparison with respect to the relationships among different variants of the *Pomorskii type*.[11] The contents of a unique manuscript of the late sixteenth–early seventeenth centuries, *Iaroslavl' GMZ no. 14982*, are similarly related to chapters of the Khludov type by D. M. Bulanin (Khludov cc 27, 28, 62, 57, 49, 31, 35, 33, 39, 41, 45, 46, 56, 59, 30, 29, 10, 11, 14, 15, 21, 22, 72, 73, 63, 12, 7, 8, 9, 13).[12]

---

letopis' 3 (1917): 37–49; E. Denissoff, *Maxime le Grec et l'occident: Contribution à l'histoire de la pensée réligieuse et philosophique de Michel Trivolis,* Université de Louvain, Récueil de travaux d'histoire et de philologie, ser. 3, no. 14 (Paris and Louvain, 1943).
  [10] Sinitsyna, *Maksim Grek v Rossii* (see n. 2).
  [11] A. T. Shashkov, "Pomorskii kodeks sochinenii Maksima Greka," *Istochnikovedenie i arkheografiia Sibiri,* ed. N. N. Pokrovskii and E. K. Romadanovskaia (Novosibirsk, 1977), 123.
  [12] Bulanin, *Perevody i poslaniia Maksima Greka* (see n. 2), 250.

These are only a few examples of the many such comparisons in the literature, but they should be enough to show that mere strings of numbers can be somewhat opaque: it is difficult to interpret them, to discern patterns in them, to sense the degree and kind of interrelationship they represent. Considering "the enormous advantages of *seeing* information rather than tabulating data,"[13] it can be useful to work instead with a holistic visual representation. Let us introduce a graphic format designed to make the interrelationship between related manuscripts intuitively clearer.

It is an extremely simple idea. Two manuscripts to be compared are represented by two columns, left and right, with one row, or line, for each composition. Whether long or short, each identifiable unit is assigned a single position.[14] In the case of Maksim's works, we use the numbers assigned to each by A. I. Ivanov in his master list of Maksim's compositions.[15] Thus, a column with the first three rows designated 242, 347, 348 represents a manuscript in which the first three compositions are nos. 242, 347, 348 in Ivanov's listing. Adjustments can be made for variants of compositions, for compositions broken into subdivisions, or for works which are not included in Ivanov's list. Such details are not important here.

Between these two columns, lines are drawn connecting identical works—in this case, identifiable by their identical Ivanov–numbers (fig. 1). We shall refer to this sort of representation as a **plectogram,** (cf. Greek πλέκω 'weave, braid', πλεκτός 'woven, braided').

In the case of two manuscripts with identical contents, the lines all form a completely parallel series, a monotonous uniformity, with the overall visual effect something like that of a Venetian blind or the "warp" on a loom (the basic cords through which the "woof," or "weft," is woven). In the case of two manuscripts whose arrangements of contents vary markedly, this complexity is represented as lines crisscrossing one another.

---

[13] E. R. Tufte, *Envisioning Information* (Cheshire, Conn., 1990), 45. This is a rich and thoughtful survey of the issues in the visual representation of information, elegantly illustrated.

[14] If such an identifiable unit consists of various subparts that may sometimes occur in different order or extent, then each of the subparts may be assigned its own row. That is, to a certain extent the division is arbitrary, a descriptive construct on as analytic a level as the comparison requires.

[15] On the notation Ivc- (Ivcc-) used in the text of the article to indicate numbers according to Ivanov's list, see note 3 above. In cases where works occurring in the manuscripts are not listed by Ivanov, additional conventional numbers have been generated for reference's sake (any number higher than 365, the final number in Ivanov's list). I intend to provide a complete key to these in a separate work now in preparation.

Figure 1 exemplifies both sorts of relationship.[16] Two late sixteenth-century manuscripts are represented: on the left, GBL Bol'shakov 16 (BMS 50), and on the right, GBL Egor. 207 (BMS 68).[17] Both consist of the compositions of Maksim Grek; their relationship is quite well studied. The collection type represented by Egor. 207 is known as Iona Dumin's collection or the "Iona Dumin type"[18] after its compiler, a prominent and very active bookman who served as archbishop of Vologda (1589–1603). It was around this time—the time of the establishment of the patriarchate in Moscow—that he assembled his new composite collection of Maksim's compositions; evidently he did so working rather closely with the new patriarch, Iov, and the tsar Boris Fedorovich Godunov. His career and his efforts on behalf of Maksim's collected works have been reconstructed in work by Sinitsyna, Bulanin, and myself.[19]

What does the plectogram comparison of Bol. 16 and Egor. 207 reveal? At first sight, perhaps, not much. As we have suggested, there are some areas with more parallels, notably the beginnings and the ends of the manuscripts, and some with fewer—in the middle a sort of kasha. But one feature does demand attention. Going down the right column, the contents of Egor. 207, we see not only that the final section starting with c 59 is essentially identical to the final section of Bol. 16, but that just before that, from cc 47 to 58, there seems to be a sort of *focusing effect.* Instead of corresponding to various sections of Bol. 16 in a helter-skelter fashion, cc 47–58 of Egor. 207 relate to its sequence in perfectly ascending order: two works from Bol. 16 cc 27–28, three from cc 35 to 37, one at c 40, four from cc 46, 47a–c, and two more from cc 52–53—just before the final correspondence

---

[16] This and similar succeeding representations have been generated on a Macintosh computer by a program written in the graphic spreadsheet application WINGZ by Informix. I would like to thank Informix representatives Stefan Zauchenberg, Bill T. Christensen, and Beth Xiarhos for their generous and expert assistance in developing this material.

[17] Inner columns represent the successive component works as identified by Ivanov-number; the outer columns represent traditional numeration contained in the manuscripts—sometimes based upon the information in published descriptions, and in some cases, partially reconstructed on the basis of tables-of-contents (*oglavleniia*) in the manuscripts. Such sources are individually indicated below. In the cases where works are subdivided by descriptive convention (cf. note 14 above), the subdivision is indicated by numbers to the right of the period: 185.1, 185.2, etc.

[18] Sinitsyna, "Rukopisnaia traditsiia" (see n. 7), 262; Sinitsyna, *Maksim Grek v Rossii* (see n. 2), 264–265.

[19] Sinitsyna, "Rukopisnaia traditsiia," 262; idem, "Rannie rukopisnye sborniki sochinenii Maksima Greka (kodikologicheskoe issledovanie)" *AE* za 1971 (1972), 137; Sinitsyna, *Maksim Grek v Rossii* (see n. 2), 264–265; D. M. Bulanin, "Vologodskii arkhiepiskop Iona Dumin i rukopisnaia traditsiia sochinenii Maksima Greka," *Istochnikovedenie literatury drevnei Rusi* (Leningrad, 1980); Bulanin, *Perevody i poslaniia Maksima Greka* (see n. 2), 232–233; Olmsted, "Early Manuscript Tradition" (see n. 6), 286–308, 422–433; "Kodikologicheskie zametki o rukopisnykh sbornikakh Maksima Greka," *TODRL* 45 (1992): 399–406.

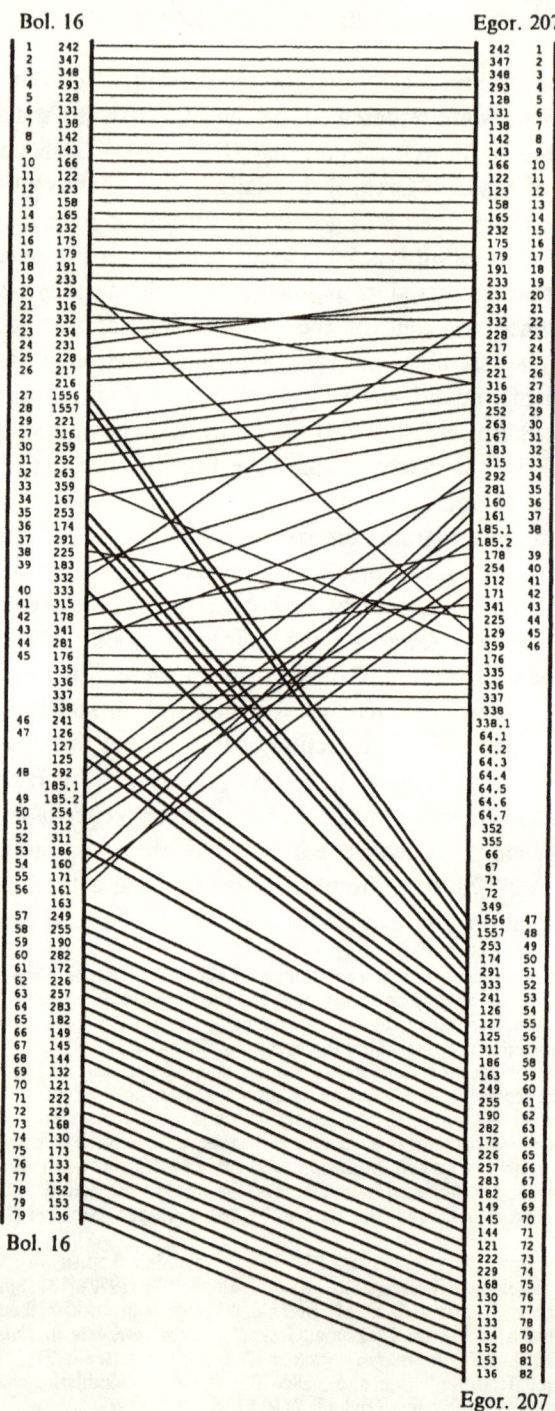

Figure 1

at Egor. 207, cc 56b–79² to Bol. 16, cc 59–82, with the omission only of Bol. 285 c 69, Ivc132.[20] It is as if after a section of unclear relationship, starting in the middle of his work the compiler of Egor. 207 had gone through Bol. 16 systematically and picked out for inclusion, in order, just those works which had not been included earlier. We shall return to this suggestion presently.

We next compare Egor. 207 with a different manuscript, GBL MDA 42 (BMS 100; this represents the "Ioasaf" type referred to above) (fig. 2). There, by contrast with what we saw in fig. 1, Egor. 207's relationship with MDA 42 is a simple one-to-one correspondence from the beginning to the end of MDA 42.[21] After this (Egor. 207, cc 47 ff.) Egor. 207 concludes with a section of works lacking in MDA 42. Here it is as if an editor had begun his assembly of Egor. 207 by taking everything from MDA 42 in order, then continued by adding works from some other source.

If we now compare the two figures (assembled in fig. 3, with Egor. 207 in the middle[22]) a striking coincidence is evident: the "focusing" section in Egor. 207 of ascending relationship to Bol. 16 begins at exactly the point—from c 47—where the exact relationship to MDA 42 ends. That is, it is evidently not a coincidence at all: we may posit that the editor first took all of MDA 42—or some close relative among manuscripts of the Ioasaf type—as primary protograph and then turned to Bol. 16, taking from it selectively just those works that had not already been included from MDA 42. It is this process which would result in exactly the relationships shown in fig. 3.

It happens that in this instance the relationships are already known, the pedigree of Egor. 207 established in some detail, and it was already clear that the Iona Dumin arrangement (Egor. 207) did indeed descend from the collection types represented by MDA 42 and Bol. 16, in that order. In this

---

[20] On the omission of this single work by Iona, some possible motivations are suggested in Olmsted, "Early Manuscript Tradition" (see n. 6), 299–300. In general, such minor evident discrepancies can be expected when one depends upon published descriptions of manuscripts, and when one uses as a term of comparison not a known specific protograph but some arbitrarily selected member of the *type* which served as prototype (frequently dictated, again, by the incidence of published descriptions). Such minor discrepancies between two obviously similar arrangements in some cases prove to be artifacts of an incomplete description; they must be investigated and explained to the degree possible—which frequently forces a degree of descriptive clarity that one might otherwise overlook. In the face of such overwhelming similarity they are not enough to cast doubt upon such reconstructions.

[21] Note one minor seeming discrepancy—the absence of Ivc338 [.1] in Egor. 207, although it is present in MDA 42, (c 63). This particular "composition" is in fact simply an addendum, a few lines in length (see n. 20).

[22] In this article the following convention will be observed: in figures consisting of three columns (i.e., representing three manuscripts), the middle will represent the blended descendent of the outer two.

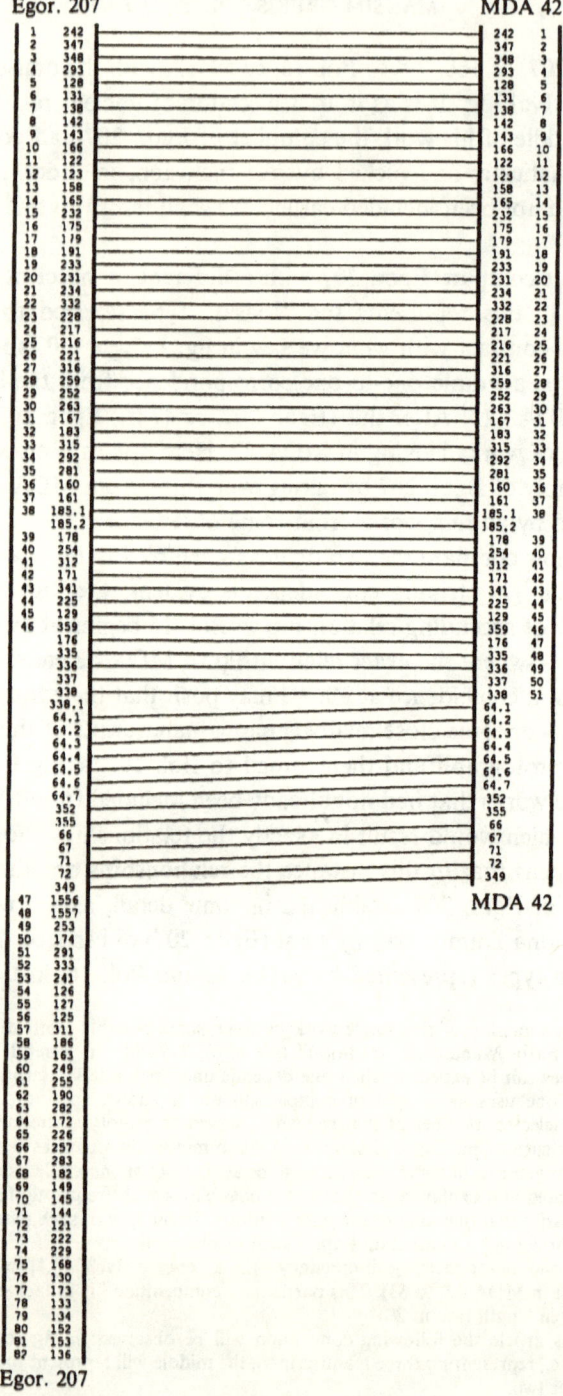

Figure 2

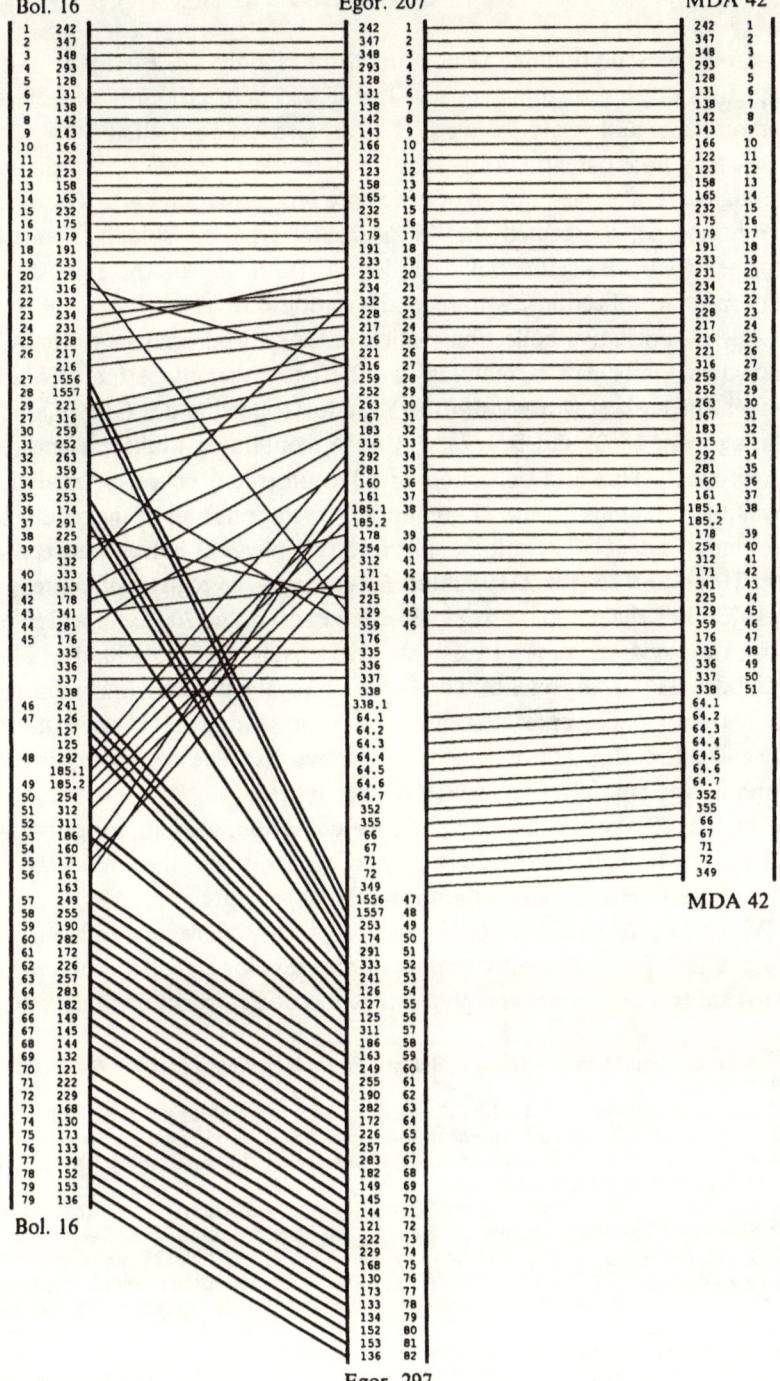

Figure 3

case our presentation in plectogram form is only an alternative way of depicting known relationships and has served here primarily to introduce, demonstrate, and verify the method of representation itself.

We may note parenthetically that the derivation of Iona's collection went through several stages, not all of which are represented in fig. 3. The secondary prototype, designated the "Rogozhskii" type by Bulanin,[23] and here represented by Bol. 16, itself was derived from one of the earliest, most authoritative collections, with secondary additions from other sources.

This authoritative collection, which dates to Maksim's own lifetime, is known in Sinitsyna's terminology as the basic variant of the "Khludov" type.[24] The earliest witnesses of the Khludov collection are GIM Khlud. 73 (dating from 1563) and Bol. 285 (by 1556, containing Maksim's autograph corrections). This is a collection of 73 enumerated chapters (analytically speaking, it contains some 81 compositions, since not all of them bear their own independent numeration), split into two physical halves, between c 25 (Ivc 216) and c 26 (Ivc 221). Khlud. 73 contains the register of contents for cc 1–73, plus the text of cc 1–25; Bol. 285 contains cc 26 ff.; we will refer to these two separate subarrangements respectively as the "Khludov I" and "Khludov II" arrangements. The latter arrangement was clearly known in the sixteenth and seventeenth centuries as representing an old and authoritative collection. Bol. 285 or some close relative was repeatedly used as protograph by the compilers of successive later types.

The Ioasaf type was a second lifetime collection, also authoritative, with a slightly differing set and arrangement of works. It and the Khludov collection probably reflect different authorial arrangements.[25]

With reference to the editorial practice which we have met in the descent of Egor. 207, it was evidently standard procedure for an editor who intended to assemble a new, more complete collection of the works of Maksim Grek

---

[23] Bulanin, "Iona Dumin" (see n. 19); Bulanin, *Perevody i poslaniia Maksima Greka* (see n. 2), 229–233.

[24] Sinitsyna, "Rukopisnaia traditsiia" (see n. 7), 262; idem, "Maksim Grek i Savonarola: O pervom rukopisnom sobranii sochinenii Maksima Greka," *Feodal'naia Rossiia vo vsemirnoistoricheskom protsesse: Sb. statei, posv. L. V. Cherepninu* (Moscow, 1972), 151 ff.; idem, "Rannie rukopisnye sborniki" (see n. 19), 135–139; idem, *Maksim Grek v Rossii* (see n. 2), 161–175, 234–236, 242–247; Olmsted, "Early Manuscript Tradition" (see n. 6), 141–169, 352–362.

[25] Sinitsyna, "Rukopisnaia traditsiia" (see n. 7), 262; idem, "Maksim Grek i Savonarola" (see n. 24), 155; Sinitsyna, "Rannie rukopisnye sborniki" (see n. 19), 130–135; Sinitsyna, *Maksim Grek v Rossii* (see n. 2), 161–175, 223–234; Olmsted, "Early Manuscript Tradition" (see n. 6), 26–45, 321–327. Cf. the preliminary plectogram depiction of the Dumin type in Olmsted, "Early Manuscript Tradition", 289, fig. 15, before Bulanin's work introducing and elucidating the intermediary role played by the "Rogozhskii" type (Bol'shakov 16 and others). We may in addition wonder whether this intermediate "Rogozhskii" step might also have been the work of Iona Dumin himself.

to proceed in just this manner: to start by copying the contents of one authoritative protograph in toto, then to add from another source (or successively from several further sources) those contents which had not already been included in the preceding step(s). When this method was used, the procedure leaves revealing formal traces, with the pattern of more or less initial confusion, medial focusing, and final agreement.

Another collection-type clearly demonstrates this same method of uniting multiple protographs. It is the so-called Pomorskii or Staroobriadcheskii (Old Believer) type,[26] a major compendium that was initiated in and guided from the Vyg Monastery probably by Andrei Denisov.[27] The work dates from 1705 until 1721. Thirteen extant copies dating from the eighteenth and nineteenth centuries, represent widespread centers of the Old Belief.[28]

The descent of the type has been studied in detail by Shashkov.[29] Its contents are fundamentally those of the so-called Solovetskii type, which originated in the 1570s and was centered in the Solovetskii Monastery, followed by additional contents from the Troitskii or First Troitskii type (TSL I), one of two major collection-types which were initiated during the 1620s and 1630s in the Troitse-Sergiev Monastery by its archimandrite, Dionisii Zobninovskii.[30] At the end are appended some additional works from a source not as yet precisely identified, but evidently close to Solov. 495/310 (BMS 151) and GPB F.XVII.13 (BMS —).[31]

The relationships of the Pomorskii type to the Solovetskii and TSL I collections are shown in fig. 4. (Khlud. 74 [BMS 31] is taken as the representative of the Pomorskii type.)[32] Again we see the one-to-one relationship between the initial section of the derived manuscript (Khlud. 74) and the

---

[26] Shashkov, "Pomorskii kodeks" (see n. 11); Olmsted, "Early Manuscript Tradition" (see n. 6), 271–273, 415–416; Bulanin, *Perevody i poslaniia Maksima Greka* (see n. 2), 239–247; Sinitsyna, *Maksim Grek v Rossii* (see n. 2), 278.

[27] Shashkov, "Pomorskii kodeks" (see n. 11), 107, 120.

[28] The known manuscripts are listed in various combinations by Sinitsyna, *Maksim Grek v Rossii* (see n. 2), 278, Shashkov, "Pomorskii kodeks" (see n. 11), 93, and Bulanin, *Perevody i poslaniia Maksima Greka* (see n. 2), 240–247.

[29] Shashkov, "Pomorskii kodeks" (see n. 11); A. T. Shashkov, "Tagil'skii sbornik sochinenii Maksima Greka (kodikologicheskie zametki)," *Rukopisnaia traditsiia XVI–XIX vv. na vostoke Rossii* (Novosibirsk, 1983), 4–14.

[30] On the TSL I type see Sinitsyna, *Maksim Grek v Rossii* (see n. 2), 273–274; Bulanin, *Perevody i poslaniia Maksima Greka* (see n. 2), 234–235; B. L. Fonkich, "O grecheskom tekste poslaniia Maksima Greka kniaziu P. I. Shuiskomu" (unpublished paper); H. M. Olmsted, "Maksim Grek's 'Letter to Prince Petr Shuiskii': the Greek and Russian texts," *Modern Greek Studies Yearbook* 5 (1989), 267–309, particularly pp. 270, 281, 306n–307n.

[31] Bulanin, *Perevody* (see n. 30), 60–63.

[32] For a published description of Khlud. 74, see A. N. Popov, *Opisanie rukopisei i katalog knig tserkovnoi pechati biblioteki A. I. Khludova* (Moscow, 1872), 158–174; the listing given by Shashkov details the contents of the various antecedents, redactions, and subtypes ("Pomorskii kodeks" [see n. 11], 122–123).

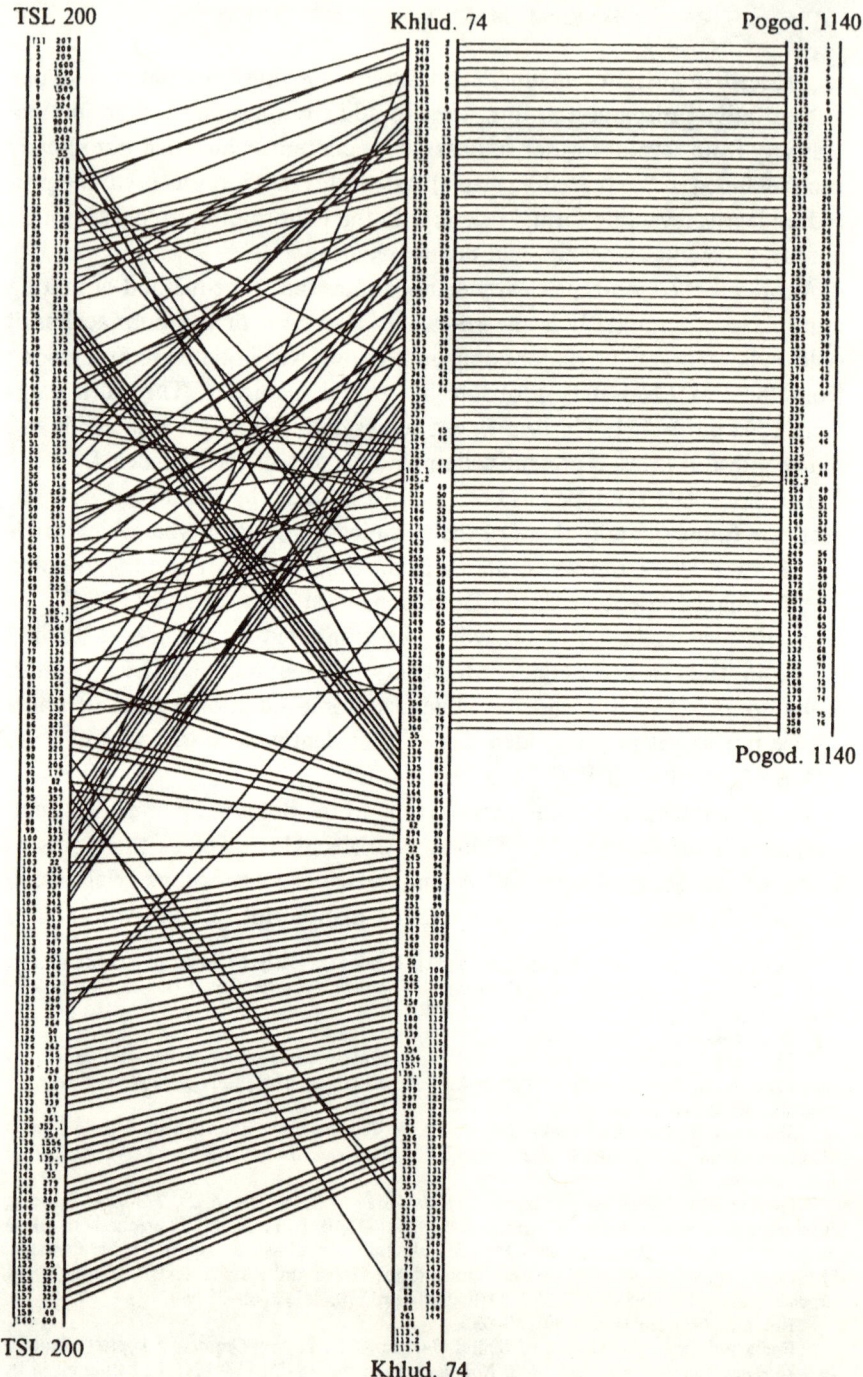

Figure 4

primary protograph (GPB Pogod. 1140 [BMS 211]),[33] together with the focusing into a consecutive sequence in the derived manuscript (Khlud 74 cc 78–131) of scattered, but ascending works from the secondary protograph (TSL 200) of works not included in the first section. Once more, the focusing is from the secondary protograph; the contents of the primary protograph are included complete. Note the introductory comments of the editor of the Pomorskii type, whose proclaimed method of work is confirmed by the plectogram in figure 4:

> ...Понеже две книзе Максима Грека обретаются, ова малая, иаже повсюду обносима есть, имеющая глав 77; ова же великая, яже во обители чюдотворца Сергия лежит, содержащая в себе 115 глав; иная же словеса сто̃ Максима во иных древних книгах обретаются. ...Чин же си есть: порядок глав и оглавлений прежде малыя книги, яков в ней содержится, цел сохранихом; по нем из великия серьгиеобительския, и из иных книг собраныя сочинивше, написахом. Занеже малая книга всюду обретается убо и главы оноя да будут оной согласны. Прочия же главы из иных книг приложены убо и в числе оглавления прилагательнаго да будут.[34]

In both cases we have examined so far, the order of preference and precedence matches the copy order.

Another of the major types, the "Nikiforov," which arose ca. 1625, evidently was assembled from a pair of protographs whose copy order did *not* match their hierarchy of preference. The prototypes were two collections from the sixteenth century—the Khludov and the Burtsev.

The first of these, the Khludov collection, we have already met for its role in the derivation of the Iona Dumin collection (figs. 1, 3). This is the collection that was split into two constituent parts, of which the second (Khludov 2), represented by Bol. 285, was the more frequently used by successive compilers. As we have noted, it was clearly known in the sixteenth and seventeenth centuries as an old and authoritative collection; it was repeatedly used

---

[33] Pogod. 1140, a close representative of the Solovetskii type, has been shown by Shashkov (ibid., 97–106) to be prototypical for this section of the Pomorskii collection. For other descriptions of the Solovetskii collection see Porfir'ev et al., *Opisanie rukopisei Solovetskogo monastyria* (see n. 1), v. 1, 473–483; and Sinitsyna, *Maksim Grek v Rossii* (see n. 2), 265–267.

[34] "For two books of Maksim Grek are to be found: one small, which is in wide circulation, containing 77 chapters; and the other large, stored in the Monastery of the Wonderworker Sergii, containing 115 chapters; other discourses of the saintly Maksim are found in other ancient books .... The order is as follows: the arrangement of chapters and contents we have kept intact first as they are found in the small book; after this we wrote from the St. Sergii Monastery copy and added from other books as well. Since the small book may be found everywhere, let the chapters of this one agree with that. The other chapters are added from other books; let them be among the added contents." Popov, *Opisanie rukopisei* (see n. 32), 158–159.

by the compilers of successive types to the extent that they had it available. The origination of the Nikiforov type is just such a use.

The Burtsev type arose ca. 1580 and achieved its widest spread and popularity in Ruthenian lands, although it circulated in Muscovy as well. Some of Maksim's compositions as represented in this type were used in Belorussia and Ukraine in the polemic struggles against Western influences. The Burtsev is a fairly close relative to the entire unsplit Khludov collection, containing nearly an identical set of compositions from the beginning, but with some differences in numeration and, more important, with a number of added works scattered through the middle to end of the collection (fig. 5).[35]

Evidently the compilers of the Nikiforov collection, like Iona Dumin, did not have the entire Khludov collection available—only the Bol. 285 half or its equivalent (Khludov 2). Wanting nonetheless to begin their new collection properly "at the beginning," with the set of works intended by Maksim as the opening section for his major apologetic collection, the compilers began with the Burtsev collection as protograph and concluded with materials from Khludov 2. In this case, however, instead of copying all of the Burtsev contents and then including from Khludov 2 only what they had not already taken (the analogue of Iona Dumin's procedure), they preferred to take from Khludov 2 whatever they could. They thus copied from Burtsev only what was not in Khludov 2 (but put the Burtsev works first in accord with Maksim's traditional arrangement), and then took the latter in toto. Iona, working with Ioasaf plus Khludov 2, in case of duplication preferred the former; the Nikiforov editors, working with Burtsev plus Khludov 2, preferred the latter. Both of them knew that the Khludov 2 works should be second in position, but, in case of duplication between the protographs, only for Iona were they second in preference as well.

The resulting Nikiforov configuration (fig. 6) has much in common with figures 1, 3 and 4, with the familiar combination of focusing and exact correspondence.[36] Here, however, the focusing occurs from the protograph which is first in copy order, since in preference it is secondary. The Khludov 2 contents, which are second in copy order but first in preference, are then included complete.

[35] Sinitsyna, *Maksim Grek v Rossii* (see n. 2), 236–242; Olmsted, "Early Manuscript Tradition" (see n. 6), 144–145, 169–208. In fig. 5 the Burtsev type is represented by BAN, Burts. 25 (BMS —), described in Sinitsyna, ibid., 241; a close relative (GBL Rum. 265 [BMS 49]) is more completely described in A. K. Vostokov, *Opisanie russkikh i slovenskikh rukopisei Rumiantsovskogo muzeuma* (St. Petersburg, 1842), 374–380.

[36] In fig. 6 the Nikiforov type is represented by Nikif. no. 79 (BMS —), described by Sinitsyna (*Maksim Grek v Rossii* [see n. 2], 237); the Burtsev, as in fig. 5.

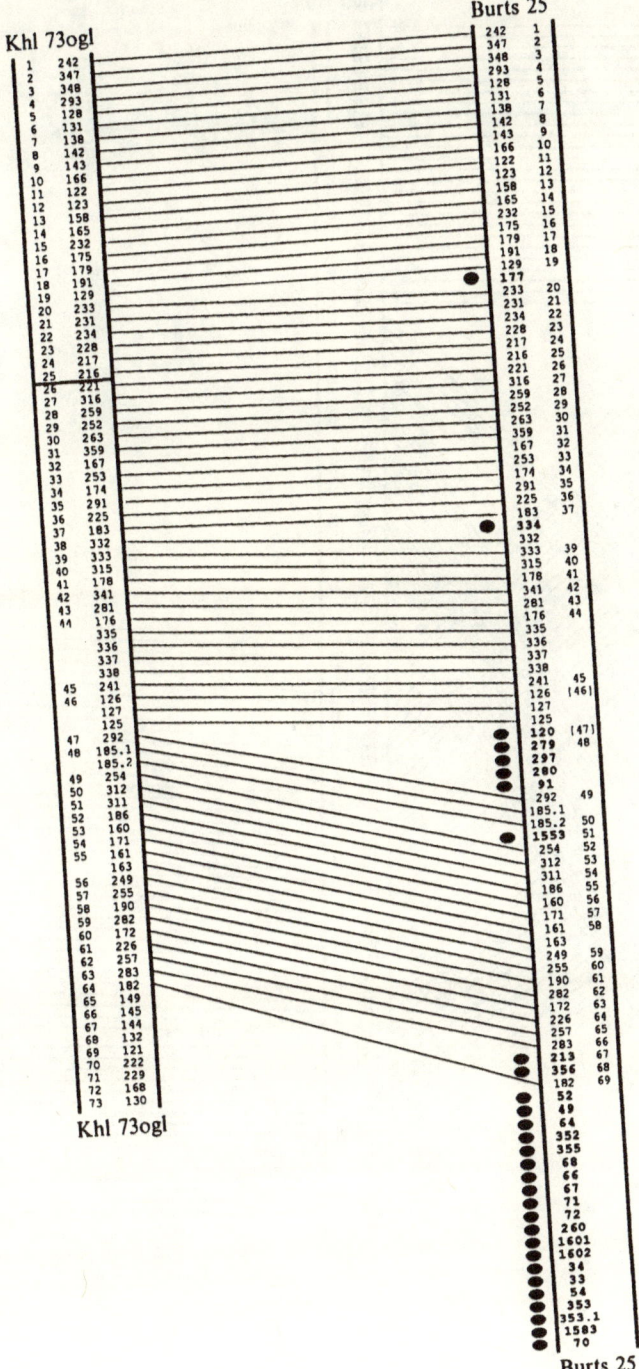

Figure 5

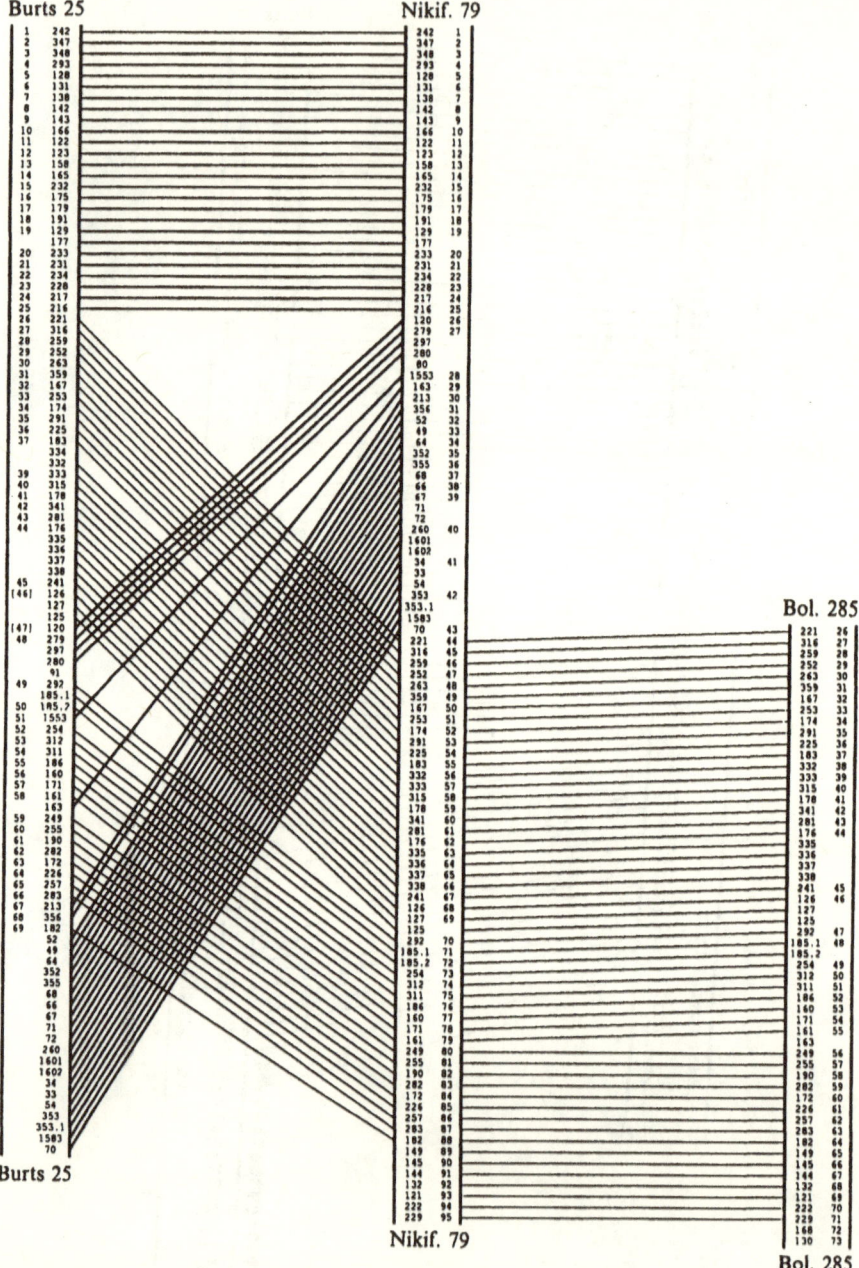

Figure 6

It is worth noting in passing that it was specifically the plectogram representation that suggested and served among the central arguments for this reconstruction.[37] In earlier literature the Burtsev and Nikiforov types had been taken as coordinate in origin, or the Nikiforov as even prior.[38] This reconstruction of the derivative relationship of the Nikiforov to the Burtsev type is affirmed also by textual evidence, and it has been accepted by Bulanin as convincing.[39]

Our last examples concern three of the collections that arose near the end of the sixteenth century:

1. *The "Synod" type*—Paris, Bibliothèque Nationale, MS Slave, 123 (henceforth BN 123) (BMS 243), late sixteenth century, and its close relative and descendent, GIM Sin. 491/191.[40]

2. *The "Second Troitskii" type* or *"151-chapter" collection* (TSL II), here represented by its prototype, TSL 201 (BMS 110), together with the "First Troitskii" type, arose in the Troitse–Sergiev Monastery in the 1620s or 1630s under Dionisii Zobninovskii.[41]

3. *The "Museum" type (Muzeinoe sobranie)*—dating from the late sixteenth or the beginning of the seventeenth century, here represented by BAN 31.4.7 (BMS —).[42]

Here we will limit ourselves to juxtaposing BN 123 and TSL 201 (fig. 7), and TSL 201 with the Museum type as represented by BAN 31.4.7 (fig. 8), and to a few comments concerning directions for future research on the interrelationships among these types. Both of the plectograms in figs. 7–8, it must be strictly understood, are presented as working aids showing the degree of existing relationship, not as proposed genealogical models.

---

[37] Olmsted, "Early Manuscript Tradition" (see n. 6), 213–216.
[38] Sinitsyna, "Rannie rukopisnye sborniki" (see n. 19), 137; Sinitsyna, *Maksim Grek v Rossii* (see n. 2), 169, 236–242; Kovtun, *Leksikografiia* (see n. 4), 135.
[39] Olmsted, "Early Manuscript Tradition" (see n. 6), 216–219; Bulanin, *Perevody i poslaniia Maksima Greka* (see n. 2), 7, 132, 195.
[40] More detailed information concerning both of these manuscripts is given below.
[41] TSL 201 is described by Arsenii, ierom., and Ilarii, ierom. *Opisanie slavianskikh rukopisei Biblioteki Sviato-Troitskoi Sergievoi Lavry* (Moscow, 1878–1879; also issued in: *ČOIDR* 1878–1879), v. 2, 207–216, and assigned to a type by Sinitsyna, "Rukopisnaia traditsiia" (see n. 7), 263; Sinitsyna, *Maksim Grek v Rossii* (see n. 2), 274–276; cf. also Bulanin, *Perevody i poslaniia Maksima Greka* (see n. 2), 236.
[42] For a description see V. I. Sreznevskii, and F. I. Pokrovskii, *Opisanie Rukopisnogo otdeleniia Biblioteki Imp. Akademii nauk* (St. Petersburg, 1910–1915), v. 2, 81–90, together with Sinitsyna, *Maksim Grek v Rossii* (see n. 2), 271–272.

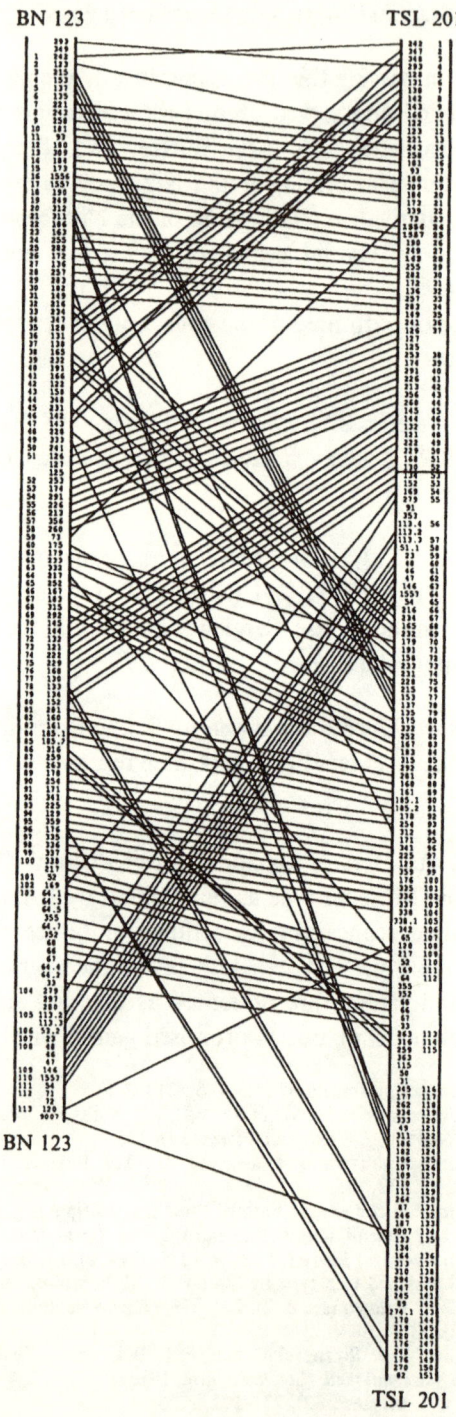

Figure 7

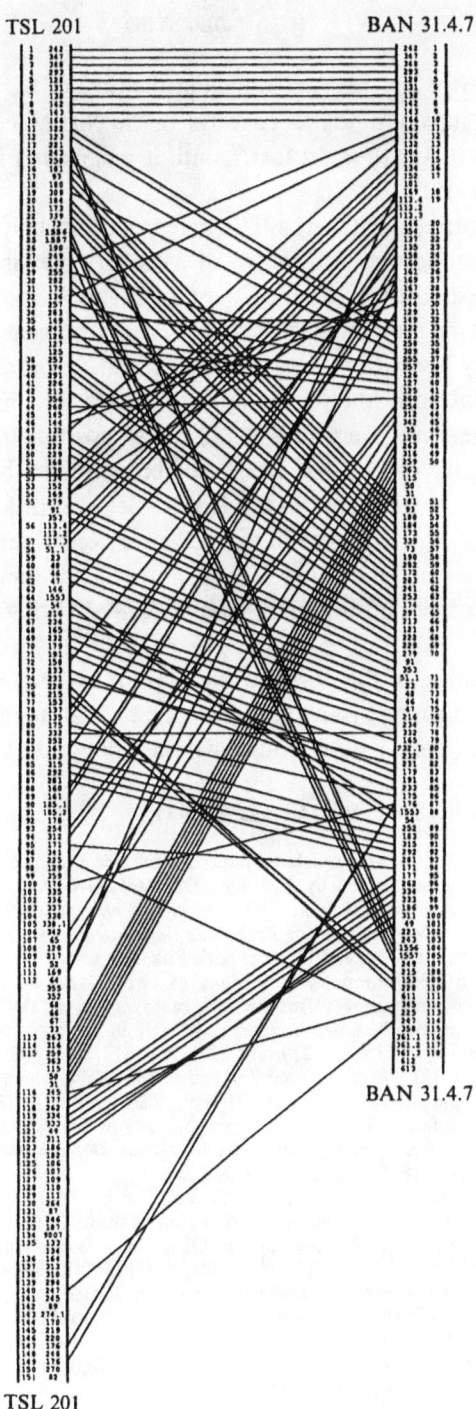

Figure 8

The manuscript BN 123 was known at the time of S. A. Belokurov, when it was in the hands of a private collector in the Nizhnii Novgorod *guberniia*. More recently it was thought lost,[43] until it reappeared in the Bibliothèque Nationale in Paris.[44]

Its close relative, GIM Sin. 491/191, reproduces many of its peculiarities and is itself among the best known of Maksim's manuscripts, having been carefully and exhaustively described by Gorskii and Nevostruev in their capital description of the Synod collection.[45] The arrangement of the contents was completely revised by the editor or copyist, but the numeration of the works as organized in the protograph is carefully retained, enough so that even before the rediscovery of BN 123 it was possible to establish it in detail.[46] The history of Sin. 491 has been reconstructed by Shashkov,[47] who surmised that it was donated to the Kirillo–Belozerskii Monastery by a certain Ioanikii Osokin around the end of the sixteenth century or the beginning of the seventeenth century. This hypothesis has now been conclusively supported by a note of donation (*vkladnaia zapis'*) that had escaped prior attention.[48]

The exact nature of the possible relationship between the TSL II and the Synod collections is not fully clear from figure 7. Among possible comparisons of either of these with various different types, these two stand strikingly

---

[43] Bulanin, *Perevody i poslaniia Maksima Greka* (see n. 2), 220; Shashkov, "Tagil'skii sbornik" (see n. 29), 10.

[44] See Belokurov, O biblioteke moskovskikh gosudarei (see n. 2), cccxiii–xiv, s.n. 243. A more thorough description is provided by A. J. Langeler, *Maksim Grek, Byzantijn en Humanist in Rusland: Een onderzoek naar enkele van zijn bronnen en denkbeelden. Proefschrift ter verkrijging van de graad van dr. in de letteren aan de Katholieke Universiteit te Nijmegen* (Amsterdam, 1986), 166–184; this book should be read together with Bulanin's review (D. M. Bulanin, "Gollandskaia dissertatsiia o literaturnom nasledii Maksima Greka," *Russkaia literatura*, no. 1[1987]: 224–230), which corrects some misprints and other errors. A few other inaccuracies in Langeler's description may be noted here: on p. 167 (c 8 in the manuscript is Ivc 243, not 260; c 13 is Ivc 309); p. 177 (c 75 is Ivc 229, not 221); pp. 181–182 (c 103 contains in addition to Ivc 64 also Ivcc 355, 352, 68, 66, 67, and 33); and p. 183 (c 112, which is on Fols. 708b v–709, not 608v–609, contains in addition to Ivc 71 [Fol. 708b v] also Ivc 72 [Fol. 709]). The Paris manuscript was identified as Belokurov's missing no. 243 by Langeler (ibid., 197–198).

[45] A. V. Gorskii, and K. I. Nevostruev, *Opisanie slavianskikh rukopisei Moskovskoi Sinodal'noi biblioteki* (Moscow, 1855–1917), v. 2, pt. 2, 520–578.

[46] We may note that BMS 243 as summarily described by Belokurov was first identified as a relative of the Synod type in Olmsted, "Ivanov on Maksim Grek" (see n. 3), 21–22, based upon this retained prototypical numeration in GIM Sin. 491/191 (*pace* Bulanin's declaration [Bulanin, "Gollandskaia dissertatsiia" (see n. 44), n. 18] that the identification had first been done by A. T. Shashkov ("Tagil'skii sbornik" [see n. 29], 10n).

[47] Shashkov, "Tagil'skii sbornik" (see n. 29), 10; idem, "Sborniki sochinenii Maksima Greka v sostave biblioteki Kirillo–Belozerskogo monastyria v XVI–XVIII vv.," *Literatura i klassovaia bor'ba epokhi pozdnego feodalizma v Rossii*, ed. E. K. Romodanovskaia; *Arkheografiia i istochnikovedenie Sibiri* (Novosibirsk, 1987), 6–8.

[48] Olmsted, "Kodikologicheskie zametki" (see n. 19).

close to one another in both contents and arrangement. Some close tie seems obvious. This supposition is supported also by significant textual agreements between the TSL II and the Synod collections against other types; these are found in a number of works (Ivcc 52, 64, 133, 134, 152, 165, 191, 216, 228, 232, 234, 332), and include firm evidence of descent from an earlier line of nonextant manuscripts dating from the lifetime of Maksim, specifically from the early 1540s. Also shared are significant dislocations of blocs of text (Ivcc 64, 134, 152). It seems unlikely, however, that either one of these types descends directly and completely from the other; more likely is some sort of blend, incorporating a tradition close to the Burtsev and GPB Q.I.219 types.[49]

One may suggest that the relationship of the Synod type is probably best drawn not with the full TSL II type as constituted at the time of Dionisii; rather, it is the shorter subset of works up through c 115 or c 123 that is involved—perhaps a late sixteenth-century prototype of the TSL II type, with the additions made in Dionisii's time.

My purpose here has been simply to indicate the striking parallels between the two types and to point out some individual features previously not noted.[50] A more detailed discussion is to follow in a subsequent study which I am preparing.

Somewhat similar is a comparison of the TSL II and the Museum type, the latter represented here by BAN 31.4.7 (fig. 8). Concerning the Museum type itself little is known. Judging by the apparent age of its first known representative (GBL Stroev 62 [=GBL Muz. 8291]), it seems to have arisen around the end of the sixteenth century.[51]

The plectogram comparison reveals a striking relationship between the two types, albeit a relationship of a different sort from the ones we have already seen. The pattern is clearly organized into several groups of works in the Museum arrangement, each one showing the focusing effect. It is tempting to see such a relationship as the result of several passes through the TSL II protograph to compile the contents of the Museum type. With minor departures, the major blocs would have been as follows. First, cc 1–10 in

---

[49] The latter is described in K. F. Kalaidovich, and P. M. Stroev, *Obstoiatel'noe opisanie slaviano-rossiiskikh rukopisei, khraniashchikhsia v Moskve v biblioteke . . . grafa Fedora Andreevicha Tolstova* [sic] (Moscow, 1825), 390–400, to which more analytic recent descriptive work has been added by Bulanin (*Perevody i Poslaniia* [see n. 2]), 78–79, 249 passim; see also Olmsted, "Early Manuscript Tradition" (see n. 6), 80–122, 339–349.

[50] N. V. Sinitsyna suggested a possible shared archaism in the TSL II and Synod types in their grouping of the first twelve compositions: "Rukopisnaia traditsiia" (see n. 7), 263; "Maksim Grek i Savonarola" (see n. 24).

[51] Sinitsyna, *Maksim Grek v Rossii* (see n. 2), 271.

order; then Muz. 11–31, then 33–50[e]; then 51–101, and finally cc 102–114—four passes through the protograph, each time with works taken in ascending order. With the exception of a few scattered works in the final section, the parallel ceases abruptly after TSL II c 123.

The Museum type dates from the end of the sixteenth century; the TSL II dates only from the 1620s. If our reconstruction is supported by further analysis, however, the inescapable conclusion is that the TSL II arrangement *preceded* that of the Museum type. It could well be that a protograph of TSL II, consisting of works only down through c 123, was used near the end of the sixteenth century as protograph for the Museum type. It would then subsequently have received added works (cc 124–151) at the time of Dionisii Zobninovskii, taking on the full configuration associated with that time and activity (cf. the similar observation above concerning the Synod type's relationship to the TSL II collection, for which here, too, a shorter prototype was posited).

During our brief presentation we have surveyed several typical configurations, moving from the certain to the increasingly conjectural. Some more general principles have emerged as well. For example, given a focusing configuration like that in fig. 1 (labelling the columns, for the nonce, A and B), we can expect with considerable confidence:

1. that A *precedes* B. The focusing is extraordinarily unlikely to occur in reverse direction; it generally signals that arrangement A was the *secondary prototype* for B;
2. that some C existed/exists which served as *primary protograph* (cf. the third column of figure 3), and it is worth searching for;
3. that *textually* B is likely to correspond more closely to A in the initial section, and to C in the final portion. Thus on the macrolevel the plectograms assist us in predicting likelihoods of proximity which remain to be tested on the microlevel. The expected results are not always borne out in detail (sometimes a more complicated sort of blending may be involved), but they allow us to structure our expectations. Departures from these expectations call for special explanations.

With a more complex and extensive set of compositions, figure 4 shows the same editorial procedure. A variation in figure 6 allows us to see that copy-order and order of precedence need not coincide, but that, *mutatis mutandis,* the focusing and one-to-one relationships still hold. Figure 7 shows a degree of close relationship whose contours have yet to be probed.

Given a pattern like the one in figure 8, one may suspect an editorial procedure of several "passes" through the protograph. In general, the device lets us see at a glance the contours of the relationship. It allows us to give focus and priority to information that otherwise would be unwieldy; it allows us to set manageably small tasks for further work in strategic sampling of textual and other relationships.

Furthermore, these powerful relationships of proximity and precedence can be quite easily deduced in the majority of cases from the *already existing* rough, incomplete chapter-by-chapter (*postateinye*) descriptions that we have for so many manuscripts from early in the nineteenth century to the present. Even partial descriptions can be pressed into use to yield this new sort of information.

Of course, the relationships are not always so tractable. Historically there were also more radical editorial reorganizations of the contents, which may generate plectograms that look more like the upper left quadrant of figure 4. Nevertheless, whatever the degree of tangle, traces of proximity tend to remain; the actual protograph will generally be closer—and look closer—than anything else does.

Plectograms cannot solve all riddles. Other types of information must be brought to bear wherever possible. They are not intended as a substitute for traditional codicological evidence, or as reason for ignoring the genre and content of the compositions in the manuscript. They are simply intended as an additional instrument for the codicologist's toolkit.

The overhead to their use must be acknowledged. Before the plectogram can be devised, one must be prepared to code or otherwise reduce the contents of a manuscript into manageably small units, for instance through reference to a master list of compositions such as Ivanov's in the case of Maksim Grek. The method works best in the context of a circumscribed body of works. If the numbers become too large and their limits too open, it becomes unworkable.

Working with plectograms as heuristic tools, one frequently has to remind oneself that although the connections may look very concrete and actual, the two manuscripts may not in fact have much to do with one another (that is, may not have close genealogical ties). Plectograms are not necessarily pictures of genealogical relationship. Instead, they are usually quite ad hoc, arbitrary comparisons, of which one tries a fairly large number to determine relative proximities. It is only when one finds the unusual match that one knows one is on to something.

Recognizing these restrictions and dangers, it is clear that plectograms can have their uses. In the face of such daunting tasks as the grouping, textual sampling, chronological placement, genealogical modeling of the major families of the hundreds of voluminous manuscripts of Maksim Grek's collected compositions—together with their interrelationships with the dozens of unanalyzed smaller miscellanies—the plectogram provides a simple visual shortcut, achievable on the basis of information that is already available. A gross, imperfect initial version (based, for example, upon a less than fully satisfactory published description) is easy to revise and to perfect as more information becomes available; this frees one to proceed with whatever is available and to extract new conclusions from old and well-known sources. It allows one to see at once both large and small levels of organization,[52] to reduce cumbersome units (each of the compositions in the manuscripts, or even large groups of compositions) to manageable size, and to grasp their interrelationship at a glance, intuitively, holistically.

It seems likely that such a device could, if put to appropriate use, be useful in other fields of inquiry. Perhaps it could find some application in studying the relationships of assemblages such as chronicles, redactions of Zlatoust, or *chet'i sborniki* in broader terms. In any event, I hope that the plectogram has drawn attention to the tremendous creative labor over the generations which a respectful posterity devoted to the collected works of Maksim Grek.

Abbreviations

Bol.	T. F. Bol'shakov Manuscript collection, f. 37, GBL
Burts.	Burtsev manuscript collection, BAN
Egor.	E. E. Egorov Manuscript collection, f. 98, GBL
GMZ	Gosudarstvennyi muzei-zapovednik (State Museum and Preserve), Iaroslavl'
Imp. An	Imperatorskaia Akademiia nauk (Imperial [Russian] Academy of Sciences), St. Petersburg.
IRLI	Institut russkoi literatury AN SSSR (Institute of Russian Literature of the Academy of Sciences of the Soviet Union)
Khlud.	A. I. Khludov manuscript collection, no. 86795, GIM
MDA	Moskovskaia dukhovnaia akademiia (Moscow Ecclesiastical Academy) Manuscript collection, f. 173, GBL
MGA MID	Moskovskii glavnyi arkhiv Ministerstva inostrannykh del

---

[52] Cf. the observations on "micro/macro design" in Tufte, *Envisioning Information* (see n. 13), 37–51.

Muz.	Muzeinoe sobranie (Museum collection), f. 178, GBL
Nikif.	P. N. Nikiforov manuscript collection, f. 199, GBL
OIDR	Obshchestvo istorii i drevnostei rossiiskikh (Society of Russian History and Antiquities), Moscow
ORIaS	Otdelenie russkogo iazyka i slovesnosti [Imp./Rossiiskoi Akademii nauk] (Division of Russian Language and Letters of the Imperial/Russian Academy of Sciences)
Pogod.	M. P. Pogodin manuscript collection, no. 558, GPB
Rog.	Rogozhskaia obshchina Manuscript collection, f. 247, GBL
Rum.	N. P. Rumiantsev Manuscript collection, f. 256, GBL
Shchuk.	P. I. Shchukin Manuscript collection, no. 23905, GIM
Sin.	Moskovskoe sinodal'noe sobranie (Moscow Synod Manuscript collection), no. 80370, GIM
Solov.	Solovetskii monastery (Solovki) manuscript collection, no. 717, GPB
TSL	Troitse-Sergieva Lavra (St. Sergii Trinity Monastery) Manuscript collection, f. 304, GBL
TSL I	First Troitskii type
TSL II	Second Troitskii type
Uvar.	A. S. Uvarov Manuscript collection, nos. 911, 80269–80271, GIM

EARLY RUSSIAN TOPOI
OF DEATHBED AND TESTAMENT

DANIEL E. COLLINS

Death scenes in early Russian writings, especially in the biographies of prominent churchmen and laymen who die from natural causes, contain a number of topoi that are connected to final religious or social duties and that are characterized by recurrent linguistic formulae. Accounts with a full complex of these topoi of deathbed and testament describe how the protagonists anticipate their demise and fulfill religious duties by receiving the last rites. In preparation for leaving this world, they pass on authority to successors. Likewise, they summon family or dependents—subjects or spiritual children—and admonish them to practice Christian virtues and in particular to love one another and obey their superiors, i.e., parents, elder brothers, rulers, or abbots. Finally, they fulfill social obligations to those who will be left behind by kissing them, blessing them, and asking their forgiveness.[1]

In his 1949 essay on the Kiev Chronicle, Igor' Eremin attributes the conformity of description in princely obituaries to the purely literary strictures of the "hagiographical canon";[2] that is, he believes that the chronicle passages imitate the death scenes in saints' lives and thus reflect a "conventional, abstract, and antirealistic" literary style.[3] This interpretation has gained wide acceptance among scholars of early Russian literature. For exam-

---

I would like to thank Henrik Birnbaum, Michael Heim, Norman Ingham, Gail Lenhoff, Nancy Ševčenko, Russell Valentino, and Ronald Vroon for their criticism of earlier versions of this paper.

[1] The topoi of deathbed and testament do not occur in any fixed order, although they often appear as a complex. Moreover, the presence of one topos does not imply that of the others. Of the many formulae and recurrent situations that could be mentioned, only the most frequent will be discussed in this paper.

[2] "Kievskaja letopis' kak pamjatnik literatury," in I. P. Eremin, *Literatura drevnej Rusi* (Moscow-Leningrad, 1966), 114–121. See also idem, *Lekcii i stat'i po istorii drevnej russkoj literatury*, 2d ed. (Leningrad, 1987), 61–63. According to Eremin, the obituaries portraying idealized princes are examples of the type of narrative he calls the "chronicle tale" (*letopisnaja povest'*). The obituaries in the oldest form of narrative, the yearly record (*pogodnaja zapis'*), include only a few terse facts—e.g., when and where the subject died and where he was buried (ibid., 62).

[3] Eremin, *Literatura drevnej Rusi*, 114.

ple, Dmitrii Lixačev states that chronicle obituaries, which were written in the generalizing style he terms "monumental historicism" (*monumental'nyj istorizm*), portray princes unrealistically, as idealized representatives of their position in the feudal hierarchy.[4] However, there is some evidence that the recurrent elements in early Russian death scenes are a reflection of social norms rather than purely literary conventions; in other words, they derive from similarities in what the authors actually saw or expected. Evidence that the topoi of deathbed and testament are not mere clichés but reflect actual social practices can be found in biographies based on personal recollections and eyewitness accounts and in nonbiographical texts such as legal documents.

The term topos is used here to denote a recurrent proposition, formula, or element that can be used in literature and other types of communication to construct representations of an event.[5] In modern usage, topoi are commonly equated with motifs, i.e., recurring elements or thematic units in literature;[6] by contrast, in classical rhetoric they were understood not just as literary clichés but also as expressions of social expectations grounded in underlying cultural norms.[7] As Heinrich Lausberg notes, classical topoi always had the potential to reflect reality:

---

[4] D. S. Lixačev, *Čelovek v literature drevnej Rusi* (Moscow, 1970), 26. See also ibid., 49, 51; idem, *Poètika drevnerusskoj literatury,* 3d ed. (Moscow, 1979), 89; and O. V. Tvorogov's remarks on monumental historicism in obituaries in *Istorija russkoj literatury X–XVI vekov,* ed. D. S. Lixačev (Moscow, 1980), 81–82. Lixačev likewise asserts that the laments and panegyrics that recur in death scenes are "far from transmitting realities; they are to a great degree literary and traditional" (*Čelovek,* 39). This overlooks the fact that funeral rites tend to be heavily ritualized (cf. the funerals of various modern heads of state) and that *de mortuis nihil nisi bonum* is a taboo common to many cultures.

[5] The concept of topos, as defined here, should be distinguished from Lixačev's somewhat similar notion of literary etiquette (= decorum), i.e., a recurrent, normative mode of representing a ceremonialized situation in literature. Although Lixačev acknowledges that many of the etiquettes in early Russian writing could reflect actual practices, he focuses on their function as devices to idealize situations in accordance with specifically literary canons. (See Lixačev, *Poètika,* 80–81, 86–91, and *Istorija,* 80–82. On the related concept of situational formula; see O. V. Tvorogov, "Zadači izučenija literaturnyx formul drevnej Rusi," *TODRL* 20 [1964]: 32.)

[6] Cf. M. H. Abrams, *A Glossary of Literary Terms,* 3d ed. (New York, 1971), 101; Sylvan Barnet et al., *A Dictionary of Literary, Dramatic, and Cinematic Terms,* 2d ed. (Boston, 1971), 71, 111; Jostein Børtnes, *Visions of Glory: Studies in Early Russian Hagiography,* trans. Jostein Børtnes and Paul L. Nielsen, Slavica Norvegica, no. 5 (Oslo, 1988), 91. It is sometimes defined more precisely as a stable complex of motifs (minimal thematic units) that recurs in various literary works (Oswald Ducrot and Tzvetan Todorov, *Encyclopedic Dictionary of the Sciences of Language,* trans. Catherine Porter [Baltimore, 1979], 219–220; David E. Aune, *The New Testament in Its Literary Environment,* Library of Early Christianity [Philadelphia, 1987], 172). See also *Dictionary of Literary Themes and Motifs,* ed. Jean-Charles Seigneuret et al., 2 vols. (New York, 1988), v. 1, xxi.

[7] According to Ernst Robert Curtius (*European Literature and the Latin Middle Ages,* trans. Willard R. Trask [Princeton, 1953], 70), the topoi (κοινοὶ τόποι, *loci communes*) of early classical judicial and political oratory are "arguments which address themselves to the hearer's

> Der Topos ist eine Form . . . die . . . mit jeweils aktuell gemeintem Inhalt gefüllt werden kann. Die Erkenntnis, daß ein in einem Text angetroffener Gedanke einem Topos entspricht, ist historisch wertvoll und auch für das Verständnis des betreffenden Textes nicht wertlos, wenn man beachtet, daß der Autor den Topos finitisiert und in den konkreten Kontext eingefügt hat, wo er seine aktuelle Funktion zu erfüllen hat.[8]

The same is true of the early Russian topoi of deathbed and testament. As will be shown below, the topoi reflected how authors expected the dying to behave and so were continually renewed by the very rituals they described. Therefore, they should be understood not as literary clichés but as manifestations of the vertical bond that existed between social responses to death and the representation of dying in narratives.[9]

Presentiment of Death

In hagiographical texts, the protagonist is commonly represented as being aware of his impending death and able to summon his spiritual father (*duxovnyj otecь*) to administer the last rites.[10] In some accounts the saints' presentiment of death must be inferred from their behavior; in others it is specified—at times as an instance of miraculous prescience—by the use of verbs such as *uvidĕti* 'see,' *poznati* 'realize,' and *prouvĕdĕti* 'know in advance,' plus noun phrases such as *svoe (konečnoe) otxoždenie k bogu* 'his (final) departure to God.' An early instance occurs in the *Life* of Feodosij of the Kiev Caves Monastery: "уже на коньць жития прѣшьдъ прѣже увѣдѣвъ.

---

mind or heart . . . which can be used on the most diverse occasions . . . intellectual themes, suitable for development and modification at the orator's pleasure . . . . Originally, then, topoi are helps toward composing orations. They are, as Quintillian (V, 10, 20) says, 'storehouses of trains of thought' ('argumentorum sedes'), and thus can serve a practical purpose." See also Heinrich Lausberg, *Elemente der literarischen Rhetorik,* 4th ed. (Munich, 1971), 38–39.

[8] Ibid., 39.

[9] On the concept of vertical bonds, see Gail Lenhoff, "Towards a Theory of Protogenres in Medieval Russian Letters," *RR* 43 (1984): 50; idem, "Categories of Early Russian Writing," *SEEJ* 31 (1987): 264.

[10] According to Dorothy Abrahamse ("Rituals of Death in the Middle Byzantine Period," *The Greek Orthodox Theological Review* 29 [1984]: 127, 129), the prescience of death was also a recurrent element ("one of the standard prerequisites of sanctity") in Byzantine hagiography, e.g., in the *Lives* of Anthony of Egypt and Evaristos the Studite. Abrahamse (126, 133–34) is inclined to treat the Byzantine topoi of deathbed as purely literary devices but notes that "for the historian . . . they present a particular problem, for their presence in a ninth or tenth century text could be motivated by hagiographical tradition and the expectation of what made a holy death, or it could reflect the continuity of actual practices in a common tradition" (129). However, it seems odd to disassociate "the expectation of what made a holy death" from "the continuity of actual practices," since conventions are motivated by norms and expectations.

еже къ б[ог]у свое отшьствие и дьнь покоя своего."[11] Later in the text, Feodosij predicts the exact time of his demise: "нарекъ имъ д[ь]нь прѣставления своего. яко въ суботу по възитии с[ъ]лнца. д[у]ша моя отлучить ся от тѣлесе моего."[12] Similarly, in Epifanij's *Life of Sergij of Radonež*, "и разумѣ свое еже къ б[о]гу отхождение."[13] Examples of this topos can be found both in probable eyewitness accounts, e.g., the *Lives* of Iona of Novgorod,[14] Evfrosin of Pskov,[15] Iosif of Volokolamsk,[16] Aleksandr Svirskij,[17]

---

[11] "Having already arrived at the end of his life, he knew in advance of his departure to God and the day of his rest." *Uspenskij sbornik XII–XIII vv.*, ed. S. I. Kotkov (Moscow, 1971), 127, col. 62a, ll. 19–23. Feodosij's *Life* was written not long after his death by Nestor of the Caves Monastery, who was tonsured under his successor, Stefan. (See *Slovar' knižnikov i knižnosti drevnej Rusi*, ed. D. S. Lixačev [Leningrad, 1987–89], v. 1, 274–275.)

[12] "He told them the day of his death: 'Saturday after sunrise, my soul will be parted from my body.'" *Uspenskij sbornik*, 128, col. 63a, ll. 25–31.

[13] *Die Legenden des heiligen Sergij von Radonež*, ed. N. S. Tixonravov, 1892; reprint, Slavische Propyläen, 17, ed. Ludolf Müller (Munich, 1967), section 1, 143 (reworked first redaction ascribed to Paxomij Logofet). Epifanij Premudryj wrote the first redaction of Sergij's *Life* from his own and other monks' recollections and preliminary notes made soon after Sergij's death. In the mid-fifteenth century, Paxomij used Epifanij's version to produce an abridged redaction, which exists in two variants; this adds that Sergij foresaw his death six months in advance (section 2, 46). The topos of presentiment of death is also found in the death scene of Abbot Nikon, Sergij's disciple and successor, in the second variant of Paxomij's redaction (section 2, 83, 103). (See V. O. Ključevskij, *Drevnerusskie žitija svjatyx kak istoričeskij istočnik* [1871; reprint, Moscow, 1988], 98–110, 114–19, 129–32; *Slovar'* [see n. 11], v. 2, pt. 1, 330–331.)

[14] *Pamjatniki starinnoj russkoj literatury*, ed. N. Kostomarov, 4 vols. (St. Petersburg, 1860), v. 4, 34. The "memoir" (*vospominanie*) about Iona (died 5 November 1470) is material for a biography rather than a full-fledged vita and was probably written in 1472 by a Novgorodian monk. (See Ključevskij, Žitija, 184–188; *Slovar'* [see n. 11] v. 2, pt. 2, 175–176.)

[15] *Žitie prepodobnogo Evfrosina Pskovskogo (pervonačal'naja redakcija)*, ed. N. Serebrjanskij, 1909; reprint, Monuments of Early Russian Literature, no. 3 (Berkeley, 1982), 54 (first redaction); *Pamjatniki*, v. 4, 98–99 (second redaction). The first redaction of the *Life of Evfrosin* (died 15 May 1481) was evidently written before 1510; its author did not know Evfrosin personally but based his account on the recollections of Evfrosin's monks. The second redaction, which conforms to traditional hagiographical norms, was written by the Pskovian priest Vasilij-Varlaam in 1547; its chief source was the first redaction. (See *Žitie Evfrosina*, i–ii, vi, xiv–xviii; Ključevskij, *Žitija* [see n. 13], 250, 252–255; *Slovar'* [see n. 11], v. 2, pt. 1, 112–113, 262–264).

[16] *Skazanija o russkix i slavjanskix svjatyx, izvlečennyja iz Velikix Minej Četiix* (St. Petersburg, 1868), v. 1, 120, 122. The main redaction of the *Life of Iosif Sanin* (died 9 September 1515) was written in 1546 by Bishop Savva Černyj, who was tonsured under him. Although essentially a factual account, it contains certain imprecisions due to faulty memories or political discretion. (See Ključevskij, *Žitija* [see n. 13], 312; *Slovar'* [see no. 11], v. 2, pt. 1, 273–275.)

[17] Iv. Jaxontov, *Žitija sv. severnorusskix podvižnikov pomorskogo kraja, kak istoričeskij istočnik* (Kazan', 1881), 371; a later passage reports that Aleksandr foretold his death a year in advance (375). The *Life of Aleksandr* (died August 30, 1533) was written in 1545 by Irodion, his successor, from eyewitness accounts, personal recollections, and, evidently, Aleksandr's last will. Jaxontov, who evidently did not know of the will, suspected the historicity of Irodion's work because it repeated passages from other lives almost verbatim (38–39, 73, 86–87). I. U. Budovnic (*Monastyri na Rusi i bor'ba s nimi krest'jan v XIV–XVI vekax* [Moscow, 1966], 322–323, n. 198) pointed out the flaw in Jaxontov's argument: "one can expound a reliable fact using a previously known text." (See also Ključevskij, *Žitija* [see n. 13], 262–63; *Slovar'* [see n. 11], v. 2, pt. 1, 440–441; L. A. Dmitriev, *Žitijnye povesti russkogo severa kak pamjatniki literatury XIII–XVII vv.* [Leningrad, 1973], 266–267.)

and Daniil of Perejaslavl',[18] and also in vitae in which the authors had to fill in biographical gaps on the basis of their knowledge of social and literary norms—for example, the *Lives* of Varlaam of Xutyn',[19] Antonij Rimljanin,[20] and Martirij of Zelenaja Pustynja.[21]

The topos of presentiment of death is sometimes added to the later redactions of a Life when it is missing or implicit in the initial version—e.g., in the second redaction of Mixail Klopskij's vita: "яко убо позна блаженный свое еже из мира исхожение и час уведе [sic] чюдный нашь старець богочестивой и аггелохранимой души от трудолюбнаго его телесе разлучение."[22] Further cases of such emendation appear in versions of the *Lives* of Avraamij of Smolensk, Ioann of Novgorod, Aleksandr Nevskij, and Dovmont.[23]

---

[18] *Žitie prepodobnogo Daniila, perejaslavskogo čudotvorca, Pověst' o obretenii moščej i Čudesa ego*, ed. S. I. Smirnov (Moscow, 1908), 69–70. The *Life of Daniil* (died 7 April 1540), attested in four redactions in seventeenth-century copies, was written in the 1550s or 1560s by an anonymous eyewitness—probably Andrej-Afanasij, later Metropolitan of Moscow. (See ibid., v–xv; Ključevskij, *Žitija* [see n. 13], 282; *Slovar'* [see n. 11], v. 2, pt. 1, 73–74, 257–258.)

[19] *Žitie Varlaama Xutynskogo*, Obščestvo ljubitelej drevnej pis'mennosti, 41 (St. Petersburg, 1881), 19 (extended redaction). The first redaction of the *Life of Varlaam* (died 6 November 1192), a short prologue version written before the late thirteenth century, was probably based on local tales and on notes made shortly after Varlaam's death. A second, more extensive redaction, found in manuscripts from the fifteenth century onwards, was the chief source of Paxomij Logofet's version (1460), which served in turn as the basis of the extended and special versions (early to mid-sixteenth century). (See Ključevskij, *Žitija* [see n. 13], 58–63, 121, 140–146; *Slovar'* [see n. 11], v. 1, 138–141.)

[20] *Pamjatniki* (see n. 14), v. 1, 268 (about Bishop Nikita, Antonij's mentor), 269 (about Antonij himself). The *Life of Antonij* (died 1147) was composed in the mid- or late sixteenth century. Some of its episodes derived from local legends; it also had factual sources, including a deed (*kupčaja*) and will (*duxovnaja*) extant in sixteenth-century copies, and perhaps also an unattested short life. (See Ključevskij, *Žitija* [see n. 13], 306–311; *Slovar'* [see n. 11], v. 2, pt. 1, 245–247; M. N. Tixomirov, "O častnyx aktax v drevnej Rusi," *Istoričeskie zapiski* 17 [1945]: 237–238; A. S. Xorošev, *Cerkov' v social'no-političeskoj sisteme Novgorodskoj feodal'noj respubliki* [Moscow, 1980], 25, n. 45.)

[21] *Pamjatniki* (see n. 14), v. 4, 65. The *Life of Martirij* (died 1 March 1603), founder of Trinity Monastery on Zelenyj Island in the swamps near Tixvin, survives in a single eighteenth-century copy. Its author may have been Metropolitan Kornilij of Novgorod, who served as Trinity's abbot until 1667 and retired there in 1695. (Ključevskij, *Žitija* [see n. 13], 346; Nikolaj Barsukov, *Istočniki russkoj agiografii*, Obščestvo ljubitelej drevnej pis'mennosti, 81 [St. Petersburg, 1882], col. 602–605; 357; *Slovar'* [see n. 11], v. 2, pt. 2, 106–107.)

[22] "How the blessed one knew of his departure from the world: our miraculous elder foresaw the time of his godly and angel-guarded soul's separation from his hardworking body." *Povesti o žitii Mixaila Klopskogo*, ed. L. A. Dmitriev (Moscow and Leningrad, 1958), 136. The first redaction of the *Life of Mixail* (died ca. 1456), called the "miracles" (*redakcii čudes*), was written in 1478 or 1479 and exists in two variants. The longer, second redaction (the "prophecies," *proročestva*) dates from the late fifteenth or early sixteenth century; Ključevskij considers it the oldest version of the *Life*. (See ibid., 62–63; Ključevskij, *Žitija* [see n. 13], 209–212, 233; *Slovar'* [see n. 11], v. 2, pt. 1, 302–305).

[23] Avramij of Smolensk: *Die altrussischen hagiographischen Erzählungen und liturgischen Dichtungen über den heiligen Avraamij von Smolensk*, ed. S. P. Rozanov, 1912; reprint, Slavische Propyläen, no. 15 (Munich, 1970), 80 (third reworked version, sixteenth–seventeenth centuries);

In using the topos of presentiment of death to fill in biographical gaps, early Russian authors probably perceived it not as a mere literary device but rather as probable truth. The dying had to be aware of death to prepare for the last rites, draw up their wills, and fulfill other social and religious obligations. Although there were provisions for shriving those who had lost their faculties (reading the formula of confession over them and giving them communion),[24] the Church obviously considered it desirable for communicants to be conscious. Moreover, actual events sometimes substantiated the topos. For example, like Feodosij, Pafnutij of Borovsk made a seemingly preternatural prediction of his own death, as recounted in Innokentij's detailed notes about his last week: "рече бо ми: 'в сий же день четверток имам премѣнитися немощи моея.'"[25] This plain-spoken assertion, which

---

the topos is absent in the first two redactions and the other reworked variants. The earliest version of the *Life of Avraamij* (late twelfth–early thirteenth centuries) was written by his disciple Efrem and refers to other eyewitnesses; though factual, it shows the influence of other vitae, especially Nestor's *Life of Feodosij*. The various reworked versions date to the sixteenth and seventeenth centuries. (See ibid., i–xiv; Ključevskij, *Žitija* [see n. 13], 52–58; *Slovar'* [see n. 11], v. 1, 126–128.)

Ioann of Novgorod: *Skazanija* (see n. 16), 28 (second redaction); the presentiment is absent in the first redaction (4). The first redaction of the *Life of Ioann* (died 7 September 1186), a short biography that survives in two variants, was probably written before the mid-fourteenth century. The longer, second redaction, written in the 1470s or 1480s, was based mainly on local legends; it is sometimes ascribed, on weak grounds, to Paxomij Logofet. (See Ključevskij, *Žitija* [see n. 13], 161–164; *Slovar'* [see n. 11], v. 2, pt. 2, 514–517.)

Aleksandr Nevskij: Mansikka, *Žitie Aleksandra Nevskogo: Razbor redakcij i tekst,* Pamjatniki drevnej pis'mennosti i iskusstva, 180 (1913; reprint, Leipzig, 1984), app., 25 (Vladimir redaction); the topos is missing in the other redactions. The Vladimir redaction, a traditional vita, was written in 1547; the death scene in particular was enhanced with hagiographical topoi. (See ibid., 110–122; Ključevskij, *Žitija* [see n. 13], 238–240; *Slovar'* [see n. 11], v. 1, 354–363; Ju. K. Begunov, *Pamjatnik russkoj literatury XIII veka 'Slovo o pogibeli Russkoj zemli'* [Moscow and Leningrad, 1965], 57–64.)

Dovmont: V. I. Oxotnikova, *Povest' o Dovmonte. Issledovanie i teksty* (Leningrad, 1985), 225 (extended redaction). The extended redaction of the *Life of Dovmont* (died 20 May 1299) dates to the late sixteenth or early seventeenth century and is less historical and more conventional than the other versions. (See ibid., 117–137; *Slovar'* [see n. 11], v. 2, pt. 2, 239–243.)

[24] Cf. a sixteenth- or seventeenth-century nomocanon: "Аще ч[е]л[овѣ]къ разболится на смерть а языкъ отыметася не покаял ся. ино покояние (!) [editor's interpolation] наð нимъ изговорити и при смерти с[вя]тое причастие дати." ("If a person is sick unto death and his power of speech is taken away and he has not confessed, pronounce the formula of confession over him and give him holy communion around the time of death." S. Smirnov, *Drevne-russkij duxovnik; Issledovanie po istorii cerkovnogo byta,* [1914; reprint, Westmead, U. K., 1970], app., 43, §8.)

[25] "He said to me, 'Next Thursday, a week from today, I shall be saved from my sickness.'" *Pamjatniki literatury drevnej Rusi. Vtoraja polovina XV veka,* ed. L. A. Dmitriev and D. S. Lixačev (Moscow, 1982), 480. Innokentij, a trusted monk, was with Pafnutij (died 1 May 1477) almost constantly during his final eight days; in 1477 or 1478, he wrote an extremely circumstantial memoir, as material for a future vita. (See Ključevskij, *Žitija* [see n. 13], 206–207; Lixačev, *Čelovek* [see n. 4], 129–130; *Slovar'* [see n. 11], v. 2, pt. 1, 404.)

proved true, is repeated nearly verbatim in Vassian Sanin's *Life* of the abbot.[26] A further actualization of the topos can be found in the biography of Kirill of Beloozero, who writes movingly of his oncoming death in the preamble of his will (ca. 1427):

> смотрих, яко постиже мя старость, впадох бо в частыя и различныя болезни, ими же ныне сдержимь есмь, человеколюбне от бога казним, ради моих грех, болезнем на мя умножившимся ныне, яко же иногда никогда же, и ничто же ми возвещающе разве смерть и суд страшный спасов будущаго века. И во мне смутись сердце мое исхода ради и страх смертный нападе на мя....[27]

In writing Kirill's *Life*, Paxomij Logofet paraphrases this passage in the third person as a transition to the death scene.[28] In the subsequent text, Paxomij repeats this preamble in the first person while quoting Kirill's entire will (with some emendations).

Last Rites

The last rites were obligatory in the early Russian Orthodox Church;[29] consequently, they are often mentioned in hagiographical death scenes—for example, in the *Life of Sergij of Radonež* in Epifanij Premudrij's version: "причаствъ же ся пр[ѣ]ч[и]стых таинъ ...."[30] Paxomij Logofet's redac-

---

[26] Vassian Sanin, later archbishop of Rostov, was also an eyewitness of Pafnutij's last days; he composed the vita sometime before 1515 from his own and others' recollections. Vassian relied heavily on Innokentij's notes in his account of Pafnutij's death. (See *Žitie prepodobnogo Pafnutija Borovskogo, pisannoe Vassianom Saninym*, ed. A. P. Kadlubovskij, in *Sbornik istoriko-filologičeskogo Obščestva pri Institute Knjazja Bezborodko* (Nežin, 1899), 143; Ključevskij, *Žitija* [see n. 13], 205–207; *Slovar'* [see n. 11], v. 2, pt. 1, 125–126.)

[27] "I have seen how old age has overtaken me, for I have fallen into frequent and varied illnesses, by which I am now held captive, punished lovingly by God because of my sins; my illnesses have multiplied now as never before, and nothing is foretold for me except death and the Savior's terrible judgment of the next age. And my heart grew troubled within me because of my demise, and the fear of death beset me ...." *Akty social'no-èkonomičeskoj istorii severo-vostočnoj Rusi konca XIV-načala XVI v.*, ed. L. V. Čerepnin, v. 2 (Moscow, 1958), no. 314, p. 277.

[28] *Pachomij Logofet. Werke in Auswahl*, ed. V. Jablonskij, 1908; reprint, Slavische Propyläen, no. 1, ed. Dmitrij Tschižewskij (Munich, 1963), xli.

[29] Cf. a sixteenth-century nomocanon: "и в см[е]рть достоит прич[а]ститися, всякому ч[е]л[ове]ку. и въ епитеми хр[и]стианомъ, ни единому ч[е]л[ове]ку, хр[и]стианину будучи, мужу, или женѣ, малу и велику, и стару и молоду, не достоит умр[е]ти без покаяния, и без причащения с тых таинъ, или в нощь или в д[е]нь." ("Both in death and in Christian penance, everyone should take communion; and no one who is a Christian—man or woman, small and large, old and young—should die without confessing and partaking of the sacraments, day or night." S. Smirnov, *Drevne-russkij duxovnik* [see n. 24], app., 115, §9).

[30] "Having partaken of the most holy sacraments ...." *Legenden des Sergij* (see n. 13), sect. 1, 67, similarly 143 (Epifanij's redaction with emendations ascribed to Paxomij Logofet. Cf. also the death scene of Nikon, Sergij's successor, in Paxomij's redaction (ibid., sect. 2, 83, 103).

tion gives a fuller and more complex description of this event: "и на самыи убо исход во ньже хотяше телеснаг[о] соуза отрѣшитис[я] вл[а]д[ы]чяго тѣла и крове причастис[я]."[31] Similar allusions to the last rites can be found in comparatively accurate biographies, such as the *Lives* of Pafnutij of Borovsk (in both Innokentij's notes and Vassian Sanin's *Life*),[32] Kirill of Beloozero,[33] Daniil of Perejaslavl',[34] and Iulianija Osor'ina.[35] They also appear in historically less reliable vitae, e.g., the *Lives* of Nifont of Novgorod,[36] Evfrosinija of Polock,[37] and Martirij of Zelenaja Pustynja.[38]

When an account of the last rites was missing in earlier redactions of a vita, it could be added as a topos in later versions; this is the case in a reworking of Avraamij of Smolensk's *Life*[39] and in Vasilij-Varlaam's and Iona Dumin's versions of Aleksandr Nevskij's *Life*.[40] The prologue redaction of the *Life of Dovmont* and the variants from the Pskov I, II, and III Chronicles mention only that he suffered a brief illness and died on 20 May.[41] By contrast, the middle redaction (sixteenth century) mentions, albeit laconically, that he took communion ("и причастився божественых даров . . ."),[42] while the extended redaction (late sixteenth or early seventeenth century) closely resembles Paxomij's Life of Sergij: "рече им и в самый исход, в онь же хотяще телеснаго соуза отрешитися, владычняго тела

---

[31] "And at the very end, when he was about to dissolve the bond of the body, he partook of the Lord's body and blood." Ibid., sect. 2, 47 (Paxomij Logofet's redaction).
[32] *Pamjatniki literatury* (see n. 29), 490; *Žitie Pafnutija* (see n. 26), 144.
[33] *Pachomij Logofet* (see n. 28), xlv.
[34] *Žitie Daniila* (see n. 18), 72.
[35] *Pamjatniki* (see n. 14), v. 1, 66. The Life of Iulianija Osor'ina of Lazarevo, near Murom (died 2 January 1604), was written in 1614 by her son, Kalistrat Družina-Osor'in, a government official. (See Ključevskij, *Žitija* [see n. 13], 322–323; Barsukov, *Istočniki* [see n. 21], 282–283.)
[36] *Pamjatniki* (see n. 14), v. 4, 6. The *Life of Nifont* (died 1156) was written in 1558 by Vasilij-Varlaam of Pskov. (See Ključevskij, *Žitija* [see n. 13], 260–262; *Slovar'* [see n. 11], v. 2, pt. 1, 114).
[37] *Pamjatniki,* (see n. 14) v. 4, 179. The earliest copy of the life of Evfrosinija (died 1173) dates to the end of the fifteenth century and shows literary traits characteristic of that period; however, it evidently had early, perhaps even pre-Mongol, sources. (See Ključevskij, *Žitija* [see n. 13], 262; *Slovar'* [see n. 11], v. 1, 147–148.)
[38] *Pamjatniki,* (see n. 14) v. 4, 66.
[39] *Erzählungen* (see n. 23), 49 (first reworked redaction, sixteenth century; ibid., x–xi).
[40] Mansikka, *Žitie Aleksandra* (see n. 23), sect. 2, 46 (Vasilij-Varlaam's redaction), 100 (Iona Dumin's redaction). Some time after 1547, Vasilij-Varlaam of Pskov used the first redaction of Aleksandr's *Life,* as it appeared in contemporary chronicles, to compose a version strongly influenced by other vitae, especially those of sovereign saints. Around 1600, Iona Dumin reworked chronicle accounts and earlier redactions to create an extended rhetorical version. (See Ključevskij, *Žitija* [see n. 13], 251, 258, 312–313.)
[41] Oxotnikova, *Povest' o Dovmonte* (see n. 23), 188, 192, 195, 199.
[42] "And having partaken of the divine gifts . . . ." Ibid., 209.

и крови причаститися в напутие живота вечнаго . . . ."[43] The formula *vladyčnago těla i krove pričastitisja* 'partake of the Lord's body and blood' or similar phrases, along with the image of communion as preparation for the final journey (*dobrago sputnika* 'good companion,' cf. *v naputie života věčnago* 'to set off for eternal life'), occur in Vasilij-Varlaam's and Iona Dunin's redactions of Aleksandr Nevskij's vita. Likewise, the formula *otrěšitisja tělesnago souza* 'be released from the bond of the body' or variants appear in the vitae of Kirill, Pafnutij (Innokentij's notes and Vassian Sanin's redaction), Mixail Klopskij (second redaction),[44] and Aleksandr Nevskij (Vasilij-Varlaam's redaction),[45] among others; cf. *razrěšitisja ot ploti* 'be released from the flesh' in the *Life of Antonij Rimljanin*.[46] These verbal topoi are evidently related to passages in the religious rites performed over the dying—e.g., the phrases "душю раба твоего всякия узы разрѣши . . . . повели да отпустится от узъ плотныхъ и грѣховныхъ" in the "prayer spoken at the departure of the soul of a priest."[47]

Because it derives from a mandatory church ritual, the topos of last rites reflects cultural expectations to an even greater degree than the topos of presentiment of death; therefore, any irregularities in the ritual require an explanation. For example, in the first redaction (variant B) of Mixail Klopskij's *Life,* Mixail's abbot violates canon law by offering him communion twice in one day: "и призва его игумен причаститися божьих тайн, и он молвяше: 'Ей, отче, взял есми от тобя божия тайны!' И рече ему игумен: 'Возьми, чядо, опять причястися божьих тайн.' И от сего всем удивльшимся."[48] This incident is not reported in the second redaction: "и паки преподбный причастився, тело христово взял на своих ногах."[49]

---

[43] "At the very end, when he was about to be released from the bond of the body, he told them that [he wanted] to partake of the Lord's body and blood to set off for eternal life . . . ." Ibid., 225.

[44] *Povesti o žitii Mixaila* (see n. 22), 137.

[45] Mansikka, *Žitie Aleksandra* (see n. 23), sect. 2, 46.

[46] *Pamjatniki* (see n. 14), v. 1, 270.

[47] "Release the soul of your servant from every bond . . . . Command that he be freed from the bonds of the flesh and of sin." "M[o]l[i]tva. glagolaema na isxod d[u]ši ot iereja," in *Staroobrjadčeskij učebnyj časovnik, perepečatannyj s izdannogo v Moskve pri patriarxe Ioasafe v 7015* (Moscow, 1908), 72r.

[48] "And the abbot called him to partake of the divine mysteries, and he said, 'Eh, father, I've [already] taken the divine sacraments from you!' And the abbot said to him, 'Take [it], my child, partake of the divine sacraments again.' And everyone was astounded by this." *Povesti o žitii Mixaila* (see n. 22), 109.

[49] "And then [or 'again'] the venerable one took communion; standing unsupported, he took the body of Christ." Ibid., 137. This appears to be based on variant A of the first redaction, where the abbot's transgression and Mixail's refusal are missing: "а дары взял на Феодосиев день на своих ногах" ("And on Feodosij's feast-day, standing unsupported, he took the gifts [sacraments].") Ibid., 97.

In the third redaction the author included the abbot's well-intentioned mistake but apparently felt that some explanation was in order; thus Mixail explains his refusal in courteous and highly bookish language: "'немногу времени пришедъшу, яко сподобихся прияти от тебе тоя святыни, и аще господь повелит в утрешний день паки сподоблюся тоя святыни.'"⁵⁰

Transfer of Power

In biographies of churchmen, the protagonists are often portrayed anointing their successors and teaching them about pastoral care—for example, in the *Life of Feodosij*:

> блаженныи же того призъвавъ и бл[а]гословивъ игумена имъ въ себе мѣсто нарече. оны же много поучивъ еже покаряти ся тому. и тако отпусти я....и пакы же призъвавъ стефана единого учааше и. еже о паствѣ с[вя]тааго того стада....И яко же пришьдъши суботѣ. и д[ь]ни освитающу. посълавъ блаженыи призъва въсю братию....и се вамъ игуменъ. его же сами изволисте того послушаите. и о[т]ця того д[у]ховьнааго себѣ имѣите. и того боите ся. и по повелѣнию его въся творите. Б[ог]ъ же... даи же вамъ бл[а]годать еже работати тому бес прирока. и быти вамъ въ единомь тѣлѣ. и единѣмь д[у]хъмь. въ съмѣрении сущемь и въ послушании.⁵¹

In its historical context, Feodosij's repeated exhortations that the monks obey their abbot were quite relevant; after his death, Stefan was forced out amid dissension in the monastery.⁵² Further transfers of power appear in

---

⁵⁰ "Only a little time has passed since I was favored to receive the sacrament from you, and if the Lord wills it, tomorrow I shall again be favored [to partake] of the sacrament." Ibid., 158.
⁵¹ "Having called [Stefan] and blessed him, the blessed one named him their abbot in his own place; and after greatly urging them to submit to [Stefan], he dismissed them .... And then, calling Stefan aside, he taught him about the care of that holy flock .... And when Saturday had come and day was dawning, the blessed one sent [someone] and summoned all the brethren .... 'Here is your abbot. Obey the one whom you yourselves have chosen, and have him as your spiritual father, and fear him, and do all things according to his command. And God ... give you the grace to work for him without vice and to be one in body and heart, in humility and obedience.'" *Uspenskij sbornik* (see n. 11), 128–129, col. 63a, ll. 18–25, 31 col. 63b, l. 3, 8–11, 22–29, col. 63c, 9–16.
⁵² D. Abramovič, *Das Paterikon des kiever Höhlenklosters*, 1931; reprint, Slavische Propyläen, 2, ed. Dmitrij Tschižewskij (Munich, 1964), 77. In Feodosij's chronicle obituary, the Caves monks are praised for their submissiveness: "въ любви пребывающе. меншии покаряющеся старѣишимъ. и не смѣюще пред ними г[лаго]лати. но все с покореньемь и с послушаньмь великымъ. такоже и старѣишии имя[ху] [editor's interpolation] любовь к меншимъ. наказаху утѣшающе. яко чада възлюбленая." ("Persisting in love, the lesser ones submitted to their elders and dared not speak before them, but with submission and great obedience withal. Likewise, the elders had love for their lessers; they instructed them comfortingly, as beloved children." *PSRL*, v. 1: *Lavrent'evskaja letopis' i Suzdal'skaja letopis' po Akademičeskomu spisku*, 2d ed. [1926; reprint, Moscow, 1962], 188.)

more or less factual biographies such as the *Lives* of Sergij of Radonež,[53] Kirill of Beloozero,[54] Daniil of Perejaslavl',[55] and Iosif of Volokolamsk.[56] Certain phrases are characteristic of these episodes; for example, the expression *o pastvě svjatogo togo stada* 'about the care of that holy flock,' seen in the *Life of Feodosij*, also occurs (with minor changes) in the *Lives* of Sergij of Radonež (Paxomij's redaction)[57] and Antonij Rimljanin.[58]

This topos reflects a real concern of dying abbots—the election and empowerment of a successor. In his will (1533), which is preserved in a sixteenth-century copy, Aleksandr Svirskij asks Archbishop Makarij of Novgorod and Pskov to choose his successor:"и азъ, государь, положу ли упованье на Бога да на тобя; а есть, государь, у Живоначалные Троицы во обители, въ нашей пустынкѣ, 4 священники, и азъ приказываю, государь, Богу да тобѣ, которого, государь, ты благословишъ въ тѣхъ 4 священникѣхъ, то имъ игуменъ."[59] In Aleksandr's vita, this petition is reported as part of an address to the Trinity monks and is juxtaposed with admonitions that resemble some of Feodosij's deathbed instructions:

> се оставляю вамъ въ себе мѣсто 4 браты во священноиноцѣхъ: Исаию и Никодима, Леонтия, Иродиона, и отъ тою же четырехъ братъ, его же Богъ восхощетъ и архиепископъ Макарий благословитъ, той да будетъ вамъ игуменъ въ мое мѣсто, и тому во всемъ да повинуетеся духовнѣ, вкупѣ же и тѣлеснѣ, того послушайте, и отца духовнаго себѣ имѣйте его, того бойтеся и повелѣния его вся творите.[60]

Convocation and Admonition

In a similar vein, the protagonists of death scenes are often depicted calling together those whom they have influenced in life—family, subjects, brethren, or spiritual children—to give them parting moral instructions—e.g., to be

---

[53] *Legenden des Sergij* (see n. 13), sect. 1, 67 (Epifanij's redaction), 143 (Epifanij's redaction with changes ascribed to Paxomij); sect. 2, 46 (Paxomij's redaction).
[54] *Pachomij Logofet* (see n. 33), xliii, xlv.
[55] *Žitie Daniila* (see n. 18), 71.
[56] *Skazanija* (see n. 16), 59–60, 123–125.
[57] *Legenden des Sergij* (see n. 13), sect. 2, 46.
[58] *Pamjatniki* (see n. 14), v. 1, 269–270.
[59] "And I, lord, will place my hope in God and in you. In Trinity monastery, in our hermitage, there are, lord, four priests, and I entrust [the matter], lord, to God and to you. Whichever of those four priests you consecrate, that is their abbot." *AI*, v. 1: 1334–1598 (St. Petersburg, 1841), no. 135, p. 195.
[60] "I leave you in my place four brothers [who are] hieromonks: Isaia and Nikodim, Leontij, Irodion; and the one of those four whom God wills and Archbishop Makarij consecrates, let him be your abbot in my place, and obey him in everything in spirit and also in flesh. Obey him and have him as your spiritual father. Fear him and do all his biddings." Jaxontov, *Žitija sv. severnorusskix podvižnikov* (see n. 17), 373.

pure physically and spiritually, live united in love, submit to their seniors, and deal faithfully and kindly with their juniors.⁶¹ The chief virtues stressed in such deathbed admonitions are obedience and brotherly love, as can be seen in Feodosij's *Life*:

> еже прѣбывати комужьдо въ порученѣи ему служьбѣ. съ вьсякыимь прилежаниемь и съ страхъмь б[о]жиемь. въ покорении и любъви. И тако пакы вься съ слъзами учааше. еже о сп[а]сении д[у]ши и боугодь-нѣмь житии. и о пощении. и еже къ ц[ь]ркви тъщание. и въ тои съ страхъмь стояние. и о братолюбии. и о покорении. еже не тъкъмо къ старѣишинамъ. нъ и къ съвъръстъныимь себѣ. любъвь и покорение имѣти.⁶²

The same themes are emphasized in the *Life of Antonij Rimljanin*. After teaching the monks how to elect abbots, Antonij bids them to live righteously and to submit to their abbot and elders:

> и пребудите у него въ постѣ, и въ молитвѣ, и въ трудехъ, въ поще-нниихъ, и во бдѣниихъ, и въ слезахъ, еще и в любвѣ межи собя, и в послушании ко игумену и къ отцемъ своимъ духовнымъ и ко старѣй-шимъ братиямъ.... И ина многа преподобный наказавъ братии, поу-чивъ яже ко спасению.⁶³

Similar deathbed admonitions can be found in relatively historical biographies such as the *Lives* of Stefan of Perm'⁶⁴ and Daniil of Perejaslavl',⁶⁵ and in vitae based on scanty information such as the *Life of Martirij of Zelenaja Pustynja*.⁶⁶

When such deathbed admonitions were brief in early redactions of a vita, the authors of later versions often expanded them with further teachings on

---

⁶¹ The deathbed admonition was also a recurrent element in Byzantine saint's lives—"either a hagiographic commonplace or a ritual act" (Abrahamse, "Rituals of Death" [see n. 10], 129).

⁶² "[He commanded] that each one persevere in the service entrusted to him with all diligence and with fear of God, in submission and in love. And so again with tears he taught [them] about salvation of the soul, and a godly life, and abstinence, and zeal for the church, and being in awe there, and brotherly love, and submission; [he taught them] to show love and submission not only to their seniors, but also to those who were of the same age as themselves." *Uspenskij sbornik* (see n. 11), 127, col. 62b1-19.

⁶³ "'And persevere with him in abstinence, and prayer, and works, and fasts, and watches, and tears, and furthermore in love among yourselves, and in obedience to the abbot and your spiritual fathers and your elder brothers' .... And the venerable one taught them many other things, inculcating that which leads to salvation." *Pamjatniki* (see n. 14), v. 1, 269.

⁶⁴ Ibid., v. 4, 157-158. Stefan's *Life* was written in the 1390s or early 1400s by his acquaintance, Epifanij Premudryj. Although Epifanij was not in Moscow when Stefan died, he based the death scene on eyewitness accounts. (See Ključevskij, *Žitija* [see n. 13], 93, 95-96; *Slovar'* [see n. 11], v. 2, pt. 1, 212-214.)

⁶⁵ *Žitie Daniila* (see n. 18), 71-72.

⁶⁶ Ibid., v. 4, 65.

the same themes. For instance, in the first redaction of the *Life of Sergij of Radonež*, Epifanij Premudryj merely alludes to the abbot's instructions: "и призва всю братию. и поучивъ ихъ о плъзѣ";[67] in the second redaction, Paxomij Logofet gives a more minute account of Sergij's admonition:

> и бесѣду простеръ и подобающая къ полъзѣ поучивъ непредкновеньно въ православии пребывати реч[е]. и единомыслие другъ къ другу хранити завѣща. имѣти же ч[и]стоту д[у]шевную и телесную. любовь нелицемѣрну. от злыхъ же и скверныхъ похотии отлучитис[я] пищу ж[е] и питье имѣти немятежьно. наипаче смирениемь украшатис[я]. страньнолюбия не забывати. съпротивословия удалятися и ни во что ж[е] вмѣняти житиа сего ч[е]сть же и славу но в мѣсто сихъ еже от б[ог]а мъздовъздаяния ожидати. и н[е]б[е]сныхъ вѣчныхъ бл[а]гъ наслаждение.[68]

When the earlier redactions of a biography lacked a deathbed admonition, later editors sometimes added the topos. This was the case, for example, in the second redaction of Ioann of Novgorod's vita.[69] In the extended redaction of Dovmont's *Life*, much of the deathbed admonition is drawn from the death scene of Sergij in Paxomij's redaction:

> призывает убо старейшины града и домочадца своя, и беседу полезну простер к ним поучив непредкновенно в православии пребывати, и единомыслие же и любовь друг ко другу имети, и всякими благими делы украшатися, и прочее мир имети.[70]

In the *Kniga stepennaja*, Grand Prince Vladimir is portrayed teaching his grieving nobles: "'нынѣ истинную обрѣтосте вѣру, въ ней же неуклонно пребывайте, и твердо стойте, и усердно крѣпитесь.'" Earlier versions of the life recount his death and burial but do not include a deathbed admonition.[71]

---

[67] "And he called all the brethren and instructed them for their benefit." *Legenden des Sergij* (see n. 13), sect. 1, 67; similarly in Epifanij's redaction with changes attributed to Paxomij Logofet (ibid., sect. 1, 143).

[68] "And he gave a discourse; and having taught [them] that which could benefit them, he told them to remain constantly in orthodoxy. And he commanded them to preserve their unanimity; to have spiritual and physical purity [and] unfeigned love; and to separate themselves from wicked and vile desires; and to take their food and drink in an orderly fashion. Most of all, [he commanded them] to adorn themselves with humility; and not to forget hospitality to strangers; to distance themselves from argument; and to consider the honor and glory of this life as nothing, but instead await reward from God and the delight of heavenly eternal blessings." Ibid., sect. 2, 47. Paxomij depicts Nikon, Sergij's successor, making a briefer deathbed admonition (ibid., sect. 2, 83, 103).

[69] *Skazanija* (see n. 16), 29–30.

[70] "Then he summoned the elders of the city and his servants and gave them a beneficial discourse, teaching them to remain constantly in orthodoxy, and to have unanimity and love for one another, and to adorn themselves with good works of every sort, and in general to have peace." Oxotnikova, *Povest' o Dovmonte* (see n. 23), 225.

[71] "Now you have found the true faith; remain steadfast in it, and stand firmly, and strengthen yourselves zealously." *Kniga stepennaja carskago rodoslovija* (see n. 95), v. 1, 174. There is no

Although these admonitions are all represented as speeches, there is some evidence that abbots, at least, wrote down their parting instructions to their flocks; in particular, the founders of monasteries often wrote a monastery rule or included specific guidelines in their last wills to ensure that the customs they established would be continued. As mentioned above, the first redaction of the *Life of Evfrosin of Pskov* alludes to such a "rule"; in his will, the autograph of which is preserved in his monastery in Pskov, Evfrosin does indeed stipulate several brief regulations for his successor, Xarlampij, and the monks.[72] The *Life of Iona of Novgorod* mentions that he composed a "testament" (*zavětъ*) concerning Otenskaja Pustyn', the monastery that he had founded.[73] The *Life of Iosif of Volokolamsk* includes two "wills"—a petition to Vasilij Ivanovič and a lengthy rule for the future abbots and monks of his monastery.[74] In the petition, Iosif asks the grand prince to choose his successor and to ensure that the monks obey the abbot and the rule:

> и тотъ бы игуменъ да и братия жили по моему велѣнию, какъ язъ имъ написалъ, и ко игумену повиновение имѣли. А иже не восхощетъ по моему велѣнию игуменъ или которая братия въ монастырѣ жити, и имутъ нѣчто общаго житиа чинъ разоряти, о семъ убо тебѣ, государю своему, челомъ бию и съ слезами молюся, да не попустиши сему быти; но не хотящаа по моему велѣнию жити, тѣхъ изъ монастыря изженути, яко да и прочая братия страхъ имутъ.[75]

In a similar fashion, Kirill of Beloozero beseeches Grand Prince Andrej Dmitrievič in his will to uphold Innokentij, his successor, and expel any disobedient monks from the monastery.[76]

---

deathbed admonition in the short prologue, reworked extended, or later reworked extended redactions (N. Serebrjanskij, *Drevne-russkie knjažeskie žitija; Obzor redakcij i teksty* [Moscow, 1915], app., 16, 21, 26, respectively). Although its textual history is controversial, Vladimir Svjatoslavič's *Life* was probably composed in the second half of the eleventh century from chronicle records; the reworked redaction was evidently written in Northern Rus' in the fourteenth century. (See *Slovar'* [see n. 11], v. 1, 288–290, and v. 2, pt. 1, 74.)

[72] *Akty, sobrannye v bibliotekax i arxivax Rossijskoj imperii Arxeografičeskoju ėkspedicieju Imperatorskoj akademii nauk*, v. 1: *1294–1598* (St. Petersburg, 1836), no. 108, p. 83.

[73] *Pamjatniki* (see n. 14), v. 4, 34.

[74] *Skazanija* (see n. 16), 120–122, 140–373.

[75] "And let the abbot and the brethren live according to my commandment, as I wrote to them, and let them show obedience to the abbot. And if the abbot or any of the brethren do not wish to live in the monastery according to my commandment, and violate the order of the shared way of life in some way, I petition you, my lord, and beseech you with tears not to permit this, but to drive those who do not want to live according to my commandment from the monastery, so that the other brethren will have fear." Ibid., 121–122.

[76] *Akty social'no-ėkonomičeskoj istorii* (see n. 27), no. 314, p. 278; *Pachomij Logofet* (see n. 28), xliii.

Deathbed instructions of this sort seem to have been expected from abbots or, at any rate, the founders of monasteries. In his account of Pafnutij of Borovsk's death, Innokentij reveals that he was concerned because the abbot had not made a testament: "азъ же от многых помыслъ борим, како хощеть после старца быти строение монастырьское, понеже старець ничто же о сих глаголеть";⁷⁷ so he actually asked him to write "a testament about the monastery order" ("завѣщание о монастырьском строении"). Pafnutij then dictated a brief rule, evidently with some reluctance, and predicted that the monks would disobey it. This conduct was apparently so unusual that Innokentij thought no one would believe it; immediately after this passage, he digresses to insist that his account is true, and he cites several witnesses to prove that Pafnutij made this prophecy.⁷⁸

Obedience and the Testament

Deathbed exhortations to obedience, usually in connection with a transfer of power, can also be found in princely biographies and chronicle death scenes. In the internecine climate of early Rus', such injunctions had not only moral but also legal and political significance because of the institution of the state will. The theme of obedience to a dead man's wishes, especially in the matter of succession, recalls the entire premise of last wills; this similarity is not accidental, since literary death scenes and wills drew their substance from the same real-world situation. Moreover, clergymen not only wrote the vitae and chronicles in which death scenes appear, but also assisted in the creation of legal testaments. From the thirteenth to the fifteenth century wills in both northeastern and northwestern Rus' almost invariably list clerics as witnesses and copyists.⁷⁹ In some cases, the documents begin with a formulaic benediction to show that they have passed

---

⁷⁷ "I [was] worried by many thoughts about how the elder wanted the monastery order to be after his death, since he had said nothing about it." *Pamjatniki literatury* (see n. 25), 496.

⁷⁸ Ibid., 496. Later Pafnutij gives further moral instructions in an address to all the brothers (498, 500).

⁷⁹ Spiritual fathers and other clerics are mentioned in all of the pre-fifteenth-century northwestern testaments in *Gramoty Velikogo Novgoroda i Pskova* (ed. S. N. Valk [Moscow and Leningrad, 1949]) that name witnesses (24 out of 28). Clergymen serve as witnesses in eight out of the ten wills in *Novye pskovskie gramoty XIV–XIV vekov*, ed. L. M. Marasinova (Moscow, 1966). Spiritual fathers are named as witnesses in 13 out of the 18 northeastern state wills from before the sixteenth century in *Duxovnye i dogovornye gramoty velikix i udel'nyx knjazej XIV–XVI vv.*, ed. L. V. Čerepnin (Moscow and Leningrad, 1950). On the participation of churchmen in will-making, see G. V. Semenčenko, "Načal'naja čast' duxovnyx gramot votčinnikov Severo-vostočnoj Rusi XIV–XV vv.," in *Istočnikovedenie otečestvennoj istorii; Sbornik statej*, 1989, ed. V. A. Kučkin (Moscow, 1989), 226–229.

through the hands of the metropolitan.[80] Such practices continued in the later medieval period; sixteenth- and seventeenth-century Muscovite wills indicate that "churchmen were regularly in attendance when testaments were drawn up."[81] Clerics were well-suited to help with wills because they were literate, exercised social and spiritual authority, and had to be present anyway to perform the last rites. In the Northwest, testators usually waited until they were near death before making their wills, in which they stated that they were "departing this world," "at the point of death," or "lying in sickness."[82] Similar remarks appear in testaments from northeastern Rus',[83] and there is evidence that the practice of making wills just before death continued in sixteenth- and seventeenth-century Muscovy.[84] Thus, the dying customarily fulfilled their final secular and religious obligations at about the same time,[85] and churchmen were on hand to help them in both duties.[86]

The evidence from death scenes suggests will-making was primarily an oral ceremony: testators dictated their wills and had them read in the presence of the heirs and witnesses.[87] The death scene of Volodimir Vasil'kovič in the Galician-Volynian Chronicle (1287) presents a vivid picture of the testamentary process. Realizing that there will be rival claimants to the succession if he dies intestate, Volodimir names his brother Mstislav heir and disinherits

---

[80] Seven of the wills in *Duxovnye i dogovornye gramoty* begin with the metropolitan's benediction. In the early cases, at least, testators sought the metropolitan's authority because they feared that their testaments would be contested; his blessing ensured compliance through the threat of religious sanctions (Semenčenko, "Načal'naja čast'," 226–228, with examples from private wills). This recalls the exhortations to obedience in death scenes.

[81] Daniel H. Kaiser, "Death and Dying in Early Modern Russia," Kennan Institute Occasional Papers, no. 228 (Washington, 1988), 8.

[82] The formula *otxodja sego světa* 'departing this life' or variants appears in *Gramoty Velikogo Novgoroda i Pskova* (see n. 90), no. 126, p. 184; no. 210, p. 237; no. 217, p. 241; no. 239, p. 256; no. 257, p. 266; no. 320, p. 308; and no. 328, p. 312; and in *Novye pskovskie gramoty* (see n. 79), no. 15, p. 57; no. 18, p. 59; and no. 33, p. 33. The formula *leža v bolezni* 'lying in illness' occurs in ibid., no. 8, p. 51; and no. 14, p. 56. The formula *pri smerti* 'at the point of death' is found in ibid., no. 10, p. 53. See also V. F. Andreev, *Novgorodskij častnyj akt XII–XV vv.* (Leningrad, 1986), 102–103; and Semenčenko, "Načal'naja čast'" (see n. 79), 232.

[83] According to Semenčenko ("Načal'naja čast'" [see n. 79], 232), testators in the Northeast usually drew up their wills before their illness was far advanced, while in Novgorod and Pskov they waited until they were on the brink of death; thus formulae indicating imminent death are more common in northwestern wills than in northeastern ones.

[84] Kaiser, "Death and Dying" (see n. 81), 5–8, 15–16.

[85] In addition to property dispositions, wills often include arrangements to pay or collect debts, i.e., to discharge various temporal obligations (Semenčenko, "Načal'naja čast'" [see n. 79], 232–233, 238, n. 41).

[86] Clergymen even took responsibility for wills after the testators' demise; wills were often stored in church and monastery archives (Kaiser, "Death and Dying" [see n. 81], 3).

[87] On the primarily oral nature of wills, see Daniel H. Kaiser, *The Growth of the Law in Medieval Russia* (Princeton, 1980), 153; and Henrik Birnbaum, "Orality, Literacy, and Literature in Old Rus'," *Die Welt der Slaven* 30 (1985): 167.

his other male relatives who have offended him. Later Volodimir has a scribe write a will that makes Mstislav heir and a second document that vouchsafes property rights to his wife. Mstislav takes an oath to respect his sister-in-law's legacy and to protect Volodimir's stepdaughter; Volodimir's boyars and local and foreign citizens serve as witnesses to the documents.[88] A similar process can be seen in other death scenes; for instance, in the Kiev Chronicle (1172), Mstislav Izjaslavič of Vladimir has his brother swear not to infringe on his children's territory.[89]

Wills in any society have a paradoxical aspect, aptly formulated in the modern aphorism that a testament is "the expression of the will of a man who no longer has any will, respecting property which is no longer his property."[90] Because of the ethic of political expediency, which made oath-breaking a frequent practice, early Russian testators could not be sure that their wills would be respected, especially with the complicated system of legal succession and the redistribution of property that took place when a prince died. In his instruction, Vladimir Monomax condemns the faithlessness of contemporary politics; he admonishes his grandsons to respect the rights and territories of their "brothers"—i.e., fellow princes: "аще ли вы будет[е] кр[е]стъ цѣловати к братьи или г кому. а ли управивъше с[е]рдце свое. на немже можете устояти. тоже цѣлуите. и цѣловавше блюдѣте. да не приступни погубите д[у]шѣ своеѣ."[91] The epithet *bratoljubecь* 'one who loves his brother' is used as a term of praise in obituaries—for example, that of Gleb Jur'evič in the Kiev Chronicle (1173): "сеи бѣ князь. братолюбець. къ кому любо кр[е]стъ цѣловашеть. то не ступашеть его и до см[е]рти."[92] The early Russian concept of the brotherhood of princes was not egalitarian but hierarchical—"younger brothers" (subordinate princes) were supposed to submit to "elder brothers." The virtue of "brother-love" (bratoljubie) gave political meaning to Christian "brotherly love" (φιλαδελφία);[93] therefore,

---

[88] *PSRL*, v. 2: *Ipat'evskaja letopis'* (1908; reprint, Moscow, 1962), col. 900–907.
[89] Ibid., col. 559.
[90] Cited in Barry Nicholas, *An Introduction to Roman Law*, Clarendon Law Series (Oxford, 1982), 252.
[91] "If you will make an oath to your brothers or to anyone, only swear if you are sure in your heart that you can uphold it; and once you have sworn, observe [it], lest you destroy your soul as transgressors." *PSRL*, v. 1 (see n. 52), 245.
[92] "He was a prince who loved his brothers; if he made an oath to anyone, he never violated it, even unto death." Ibid., v. 2 (see n. 88), 563. On epithets in chronicle obituaries, see Eremin, *Lekcii i stat'i* (see n. 2), 62.
[93] See D. S. Lixačev, "Voprosy ideologii feodalov v literature XI–XIII vv.," *TODRL* 10 (1954): 87–88; and Norman W. Ingham, "The Martyred Prince and the Question of Slavic Cultural Continuity in the Early Middle Ages," in *Medieval Russian Culture*, ed. Henrik Birnbaum and Michael S. Flier, California Slavic Studies, no. 12 (Berkeley, Los Angeles, and London, 1984), 47–48.

testators could use the threat of divine retribution to ensure that their survivors lived in peace with one another and obeyed their successors.

Thus, death scenes and wills have the same real-world context and an identical purpose—to inculcate obedience, whether for purely moral or for pragmatic legal and political reasons.[94] In a very early example of a deathbed admonition in the Primary Chronicle (1054), Jaroslav Mudryj summons his sons, advises them to live in unity, and tells them how he will divide their patrimony; he predicts that princely feuding will wreak devastation upon Rus'. With its emphasis on brotherly love and property division, this passage recalls a will in both theme and language:

наряди с[ы]ны своя рекъ имъ. се азъ отхожю свѣта сего с[ы]н[о]ве мои. имѣите в собѣ любовь. понеже вы есте брат[ь]я единого о[т]ца и м[а]т[е]ре. да аще будете в любви межю собою. Б[ог]ъ будеть в васъ. и покоривыть [сиц] вы противныя подъ вы. и будете мирно живуще. аще ли будете ненавидно живуще. в распряхъ и котораюещеся то погыбнете сами. [и] [погубите] [editor's interpolations] землю о[те]ць своихъ и дѣдъ своихъ иже налѣзоша трудомь своимь великымъ. но пребываите мирно послушающе брат брата. се же поручаю в собе мѣсто столъ старѣишему с[ы]ну моему и брату вашему Изяславу Кыевъ. сего послушаите якож[е] послушасте мене. да то вы будеть в мене мѣсто. а С[вя]тославу даю Черниговъ. а Всеволоду Переяславль. [а Игорю Володимерь] [editor's interpolation] а Вячеславу Смолинецкъ. и тако раздѣли имъ грады. заповѣдавъ имъ не преступати предѣла братня. ни сгонити рекъ Изяславу. аще кто хощеть обидѣти брата своего. то ты помагаи егоже обидять. и тако уряди с[ы]ны своя пребывати в любви.[95]

---

[94] As expressions of the wishes of the dead, wills naturally had religious as well as legal significance; cf. the Muscovite terms *duxovnaja* and *duševnaja (gramota)* 'will,' which derive from *duxъ* 'spirit' and *duša* 'soul,' respectively. The religious language of several characteristic testamentary formulae may have made wills useful and accessible for hagiographic writing. Wills often begin with a cross or a religious *invocatio* (dedication), e.g., in Ivan Kalita's will, "во имя о[т]ця и с[ы]на и с[вята]го д[у]ха" ("in the name of the Father and the Son and the Holy Spirit"; *Duxovnye i dogovornye gramoty* [see n. 79], no. 1a, p. 7). Testators almost invariably name themselves with the formula *se jazъ grěšnyi xudyi rabъ b[o]žii* ('I, a sinful wretched servant of God'). The use of *blagosloviti* 'bless' as a synonym of *prikazyvati* 'bequeath, entrust' or *dati* 'give' may also be significant in this regard; cf. the will of Semen Ivanovič (1353): "а чимъ мя бл[а]г[о]с[ло]вилъ о[те]ць мои . . ." ("and with that which my father blessed me . . ."; ibid., no. 3, p. 13). See A. S. Lappo-Danilevskij, *Očerk russkoj diplomatiki častnyx aktov* (Petrograd, 1918), 135–136; S. M. Kaštanov, "Diplomatičeskij sostav drevnerusskogo akta," *Vospomogatel'nye istoričeskie discipliny* 2 (1969): 145, n. 8; idem, *Očerki russkoj diplomatiki* (Moscow, 1970), 40–41; Semenčenko, "Načal'naja čast'" (see n. 79), 229–230.

[95] "He admonished his sons, telling them, 'I am leaving this life, my sons. Love one another, because you are brothers, with a single father and mother. And if you love one another, God will be among you and will make all those who oppose you subject to you, and you will live in peace. But if you live in animosity, in feuds and quarrels, you yourselves will perish, and you will ruin the land of your fathers and grandfathers, which they acquired by their own great

Other texts, e.g., the obituary of Mixail Aleksandrovič of Tver' (1399), explicitly mention wills.[96]

Because they originated in the same context, wills could serve as sources for literary death scenes. For example, in his chronicle obituary, Dmitrij Donskoj is portrayed dividing his realm among his sons. Dmitrij first urges his sons to love one another and obey their eldest brother:

> И рече сыномъ своимъ: «Вы же, сынове мои, плод чрева моего, бога боитеся, помните писаное: 'Чьсти отца и матере, да благо ти будет.' Миръ и любовь межи собою имѣйте. Аз бо предаю вас богови и матери вашей, и под страхомь ея будите всегда. Обяжите собѣ заповѣдь мою на шию свою, и вложите словеса моя в сердце ваше. Аще ли не послушаете родитель своихъ, помянѣте писаное: 'Клятва отчяя домъ чядом раздрушит, и матерне въздыхание до конца искоренить.' Аще ли послушаете — длъголѣтни будете на земли и в благыхъ пребудет душа ваша, и умножится слава дому вашего, врази ваши падут под ногами вашими, и иноплеменници побѣгнут от лица вашего, и облегчится тягота земли вашей, и умножатся нивы ваша обильемь.... все творите с повелѣниемь родителя своего.[97]

The author presents this testament primarily as an oral act, and only as if by afterthought as a written text; nevertheless, he makes obvious citations from Dmitrij's actual will,[98] which contains several exhortations to obedi-

---

labor. Instead, remain in peace, brother obeying brother. I entrust my throne of Kiev to my eldest son and your brother, Izjaslav, in my place. Obey him as you do me; let him take my place for you. And to Svjatoslav I give Černigov, and to Vsevolod Perejaslavl', and to Igor' Vladimir, and to Vjačeslav Smolensk.' And he thus divided the cities among them, having commanded them not to transgress a brother's share or to drive [him] out. He said to Izjaslav, 'If anyone offends his brother, help the offended party.' And so he enjoined his sons to persevere in love." *PSRL*, v. 1, 161. In the *Kniga stepennaja carskago rodoslovija, soderžaščaja istoriju rossijskuju s načala onyja do vremen gosudarja carja i velikogo knjazja Ioanna Vasil'eviča,* ed. Gerard Friderik Miller, 2 vols. (Moscow, 1775), v. 1, 224, only the homiletic portions of the testament are retained.

[96] *PSRL*, v. 7: *Letopis' po voskresenskomu spisku* (St. Petersburg, 1856), 74; cf. ibid., vols. 11–12: *Patriaršaja ili Nikonovskaja letopis'* (1897–1901; reprint, Moscow, 1965), 180.

[97] And he said to his sons, 'My sons, fruit of my loins [literally, 'belly'], fear God. Remember that which is written: "Honor thy father and thy mother, that it may go well with thee." Have peace and love among yourselves. I entrust you to God and your mother; and always be in fear of her. Tie my commandment about your neck, and place my words in your heart. If you do not obey your parents, remember that which is written: "A father's curse destroys the children's house, and a mother's sighing tears it down completely." If you obey, you will live long in the land and your soul will be blessed, and the glory of your house will increase, your enemies will fall beneath your feet, and foreigners will flee from before your face, and the burden of your land will be eased, and your fields will give forth abundantly . . . Do everything according to your parent's commandment.'" *Pamjatniki literatury. XIV–ser. XV veka*, 216.

[98] Dmitrij's will was written between 13 April and 16 May 1389 (L. V. Čerepnin, *Russkie feodal'nye arxivy XIV–XV vekov,* 2 vols. [Moscow and Leningrad, 1948–1951], v. 1, 59).

ence, albeit more laconic ones. Immediately after that document's incipit, Dmitrij appoints his wife executrix and entrusts his sons to her guidance: "приказываю дѣти свои своеи княгинѣ. А вы, дѣти мои, жывите заодин, а м[а]т[е]ри своее слушаите во всем";[99] the corresponding statement in the biography ("миръ и любовь межи собою имѣите. Аз бо предаю вас богови и матери вашеи, и под страхомь ея будите всегда")[100] gives Dmitrij's wife a moral rather than a legal authority. In fact, her status as executrix gave her the right to reapportion her sons' patrimony, should one of them die or lose his share; thus Dmitrij feared that his sons might resent or resist their mother's interference and envy their brothers' shares, and he repeatedly commands them to obey her in the will:

> А по грѣхом, которого с[ы]на моего б[ог]ъ отъимет, и княгини моя подѣлит того удѣлом с[ы]н[о]въ моих. Которому что дастъ, то тому и есть, а дѣти мои изъ ее воли не вымутьс[я].... А у которого с[ы]на моего убудет о[т]ч[и]ны, чѣмъ есмъ его бл[а]г[о]с[ло]вилъ, и княгини моя подѣлит с[ы]н[о]въ моихъ изъ их удѣловъ. А вы, дѣти мои, м[а]т[е]ри слушаите. А по грѣхом, отъимет б[ог]ъ с[ы]на моего, князя Василья, а хто будет подъ тѣм с[ы]нъ мои, ино тому с[ы]ну моему княжъ Васильевъ удѣл, а того удѣломъ подѣлит их моя княгини. А вы, дѣти мои, слушаите своее м[а]т[е]ри, что кому дастъ, то тому и есть.[101]

At the end of the will's dispositions, Dmitrij reinforces his wife's authority with a sanction: "а вы, дѣти мои, слушаите своее м[а]т[е]ри во всем, изъ ее воли не выступаитеся ни в чем. А которыи с[ы]нъ мои не имет слушати свое м[а]т[е]ри, а будет не въ ее воли, на том не будет моего бл[а]г[о]с[ло]в[е]нья."[102] Similarly, in the biography, Dmitrij describes the consequences of disobedience, but without reference to his wife's legal powers and with the sanctions couched in biblical terms. The theme of submission is taken even further in the biography than in the will; Dmitrij

---

[99] "I entrust my children to my wife. And you, my children, live in unity, and obey your mother in everything." *Duxovnye i dogovornye gramoty* (see n. 79), no. 12, p. 33.

[100] "Have peace and love among yourselves. I entrust you to God and to your mother; and always be in fear of her." *Pamjatniki literatury. XIV–ser. XV veka* (see n. 98), 216.

[101] "And if because of sins God takes away any of my sons, my wife will divide his share among my [other] sons. Whatever she gives to anyone is his; and my children must not disobey her wish. And if any of my sons loses the patrimony with which I blessed him, my wife will provide for him from out of the shares of my [other] son; and you, my sons, obey your mother. And if because of sins God takes away my son, Prince Vasilij, whichever of my sons comes after him [in rank] will get Prince Vasilij's share; and my wife will divide his [former] share among [my other sons]. And you, my children, obey your mother; whatever she gives to anyone is his." *Duxovnye i dogovornye gramoty* (see n. 79), no. 12, p. 35.

[102] "And you, my children, obey your mother in everything; do not go against her will in anything. And if any of my sons does not obey his mother, and does not submit to her, my blessing will not be upon him." Ibid., p. 36.

is depicted admonishing his boyars as well: "послужите княгини моей и чядом моимъ от всего сердця своего, въ время радости повеселитеся с ними, и въ время скръби не оставите их: да скръбь ваша на радость преложится."[103]

The common theme of obedience even made it appropriate to quote legal documents directly in literary death scenes; a striking example can be found in the *Life of Fedor Černyj of Jaroslavl'*. On the day before his death, Fedor summons his family and commands them to live in peace:

> призва княгиню свою и дѣти своя. и начатъ г[лаго]лати о любви. учити и наказати и пребывати во единои любви и г[лаго]ла имъ дѣти мои. аще кто в васъ сблюдеть слово мое. бл[а]г[о]с[ло]в[ле]ние мое будеть на немъ. аще ли кто въ васъ не соблюдеть. бл[а]г[о]с[ло]вления моего не буди на немъ.[104]

Fedor's command that his sons follow his word recalls the blessing for obedience in Vasilij Dmitrievič's first will (1406–1407): "а ты, с[ы]нъ мои, княз[ь] Иван, держи мат[е]рь свою во чти и в матерствѣ, как богъ реклъ, а мое бла[го]словен[ь]е на тоб[ѣ]."[105] Moreover, the last sentence of the passage strongly resembles the sanction formulae found in state wills—cf. Dmitrij Donskoj's testament: "а хто сю грамоту мою порушитъ, судит ему б[ог]ъ, а не будет на нем м[и]л[о]сти б[ож]ии, ни моего бл[а]г[о]с[лове]нья ни в сии вѣк, ни в будущии".[106] Such formulae were a traditional part of the diplomatics of wills in both northwestern and northeastern Rus'.[107]

It is unknown whether Fedor actually made a will; there is no mention

---

[103] "Serve my wife and children with all your heart. Rejoice with them in times of joy; do not abandon them in times of grief. May your grief be turned into joy." *Pamjatniki literatury. XIV–ser. XV veka* (see n. 98), 216, 218.

[104] "He called his wife and his children and began to speak about love, to teach and admonish them to be united in love. And he said to them, 'My children, if any of you observes my dictum, my blessing will be upon him; but if any of you does not observe [it], let my blessing not be upon him.'" Serebrjanskij, *Drevne-russkie knjažeskie žitija* (see n. 71), app., 91–92 (prologue redaction). The prologue version of the *Life of Fedor Rostislavič* (died 19 September 1299), usually considered the first redaction, was based on a contemporary account of Fedor's death in a lost local chronicle. (See ibid., 224; Ključevskij, *Žitija* [see n. 13], 171; *Slovar'* [see n. 11], v. 1, 179–181; Gail Lenhoff, "Die nordostrussische Hagiographie im literarischen Prozess: Die Vita des Fürsten Fedor Černyj," in *Gattung und Genealogie der slavisch-orthodoxen Literaturen des Mittelalters (Dritte Berliner Fachtagung, 1988)*, ed. K.-D. Seeman [forthcoming].)

[105] "And you, my son, Prince Ivan, hold your mother in honor and the respect due to a mother, as God said, and my blessing [be] upon you." *Duxovnye i dogovornye gramoty* (see n. 79), no. 20, p. 57.

[106] "And if anyone violates this my writ, God will judge him; and God's mercy will not be upon him, nor my blessing either in this age or in the one to come." Ibid., no. 12, p. 36.

[107] Similar formulae appear in the wills of Ivan Ivanovič, Vasilij Dmitrievič, Ivan III, and Ivan IV (ibid., no. 4a, p. 17; no. 21, p. 59; no. 89, p. 364; and no. 104, p. 444). See Andreev, *Novgorodskij častnyj akt* (see n. 82), 108; and Kaštanov, *Očerki* (see n. 94), 42–43.

of one in his vita or other sources. The oldest attested document from Jaroslavl', a charter of grant (*žalovannaja*) from Fedor's grandson Vasilij Davydovič to Savior Monastery (ca. 1320s), may incorporate a lost writ from Fedor's time.[108] Significantly, its *sanctio* bears a strong resemblance to the phrase "бл[а]г[о]с[ло]вления моего не буди на немъ" ("my blessing will not be upon him") in Fedor's life: "а через сю грамоту кто посягнет на дом святого Спаса, и милости святого Спаса не буди на нем."[108] The apodosis in both these sanctions has the structure *noun* (a desired state of grace or blessing) + *possessive* (the giver of that desired state) + *ne budi na nemъ* (whoever violates the command).[110] Thus, Vasilij Davidovič's charter provides evidence that a legal formula similar to the one in Fedor's *Life* was known in Jaroslavl' and in Savior Monastery around the time when the first redaction was composed there.

Parting Forgiveness and Blessings

Confessions of sin and prayers for forgiveness were an important part of the early Russian services for the dying and the dead.[111] Likewise, in death scenes the protagonists publicly ask forgiveness for their trespasses (*prašati proščenie*) and grant forgiveness (*dati* or *spodobljati proščenie*) to all who have trespassed against them—e.g., in the *Life of Fedor of Jaroslavl'*: "испо-вѣдаяся пред всѣми. еже согрѣши къ кому. или нелюбие подержа. или кто к нему согрѣши враждова нань. всѣ бл[а]г[о]с[ло]ви и прости. во всемь винна собе сотвори пред б[о]гомъ."[112] This exchange of pardons, a

---

[108] *Akty social'no-èkonomičeskoj istorii* (see n. 27), v. 3 (Moscow, 1964), no. 190, p. 204, attested only in eighteenth- and early nineteenth-century copies. In the incipit, Vasilij refers to Fedor's document: "по деда своего грамоте" ("in accordance with my grandfather's writ"). M. S. Čerkasova ("Drevnejšaja jaroslavskaja žalovannaja gramota XIV v.," *Vospomogatel'nye istoričeskie discipliny* 19 [1987]: 41–43) argues that it incorporates a lost writ from Fedor's reign, since the abbot is termed *arximandrit* (his title under Vasilij) in the incipit, but *igumen* elsewhere.

[109] "And if anyone in violation of this writ encroaches on the house of the Holy Savior, let the mercy of the Holy Savior not be upon him." *Akty social'no-èkonomičeskoj istorii*, v. 3, no. 190, 204. As is usual, the formula invokes the monastery's patron (see Andreev, *Novgorodskij častnyj akt* [see n. 82], 108, n. 125).

[110] The fact that the precise formula seen in Fedor's *Life* is unattested is immaterial. Although the *sanctio* of wills had become more or less standardized in the Northwest by the late fourteenth century (ibid., 108–109), there was no set formula in the Northeast as late as the sixteenth century.

[111] Cf. "Čin byvaemyi na razlučenie d[u]ši ot tela, vnegda bratu iznemogajušču," "Kanon za umeršix obščij," and "Kanon za edinoumeršago," in *Staroobrjadčeskij učebnyj časovnik* (see n. 47), 67v ff., 73v ff., and 78v ff.

[112] "Before everyone he confessed if he had sinned or nurtured hatred against anyone, or if anyone had sinned against him [or] borne him enmity. He blessed and forgave everyone; he made himself responsible before God in everything." Serebrjanskij, *Drevne-russkie knjažeskie žitija* (see n. 71), app., 91.

ritualistic means of discharging social and religious debts, is mentioned in other death scenes, including those of Pimen of the Kiev Caves,[113] Kirill of Beloozero,[114] and Iulianija Osor'ina;[115] moreover, it is added as a topos in redactions of the *Lives* of Aleksandr Nevskij[116] and Mixail Klopskij.[117] The *Life of Evfimij of Novgorod* reports four such exchanges: when the leading citizens and clergy of Novgorod learned that he was dying; when the populace met him on his way to Holy Theotokos Monastery; when the monks received him at the cloister; and when he was about to die.[118] In addition, at the beginning of his illness, Evfimij sends a letter (*proščalьnaja gramota*) to Metropolitan Iona of Kiev, to obtain his blessing and forgiveness.[119] Iona's actual reply (1458), which arrived too late, is preserved in a sixteenth-century copy. After blessing Evfimij and expressing sadness about his illness, Iona informs Evfimij that he has offended him by harboring Kievan exiles, urges him to ask God's forgiveness, and offers his own pardon.[120]

Besides asking for and granting forgiveness, the protagonists of death scenes are often depicted blessing (*blagosloviti*) everyone present or giving them "peace" (*podati mirъ*, cf. Greek τὴν εἰρήνην δίδοσθαι) or "(final) love and peace" (*konečnuju ljubovь i mirъ*)—e.g., in the death scene of Mixail Aleksandrovič in the Simeon Chronicle: "онъ же смирено всѣмъ поклонився, конечную любовь и миръ имъ подавъ."[121] Similar formulae occur in the lives of Fedor of Jaroslavl',[122] Dmitrij Donskoj,[123] and Iulianija Osor'ina;[124] in later redactions of the vitae of Aleksandr Nevskij,[125] and Mixail Klopskij (second and third redactions).[126] Furthermore, in many death scenes, the protagonist gives everyone present a "final kiss," as in the

---

[113] Abramovič, *Das Paterikon des kiever Höhlenklosters* (see n. 52), 183.
[114] *Pachomij Logofet* (see n. 28), xlv.
[115] Ibid., v. 1, 66.
[116] Mansikka, *Žitie Aleksandra* (see n. 23), app., 25 (Vladimir redaction), 46 (Vasilij-Varlaam's redaction).
[117] *Povesti o žitii Mixaila* (see n. 22), 137 (second redaction), 158 (Tučkov's redaction).
[118] *Pamjatniki* (see n. 14), v. 4, 21. *The Life of Archbishop Evfimij II of Novgorod* (died 11 March 1458) was written by Paxomij Logofet. Its detailed death scene was evidently based on Paxomij's recollections and other eyewitness accounts. (See Ključevskij, *Žitija* [see n. 13], 153, 155–156; *Slovar'* [see n. 11], v. 2, pt. 2, 172.
[119] Ibid., v. 4, 22.
[120] *AI* (see n. 59), no. 269, pp. 500–501.
[121] "He humbly bowed to all after giving them final love and peace." *PSRL,* v. 18 (see n. 96), 147; cf. ibid., v. 7 (see n. 96), 73; ibid., vols. 11–12 (see n. 96), 181; v. 15, pt. 1 (see n. 96), col. 172–173.
[122] Serebrjanskij, *Drevne-russkie knjažeskie žitija* (see n. 71), app., 92.
[123] *Pamjatniki literatury. XIV-ser. XV veka* (see n. 98), 218.
[124] Ibid., v. 1, 66.
[125] Mansikka, *Žitie Aleksandra* (see n. 23), app., 46 (Vasilij-Varlaam's redaction).
[126] *Povesti o žitii Mixaila* (see n. 22), 137 (second redaction), 158 (Tučkov's redaction).

Life of Feodosij: "посълавъ блаженыи призъва братию. и тако по единому вься цѣлова плачюща ся и кричаща."[127] This topos of a farewell kiss also appears in the vitae of Varlaam of Xutyn',[128] Mixail Aleksandrovič (in the Voskresenskaja and Nikon Chronicles),[129] Aleksandr Svirskij,[130] and others.

The biographies of Pafnutij of Borovsk clearly indicate that these topoi were based on the social norm. Innokentij recounts how Pafnutij called the monks into his cell one by one to ask their forgiveness, but he offended a monk from another monastery by refusing to bless him. Later he again asked the monks, including a priest whom he had hitherto spurned, to pardon him. However, Pafnutij refused to admit boyars, common people, and messengers that had come from the local prince Mixail, Grand Prince Ivan Vasil'evič, dowager Grand Princess Marija, Grand Princess Sofija, and Metropolitan Gerontij to ask his forgiveness and bid him peace. He rejected money sent with letters asking for his prayers and forgiveness on the grounds that he needed prayer and forgiveness more than anyone. Finally, Pafnutij balked at going to church on his last day when he saw that the courtyard was crowded with well-wishers seeking his farewell benediction. In all of these cases, the outsiders who expected to get Pafnutij's blessing were offended; Innokentij himself confesses his embarrassment and even remonstrated with Pafnutij about the Grand Prince's messengers.[131] In the vita, Vassian Sanin felt it necessary to make Pafnutij's conduct conform to expectations; thus he reports that Pafnutij received all the visitors:

> самодержецъ всея русии, князь великии иванъ васильевичь, и сынъ его благовѣрныи великии князь иванъ ивановичь, и пресвященныи митрополитъ героньтие, и отъ всѣхъ предѣлъ князи и боляре... присылаху посѣщати его и милостыню многу посылаху ко блаженному просяще отъ него молитвы и благословения и прощения, и се сотвориша множицею. святыи же миръ и благословение и прощение всѣмъ подасть....[132]

---

[127] "The venerable one sent [someone] and summoned all the brethren, and kissed them all, as they wept and wailed." *Uspenskij sbornik* (see n. 11), 128–129, col. 63b 12–13.
[128] *Žitie Varlaama* (see n. 19), 19.
[129] *PSRL*, v. 7 (see n. 96), 73–74; vols. 11–12 (see n. 119), 180.
[130] Jaxontov, *Žitija sv. severnorusskix podvižnikov* (see n. 17), 375.
[131] *Pamjatniki literatury. 2-a pol. XV veka* (see n. 25), 482, 486, 488, 490, 492, 494, 502, 504.
[132] "The ruler of all Russia, Grand Prince Ivan Vasil'evič, and his son, pious Grand Prince Ivan Ivanovič, and the most holy Metropolitan Gerontij, and princes and boyars from all parts ... sent [messengers] to visit the venerable one and sent him many gifts, asking him for prayer and blessing and forgiveness; and they did this many times. And the saint gave peace and a blessing and forgiveness to all ...." *Žitie Pafnutija* (see n. 26), 144. However, even Vassian depicts Pafnutij hiding from the crowd in the courtyard (ibid., 145–146).

Conclusions

Similar or identical linguistic and situational formulae recur in early Russian texts (eleventh-seventeenth centuries) that record the final hours of righteous princes, churchmen, and other members of the social elite. All the topoi discussed in this paper relate to the social and religious obligations that had to be fulfilled during the transition from earthly to eternal life. Hagiographical commonplaces have often been regarded as purely literary devices; however, diverse evidence suggests that the topoi of deathbed and testament reflect actual practices in early Russian society. First, the situations represented by the topoi appear in historically reliable biographies based on eyewitness accounts and personal recollections, including Innokentij's circumstantial notes on the death of Pafnutij. Second, the situations have parallels in nonliterary texts such as service books, nomocanons, and legal documents, in which the commonplaces of biographical writing would have no function. Third, the situations were added to later versions of lives when the death scenes in early redactions contained unexpected details. Editors evidently felt it necessary to make their texts conform to the social norm.

When early Russian authors used the topoi of deathbed and testament to fill in gaps in biographical information, they evidently viewed the commonplaces not only as echoes of familiar literature, but also as representations of customary social practices—i.e., as probable truth. To be valid for writing, topoi must fulfill some social expectation; like any other conventional form, they must be accepted by the community. Topoi become clichés only when society no longer regards them as reflections of appropriate conduct, that is, when significant cultural changes have taken place. Since saints' lives and other types of early Russian biographical literature were written to provide norms for behavior, their characteristic topoi were continually renewed by the community's acceptance and, ideally, imitation. For example, according to Innokentij's notes, Pafnutij complained that he had wasted sixty years dealing with worldly people and affairs, to the tribulation, not the benefit, of his soul.[133] This statement is obviously a variant of the *vanitas* topos, which dates back at least to Ecclesiastes and which appeared in the General Canon for the Dead;[134] yet it is so idiosyncratic in form that there can be little doubt that he actually said it.[135] Pafnutij's thoughts turned to

---

[133] *Pamjatniki literatury. 2-a pol. XV veka* (see n. 25), 502, 504.
[134] "Kanon za umeršix obščij," in *Staroobrjadčeskij učebnyj časovnik* (see n. 47), 74r.
[135] See *Slovar'* (see n. 11), v. 2, pt. 1, 404.

a theme that was both familiar and appropriate to his circumstances; the fact that his words had literary reverberations is hardly surprising, considering the high value of *auctoritas* in early Russian culture.[136]

Last wills and the admonitions in literary death scenes were responses to rituals connected with dying in early Rus'. In essence, will-making was a form of oral admonition: the dying addressed their heirs and successors and dictated their final wishes in the presence of witnesses. Testators tried to inculcate the virtues of brotherly love and obedience in order to safeguard their wills and ensure loyalty to their successors through the threat of divine displeasure. Since the dying discharged their final legal obligations at about the same time as their spiritual ones, churchmen were on hand to observe and assist in will-making; hence the clerical authors of death scenes naturally associated the testamentary process with the last rites and other deathbed rituals. This explains why wills and biographies share verbal and situational elements and especially why they both emphasize obedience and brotherly love. The commonalities of form and content in such diverse texts bear witness to the strong influence that social institutions exerted on early Russian writing.

---

[136] On the early Russian attitude to *auctoritas,* see Lixačev, *Poètika drevnerusskoj literatury* (see n. 4), 92–93; and B. A. Uspenskij, *Istorija russkogo literaturnogo jazyka (XI–XVII vv.),* Sagners slavistische Sammlung, no. 12 (Munich 1987), 55–59.

EXTENDING THE LIMITS
OF THE TEXT

PILGRIMAGE, PROCESSION AND SYMBOLIC SPACE IN SIXTEENTH-CENTURY RUSSIAN POLITICS

NANCY S. KOLLMANN

One of the most poignant essays I have read in early Russian history concerns the untimely death in 1560 of Ivan IV's first wife, Anastasiia Romanovna. In 1945, S. B. Veselovskii pondered its cause: did Adashev and Sylvester mastermind a plot to kill the young woman? Did the boyars? Or was someone else responsible? He reached this sad conclusion:

> her health was undermined by her early marriage and frequent childbirths and was definitively shattered by continual trips with her husband on pilgrimage and the hunt.

Veselovskii showed that Anastasiia gave birth six times in eight years while accompanying her husband and family on extended pilgrimages virtually every year, often twice a year. Ivan himself, Veselovskii concluded, drove her to her death.[1]

My purpose here is not to explore the perils of childbirth in early modern Russia, but to consider a tangential aspect of Anastasiia's story: Ivan's travels. Why did Ivan traverse his realm on pilgrimages, hunting expeditions, and processions so determinedly? Is there significance in these outings deeper than their ostensible purposes of prayer and recreation?

Undoubtedly so, on many levels. On one level they likely had a very straightforward meaning: rulers may have traveled to monasteries simply to pray and render respect to the Church. These travels may also have had more prosaic goals: fresh air for the children, fresh food from the countryside, the welcome diversions of a pastoral setting. Such homely desires might well have provided the most conscious level of meaning in Ivan IV's peregrinations.

At the same time tours might have had political utility. Like Charlemagne's circuits of his realm and Kievan grand princes' rounds, sixteenth-

---

[1] S. B. Veselovskii, "Bolezn' i smert' tsaritsy Anastasii," in *Issledovaniia po istorii oprichniny* (Moscow, 1963), 92–95.

century processions to monasteries may have been occasions for collecting taxes, rendering justice, and showing the flag. Unfortunately, surviving records give only the barest of accounts: they hint neither at the public's reaction to a grand prince's procession nor at associated secular activities. But clearly such activities might have been combined with religious pilgrimages.

Symbolically Ivan's travels may have had even deeper meaning. Such processions were, after all, ritualized activities, a form of nonverbal communication subject to analysis. Social anthropology has provided inspiration for such an approach, particularly in its social interpretation that sees ritual as intimately connected with community beliefs and life. This view has its roots in Emile Durkheim, who argued that rituals—events as various as liturgies, puberty rites, coronations or pilgrimages—have both passive and dynamic effects. While fundamentally "symbolic representations of social relationships," they also provide a living experience of the community assembled and its expressed values, and thereby physically and personally integrate individuals consensually into the dominant social value system.[2]

Arnold van Gennep expanded Durkheim's perception of ritual as dynamic; he saw certain rituals as "rites of passage" that transform individuals: first, isolating them from a given physical, social, or religious community, then transforming and reintegrating them into the community as fuller embodiments of its values.[3] Such a social interpretation of ritual rests on a concept of sacred and profane space, sacred not only in religious terms but in the broader sense of hallowed as a component part of a particular social, political, or cultural community. Ritual activity demarcates space as sacred or profane; it transforms profane space into sacred space and outsider into insider.[4] Following these leads, historians have found ritual in the most various situations—riots, judicial punishments, festivals—and have argued that it communicates. Ritual acts out stylized political relations and displays real tensions, providing catharsis for the ruling strata and the populace.[5]

Clifford Geertz offers special insights for those interested in public pro-

[2] Emile Durkheim, *The Elementary Forms of the Religious Life*, trans. Joseph Ward Swain (London, 1915), 257–258.

[3] For a summary, see Edmund R. Leach, "Ritual," *International Encyclopedia of the Social Sciences* 13 (New York, 1968).

[4] Victor Turner follows Van Gennep: *The Drums of Affliction: A Study of Religious Processes among the Ndembu of Zambia* (Ithaca, N.Y., 1981); idem, *Dramas, Fields, and Metaphors: Symbolic Action in Human Society* (Ithaca, N.Y., 1974), chaps. 1 and 5.

[5] Cf. Natalie Zemon Davis, *Society and Culture in Early Modern France* (Stanford, 1975). For examples in the Russian context, see my "Ritual and Social Drama at the Muscovite Court," *SR* 45, no. 3 (1986): 486–502, and Richard Wortman, "Rule by Sentiment: Alexander II's Journeys through the Russian Empire," *American Historical Review* 95, no. 3 (1990): 745–771.

cessions such as pilgrimages.[6] Declaring that politics *is* symbolic—"a world wholly demystified is a world wholly depoliticized"—Geertz explores how the "active centers of the social order" embody social values; he envisions these centers not necessarily as physical places but as acts or "leading ideas" associated with "leading institutions." When kings use ceremony—coronations, progresses, fêtes, gift-giving—to "take symbolic possession of their realm," Geertz declares, they thereby "locate the society's center and affirm its connection with transcendent things by stamping a territory with ritual signs of dominance." Geertz suggests for us that Muscovite grand princes' pilgrimages had meaning as demonstrations of authority, as demarcations of sacred space, and as manifestations of the theoretical order of the realm.

The social interpretation of ritual has not escaped criticism.[7] In Geertz's interpretation, and even more strongly in Durkheim, ritual builds consensus, integration, and affirmation of social values. Historians protest that this approach is aestheticizing. Ronald G. Walters notes, for example, that for Geertz "reality is a drama in which the focus is upon symbolic exchanges, not social consequences," whereas, he warned, "in history the play is not the whole thing . . . symbolic dramas, however interesting in their own right, can serve larger purposes of power, domination, exploitation and resistance." Steven Lukes similarly points out that since societies are rent with conflicting value systems, rituals more often serve to "mobilize" a dominant ideology than to affirm consensus. Suzanne Desan suggests that the violence in some public rituals can act out social tensions: it "contributes not only to the definition of community and meaning, but also to the transformation of symbolic systems and the realignment of power, status, and roles within the community."[8]

---

[6] "Centers, Kings, and Charisma: Reflections on the Symbolics of Power," in *Local Knowledge* (New York, 1983), 121–146, also in Sean Wilentz, ed., *Rites of Power. Symbolism, Ritual, and Politics Since the Middle Ages* (Philadelphia, 1985), 13–40. See also Victor Turner, "The Center Out There: Pilgrim's Goal," *History of Religions* 12, no. 3 (1973): 191–230; Victor Turner and Edith Turner, *Image and Pilgrimage in Christian Culture. Anthropological Perspectives* (New York, 1978), esp. chap. 1.

[7] Steven Lukes, "Political Ritual and Social Integration" in *Essays in Social Theory* (London, 1977), 52–73; Ronald G. Walters, "Signs of the Times: Clifford Geertz and Historians," *Social Research* (Autumn 1980): 537–556; David Cannadine, "The Context, Performance and Meaning of Ritual: The British Monarchy and the 'Invention of Tradition', c. 1820–1977" in Eric Hobsbawm and Terence Ranger, eds., *The Invention of Tradition* (Cambridge, 1983), 101–164; Sean Wilentz, "Introduction: Teufelsdrockh's Dilemma . . . ." in idem, ed., *Rites of Power* (see n. 6), 1–10; Suzanne Desan, "Crowds, Community, and Ritual in the Work of E. P. Thompson and Natalie Davis," in Lynn Hunt, ed., *The New Cultural History* (Berkeley, 1989), 47–71; Gabrielle M. Spiegel, "History, Historicism, and the Social Logic of the Text in the Middle Ages," *Speculum* 64 (1989): 59–86.

[8] Walters, "Signs of the Times" (see n. 7), 556; Lukes, "Political Ritual" (see n. 7); Desan, "Crowds" (see n. 7), 71.

The controversy, however, is not over ritual's social functions but over the extent of its effects. Historians accept that ritual is a "communicative aspect of behavior," in Edmund Leach's phrase, but they expect it to function differently for different observers and in different circumstances. Through one observer's eyes a ceremony imposes a political vision, whereas for another it affirms accepted values. One participant may cathartically challenge dominant values in a ritual, whereas another may regard it as a transformative odyssey through space defined by community values as sacred. The uniting thread is an effort to define and consolidate the community. Perhaps Ivan IV's pilgrimages at some level attempted that.

Expansion and consolidation of power, after all, were the dominant goals of sixteenth-century Muscovite politics. It is well to remember that politically and institutionally Muscovy was only minimally centralized well into the sixteenth century and that the court—that is, the grand prince and his boyars—made bringing the disparate and expanding realm more firmly under Moscow's authority its primary task.[9] The coercive and institutional mechanisms they devised from Ivan III's reign through Ivan IV's are familiar: regional elites were integrated into the Moscow servitor stratum; the *pomest'e* system was disseminated over the central lands; the brigandage and land reforms enlisted local cavalrymen in social control; a bureaucratic network centered in the Kremlin chanceries was inaugurated.[10]

Simultaneously the court embellished the center and the ruler through ideas and images. The Kremlin architectural ensemble was made glorious, starting with the Cathedral of the Assumption in the 1470s and culminating in Saint Basil's in the 1550s.[11] Mammoth histories compiled at the metropolitan's and grand-princely courts—the Nikon Chronicle in the 1520s, the Brief Chronicle of the Beginning of the Tsardom in the 1550s, the Book of Degrees and the Great Menology in the 1560s, the Illuminated Chronicle in

---

[9] This theme is implicit in the following works: M. N. Tikhomirov, *Rossiia v XVI stoletii* (Moscow, 1962), chap. 3; A. A. Zimin, "O politicheskikh predposylkakh vozniknoveniia russkogo absoliutizma," in *Absoliutizm v Rossii (XVI–XVIII vv.)* (Moscow, 1964), 18–49; S. M. Kashtanov, *Finansy srednevekovoi Rusi* (Moscow, 1988).

[10] The literature on this topic is vast. See A. A. Zimin's monographs: *Rossiia na rubezhe XV–XVI stoletii* (Moscow, 1982); *Rossiia na poroge novogo vremeni* (Moscow, 1972); and *Reformy Ivana Groznogo* (Moscow, 1960). See Ann M. Kleimola's numerous articles, including "The Changing Face of the Muscovite Aristocracy . . . ." *Jahrbücher für Geschichte Osteuropas* 25 (1977): 481–493 and "The Muscovite Autocracy at Work . . . ," in *Russian Law: Historical and Political Perspectives*, ed. William E. Butler (Leyden, 1977), 29–50. See Gustave Alef's collected articles in *Rulers and Nobles in Fifteenth-Century Muscovy* (London, 1983) and his *Origin of Muscovite Autocracy: The Age of Ivan III* (Berlin, 1986) (= *Forschungen zur osteuropäischen Geschichte* 39).

[11] An excellent examination of this issue is N. Ia. Tikhomirov and V. N. Ivanov, *Moskovskii kreml'. Istoriia arkhitektury* (Moscow, 1967).

the 1570s—declared Moscow the center of the East Slavic and the Orthodox world.[12] Some writers elevated the tsar as autocrat with Agapetan rhetoric, while secular tales concocted an imperial genealogy for the ruling dynasty.[13] The court adopted the habit of coronation: an isolated experiment in dire political straits in 1498, it became established tradition after 1547. Special veneration was accorded relics of dynasty members and hierarchs of special significance to the court;[14] Kremlin churches were decorated with frescos of the grand-princely dynasty and Biblical typology depicting Moscow's greatness.[15] In this context the ruler's pilgrimages and processions appear as tools in the symbolic definition of the center in the person of the grand prince, his elite, and the sacred space demarcated by their pious rounds.

The chronology of grand-princely pilgrimages itself suggests a connection with state efforts to consolidate authority. Moscow's grand princes began to travel regularly on pilgrimage and procession starting in the early sixteenth century. Chronicles, the only source for such travels in this era, whether associated with the grand prince or independent, mention only sporadic pilgrimages by grand princes in the fifteenth century.[16] Vasilii II journeyed to the Trinity-Saint Sergius Monastery several times, and Vasilii, first son of Ivan III's second wife Sophia Paleologue, was baptized there in 1479.[17] But pilgrimages begin to be recorded regularly in the early sixteenth century: in

---

[12] See A. A. Zimin, *I. S. Peresvetov i ego sovremenniki* (Moscow, 1958); David B. Miller, "The *Velikie Minei Chetii* and the *Stepennaia Kniga* of Metropolitan Makarii and the Origins of Russian National Consciousness," *Forschungen zur osteuropäischen Geschichte* 26 (1979), 263–382.

[13] Agapetus: Ihor Ševčenko, "A Neglected Byzantine Source of Muscovite Political Ideology," *Harvard Slavic Studies* 2 (1954): 141–179. Other tales: A. L. Gol'dberg, "Istoriko-politicheskie idei russkoi knizhnosti XV–XVII vekov," *Istoriia SSSR* 1975, no. 4: 60–77; A. A. Zimin, *Rossiia na rubezhe* (see no 10), 148–160; R. P. Dmitrieva, *Skazanie o kniaz'iakh vladimirskikh* (Moscow and Leningrad, 1955).

[14] Relics of Saint Peter: *PSRL*, v. 23, 192–193; v. 8, 170–173; v. 12, 143–147 (all 6980); *PSRL*, v. 23, 193–195; v. 8, 201–203; v. 12, 192–196 (all 6987). Relics of dynasty: *PSRL*, v. 23, 197–198; v. 8, 248–249; v. 13, 6–8 (all 7016). New sepulcher for Saint Aleksii: *PSRL*, v. 29, 16–17; v. 13, 84 (both 7043).

[15] Daniel Rowland, "Biblical Military Imagery in the Political Culture of Early Modern Russia: The Blessed Host of the Heavenly Tsar" (this volume); Michael Cherniavsky, "Ivan the Terrible and the Iconography of the Kremlin Cathedral of Archangel Michael," *Russian History* 2, no. 1 (1975): 3–28.

[16] This essay is based on a systematic survey of all the important chronicle sources of the fifteenth and sixteenth centuries: the Trinity, Ermolin, Typography, Vologda-Perm, L'vov, Moscow Compendium of the End of the Fifteenth Century, Ioasaf, Voskresenskaia, Nikon, Vladimir Brief Chronicle, Postnikov Brief Chronicle, Brief Chronicle of the Beginning of the Tsardom, and the Piskarev, Bel'skii and Moscow Brief Chronicles, all in their texts from the late fourteenth century to the end of each account: PSRL, vols. 8, 11–13, 20, 23, 24, 25, 26, 29, 30, 34; *Ioasafovskaia letopis'* (hereafter *Ioasaf*), ed. A. A. Zimin (Moscow, 1957); *Troitskaia letopis'. Rekonstruktsiia teksta*, comp. M. D. Priselkov (Moscow and Leningrad, 1950).

[17] Vasilii II: *PSRL*, v. 23, 152 (6953); v. 25, 264–266 (6954); v. 23, 154 (6957); v. 25, 272 (6960). Baptism: *PSRL*, v. 23, 179; v. 24, 197; v. 25, 323; (all 6987). It is possible that Vasilii II's son Ivan was christened there in 1440: *PSRL*, v. 23, 150 (6948).

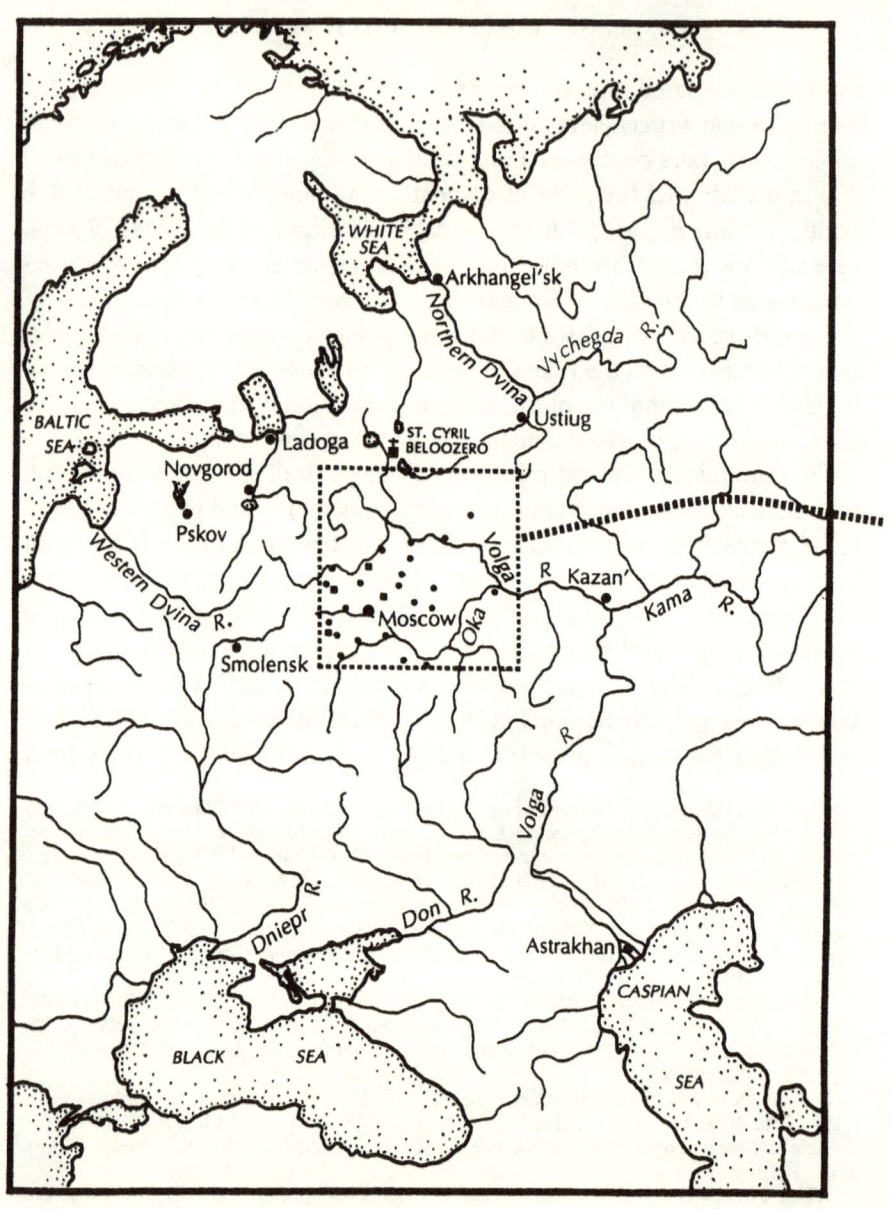

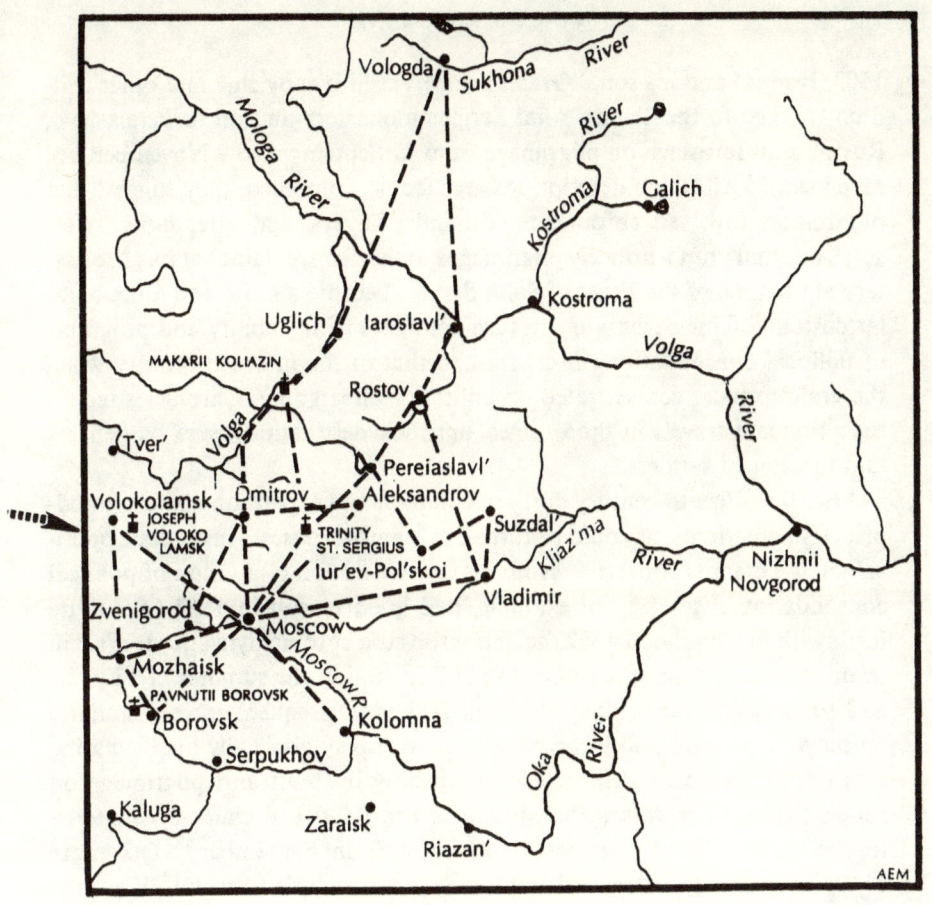

RUSSIA IN THE SIXTEENTH CENTURY

☦ Monastery   --- Pilgrimage routes
• Town

1503, Ivan III and his son, "Grand Prince Vasilii Ivanovich," and other children traveled to the Trinity-Saint Sergius monastery and on to Pereiaslavl', Rostov and Iaroslavl' on pilgrimage from 21 September to 9 November (see map inset).[18] Although descriptions are laconic, combined, they suggest that pilgrimages involved entourages of family, boyars, and attendants. After 1503, autumn grand-princely pilgrimages to the Trinity-Saint Sergius Monastery at the time of the Feast of Saint Sergius became a more and more regular custom.[19] This chronology in turn coincides with stability and programs of political consolidation, in contrast to that of the fifteenth century when the grand princes concentrated on military campaigning. Chronicles record their frequent travels in those times, but their destinations were battlefields and threatened borders.

After the fifteenth-century flurry of conquest and expansion abated, grand-princely peregrinations could be turned to many purposes—immediate political goals, personal concerns, symbolic demonstration of a vision of political consolidation. Ivan III, for example, had good reason in 1503 to venture forth with his family: in 1502, he had resolved a chronic dynastic struggle in favor of his elder son, the future Vasilii III,[20] and in the summer of 1503, he had suffered a serious illness.[21] Vasilii III's more frequent travels similarly reflect personal and political concerns while also symbolically disseminating a vision of the realm. He traveled frequently on hunt and pilgrimage on routes that both traversed the Muscovite heartland and claimed new territory as "sacred," that is, as part of his realm. From September to December 1510, for example, he traveled from Pereiaslavl' to Iur'ev, Suzdal', Vladimir, and Rostov, a roundabout route through the central Muscovite lands (see map).[22] He is next recorded in the spring of 1515 visiting Volokolamsk for the hunt, a significant trip inasmuch as he had acquired that appanage principality only in 1513. He pilgrimaged to the Trinity Monastery and then "around his towns" in the autumn of 1516, went there again in June 1518 to pray on the eve of battle, and returned to Volokolamsk in September 1518. In the spring of 1519, he pilgrimaged to Ostrov near Pskov and sum-

---

[18] *PSRL*, v. 26, 296; v. 20, 374; v. 8, 243 (all 7012); *Ioasaf*, pp. 145–146.
[19] They are recorded in 1503, 1510, 1516, 1528, 1530, 1532, 1533, 1537–1543, 1545–1546, 1548, 1554, 1556, 1559, 1561, 1563–1566. Veselovskii remarked that they were the custom since the fifteenth century, but he provides no citations: "Bolezn'" (see n. 1), 93.
[20] *PSRL*, v. 26, 295 (7010). My essay on this topic gives bibliography: "Consensus Politics: The Dynastic Crisis of the 1490s Reconsidered," *RR* 45 (1986): 235–267.
[21] *PSRL*, v. 26, 296; v. 20, 374; *Ioasaf*, p. 145 (all 7011).
[22] *PSRL*, v. 34, 10; v. 26, 301–302 (both 7019). Richard Wortman notes Alexander II's similar attention to pilgrimage and patronage of monasteries in the heartland: "Rule by Sentiment" (see n. 5), 758–759 and n. 44.

mered in his village Vorontsovo in the Moscow area.[23] His later travels might be linked with his personal concerns: in 1525, the year of his dramatic divorce, he went on pilgrimage from summer to autumn to Volokolamsk and Mozhaisk; he went hunting in Mozhaisk in September 1526 with his new wife and probably also displayed her on his winter pilgrimage in late 1526 to the Assumption Monastery at Tikhvin, between Novgorod and Ladoga.[24] Returning to the north in the autumn of 1528, he made an extended circuit north to major monasteries in Pereiaslavl', Rostov, Iaroslavl', Vologda, and Beloozero (see maps), perhaps here to pray for an heir.[25] Vasilii III brought his firstborn son, Ivan, for christening to the Trinity-Saint Sergius Monastery in August 1530,[26] a trip that also displayed the much-needed male heir to the elite and to the Muscovite populace. In later generations Muscovite heirs were shown formally from a Kremlin porch to an assembled crowd;[27] here the public display is equally formal and significant.[28]

Immediately after Ivan's birth and christening, Vasilii III took his wife and son again on pilgrimage to the Trinity Monastery and then on to hunt in Volokolamsk and Mozhaisk, from September through November 1530. The trip offered an extended opportunity to display the heir in the western perimeter of the Muscovite heartland. Vasilii III repeated his September pilgrimage to the Trinity Monastery in 1532.[29] In March 1533, he ventured to the southerly stretches of the heartland, to the Nikola of Zaraisk Monastery on the Osetr River between Kolomna and Tula. Vasilii III's last pilgrimage took him in the autumn of 1533 to the Trinity Monastery, then on to Volokolamsk for the hunt; he returned home unexpectedly and died soon thereafter.[30]

---

[23] 1515: *PSRL*, v. 26, 305 (7023). 1516: *PSRL*, v. 30, 142 (7024); June 1518: *PSRL*, v. 20, 396; *Ioasaf*, p. 173 (both 7026). Sept. 1518: *PSRL*, v. 30, 144 (7027); 1519: *Ioasaf*, p. 177 (7027).
[24] Volokolamsk: *PSRL*, v. 34, 15 (7033); Mozhaisk: *PSRL*, v. 20, 404; v. 34, 15 (both 7035). Tikhvin: *PSRL*, v. 30, 201 and 176; v. 34, 15 (both 7035).
[25] *PSRL*, v. 34, 16; v. 26, 314 (both 7037).
[26] *PSRL*, v. 26, 314; v. 8, 273–274 (both 7038).
[27] Grigorii Kotoshikhin, *O Rossii v carstvovanie Alekseja Mixailoviča*, text and commentary by A. E. Pennington (Oxford, 1980), 32.
[28] The Trinity-Saint Sergius Monastery was the usual place for baptizing first-born sons in the ruling family: see nn. 17 and 26 above. Other offspring were christened at monasteries or convents in the Kremlin or in Moscow. Ivan's first-born son's christening: *PSRL*, v. 13, 522–523 (7061). His brother's birth: *PSRL*, v. 26, 315 (7041). Ivan's other offspring, with their names and the places where they were christened: *PSRL*, v. 29, 57 (7057; Anna; New Maiden Convent); *PSRL*, v. 29, 59 (7059; Mariia; no place); *PSRL*, v. 13, 239 (7062; Ivan; Chudov Monastery); *PSRL*, v. 13, 265 (7064; Evdokiia; Chudov); *PSRL*, v. 13, 283 (7065; Fedor; Chudov). Ivan's nephew, Prince Vasilii Iur'evich: *PSRL*, v. 13, 317 (7067; Chudov).
[29] 1530: *PSRL*, v. 8, 276; v. 20, 409 (both 7039). 1532: *PSRL*, v. 20, 414 (7041).
[30] Zaraisk: *PSRL*, v. 20, 416 (7041). Volokolamsk: *PSRL*, v. 8, 285–286; v. 29, 9–10; v. 34, 17–24 (all 7042).

Political instability, rather than piety and consolidation, may have motivated Ivan's early pilgrimages and dictated their unprecedented frequency. He made pilgrimages at least annually, or even twice annually, starting from about age six. Such public processions not only demonstrated that he and his family were alive and well, they also displayed the current boyar hierarchy. In June 1536, for example, the six-year-old Ivan and his younger brother traveled "for the first time after his father's death" to the Trinity-Saint Sergius Monastery to pray and distribute alms; he was accompanied by his nurse Agrafena Cheliadnina (sister of boyar Prince I. F. Telepnev-Obolenskii), the prevailing boyar triumvirate (Princes I. D. Penkov, Telepnev-Obolenskii, I. I. Kubenskii), "other boyar wives and many boyars and *deti boiarskie* [lesser servitors]."[31] A year later, he traveled there again for a week's pilgrimage with his mother, brother, and probably an entourage, and again in September 1537, when he again heard services and distributed alms and upkeep (*korm*) to the monastery's abbot and monks.[32] In January 1538, Ivan traveled westward on a week's pilgrimage to the Monastery of Saint Nikolai in Mozhaisk, while in September the increasing eminence of boyar Prince V. V. Shuiskii—evidenced by his June 1538 wedding to Ivan IV's kinswoman—was affirmed when he and his brother Ivan, also a boyar, accompanied Ivan IV on a week's pilgrimage to the Trinity-Saint Sergius Monastery, along with boyar Prince I. I. Kubenskii.[33]

Such treks with family and varying groups of boyars to the monastery continued in May and September 1539, June 1540, September 1540, September 1541, May and September 1542. Several accounts note that Ivan was accompanied by "many princes and lesser servitors" and that while at the monastery he attended liturgies, dined with the abbot and monks, and distributed alms and upkeep to the monastery.[34] In December 1542, the twelve-year-old Ivan added a two-week pilgrimage westward to the Borovsk, Mozhaisk and Volokolamsk area with his young cousin and "many boyars"; and in the autumn of 1543 Ivan with his brother and boyars traveled for two months from the Trinity Monastery to these same possessions west of Moscow.[35] In March 1544 the fourteen-year-old Ivan, accompanied by his brother and "many boyars," combined pilgrimages to the Trinity Monastery at Koliazin near Kashin (where he prayed and distributed alms and upkeep)

---

[31] *PSRL*, v. 29, 27 (7044).
[32] June 1537: *PSRL*, v. 29, 30 (7045). September: *PSRL*, v. 29, 30 (7046).
[33] January: *PSRL*, v. 29, 31 (7046). Wedding: *PSRL*, v. 29, 32; v. 34, 26 (both 7046). September: *PSRL*, v. 29, 33–34 (7047).
[34] *PSRL*, v. 29, 35 (7047), 35–36 (7048), 37 (7048), 38 (7049), 41 (7050), 43 (7050), 44 (7051).
[35] December: *PSRL*, v. 29, 44 (7051). Autumn: *PSRL*, v. 29, 45 (7052).

and to the Trinity-Saint Sergius for bear hunting. A year later, in May 1545, Ivan, his brother, and a cousin devoted two months to a circuit through his northerly lands. He went from the Trinity-Saint Sergius Monastery to Pereiaslavl', Rostov, Iaroslavl', the Saint Cyril and Therapontus (Ferapontov) Monasteries in Beloozero, to Vologda, to the Cornelius (Kornilov) and Pavel Obnorskii Monasteries and to the Boris and Gleb Monastery at Ust'e. At all these stops he distributed alms and upkeep generously.[36]

Later in the autumn of 1545 for another two months he and his brother traveled to the Trinity-Saint Sergius Monastery and on to hunting; Ivan then returned to Moscow while his brother went on to Mozhaisk.[37] In December he went off in the direction of Vladimir for hunting, and in the autumn of 1546, the sixteen-year-old Ivan with brother and cousin devoted three months to a circuit of monasteries to the west and northwest where he generously distributed alms and upkeep to the monasteries. He went from the Trinity Monastery to Volokolamsk, Rzhev, Staritsa, Tver', Novgorod, Pskov, and the Pechora Monastery outside Pskov; on the way home he stopped to pray in Tikhvin and surveyed his villages in those areas.[38] Ivan's travels became more far reaching as he matured. Stretching out from Moscow to the east, north and northeast, they showed off the political hierarchy, displayed the young tsar's vitality, authority, and piety; and they bestowed his patronage on major monastic centers in the key territories of his realm.

When the minority rivalries were resolved with Ivan's coronation and wedding in January and February 1547, Ivan's travels reflected personal needs and political policies. Immediately after his coronation, Ivan journeyed briefly to the Trinity Monastery to venerate Saint Sergius's relics and to seek the brothers' and abbot's prayers for his health and his tsardom. He returned there humbly, "on foot," with his brother and new wife just after his wedding to give thanks.[39] A year later in June, Ivan again traveled on foot to the Trinity Monastery with his wife and brother to hear services and give gifts; in September 1548, his wife Anastasiia pilgrimaged there on foot, followed a week later by Ivan.[40] Their humility was perhaps prompted by their prayers for a numerous and healthy progeny. In the latter case Ivan went on a tour and hunting expedition to the north and west parts of the Muscovite heartland, to Aleksandrov, Dmitrov, Zvenigorod, Mozhaisk.

---

[36] March: *PSRL*, v. 29, 46 (7052). May: *PSRL*, v. 29, 47 (7053).
[37] *PSRL*, v. 29, 47 (7054).
[38] December: *PSRL*, v. 29, 47 (7054). Autumn: *PSRL*, v. 30, 149; v. 29, 49; v. 34, 28 (all 7055).
[39] January: *PSRL*, v. 29, 50–51 (7055). February: *PSRL*, v. 29, 51 (7055).
[40] June: *PSRL*, v. 29, 56 (7056). September: *PSRL*, v. 29, 56 (7057).

Because the court's attention was preoccupied with the campaign against Kazan', few pilgrimages are recorded for the next few years. In August 1549, however, Ivan's prayers were answered with the birth of his first child, a daughter. Anna was christened in Moscow, at the New Maiden Convent where a church was built and consecrated in her honor. Their second daughter, born in March 1551, was christened, probably in the Kremlin; the family made a special trip to the Trinity Monastery in December 1552 to baptize the couple's first son, Dmitrii.[41] That son, however, died on an extended pilgrimage from May to June 1553 that went from the Trinity Monastery to several monasteries near Dmitrov, then by the Volga north to Uglich and further on to Beloozero, returning home by the river route with stops at Iaroslavl', Rostov, and Pereiaslavl'.[42] One shares Veselovskii's empathy for Ivan's long-suffering wife and family.

In Ivan's pilgrimages from the early 1550s through the 1560s, prayer and thanksgiving were seemingly subordinated to more overt political goals. In October 1554, Ivan IV put pressure on his cousin Prince Vladimir Andreevich of Staritsa by visiting him and his lands when he also toured his own holdings in the Volok and Mozhaisk areas.[43] Ivan's travels also promoted him as spiritual leader when he used his pilgrimages to found churches or patronize monasteries. In the autumn of 1556, for example, Ivan pilgrimaged from the Trinity Monastery on to Pereiaslavl' where he oversaw the transformation of the Nikita Monastery from eremitic to cenobitic rule; in 1563 and 1564, he was present at the consecration of new churches in Mozhaisk and Pereiaslavl' respectively.[44] Ivan's September pilgrimages to the Trinity-Saint Sergius Monastery continued "as was his royal custom," often combined with circuits of his villages or other monasteries; they are recorded in 1554, 1556, 1559, 1561 (when his new wife accompanied him), and from 1563 to 1566. He also made some brief spring pilgrimages to the Trinity Monastery in May 1556 and May 1566.[45]

---

[41] For reference to these births and christenings, see n. 28 above.

[42] *PSRL*, v. 13, 231–232 (7061).

[43] *PSRL*, v. 13, 252 (7063). Sources are sketchy after the 1560s; the Alexander Nevskii and other later editions of the Nikon Chronicle, and the Piskarev Brief Chronicle (*PSRL*, vols. 13, 29, 34) record no grand-princely pilgrimages and their record picks up again only in the early seventeenth century.

[44] Pereiaslavl': *PSRL*, v. 13, 273–274 (7065). Mozhaisk: *PSRL*, v. 13, 370 (7072) and 383 (7072).

[45] Quotation is from 1556: *PSRL*, v. 13, 273–274 (7065). September pilgrimages: 1554: *PSRL*, v. 13, 245 (7063). 1556: *PSRL*, v. 13, 273–274 (7065). 1559: *PSRL*, v. 13, 320 (7068). 1561: *PSRL*, v. 13, 339 (7070). 1563: *PSRL*, v. 13, 370 (7072). 1564: *PSRL*, v. 13, 386–387 (7073). 1565: *PSRL*, v. 13, 399 (7074). 1566: *PSRL*, v. 13, 404 (7075). May 1556: *PSRL*, v. 13, 270 (7064). May 1566: *PSRL*, v. 13, 402 (7074).

Ivan's travels were unprecedentedly lengthy: two months from October to November 1559 to Mozhaisk monasteries, including that of Saint Nikola of Zaraisk; two months in the spring of 1563 to the Upper Oka area, rarely before visited by grand princes.[46] In September and October 1563, he combined a pilgrimage to the Trinity Monastery with a tour of Staritskii's lands and other holdings west of Moscow. He repeated a similar tour in May 1564 in Prince Vladimir Andreevich's lands.[47] In the summer of 1564, he toured the heartland, moving towards Smolensk; the trip included Pereiaslavl', Mozhaisk, Viaz'ma, and Vereia. For three weeks in June 1565, he traveled around the central heartland, visiting Pereiaslavl' and Aleksandrov.[48] For three months in autumn 1565, he went to far northern outposts, starting at the Trinity Monastery and Aleksandrov and Pereiaslavl', moving to Rostov, Iaroslavl', Vologda and Beloozero. For two months in the autumn of 1566, Ivan traveled to the Volok and Viaz'ma areas.[49] He spent four and a half months touring the Trinity-Saint Sergius Monastery, Vologda, and the Saint Cyril Beloozero Monastery in early 1567, and in late 1567 he traveled to Novgorod. He was there again with his son in June 1571 to participate in a cross procession, yet again at Christmastime, and he apparently spent most of the summer in Novgorod and neighboring monasteries that year.[50]

Ivan's pilgrimages were numerous and varied enough to encompass all the levels of meaning that such public processions can have. Let us here pause to consider their symbolic, spatial significance more closely by reflecting on the routes the grand princes favored. In their pilgrimages Moscow's grand princes and elite seem to have been marking the sacred territory of the geographical center of the realm as well as displaying the individuals who constituted its living centers, in Geertz's imagery. In addition to frequent visits to the Trinity-Saint Sergius Monastery, grand princes regularly traversed the heartland of Muscovy: in numerous variations they traced an easterly circuit from Moscow to the Trinity Monastery, on to Pereiaslavl', to some combination of the old Russian towns—Rostov, Suzdal', Vladimir, Iaroslavl'; occasionally they ventured north to the favored monasteries of the White Lake region; they traced a westerly round to Volokolamsk, Mozhaisk, and their environs. Only relatively rarely did grand princes venture to far-

---

[46] Mozhaisk: *PSRL*, v. 13, 320 (7068). Upper Oka: *PSRL*, v. 13, 366–367 (7071).
[47] 1563: *PSRL*, v. 13, 370 (7072). 1564: *PSRL*, v. 13, 383 (7072).
[48] 1564: *PSRL*, v. 13, 384 (7072). 1565: *PSRL*, v. 13, 396–397 (7073).
[49] 1565: *PSRL*, v. 13, 399 (7074). 1566: *PSRL*, v. 13, 404 (7075).
[50] Early 1567: *PSRL*, v. 13, 407 (7075). Later: *PSRL*, v. 30, 157 (7076). June 1571: *PSRL*, v. 30, 161–162 (7079). Christmas: *PSRL*, v. 30, 159–160 (7080). Summer: *PSRL*, v. 30, 195–196, 162, 194 (7080; entries are out of chronological order).

flung and historically non-Muscovite centers—Pskov, Novgorod, Smolensk, the upper Oka region—and never was it recorded that they traveled to the farthest reaches of their realm, to the Urals or Arkhangel'sk, for example. Their concern seems to have been to define the center, by demonstrating the ruler and his entourage to the populace, by patronizing church institutions and distributing alms, by making contact with the local elite then being enlisted into local government and into the expanding army.

Clearly Ivan's actions and destinations on pilgrimage portrayed him as a Christian, pious, and grand ruler. Accounts of pilgrimages are, however, too laconic to illustrate the particular vision of rulership that the entourage might have presented, but we can construct that from accounts of Ivan IV's more formal processions, in particular those associated with battle and victory. Here too we can trace an elevation in the court's use of ritual and display over that of the fifteenth century. A fifteenth-century chronicle noted simply that happy crowds greeted Vasilii II in Murom, Vladimir, and the Trinity Monastery as he returned victorious from battle in 1445.[51] Descriptions of Ivan III's entries into conquered Novgorod show them also to have been relatively simple, although they were, to be sure, ritualized activities. When, in 1475, Ivan III arrived "in peace" in Novgorod by way of Volok, Torzhok, and other regions, he was escorted into the city by the archbishop with a cross procession. Gifts were exchanged, banquets shared, and judgments rendered by the grand prince.[52] When Ivan III finally conquered the city in 1478, he culminated his victory with ceremony symbolic of the transfer of political legitimacy: he processed into Novgorod with all his male kinsmen; he heard services at the Holy Sophia Cathedral; he ordered exiled to Moscow not only recalcitrant city leaders but also the republic's symbol of legitimacy, its town meeting bell.[53]

Here secular power is combined with Orthodox ritual to impose control on Novgorod and symbolically to consecrate conquered space as sacred, i.e., as part of the grand prince's realm. The same dual mechanisms—ritual and force—are evident in descriptions of Moscow's takeovers of Tver' in 1485, of Smolensk in 1514, and of Narva (Rugodiv) in 1558.[54] The unambiguous

[51] *PSRL*, v. 23, 152 (6953).
[52] *PSRL*, v. 20, 313–319 (6984). The procession's participants are listed in *RK*, 17 (6984).
[53] *PSRL*, v. 25, 311–323; v. 20, 320–335 (both 6986). Participants listed in *RK*, 18 (6986). See other, more laconic descriptions of his trips to Novgorod. In 1460: *PSRL*, v. 25, 276–277 (6968). In 1471–1472: *PSRL*, v. 23, 191–192; v. 25, 287–292 (both 6979–6980). In 1479: *PSRL*, v. 24, 197–198 (6988). Participants: *RK*, 19 (6988). In 1495/96: *PSRL*, v. 26, 289–290; v. 20, 363 (both 7004). Participants: *RK*, 24–26 (7003). In 1509: *PSRL*, v. 26, 301 (7018). Participants: *RK*, 44 (7018).
[54] Tver': *PSRL*, v. 26, 277–278; v. 15, 500 (both 6994). Smolensk: *PSRL*, v. 8, 255–257; v. 23, 200–201; v. 26, 303–304 (all 7022). Narva: *PSRL*, v. 13, 295–296 (7066).

ritual in the case of Narva demonstrates how central the symbolic level was to the accomplishment of conquest and integration. When this Livonian city was captured, Ivan IV ordered from Moscow that the Novgorod archbishop travel there, enter the town with crosses, build and consecrate churches, and process with crosses through the town and around its perimeter, blessing it with holy water to "restore it from the Latin and Lutheran faith and confirm it in the immaculate Christian Orthodox faith." In this way the city was made sacred, part of the Muscovite community. Subsequently holy icons from Narva were ceremoniously sent to Moscow for restoration and copying, thereby affirming the spiritual communion of that newly Orthodox outpost with the center.[55]

The fairly straightforward Novgorod processions pale in comparison with the dramatic descriptions of Ivan IV's setting off for and returning from battle in 1552 and 1562.[56] Here pilgrimage and cross processions were intertwined with military domination to consecrate an armed conquest and to demonstrate the tsar's divine authority to rule. Setting out for Kazan' in 1552, the tsar bade farewell to his wife and the metropolitan; he venerated the icons and relics in the Kremlin Assumption Cathedral and set out on his horse in full military garb. On the way to Kazan' Ivan visited several churches and monasteries and venerated icons at the Vladimir Assumption Cathedral. In Murom he prayed at the shrine of Saints Peter and Fevronia; throughout his journey he exchanged letters with the metropolitan in Moscow. As he approached Sviiazhsk, the Russian stronghold outside Kazan', the tsar was met "at the city gates" by all the Orthodox people of the town. He processed to the cathedral and offered thanks. On the eve of battle a few days later Ivan prayed and heard the liturgy. After he had conquered the city, he ordered a church built on the spot where his banner had stood. He rode victoriously into the town, following the crosses borne by his spiritual father. He occupied the Kazan' tsar's court where "for many years much Christian blood had flowed," and implanted the cross there. Later the tsar marked a spot in Kazan' for the building of a church and processed with

---

[55] *PSRL*, v. 30: 190; v. 13, 305 (7066). This is a fascinating practice, deserving of further study. See examples of veneration of local icons in Moscow: 1395: *PSRL*, v. 23, 134; v. 26, 282–285; (both 6903). 1401: *PSRL*, v. 23, 138; v. 11, 184–185 (both 6909). On these relics, see also *PSRL*, v. 23, 136–137 (6906). 1456: *PSRL*, v. 25, 273–274 (6964). 1514: *PSRL*, v. 8, 254; v. 34, 11 (both 7022). See examples of restoration and copying of local icons in Moscow: Vladimir: *PSRL*, v. 30, 141 (7022); *PSRL*, v. 34, 11, 13 (7022, 7026, 7028); *Ioasaf*, pp. 173–174 (7026), 180–181 (7028). Rzhev: *PSRL*, v. 23, 205; v. 20, 411 (both 7039); *PSRL*, v. 34, 173; v. 29, 36 (both 7048). Viatka: *PSRL*, v. 34, 189 (7062, 7068); v. 13, 254 (7063), 273 (7064). Novgorod: *PSRL*, v. 30, 174 (7069).

[56] 1552: *PSRL*, v. 29, 73–116 (7060–61). 1562: *PSRL*, v. 13, 341, 346–367 (7070–71).

crosses around the city walls to bless them. The church was quickly built and consecrated; Ivan worshipped there and set off to Moscow.

At various stages on the return journey Ivan was greeted by honored envoys of the metropolitan and his own family; he paused at monasteries in Suzdal' and Vladimir as well as at the Trinity-Saint Sergius Monastery to give thanks. Outside Moscow he was met by a huge crowd and at the Sretenskii Monastery on the edge of the city Metropolitan Macarius met him with a grand cross procession. Accepting their praises humbly, the tsar changed from his military clothes to his tsar's garb, with cross, crown, and regalia. Then he processed humbly, on foot, in a cross procession into Moscow, into the Kremlin, and to the Assumption Cathedral where he gave thanks before the icons and relics that he had venerated on his departure. He concluded his thanksgiving with three days of banquets and gifts to his men and largesse distributed to the whole land.

This procession and the equally elaborate one recorded for the campaign against Velikie Luki in 1562 highlight the cardinal characteristics of royal power in Muscovite ideology in the sixteenth century. The tsar girded himself in battle dress, but readied himself with spiritual exercises. At key points he was met as a spiritual leader with a cross procession, and thus did he enter the vanquished city, making a circuit of its perimeter to consecrate it as sacred space and founding churches to create enduring representations of God's blessing on the Muscovite realm. Victorious in Christ, the tsar processed home as God's servant, not as a conquering hero. Greeted by cross processions and spiritual leaders outside Moscow, he relinquished his warrior garb to dress as the shepherd of God's flock on earth, increasingly submitting himself with humility to the Godhead as he neared—on foot—the symbolic center of the state, the Kremlin. He celebrated the victory by bestowing his mercy and generosity on his army and people, thus making the victory an occasion for community cohesion. The procession thus depicts the cosmic order of the Muscovite state, in which the grand prince functioned as God's lieutenant on earth and shepherd of his flock.[57] He was the spiritual surrogate whose performance of religious ritual on behalf of his people sanctified them and his realm, thus justifying the social order. He and his men symbolized that order, which was known by the crosses, pilgrimages, commemorative icons, churches, and ritual that demarcated it.

---

[57] On Muscovite political ideology, see V. Val'denberg, *Drevnerusskie ucheniia o predelakh tsarskoi vlasti* (Petrograd, 1916); see also Daniel Rowland, "Did Muscovite Literary Ideology Place Limits on the Power of the Tsar (1540s–1660s)?" *RR* 49, no. 2 (1990): 125–156; N. S. Kollmann, "Muscovite Theories of Autocracy" (forthcoming).

These processions were not mere symbol; they were dynamic components of political life. Muscovite sovereigns and their elites physically acted out their theoretical relationships with God and the people. In doing so, they communicated a cohesive ideology that legitimated their power by associating it with God's benediction. Moreover, they demonstrated not only Muscovy's political ideology but also its social and political hierarchy. They gave onlookers opportunity to identify with the dominant value system, and they imposed that value system on recalcitrant observers. They used public processions to record the vagaries of factional infighting, to demonstrate the health and vitality of the political leadership, to distribute alms, and to embody piety. As passive communication or cathartic community experience, public processions in Muscovy defined, demarcated, affirmed, and modified the community.

In conclusion, I want to reflect on the problem of representation and reality. Can we be sure that this symbolic meaning existed anywhere but in the minds of the chroniclers who described these rituals? After all, much of the power we see in grand-princely ritual activity stems from the chroniclers' literary skill: ritual activity was often placed at the narrative center of chronicle compositions. The Nikon Chronicle, for example, ends with accounts of Saint Alexius the Wonder-worker's miracles in Moscow, subtly building a cult of Moscow, while the "Brief Chronicle of the Beginning of the Tsardom" ends with Ivan IV's triumphant return to Moscow from the Kazan' campaign summarized above.[58] Was this ritual activity as important in fact as on paper?

Probably so. The attention sixteenth-century chroniclers and other writers lavished on ceremony bespeaks its centrality in the literary representation of an enhanced autocracy *and* in the daily life of the court. The same ecclesiastical and grand-princely cohorts who patronized these works also participated in the rituals they describe. Both media—literary production and physical embodiment—were part of the wide-ranging efforts to consolidate the tsardom (discussed above) that the Kremlin court—probably various, uncoordinated secular and ecclesiastical groups in that court—advanced in the sixteenth century. We cannot say who precisely engendered this drive to enhance the court's ritual, ideological and symbolic expression. We know that both the grand-princely and the metropolitan's courts patronized chronicle compilation and other artistic creation redolent with these themes;

---

[58] Nikon: *PSRL*, v. 13, 32–33 (7027). These texts had appeared earlier: *PSRL*, v. 26, 309–310; v. 8, 265–267; *Ioasaf*, pp. 175, 177–178 (all 7027). Brief Chronicle: *PSRL*, v. 29, 73–116 (7060, 7061).

we know that boyars participated in these rituals. All stood to gain from political consolidation and all probably played a role in promoting symbolic means of enhancing it. In western Europe both rulers and aristocrats wielded ritual to promote political rivalries, while in Muscovy the self-interested parties—court elite, ruler, and, we should add, the Church as well—show less indication of using ritual to undercut each other. Rather, the discourse of Muscovite symbolic activity was united around themes of theocracy, Orthodoxy, political and social consensus.

So ritual activity was important in real politics as well as in literary discourse; in fact, the distinction between them is false. It is a different issue whether this symbolic discourse had meaning beyond the court elite. In the absence of direct source testimony, other patterns of source evidence suggest that nonverbal means of communication were well developed in Muscovy, complementing the circumscribed nature of literacy in the sixteenth century. Only a small, generally ecclesiastical stratum could read, and what it had available to read was confined to the religious worldview displayed in ritual and visual imagery. With so self-contained a sphere for the written word, visual means of communication took on singular importance; frescos, icons, iconostases, liturgy, music, and cross processions were the primary means of transmitting God's word. The grand-princely processions shared that message and symbolic medium. A Muscovite audience would have read these pilgrimages and processions as demonstrations of the splendor of the ruler, of the power of his entourage, of his intimacy with the prelates of the Church, of his devotion to the service of God. Whether it was a welcome message, or one rammed down the throats of recalcitrant Tverians, Novgorodians, and Kazanians, communication through ritual would have occurred.

One similarly should ask whether the hard-boiled court elite, boyars and rulers alike, believed in the theocratic vision that they acted out in procession and pilgrimage. This again is a question of interpretation, since we have no direct testimony from a participant, but it is a less important question.[59]

Even if the actors were not conscious of the symbolic significance of their travels, the meaning was still there. Even if they were cynical stand-ins in a charade they viewed as pointless, the ritual should still have seemed theocratic and grand to observers. But the argument can be made that, while the court's pragmatic policies were hardly religious or messianic, the myth with

---

[59] One longs for a Muscovite counterpart to Agostino Steuco, a Venetian Catholic theologian who argued in 1530 that public ritual was essential to maintain morality, domestic peace, civic stability, and justice in society: *Opera omnia*, 3 vols. (Venice, 1590), v. 3: ff. 1r–24v. I thank Ronald Delph for the reference.

which the dominant elite cemented its authority and constructed its spiritual and ethical system was religious. The donations of boyars and grand princes to Orthodox monasteries in memory of clan and family and the visual world of Kremlin frescos and battle banners with which they surrounded themselves testify to the penetration of Orthodox beliefs in the Muscovite elite.[60] Perhaps to them, too, the processions we have looked at here communicated, providing a dominant myth to justify privilege and power, to forge links with a broader cosmic order, and to give them a hope of permanence and righteousness.

[60] On the visual world, see Rowland, "Biblical Military Imagery" (see n. 15). On the religious life of later boyars, see Robert O. Crummey, *Aristocrats and Servitors. The Boyar Elite in Russia, 1613–1689* (Princeton, 1983), chap. 6. One could assemble similar evidence for the earlier elite: their wills were laden with pious donations; their families were enrolled in commemorative registers (*sinodiki*) in the monasteries they patronized. See wills (*dukhovnye gramoty*) included in *Akty sotsial'no-ekonomicheskoi istorii severo-vostochnoi Rusi kontsa XIV–nachala XVI v.*, 3 vols. (Moscow, 1952–1964) and *Akty Russkogo gosudarstva, 1505–1526 gg.* (Moscow, 1975). See also S. B. Veselovskii's essays on boyar clans: *Issledovaniia po istorii klassa sluzhilykh zemlevladel'tsev* (Moscow, 1969).

BIBLICAL MILITARY IMAGERY IN THE POLITICAL CULTURE OF EARLY MODERN RUSSIA

THE BLESSED HOST OF THE HEAVENLY TSAR

DANIEL ROWLAND

"He deemed us soldiers of the Christian Faith
Willing to die for God. The hour of proof
Is come. The foes of Charles and God are here
Before you. Now confess your sins, and pray
God's bounteous mercy. Then shall I absolve you,
And if you die, the crown of martyrdom
Is yours, and yours great Paradise." He spake,
And so the Franks, dismounting, knelt them down,
And Turpin signed them with the cross of God,
And for a penance bade them deal stout blows.

Archbishop Turpin's sermon, The Song of Roland

But the fight for our planet, physical and spiritual, a fight of cosmic proportions, is not a vague matter of the future; it has already started. The forces of Evil have begun their decisive offensive.

Aleksandr Solzhenitsyn, Harvard Speech, 1978

What a foolish notion
That killing is devotion
Holly Near

In a recent review in *The Atlantic,* Neil Postman described the importance of mutually shared stories in the lives of nations, disciplines, and people:

> Human beings require stories to give meaning to the facts of their existence. I am not talking here about those specialized stories that we call novels, plays, and epic poems. I am talking about the more profound stories that people, nations, religions, and disciplines unfold in order to make sense out of the world. For example, ever since we can remember all of us have been telling ourselves stories about ourselves, composing life-giving autobiographies in which we are the heroes and heroines.[1]

The author would like to thank all conference participants for their comments. He owes a special debt to Nancy Ševčenko, who expended a lot of her valuable time helping a neophyte art historian.

[1] Neil Postman, "Learning by Story," *The Atlantic* 264, no. 6 (December 1989): 122.

What stories did early modern Russians tell themselves about their state, why it existed and why it deserved their allegiance? What image or images did Muscovites have of themselves as a political entity? What story did they see in history, and what role did they envision for themselves? These are some questions to which I hope my paper will provide a partial answer by briefly examining one set of overlapping Biblical images. These images depicted the Muscovite state as a re-embodiment of the ancient Israelite army and simultaneously as what the Israelites themselves thought their own army to have been—an earthly representation of the forces of God engaged in a cosmic struggle against the forces of evil.

In states as diverse as medieval Java, Elizabethan England, and nineteenth-century Morocco, commonly believed stories about the state were of enormous political importance because they helped to generate a consensus that made government possible.[2] In Muscovy, the need for such a consensus was particularly urgent because the government, like that of an early medieval Western European state, was relatively weak. In 1450, 1500, or even 1600, Muscovy was economically poorer than most other contemporary European states, had a more rudimentary bureaucratic system, and yet succeeded remarkably well in expanding both its borders and its influence. Faced with relatively slender economic resources and an inability to compel obedience through brute force alone (though brute force was relied upon often enough), Muscovite rulers were of necessity dependent on shared stories, on the "symbolics of power" in Clifford Geertz's phrase, to maintain and expand their power. The idea of heavenly host was, at least potentially, an important source of Russian political loyalty because it was framed in military images that would have been immediately accessible to the most powerful group outside of the tsar himself—the military elite who formed the core of both the court and the army. It also gave this class a divinely sanctioned role to play in world history and God's invincible protection while they were playing it.

Most of the abundant evidence we will be discussing was located in the Moscow Kremlin, the social, political, and symbolic center of the Muscovite state. The Kremlin seems to fit perfectly Geertz's definition of a "glowing center." Such centers are "essentially concentrated loci of serious acts; they consist in the point or points in a society where its leading ideas come together with its leading institutions to create an arena in which the events

---

[2] Clifford Geertz, "Centers, Kings, and Charisma: Reflections on the Symbolics of Power," in Sean Willenz, ed., *The Rites of Power* (Philadelphia, 1985), 13–38.

that most vitally affect its members' lives take place."[3] Such centers convey particular importance to the symbolic events that occur in them and charisma to the people who frequent them. The placement in the Kremlin of multiple images depicting the theme of the host of the heavenly tsar suggests that this idea was of exceptional importance.

The very abundance of evidence on this theme presents a methodological problem: space limitations of this essay require me to deal briefly with a large number of works on a general level. The biggest danger inherent in this approach is that future research may (and probably will) result in the redating of some of the works I describe. Although many of the works themselves were painted in the seventeenth century, they seem to have been carefully based on earlier paintings that had deteriorated or been destroyed. The date and nature of the earliest iconographical programs and their relationship to what we now see or what was described in the 1670s may never be known with certainty. In theory, all general overviews should await the completion of careful and skeptical investigations into the authenticity and dating of each of the monuments concerned. Since in the case of biblical military imagery in Muscovy, this point will probably never be reached to everyone's satisfaction, I have decided simply to proceed on the basis of present knowledge and to warn my readers of the danger that some pieces of evidence could turn out to come from the seventeenth rather than from the sixteenth century. I hope that this essay will demonstrate that the main ingredients of the idea of the Muscovite army as the "host of the Heavenly Tsar" were already present in Moscow by 1500. The dating of the murals in the Archangel Michael Cathedral remains uncertain, for example, but most of the scenes from the "life" of Michael, discussed below, can already be found in the same church's St. Michael icon that scholars believe was painted around 1400. These scenes were described in the twelfth century by a Byzantine writer.[4]

Limitations of both space and knowledge prevent me from following the traditional path of explaining this theme by tracing in detail the origins of each of its constituent parts. This traditional method would set Muscovite works of art produced at a given moment against earlier examples of the same tradition, and, by throwing into relief what was new, would show the intention of the painter or program designer. Earlier developments are important to show that the basic ingredients of the theme of the blessed host of the Heavenly Tsar had been around for some time, that they were commonplaces in the Orthodox world, both within the cultural sphere of Rus'

---

[3] Ibid., p. 14, with further references to the work of Edward Shills.
[4] See notes 21 and 24 below.

and outside of it, and that these ideas would have therefore been easily accessible to most people, lay as well as clerical. By design as well as necessity, therefore, I have concentrated below on establishing a plausible reading of several visual texts in the light of Muscovite cultural ideas of the period roughly from 1550 to 1630. In spite of uncertainties of dating, I believe that this reading provides evidence of an important and powerful idea, of a story that, although it has been relatively ignored in recent times, may have given meaning to the lives of many Muscovites.

An emphasis on audience leads to a study of visual rather than textual evidence. In a society that was overwhelmingly illiterate, images were accessible to many more people than written texts were, and there were many more of them. As objects, they were also more powerful. M. T. Clanchy tells the fascinating story of an oral tradition from the reign of Edward I in which the Earl of Warenne shows a rusty sword in court to demonstrate the feudal rights acquired by his ancestors at the Norman Conquest. For the Earl, the sword was worth much more than words on a paper. Painted or embroidered images were narrative objects whose meaning did not depend on literacy. On a wall they were passive, but as battle standards like the sword of the Earl of Warenne they became active symbols.[5]

Historians have paid remarkably little attention to this visual evidence. Although both Michael Cherniavsky and David Miller, among American historians, have pointed to a virtual explosion of building and decorating in early modern Russia,[6] conclusions drawn from this material have yet to enter the mainstream of our conceptions about Muscovy. There are other reasons more compelling than the possibly provincial American views of Muscovy. One of the striking features of Muscovite literary life is that much more energy was spent on editing and compiling previously existing works than was expended on the composition of original works.[7] Original texts on general or abstract political subjects are particularly hard to find. Under these circumstances, the mural cycles in the Kremlin and the increasingly complex and didactic icons that were closely related to them may represent the best evidence we have of Muscovy's historical imagination and her political image of herself. Further, it was far harder to copy a mural cycle from another

---

[5] M. T. Clanchy, *From Memory to Written Record: England: 1066–1307* (Cambridge, Mass., 1979), 21–28.

[6] Michael Cherniavsky, "Ivan the Terrible and the Iconography of the Kremlin Cathedral of the Archangel Michael," *Russian History/Histoire Russe* 2, no. 1 (1975):3–28; David Miller, "The Viskovatyi Affair of 1553–1554: the Emergence of Autocracy and the Disintegration of Medieval Russian Culture," *Russian History/Histoire Russe* 8, no. 3 (1981):293–332.

[7] A. I. Sobolevskii, *Perevodnaia literatura Moskovskoi Rusi XIV–XVII vekov* (St. Petersburg, 1903), vi.

time and place than it was to copy a text, which could be easily transported.

Three sixteenth-century visual works serve admirably to illustrate the range of meanings conveyed in the theme of the blessed host of the Heavenly Tsar and provide evidence for the particular reading of other works which forms the basis of this essay. The most fully investigated is the "Church Militant" icon (pl. 1), which provides the title to this paper. This icon, measuring seven feet in length, was given its current name, the "Church Militant," only in the eighteenth century. It was painted apparently to commemorate Ivan IV's victory over Kazan' in 1552 and to memorialize the holy martyrs who fell during the victorious campaign. Thereafter it was placed prominently near the tsar's place in the Kremlin's Dormition Cathedral, and was listed in an early seventeenth-century description under the title "Blessed is the Host of the Heavenly Tsar." V. I. Antonova made the important discovery that this title comes from a liturgical text commemorating holy martyrs[8] (a point to which we will return), but the icon is also closely linked to two Biblical chapters, Daniel 12 and Revelation 19. In Daniel's vision, the Archangel Michael leads the heavenly host against an unnamed northern king in the last days:

> And at that time shall Michael stand up, the great prince [*kniaz' velikii* in the Ostrih Bible] who standeth for the children of thy people, and there shall be a time of trouble such as never was since there was a nation even to that same time; and at that time thy people shall be delivered, every one that shall be found written in the book. (Daniel 12:1)

(Notice here how the language of the Slavonic Bible facilitates the transfer of meaning to a Muscovite military and political context. Moscow had long had its own *velikii kniaz'* standing for the children of God's people.)

In Revelation 19, Christ on a white horse leads an army, conventionally interpreted as an army of martyrs, against the forces of evil at Armageddon:

> 11. And I saw heaven opened and, behold, a white horse; and he that sat on him was called Faithful and True, and in righteousness he doth judge and make war....
> 14. And the armies that were in heaven followed him upon white horses, clothed in fine linen, white and clean.
> 15. And out of his mouth goeth a sharp sword, that with it he should smite the nations, and he shall rule them with a rod of iron; and he treadeth the winepress of the fierceness and wrath of Almighty God.
> 16. And he hath on his vesture and on his thigh a name written, KING OF KINGS AND LORD OF LORDS.

---

[8] V. I. Antonova and N. E. Mneva, *Katalog drevnerusskoi zhivopisi XI–nachala XVII vv.*, 2 vols. (Moscow, 1963), 2:131.

In the icon, Ivan IV follows the Archangel Michael in leading the troops of Muscovy as the heavenly host back from Kazan'. Angels fly to those fallen in battle bringing martyrs' crowns. All are seen returning from Kazan'/ Sodom? Jericho? to Moscow/Jerusalem in the three-column formation typical of the main part of the Muscovite army in the sixteenth century.

Generations of scholars have argued about the identity of the various figures in the three columns, seeing there Saints Vladimir, Boris and Gleb, Dmitrii Donskoi and so forth. A recent and persuasive reinterpretation by I. A. Kochetkov, however, argues from the absence of princely insignia on almost all of these figures and from other evidence that the identification with historical figures beyond Ivan (and possibly three others) was not intended.[9] What we have then is a straightforward depiction of a contemporary event, Ivan's return from Kazan', in which the story of the Muscovite conquest of Kazan' is told in terms of imagery borrowed from the books of Daniel and Revelation as a type of the cosmic struggle of good against evil in the last days.

In her admirably thorough discussion of this icon in the Tretiakov Gallery Catalogue,[10] V. I. Antonova mentions several similar compositions created within the fifty years or so following the painting of this icon. Two of these compositions illustrate important variations on the theme of the Church Militant. The first is a smaller, later, and cruder version of the Church Militant icon (pl. 2), which has the same basic features: an army in three columns led by the Archangel Michael on a winged horse moving toward a heavenly Jerusalem on the left from some city on the right, with angels bringing crowns.[11] A crucial difference, however, is that many of the members of the host of the Heavenly Tsar are identified by inscriptions: the Byzantine emperors Leo and Constantine, plus David and Solomon and Saints Vladimir, Boris and Gleb. A badly damaged inscription appears to take us back again to Revelation 19 (but this time verse 18) as well as to the *stikhira* for martyrs in the fifth tone to be sung in the morning service on Saturdays.[12] A second example adduced by Antonova is the battle standard of Ivan IV of 1560 (of which I have not found an illustration). Here the Archangel Michael on a winged horse is followed by Christ leading a heav-

---

[9] I. A. Kochetkov, "K istolkovanii ikony 'Tserkov' voinstvuiushchaia' (Blagoslovenno voinstvo nebesnogo tsaria)," *TODRL* 38 (1985): 185–209.

[10] Antonova and Mneva, *Katalog* (see n. 8), v. 2, 128–134.

[11] M. P. Stepanov, *Khram usypal'nitsa Velikago Kniazia Sergiia Aleksandrovicha vo imia Prepodobnago Sergiia Radonezhskago v Chudovom monastyre v Moskve* (Moscow, 1909), 104–105, plate 36.

[12] Kochetkov, "K istolkovanii" (see n. 9), 209.

enly host of angels. An inscription on the banner from Revelation 19:11–14 shows this to be the second coming of Christ, although the Revelation text, of course, makes no mention of Michael.

Biblical references help to explain the meaning of these images. Although there is no equivalent to the phrase "the host of the Heavenly Tsar," rough synonyms like "the host of the Lord" or "His host" do occur. In some passages, particularly in Daniel and Revelation, these expressions refer to a heavenly host in the literal sense of the forces of God or Christ arrayed in a cosmic battle in heaven against the forces of Satan at the end of time (Daniel 12:1; Revelation 12:7 and 19:11–21, for example). In other passages, they refer to the army of Israel, or, by extension, to Israel as a whole. The Chosen People (or their army) were thus seen as the embodiment of the heavenly host at a given time and place (see Exodus 7:4; I Samuel 17:26, 45).

The above three works show how the Muscovites understood and appropriated this imagery. The battle standard was meant to invoke the aid of the heavenly host in the cosmic sense during very real earthly battles. The "Church Militant" icon shows the Muscovite army returning from an actual battle (against Kazan') as the embodiment of the heavenly host, led and aided by the Archangel Michael. In the third example, the icon with identified figures, historical personages from David and Solomon to Boris and Gleb have ascended to join the heavenly host in the battle against evil, possibly understood in this instance as the Tatars of Kazan'. (Note how well this last image coincides with the Muscovite rulers' well-documented desire to emphasize their dynastic links to earlier, particularly Kievan, members of the Riurikovich clan and their political links to Byzantium.)

This interpretation is supported by official pronouncements, particularly by Metropolitan Makarii. Perhaps the best example is his letter to Ivan and his "Christ-loving host" in Sviiazhsk on the eve of the conquest of Kazan'.[13] Makarii states that the Tatars were agents of "the dragon (*zmii*), the cunning enemy, the devil (*diavol*)" and asks that God send the Archangel Michael and other "incorporeal powers" to help the Muscovite army in its fight against Kazan', just as Michael helped Abraham against the king of Sodom, Joshua against the Canaanites at Jericho, Gideon against the Midianites, and Hezekiah against Sennacherib. The Muscovite host will be strengthened by the prayers of the Theotokos, the Apostles, the Church fathers, and

---

[13] The letter is found in *AI*, v. 1 (1841), 290–296; it was incorporated in the *Letopisets nachala tsarstva* published in *PSRL* 29 (1965): 86–90. Other documents associated with the Metropolitan are described in Jaroslaw Pelenski, *Russia and Kazan': Conquest and Imperial Ideology (1438–1560's)* (The Hague and Paris, 1974), 194–213.

various Rus' saints including Alexander Nevskii and helped by the aid (*pomoshchiiu i pospesheniem*) of Michael together with four military saints ("passion-sufferers")—George, Dmitrij, Andrej, and Theodore Stratilates—together with Ivan's ancestors Vladimir, Boris and Gleb. God will send his angels and all the holy martyrs as helpers (*posobniki*) to defeat the enemy. Those who shed their blood in the cause will have all of their sins forgiven, and those who die will go to heaven. Only the apocalyptic dimension of this theme is not explicitly mentioned.

The use that Muscovites made of these images depended on what we might call a typological sense of time, a view that may seem alien to us but would have been perfectly natural to anyone reared in an Orthodox liturgical culture. The same cosmic event—the struggle of God's forces against the forces of evil, surely one of the major preoccupations of the Muscovite historical imagination—was imagined as occurring many times: in the Old Testament, in Byzantium and Kiev, in the sixteenth-century "present," and at the Apocalypse. One version of this struggle was understood as implying the others. Given this typological sense of time, a military serviceman fighting in Kazan' or Livonia could easily imagine himself as part of a cosmic struggle lasting from the Old Testament to the Apocalypse.

These images had powerful resonances in other parts of Muscovite culture. The theme of holy martyrs is perhaps the best example. The veneration of martyrs plays a major role in Orthodox worship; liturgical texts about martyrs consistently use military imagery to describe them and thus reinforce the idea of an actual army of martyrs found in Muscovite sources and in Revelation 19. They are called "faithful soldiers" of Christ who "were not terrified by the threats of the tyrants," as "mighty defenders of the inhabited earth" who gave us "a rampart which cannot be destroyed."[14] A single martyr is called a *muchenik voinstva Khristovi*.[15] Note the irony here: a military metaphor to express spiritual strength (martyrs obviously lacked military strength) is taken so literally that it becomes a potent inspiration for military conquest.[16] The recurrent theme of a battle against "tyrants" brings up an interesting linguistic point: the Slavic word *muchitel'* signified both one who torments martyrs (*mucheniki*) and a tyrant, an illegitimate, Godless

---

[14] Kochetkov, "K istolkovanii" (see n. 9), 204–206; Mother Mary and Archimandrite Kallistos Ware, *The Lenten Triodion* (London and Boston, 1978), 669, 686, 685, 668–699 passim.

[15] *Mineia obshchaia* (Moscow, 1649), f. 71.

[16] For an excellent discussion of the militarization of martyr images in Serbia and the development of this theme in Rus' (particularly in Novgorod) at the turn of the fifteenth century when conflict with the Tatars was also a major concern, see O. A. Podobedova, "Voinskaia tema i ee znachenie v sisteme rospisej tserkvi Spasa na Kovaleve v Novgorode," *Drevnerusskoe iskusstvo. Monumental'naia zhivopis' XI–XVII vv.* (Moscow, 1980), 196–209.

ruler.[17] Since the persecutors of the early martyrs were usually pagans, this military martyr imagery could naturally be applied to a struggle against the Muslim Tatars, as in fact was done by Metropolitan Makarii just before the battle for Kazan'.[18] The role of martyrs thus links the Muscovite present to the Apocalypse of Revelation 19.

The "King of Kings" who will lead the army of martyrs in Revelation 19 was also an important image in Muscovy. The central prayer of Ivan the Terrible's coronation service was addressed to the "King of Kings and Lord of Lords".[19] The God invoked in the coronation service is thus the commander of the heavenly host. Further there was in Muscovy an icon type called "the King of Kings" (*tsar' tsarem*). The psalm that serves as the scriptural basis for this type (Septuagint 44, RSV 45) seems to be an ode for a royal wedding in which David and "the queen in gold of Ophir" foreshadow Jesus and Mary.[20] Verses of the psalm specifically invoke earthly kingship and extend the typological reference to a contemporary ruler and his queen:

> Gird thy sword upon thy thigh, O most Mighty, with thy glory and thy majesty . . . . Thine arrows are sharp in the heart of the King's enemies; whereby the people fall under thee . . . . Thou lovest righteousness, and hatest wickedness: therefore God, thy God, hath anointed thee with the oil of gladness above thy fellows." (Psalm 45:3, 5, 7)

The King of Kings was thus a common link connecting the Old Testament, Muscovy, and the Apocalypse; Christ as the commander of the heavenly host was prefigured by David and represented in the "present" by the Muscovite tsar. This identity in turn activated a number of Biblical texts like Psalm 45 or Revelation 19 and gave them current political significance.

The idea of a contemporary ruler and his army as a counterpart to Michael and the heavenly host was found well beyond the limits of the Church Militant icon. Both canonical and apocryphal biblical texts supported the conviction that each nation had an angel as its heavenly protector. The Archangel Michael became the first of the angels and their general in the battle against Satan and was appointed by God to protect Israel. From the time of

---

[17] Daniel Rowland, "Did Muscovite Literary Ideology Place Limits on the Power of the Tsar (1540's–1640's)?" *The Russian Review* 49 (1990): 125–155.
[18] *PSRL* 29 (Moscow, 1965): 89–90; Kochetkov, "K istolkovanii" (see n. 9), 190.
[19] E. V. Barsov, *Drevne-russkie pamiatniki sviashchennago venchanniia na tsarstvo, v sviazi s grecheskimi ikh originalami*, ČOIDR 1883, bk. 1 (repr., The Hague, 1969), 51, 76.
[20] Antonova and Mneva, *Katalog* (see n. 8), v. 1, 135–136. For further discussion of this icon type, see E. Ia. Ostashenko, "Ob ikonografii tipa ikony 'Predsta tsaritsa' Uspenskogo sobora Moskovskogo Kremlia," *Drevne-russkoe iskusstvo. Problemy i atributsii* (Moscow, 1977), 175–187.

Constantine, Michael's cult was associated with the Imperial family. The archangel's presence in imperial triumphal iconography may have been connected with the need to replace the pagan Nike or winged victory with a Christian counterpart. That the Byzantine court reflected the heavenly court of Jesus and his angels in the heavenly Jerusalem was an idea developed in this early period, with archangels appearing in the dress of Byzantine court officials. Churches were dedicated to Michael from the fourth century on. The earliest known example of an entire mural cycle dedicated to the archangel is in Hagia Sophia in Kiev, with similar cycles appearing in the Mirozh Monastery in Pskov (founded 1156) and, in a very full set of images, on the south doors of the nativity cathedral at Suzdal' (executed in the 1230's). Impressive murals about Michael can be found in the Balkans, particularly in Lesnovo.[21]

The fully developed idea of a Rus' army as a heavenly host first appears, as far as I know, in the thirteenth-century *Vita* of Alexander Nevskii. Just before the battle with the Swedes, Archbishop Spiridon reminds Alexander of the military value of God's help: "God is not in military power but in truth [*ne v silakh Bog a v pravde*]. Let us remember the psalmist who said: 'Some came with weapons and some came with horses, but we called the Lord God to our help and they were defeated and fell, but we got up and stood straight.'"[22] Spiridon's argument is practical and simple. God's help can give victory even to those at a military disadvantage. This promise is amplified when one of Alexander's men has a vision in which Boris, in a heavenly ship with his brother, says to the latter, "Brother Gleb, order them [the heavenly oarsmen] to row so that we can help our clansman [*srodniku svoemu*] Prince Alexander." This is followed by

---

[21] The literature on the cult of the Archangel Michael, East and West, is extensive. I have based my brief comments on an excellent recent summary with ample references to other sources: Mina Martens, Andre Vanrie, and Michel de Waha, *Saint Michel et sa Symbolique* (Brussels, 1979). The classic account of Lesnovo and its predecessors is N. L. Okunev, "Lesnovo" in *L'Art byzantin chez les Slavs: Les Balkans*, 2 vols. (Paris, 1930) v. 1, pt. 2, 222–259, though recent issues of *Zograf* have important supplementary information. V. I. Sventsitskaia has written an excellent brief history of the cult and early images of the archangel in Rus' as part of a description of a fourteenth-century icon of Michael: "Master ikony 'Arkhangel Mikhail s deianiiami' vtoroi poloviny XIV v. iz sela Storonna na Boikovshchine," *Pamiatniki cultury. Novye otkrytiia* (Moscow, 1989), 192–209. A crucial literary source for mural cycles and icons is an account of Michael's miracles by the late twelfth-century deacon Pantoleon of Constantinople, found in J.-P. Migne, *PG* 140 (Paris, 1887), 574–591. Pantoleon explicitly locates Michael in many scenes that became traditional in Michael's iconography but where canonical texts omit him. I have so far not been able to find evidence of a Slavic translation of this work that was available in Muscovy.

[22] *Pamiatniki literatury drevnei Rusi: XIII vek* (Moscow, 1981), p. 428. A thirteenth-century chronicle source credits Michael and other angels with helping Vladimir Monomakh against the Polovtsians. See Sventsitskaia, 193, 207.

a marvelous miracle similar [to the one that occurred] in olden times during the reign of King Hezekiah. When Sennacherib, king of Assyria, approached Jerusalem, wishing to plunder the holy city of Jerusalem, suddenly there appeared the angel of the Lord who killed 185,000 [Assyrian soldiers] and when the next morning came, the bodies were found there. The same occurred during the victory of Alexander, when he defeated the king. On the other shore of the River Izhora, which Alexander's troops did not reach, there were found a very large number [of enemy corpses] killed by the angel of the Lord.[23]

Here we have all the basic features of the iconography of the heavenly host: a contemporary battle seen as an analogue of an Old Testament conflict, help from an angel of the Lord, the protection of deceased princely clansmen (who were also martyrs), victory achieved by means of divine intervention. We saw earlier how military metaphors used to describe the spiritual strength of martyrs were taken literally in Muscovy. A few centuries after the death of the two brothers who peacefully accepted death rather than offer violent resistance, they were themselves turned into warrior-saints whose major function was to fight for the Rus' land.

Plate 3, a thirteenth-century illustration of the Archangel Michael's visit to Joshua on the eve of the battle of Jericho, presents a slightly different Old Testament aspect of this theme. Significant here is the fact that Michael has been read into the story in place of "the *voevoda* of the host of the Lord" in the Ostrih Bible version of the story (Joshua 5:14). I would argue that this insertion of Michael into biblical stories where he is absent in the relevant canonical texts shows a desire to strengthen and clarify the theme, though whether this addition occurred in Byzantium, in Rus', or in both is not yet clear. Notice also here the tiny size of Joshua groveling at the feet of Michael.

A large icon of Michael with scenes from his life dating apparently from around the year 1400 contains further evidence for the development of this theme.[24] The border scenes include the meeting with Joshua (pl. 4) and Michael's slaughtering the 185,000 Assyrian troops to help Hezekiah (pl. 5), as described in the Nevskii *Vita*. The famous fifteenth-century Novgorod icon of the Battle of the Novgorodians against the Suzdalians (currently dated to the 1460s) brings the heavenly host theme into Rus' history. Michael in the bottom register (pl. 6) leads the victorious Novgorodians

---

[23] *Pamiatniki literatury drevnei Rusi: XIII vek* (see n. 22), 430–432.

[24] For a good description of this icon with excellent plates, see V. Mashnina, *Arkhangel Mikhail: ikona "Arkhangela Mikhaila s deianiami" iz Arkhangelskogo Sobora Moskovskogo Kremlia*, Publikatsiia odnogo pamiatnika, no. 1 (Leningrad, 1968).

against the Suzdalians. Notice the anticipation of the Church Militant iconography in the depiction of Saints Boris, Gleb, George, and Alexander Nevskii who lead the Novgorodian host.[25] Plate 7 shows an early sixteenth-century icon of Saints Vladimir, Boris, and Gleb. In the bottom register, Michael helps the forces of Iaroslav defeat the army of Sviatopolk.[26]

The theme of the host of the Heavenly Tsar appeared frequently in the mural cycles in the Moscow Kremlin, at least after 1547. The destruction wrought by the Moscow fire of that year makes it hard to say what importance the original wall paintings in the Kremlin churches gave to this theme. Some early murals may survive, however. In 1508, Feodosii, the son of the famous icon-painter Dionisii, painted Michael and Joshua just before the battle of Jericho (Pl. 8) as part of the decoration of the Annunciation Cathedral.[27] The importance of the scene is emphasized by its position next to the door through which Vasilij III entered and left his family church, on the west wall of the choir gallery where the princely family sat. Is it too much to suggest that the inventors of the program for this church wanted Vasilij to see himself as (among other things) a new Joshua? Comparisons of Rus' princes with Old Testament military heroes were literary commonplaces of the time, and this interpretation would have been a natural one. The significance of Joshua and Michael as prototypes and protectors of Muscovite military leaders is illustrated in two later battle standards. The first is an early seventeenth-century banner showing Joshua and Michael under the protection of the God of Sabaoth (pl. 9). The second (pl. 10) is a much less elaborate banner painted on linen. It apparently belonged to Ermak, the conqueror of Siberia, and shows him in his late sixteenth-century battle gear being blessed by Michael as Joshua was blessed by Michael in the previous banner and in the Annunciation Cathedral mural.

On the vault beneath the gallery in the Annunciation Cathedral the Second Coming (pl. 11) was painted with an inscription condensed from the crucial Revelation 19:11, the first verse of the passage quoted on the battle standard of 1560. Notice the similarity of images to those found on the Church Militant icon—the mounted warriors with nimbi, the archangels (but this time two in number), the central figure on a horse. From the point

---

[25] I follow the identification of the haloed figures made in E. S. Smirnova, V. K. Laurina, and E. A. Gordienko, *Zhivopis' Velikogo Novogoroda. XV vek* (Moscow, 1982), 229.

[26] Antonova and Mneva, *Katalog* (see no. 8), v. 2, 60.

[27] My description is based on G. Sokolova's *Rospis' Blagoveshchenskogo sobora. Freski Feodosiia (1508) i khudozhnikov serediny XVI v. v Moskovskom Kremle* (Leningrad, 1970). I have not been able to see I. Ia. Kachalova, N. A. Maiasova, and L. A. Shchennikova, *The Annunciation Cathedral of the Moscow Kremlin* (Moscow, 1990), which apparently redates the "Feodosii" murals to the middle of the sixteenth century.

of view of someone standing on the floor below the gallery, directly over this image of Christ as the leader of the heavenly host sat the grand prince, the current embodiment (if my hypothesis is correct) of that ideal. If the apocalyptic dimension of the Church Militant iconography needs further illustration, then a late sixteenth-century icon of the Last Judgment from Stockholm (Pl. 12) provides it, with its three columns of holy warriors led by the Archangel Michael.[28]

One might expect this theme of host of the Heavenly Tsar to appear in the Golden Palace (*Zolotaia palata*), which served as the chief reception room for Ivan IV and which was decorated sometime between the 1547 fire and 1553–1554, when several of the murals were mentioned in documents connected with the so-called Viskovatyi Affair.[29] We do not find images of the Church Militant type, but there were a large number of scenes depicting the victories of the "armies of the Lord" under Moses, Joshua, and Gideon over their various enemies. If the hypothesis about the overlapping ideas that constituted the theme of the host of the Heavenly Tsar is correct (and Makarii's letter to Ivan IV and his troops indicates that it is), these images may be treated as part of the theme. This hypothesis is strengthened by the placement of the Joshua scenes on the walls of the anteroom (*seni*), parallel with a series of scenes from the History of Rus' (the Christianization, transfer of regalia to Vladimir Monomakh) on the walls of the main room. Plate 13 shows a reconstruction of two of the Joshua scenes.[30] We see not the Archangel Michael, but God Himself directing military operations. The inscription of the left-hand scene—"the Lord gave Akhil into the hand of Joshua, and Joshua seized him and killed him" (a reference to Joshua 10:30?) emphasizes this divine intervention.[31] These graphic depictions of the bloody destruction of Israel's enemies would have been entirely accessible to

[28] Helge Kjellin, *Ryska Ikoner* (Stockholm, 1956), 298–312.

[29] The murals were painted out in the 1670's and destroyed when the Golden Palace was pulled down in 1752. We know them from a very careful description compiled by the icon painter Simon Ushakov and twice published: S. P. Bartenev, *Moskovskii kreml' v starinu i teper'* (Moscow, 1916), 183–193; I. E. Zabelin, *Materialy dlia istorii, arkheologii, i statisiki goroda Moskvy*, 2 vols. (Moscow, 1884), 1:1238–1255. The dating of the murals Ushakov described is a complicated question, too complicated to be resolved here. Watermark analysis most kindly carried out by D. M. Bulanin has shown that an early manuscript (GPB, Pogodin Collection, n.1564) containing the Viskovatyi documents dates from the 1550s or the 1560s. This evidence suggests that most or all of the iconographical scheme described by Ushakov was already in place by 1553–1554, although it may have been repainted one or more times as a result of fires or natural deterioration.

[30] O. A. Podobedova, *Moskovskaia shkola zhivopisi pri Ivane IV: raboty v Moskovskom kremle 40-kh–70-kh godov XVI v.* (Moscow, 1972), appendix by K. K. Lopialo.

[31] Bartenev, *Moskovskii kreml'* (see n. 29), 192.

the boyars who frequented the room and were probably far more meaningful to them than was the elaborate Holy Wisdom iconography on the vaults.

These military scenes were not repeated when the Palace of Facets, the other main reception hall in the Kremlin, was furnished with an elaborate cycle of wall paintings in the late sixteenth century under Tsar Fedor Ivanovich and his regent Boris Godunov. (They were replaced by a large series of scenes on the life of Joseph, seemingly to illustrate the importance of Boris's position as regent.) The vault of the chamber, repainted in the nineteenth century according to a detailed description compiled in 1672 by Simon Ushakov,[32] may still contain some material on this theme, but in a surprising form. In depicting the days of creation, the artists inserted a non-canonical (but iconographically traditional) preliminary moment when the nine Angelic ranks of the heavenly hierarchy were created. In this scene and two subsequent ones—the Fourth Day (pl. 14) with the creation of the sun and moon, and the Seventh Day when God rested—the artist takes the opportunity to go well beyond the Genesis account to show the host of the Heavenly Tsar as a heavenly court, which I suggest was meant and taken as a heavenly archetype for the actual court of the earthly tsar of Muscovy, which met in the space immediately below and which was depicted on an adjacent wall. As in Muscovy, the chief warriors of the heavenly host were also counselors of the heavenly court. Comparisons between the Heavenly Tsar and Tsardom and the earthly tsar and tsardom were commonplaces in Muscovite literature, particularly in the works of Joseph Volotskii.[33]

The Palace of Facets murals tempt us toward the civil side of this imagery, though the scene of the Fourth Day does have an Archangel gracefully spearing Satan and thus maintains a military action. The murals in the Archangel Michael Cathedral, however, bring us firmly back to the military theme and form a fitting conclusion to this discussion.[34] The north and

---

[32] Zabelin, *Materialy* (see n. 27), 1255–1271; Aida Nasibova, *The Faceted Chamber in the Moscow Kremlin* (Leningrad, 1978), 11–12.

[33] David Goldfrank, ed. and trans., *The Monastic Rule of Iosif Volotsky* (Kalamazoo, Michigan, 1983), 71–72 with further references.

[34] The dating of these murals presents problems similar to those presented by the two Kremlin palaces just discussed. Most of the images now visible were painted in 1666 when the cathedral was redecorated on orders from Tsar Aleksei Mikhailovich. Both Iu. N. Dmitriev and E. S. Sizov have concluded for several reasons that in 1666 the painters were quite careful to replicate the sixteenth-century images they were "repairing." First, it was standard practice at the time to make a careful written description of the murals to be repainted so that the new should follow the old as closely as possible. Second, the tsar himself ordered that the new painting be done "protiv prezhnego." Third, two restorations and investigations carried since World War II reveal that surviving fragments of pre-1666 painting coincide very well with adjoining 1666 sections. Sizov suggests a date of 1564–1565 for the original decoration of the cathedral: Sizov, "Datirovka rospisi Arkhangel'skogo sobora i istoricheskaia osnova ee siuzhetov," *Drevnerusskoe*

especially the south walls contained a virtual compendium of Old Testament military stories into which Michael was inserted if the canonical books of the Bible did not already give him a place. On the north wall we find David and the Archangel Michael, the episode of Michael's killing the Assyrian troops mentioned in the Nevskii *Vita,* and Michael's [sic, cf. Dan. 8:16] showing Daniel the four kingdoms of Daniel's famous vision. On the south wall we see in descending order: Abraham fighting his enemies with the help of Michael, "The Archangel Michael Appoints Moses Prince"(!) (pl. 15), Michael and Joshua, and Michael appearing to Gideon and the subsequent routing of the Midianites (pl. 16). The presence of Michael in stories where the canonical biblical texts give him no role emphasizes the idea of the Israelite army as the host of the Heavenly Tsar. In fact, the two walls taken together constitute a sustained hymn to the blessed host of the Heavenly Tsar in its Old Testament guise, made recognizable by the unifying presence of Michael.

The contemporary Muscovite or Rus' dimension of this theme was provided immediately below. The Cathedral of the Archangel Michael served as the necropolis of the house of Moscow, and the tombs of the members of the Riurikid clan line the walls, particularly the southern wall. They are accompanied by portraits of the most important clan members. Since these images and tombs have been discussed at length, most recently by Sizov and Cherniavskii,[35] I do not need to list them here. What has not been discussed as far as I know is the connection between these images and tombs on the ground level of the cathedral and the Old Testament scenes above them. This connection is precisely the theme of the heavenly host. In the more sacred space of the upper walls, in the sacred time of the Old Testament, a victorious and sacred battle between the forces of good and evil is proceeding. Again and again, the Israelite armies triumph through the intervention of the Archangel Michael, against whom no enemy can stand. The Old Testament heroes have as their earthly counterparts on the ground level of the cathedral the present embodiment of the blessed host of the Heavenly Tsar, the members of the house of Moscow and their ancestors. Thus the Riurikid clan is shown as the collective descendant of Abraham, Moses, Joshua, Gideon, David, and Hezekiah, as the inheritor of God's protection and the military advantages that that protection brings, advantages graphically symbolized by the Archangel Michael.

---

iskusstvo. XVII vek (Moscow, 1964), pp. 160–174; Dmitriev, "Stenopis' Arkhangel'skogo sobora," Ibid., 138–159. The latter article has useful diagrams of the iconographic program on the walls of the cathedral on pp.158–159.

[35] Sizov, "Datirovka" (see n. 34); Cherniavsky, "Ivan the Terrible" (see n. 6).

This point could be put in terms closer to the Muscovites' own political vocabulary. If we think of the Archangel Michael Cathedral as a kind of giant genealogical book or *rodoslovnaia kniga* of the grand princely clan, with both the tombs and portraits in place on the lower parts of the cathedral, then the genealogy is extended by implication as one ascends to the upper walls to include such Old Testament figures as Abraham, Moses, and David. This interpretation coincides with the program of the late sixteenth-century "Church Militant" icon where David and Solomon join Vladimir, Boris, and Gleb in the ranks of the heavenly host, as well as with Makarii's ideas as expressed in his letter to Ivan and his troops.

I have offered considerable evidence to demonstrate the importance of the theme of the host of the Heavenly Tsar in Muscovy in general and in the Kremlin, the symbolic center of the state, in particular. From the point of view of the creators of the images and texts surveyed, the theme had clear advantages. For the ruler, it provided an image of invincible power under God's protection and glorified the royal clan both politically and genealogically. It thus builds on a well-known motif in Muscovite literature—the glorification of the ruler. What is of particular interest is that these images also provide a crucial role to the Muscovite army. The army is the center of attention in several of these image types (the Church Militant and the Old Testament scenes where the Israelite troops are depicted) and is implied in the other images, such as those depicting the Archangel Michael and Joshua. The theme of the host of the Heavenly Tsar thus provides a role in sacred history not only for the ruler but also for his military elite. As they battle against their enemies, the boyars and their subordinates are cast in the role of God's own warriors, aided by the unconquerable sword of the Archangel Michael and assured of martyrs' crowns should they fall in battle.

The theme of the heavenly host fits well with the Orthodox culture of Muscovy. Its striking historical sweep from the Old Testament to the Apocalypse accords well with the historical cast of the Rus' imagination. It mined a very rich vein of liturgical literature on martyrs and a long tradition, stretching back to Byzantium, venerating Michael as the protector of princes and their armies. It also drew on a plentiful but little-examined group of biblical texts that appear to have taken on political significance in Muscovy. Finally, the use of common terms—*tsar', voevoda, velikii kniaz', voinstvo*—facilitated the transfer of meaning from the sacred to the secular realms.

We can say, then, that the theme of the host of the Heavenly Tsar was intended by the framers of official ideology to strengthen the state by giving a sacred role to both the ruler and his nobility. The really tantalizing question is whether the hard-bitten military men of Muscovy took these images seriously or even understood them. As they prepared to attack Kazan' or slogged through the endless campaigns of the Livonian War, did they really see themselves as the embodiment of the heavenly host?

Because the men concerned were for the most part illiterate, we have little or no direct evidence on this point. Yet I believe that various pieces of indirect evidence suggest that they might well have. The battle standards we have discussed must surely have been chosen because they had at least some meaning for the troops. The touching depictions of Ermak and the Archangel Michael on a simple linen banner in particular seem to reflect the personal sentiment of the Siberian explorer and conqueror. There seems to be a fairly good fit between the little we know of the culture of the military elite and this theme. Two major components of that theme—fighting and clan honor—were also the principal preoccupations of the Muscovite aristocracy. We have discussed common vocabulary, but visual representations of Christ's army or the Israelite army in the Old Testament looked like the Muscovite army. And of course all these armies were imagined as doing the same thing: they slaughtered ungodly enemies with fire and sword. The idea of receiving help from one's clan had pagan roots and had been a motif in East Slavic literature since the composition of the Primary Chronicle.[36]

Seeing oneself as a member of God's army would surely have provided spiritual comfort amid the violence and danger of war. Almost all Christian states since the time of Christ have attempted to convey this message in one form or another. Perhaps the best analogy to the great boyars who formed the backbone of the Muscovite army is the aristocracy of early medieval Europe. The *chansons de geste* provide useful evidence on the views of this class, since these songs were performed at the pleasure of, and for pay by, the secular courts of Europe. A thoroughly militarized version of Christianity quite similar to the Muscovite idea of the host of the Heavenly Tsar (but admittedly less well developed) can be found in the *Song of Roland*, for example, particularly in Archbishop Turpin's sermon before the battle of Roncevaux.

No doubt secular and even pagan ideas played their part in military minds, but there is no reason to suppose that military men could not have

---

[36] Gail Lenhoff, *The Martyred Princes Boris and Gleb: A Socio-cultural Study of the Cult and the Texts* (Columbus, Ohio, 1989), 34–37; Helen Y. Prochazka, "On Concepts of Patriotism, Loyalty, and Honour in the Old Russian Military Accounts," *SEER* 63, no. 4 (1985): 492.

been part of both cultures, religious and secular. Aristocrats, after all, did sometimes become important churchmen. The slender evidence at our disposal thus tends to indicate that the theme of the host of the Heavenly Tsar constitutes a successful symbol. It may well have provided a most useful story for members of the Russian elite to tell themselves to justify their sacrifices and strengthen their courage. If so, we are entitled to see in this powerful symbol an important political force strengthening the cohesion and military might of the Muscovite state.

Plate 1. "Blessed is the Host of the Heavenly Tsar," 1550s, Tretiakov Gallery, photo from M. W. Alpatov, *Art Treasures of Russia* (New York: Harry N. Abrams, n.d.), plate 78, p.140. Reproduced by permission.

Plate 2. "Blessed is the Host of the Heavenly Tsar," a late sixteenth-century copy of figure 1, Museum of the Moscow Kremlin, photo courtesy of Daniel Clarke Waugh. Reproduced by permission.

Plate 3. Joshua and the Archangel Michael before the Battle of Jericho, thirteenth century, Dormition Cathedral of the Moscow Kremlin, photo from M. V. Alpatov, *Early Russian Icon Painting* (Moscow: Iskusstvo, 1984), plate 44. Reproduced by permission.

Plate 4. Joshua and the Archangel Michael before the Battle of Jericho. Border scene from the icon "The Archangel Michael with Scenes from his Life," ca. 1400, Museum of the Moscow Kremlin (The Cathedral of the Archangel Michael), photo from V. Mashnina, *Arkhangel Mikhail* (see n. 24), pl. 19.

Plate 5. The Archangel Michael Helps Hezekiah Defeat 185,000 Assyrian Troops. Border scene from the icon "The Archangel Michael with Scenes from his Life," ca. 1400, Museum of the Moscow Kremlin (The Cathedral of the Archangel Michael), photo from V. Mashnina, *Arkhangel Mikhail* (see plate 4), plate 12.

Plate 6. The Battle between the Novgorodians and the Suzdalians, 1460s, The Novgorod Architectural-Historical Museum, photo from M. V. Alpatov, *Treasures of Russian Art of the XI–XVI Centuries* (Leningrad: Aurora, 1971), plate 139.

Plate 7. Saints Boris, Vladimir, and Gleb with scenes from the Lives of Saints Boris and Gleb, early sixteenth century, Tretiakov Gallery, photo from Alpatov, *Treasures* (see plate 6), plate 210.

Plate 8. Joshua and the Archangel Michael before the Battle of Jericho, sixteenth century, Annunciation Cathedral of the Moscow Kremlin, photo from G. Sokolova, *Rospis' Blagoveshchenskogo sobora* (Leningrad: Aurora, 1969), plate 22.

Plate 9. Battle Standard with images of Joshua, the Archangel Michael, and the Lord Sabaoth (known as "the Standard of Sapiega"), early seventeenth century, Tretiakov Gallery, photo from N. Maiasova, *Drevnerusskoe shit'e* (Moscow: Iskusstvo, 1971), plate 54.

Plate 10. Battle Standard with images of the Archangel Michael and Ermak, late sixteenth century, The Armory Palace of the Moscow Kremlin, photo from *Oruzheinnaia palata* V. N. Ivanov, ed. (Moscow: Moskovskii rabochii, 1964), page 68.

Plate 11. "And I Saw Heaven Opened, and Behold a White Horse, and He that Sat Upon Him was Called Faithful and True, and in Righteousness He Doth Judge and Make War," sixteenth century, Annunciation Cathedral of the Moscow Kremlin, photo from Sokolova, *Rospis'* (see plate 8), plate 3.

Plate 12. The Apocalypse, late sixteenth century, National Museum, Stockholm, photo from Helge Kjellin, *Ryska Ikoner* (Stockholm: Svensk Literatur, 1956), plate 184. Reproduced by permission.

Plate 13. Joshua Conquering the Promised Land, reconstruction of lost murals in the Golden Palace of the Moscow Kremlin, drawing by K. K. Lopialo in O. A. Podobedova, *Moskovskaia shkola zhivopisi pri Ivane IV* (Moscow, 1972).

Plate 14. The Fourth Day of Creation. The Creation of the Sun, Moon, and Stars, nineteenth century (1882) after the late sixteenth-century scheme, the Palace of Facets of the Moscow Kremlin, photo from Aida Nasibova, *The Faceted Chamber in the Moscow Kremlin* (Leningrad: Aurora, 1978), plate 33. Reproduced by permission.

Plate 15. The Archangel Michael Appoints Moses Prince, seventeenth century based on sixteenth-century scheme, the Archangel Michael Cathedral of the Moscow Kremlin, photo from Iu. N. Dmitriev, "Stenopis' Arkhangel'skogo sobora Moskovskogo Kremlia," in *Drevnerusskoe iskusstvo. XVII vek* (Moscow: Nauka, 1964), plate facing p. 150.

Plate 16. The Archangel Michael Helps Gideon Defeat the Midianites, seventeenth century based on sixteenth-century scheme, photo from Jiri Burian and Oleg Shvidkovsky, *The Kremlin of Moscow* (New York: St. Martin's Press, 1975), plate 91. Reproduced by permission.

BREAKING THE CODE

THE IMAGE OF THE TSAR
IN THE MUSCOVITE PALM SUNDAY RITUAL

MICHAEL S. FLIER

Introduction

Of all of the customs and rituals described by foreign observers during their visits to medieval Muscovy in the sixteenth and seventeenth centuries, perhaps none is so impressive and intriguing as the religious procession held in Moscow one week before Easter. The annual Palm Sunday Ritual (*Deistvo v nedeliu Vaii*) brought together in an elaborate ceremony the most important personages in the realm on a stage no less dramatic and culturally charged than Cathedral Square inside the Kremlin and, somewhat later, Red Square outside its walls. From numerous extant descriptions,[1] we know that the Ritual was one of the major public events of the Church calendar, rivalling the Blessing of the Waters on Epiphany Day, 6 January. So important was its status in the spiritual life of medieval Moscow, that after the Poles decided to ban the Ritual during their 1611 occupation of the city, the threat of a popular riot forced them to reconsider and allow the Ritual to be performed.[2]

The research for this study was supported by a grant from the UCLA Committee on Research and by a University of California President's Fellowship in the Humanities for 1990. Citations of foreign descriptions of Russia include, when available and relevant, the dates of the journeys themselves enclosed in angled brackets < > and the dates of writing or first publication enclosed in square brackets [ ]. Multiple dates of publication refer to relevant revised editions. Unless otherwise indicated, translations are mine. I am grateful to Ia. S. Lur'e, who provided valuable comments and suggestions on an earlier version of this paper.

[1] For a review of the foreign accounts of the Palm Sunday Ritual in Moscow, see Konstantin Nikol'skii, *O sluzhbakh russkoi tserkvi, byvshikh v prezhnikh pechatnykh bogosluzhebnykh knigakh* (St. Petersburg, 1885), 45–97.

[2] Konrad Bussov <1584–1613>, *Moskovskaia khronika. 1584–1613*, dual-lang. ed., ed. I. I. Smirnov et al., trans. S. A. Akuliants (Moscow and Leningrad, 1961), 185, 320–321. Not the tsar, but a nobleman, Andrei Gundarov, led the ass. Bussov identifies the Muscovite celebration of Palm Sunday as second in importance only to the observance of St. Nicholas Day (apparently the spring celebration on 9 May rather than the winter celebration on 6 December). Cf. B. A. Uspenskii, *Filologicheskie razyskaniia v oblasti slavianskikh drevnostei (Relikty iazychestva v vostochnoslavianskom kul'te Nikolaia Mirlikiiskogo)* (Moscow, 1982), 6.

The earliest description of the Ritual in Moscow is recorded by an anonymous member of Anthony Jenkinson's English entourage who witnessed it in the spring of 1558:

> On Palme sunday they have a very solemne procession in this maner folowing.
>
> First, they have a tree of a good bignesse which is made fast upon two sleds, as though it were growing there, and it is hanged with apples, raisins, figs and dates, and with many other fruits abundantly. In the midst of the same tree stand 5. boyes in white vestures, which sing in the tree before the procession: after this there folowed certaine yong men with waxe tapers in their hands burning, and a great lanterne that all the light should not goe out: after them followed two with long banners, and 6. with round plates set upon long staves: the plates were of copper very ful of holes and thinne: then folowed 6. carrying painted images upon their shoulders, after the images follow certaine priests to the number of 100. or more, with goodly vestures, whereof 10. or 12. are of white damaske, set and imbrodered round about with faire and orient pearles, as great as pease, and among them certaine Saphires and other stones. After them followed one halfe of the Emperours noble men: then commeth the Emperours majestie and the Metropolitaine, after this maner.
>
> First, there is a horse covered with white linnen cloth down to the ground, his eares being made long with the same cloth like to an asses eares. Upon this horse the Metropolitane sitteth sidelong like a woman: in his lappe lieth a faire booke [the Gospels], with a crucifix of Goldsmiths worke upon the cover, which he holdeth fast with his left hand, and in his right hand he hath a crosse of gold, with which crosse he ceaseth not to blesse the people as he rideth.
>
> There are to the number of 30. men which spread abroad their garments before the horse, and as soone as the horse is past over any of them, they take them up againe and run before, and spred them againe, so that the horse doth always go on some of them. They which spred the garments are all priests sonnes, and for their labours, the Emperour giveth unto them new garments.
>
> One of the Emperours noble men leadeth the horse by the head, but the Emperour himselfe goyng on foote, leadeth the horse by the ende of the reine of his bridle with one of his hands, and in the other of his handes he had a braunch of a Palme tree: after this followed the rest of the Emperours Noble men and Gentlemen, with a great number of other people. In this order they went from one church to another within the castle [Kremlin],[3] about the distaunce of two flights shot: and so returned agayne to the Emperours Church [Cathedral of the Dormition], where they made

---

[3] Although anachronistic for the probable beginnings of the Muscovite Palm Sunday Ritual (1550s?, before the completion of the Cathedral of the Intercession on Red Square), the early seventeenth-century map of "Kremlenagrad" (plate 1) provides the clearest plan for charting the Ritual's subsequent development.

an end of their service. Which being done, the Emperours majestie and certaine of his noble men, went to the Metropolitaine his house to dinner, where of delicate fishes and good drinks there was no lacke.[4]

From later accounts we learn that the branches of the tree were distributed by the metropolitan to the assembled throng along with gifts to ranking members of the court.[5] The tsar was given 200 rubles by the metropolitan, which foreigners interpreted as payment for service rendered.[6]

Sometime between 1564 and 1576, Heinrich von Staden, a German mercenary in the service of Ivan IV's Oprichnina, recorded the same ritual.[7] His description reveals one important difference in the Ritual as compared with that seen by Jenkinson: the procession moves beyond the Kremlin walls to the Jerusalem Chapel of the Cathedral of the Intercession on Red Square (see plate 1, no. 1A) before returning to the Dormition (plate 1, no. 20).[8] This second version, with the extension to Red Square, is confirmed in the account of Prince Daniel von Buchau, ambassador of the Holy Roman Empire to Muscovy, who witnessed it in 1576:

> On the Sunday that derives its name from the palm branches spread before Christ entering Jerusalem—during the singing by youths of the words of the psalm "Blessed is he that cometh in the name of the Lord, Hosanna in the highest!"—the Muscovite metropolitan seated on an ass and the archbishops process to the cathedral named for the city of Jerusalem.
>
> Usually the grand prince himself leads the ass of the metropolitan; a wooden cross is carried before him, as it is before the other bishops.[9]

---

[4] The commentary of Anthony Jenkinson and his entourage <1557–1558 [publ. 1589]> in Richard Hakluyt, *The Principall Navigations Voiages and Discoveries of the English Nation*, facsim. ed., intro. David Beers Quinn and Raleigh Ashlin Skelton (Cambridge, 1965), 341–342.

[5] See Ivan Zabelin, *Domashnii byt russkogo naroda v XVI i XVII st.*, 2 vols., 3d exp. ed. (Moscow, 1895), v. 1, pt. 1: *Domashnii byt russkikh tsarei v XVI i XVII st.*, 414–415.

[6] Giles Fletcher <1588–1589 [publ. 1591]>, *Of the Russe Commonwealth*, facsim. ed. with variants, intro. Richard Pipes, glossary–index comp. John V. A. Fine, Jr. (Cambridge, Mass., 1966), 105; Adam Olearius <1634,1636,1639,1643 [publ. 1647, 1656]>, *The Travels of Olearius in Seventeenth-Century Russia*, 2d ed., ed. and trans. Samuel H. Baron (Stanford, 1967), 100. The figure of 100 is reported by Antonio Possevino <1582 [publ. 1584, 1882]>, *The Mission to Muscovy*, in Hugh F. Graham, ed. and trans., "The *Mission Muscovitica*," *Canadian–American Slavic Studies* 6, no. 3 (1972): 475; and by Samuel Collins <1657–1666>, *The Present State of Russia in a Letter to a Friend at London, Written by an Eminent Person Residing at the Great Tzars Court at Mosco for the Space of Nine Years* (London, 1671), 17.

[7] Heinrich von Staden <1564–1576? [publ. 1578–1579]>, *The Land and Government of Muscovy: A Sixteenth-Century Account*, trans. and ed. Thomas Esper (Stanford, 1967), 22, 41.

[8] Nikol'skii's objection to Jenkinson's limitation of the Ritual to the Kremlin in 1558 is unfounded: *O sluzhbakh* (see n. 1), 55. The Ritual was apparently not extended to Red Square until after the consecration of the chapels of the Church of the Intercession on the Moat on 1 October 1560: *PSRL*, v. 13, 320 <7069>.

[9] Daniel, prince of Buchau, <1576, 1578 [written 1577, published 1668, 1679, 1681, 1687]>, "Nachalo i vozvyshenie Moskovii," trans. I. A. Tikhomirov, *ČOIDR*, 1876, bk. 3, sec. 2, 40. Miroslav Labunka incorrectly characterizes Daniel's testimony as the oldest western description of the ritual, overlooking those of Jenkinson's entourage and Staden: "The Legend of the

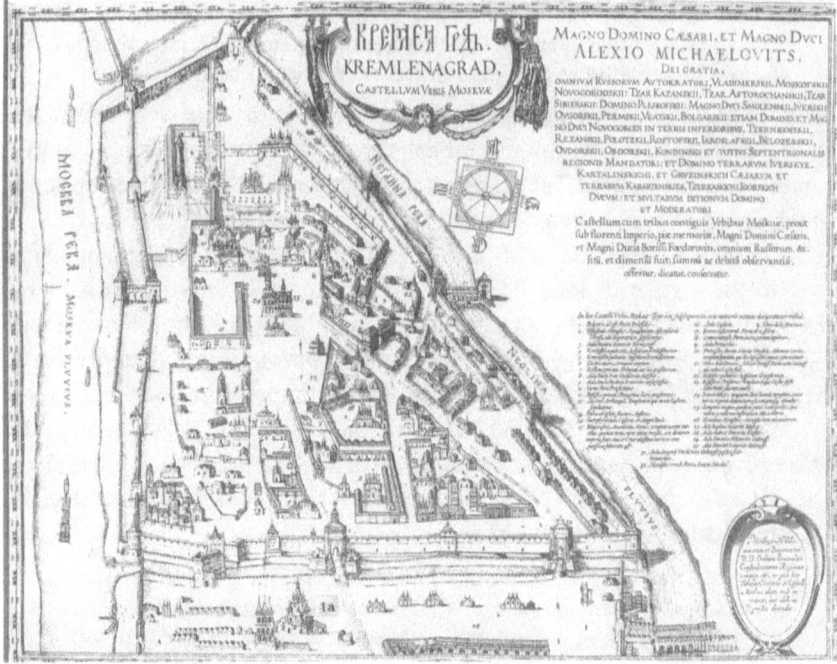

Plate 1. *Plan of the Moscow Kremlin* [Kremlenagrad]. Early 1600s. Supplement to M. V. Posokhin et al., eds., *Pamiatniki arkhitektury Moskvy. Kreml'. Kitai-gorod. Tsentral'nye ploshchadi.* (Moscow, 1982). Reproduced with permission. 1. Savior (Frol) Gates. 1A. Cathedral of the Intercession on the Moat (Saint Basil's Cathedral), Red Square, and Lobnoe Mesto. 12. Cathedral of the Archangel Michael. 14. Cathedral of the Annunciation. 20. Cathedral of the Dormition.

A third version, introduced in 1656, distinguished a procession on foot from the Dormition to the Intercession, and the Procession on the Ass (*Shestvie na osliati*) from Lobnoe Mesto in Red Square back to the Dormition.

Novgorodian White Cowl: The Study of Its 'Prologue' and 'Epilogue'," unpublished doctoral dissertation (Columbia University, 1978), 257, n. 1. In ignoring the English testimony, Labunka follows a tradition apparently begun by Nikol'skii and followed by later researchers. See Konstantin Nikol'skii, *O sluzhbakh* (see n. 1), 54–55; Georg Ostrogorsky, "Zum Stratordienst des Herrschers in der byzantinisch-slavischen Welt." *Seminarium Kondakovianum*, v. 7 (1935), 195; Robert O. Crummey, "Court Spectacles in Seventeenth-Century Russia: Illusion and Reality," in *Essays in Honor of A. A. Zimin,* ed. Daniel C. Waugh (Columbus, 1985), 143, n. 10. Snegirev seems to accept the English account, but ascribes it to Hakluyt rather than Jenkinson and mistakenly attributes the first version of the ceremony (confined to the Kremlin) to the chronicle of Martin Behr [Konrad Bussov]: I. M. Snegirev, *Russkie prostonarodnye prazdniki i suevernye obriady,* 4 pts. (Moscow, 1838), pt. 3, 161–164.

Plate 2. *The Palm Sunday Ritual in Moscow*, 10 April 1636. Engraving from Adam Olearius, *Vermehrte Newe Beschreibung Der Muscowitischen und Persischen Reise* (Schleswig, 1656), p. 132a.

Plate 3. *The Palm Sunday Ritual in Moscow*, 23 March 1662. Engraving from F. Adelung, *Al'bom Meierberga. Vidy i bytovye kartiny Rossii XVII veka* (St. Petersburg, 1903), pl. 73.

The earliest engravings of the Palm Sunday Ritual in Moscow are from the seventeenth century, but they reproduce many of the elements found in the earlier accounts. In plates 2 and 3 we see the artist's rendering of the 1636 and 1662 ceremonies described by Adam Olearius and Baron Augustin Meyerberg, respectively.

Arguably the most problematic aspect of the Palm Sunday Ritual in Moscow is its presentation of the tsar in an uncharacteristically subservient role vis-à-vis the head of the Church, that is, as the metropolitan's equerry or groom. Since the ruler mentioned in the accounts above is Tsar Ivan IV, this particular royal image is remarkable indeed. Is Ivan breaking the code that otherwise appears to place him at the apex of Muscovite society without institutional restraint?[10] Or is the image of the tsar to be understood as a rare direct representation of the "political culture" of the Muscovite court, indicating "the realities of an informal, 'corporate,' and oligarchic political system" otherwise "masked by a facade of complex protocol, hierarchic nomenclature, and ecclesiastical trappings elaborated with great inventiveness and false circumstance?"[11] Or could the Muscovite audience for whom the Ritual was intended have viewed the tsar's role differently, as a consequence of time, place and event, a transformed context in which a comparison of relative dignity of worldly office would not have been appropriate?

I propose to review the material relevant to these issues and to suggest an alternative iconographical analysis that serves to "break the code" represented by the Ritual, thereby demonstrating how it actually enhanced rather than diminished the authority of the tsar. In particular I will scrutinize the symbolic value of the equerry service in defining the image of the tsar in the Ritual. Before presenting this analysis, however, I must review briefly the function of Palm Sunday itself.

Palm Sunday in the Orthodox Calendar

Among the Sundays of the paschal season, Palm Sunday alone shares with Easter the property of correlative perspective. Both serve simultaneously as the climax of the preceding week and the beginning of the next.[12] In its retrospective function, Palm Sunday concludes Palm Week, a period devoted

---

[10] Richard Hellie, "What Happened? How Did He Get Away with It? Ivan Groznyi's Paranoia and the Problem of Institutional Restraints," in *Ivan the Terrible: A Quarcentenary Celebration of his Death* [= *Russian History* 14, nos. 1–4], ed. Richard Hellie, 219, 221.

[11] Edward L. Keenan, "Muscovite Political Folkways," *RR* 45, no. 2 (1986): 129.

[12] See Michael S. Flier, "Sunday in Medieval Russian Culture: *Nedelja* versus *Voskresenie*," in *Medieval Russian Culture*, ed. Henrik Birnbaum and Michael S. Flier. California Slavic Studies, v. 12. (Berkeley, Los Angeles, London, 1984), 124–131.

to the events surrounding Lazarus in Bethany that lead to his Resurrection or Raising, celebrated on Palm Saturday, the preceding day. Lazarus, already dead four days and mouldering in the grave, is restored to life by Christ in historical time. In its anticipatory function, Palm Sunday marks the beginning of Passion Week. The celebration of Christ's historical Entry into Jerusalem sets into motion the series of events that culminates with his Resurrection on Easter Sunday. In both functions, Palm Sunday serves as an index to the victory over human death, and as such has eschatological force; it is emblematic of the promise of the General Resurrection at the Last Judgment (Rev. 20:12–15). The link between the Raising of Lazarus and the General Resurrection is made explicit in the troparion of the General Resurrection that recurs throughout the services on Palm (Lazarus) Saturday and Palm Sunday:

> Giving us before Thy Passion an assurance of the general resurrection, Thou hast raised Lazarus from the dead, O Christ our God. Therefore, like the children, we also carry tokens of victory, and cry to Thee, the Conqueror of death: Hosanna in the highest; blessed is He that comes in the Name of the Lord.[13]

With its concentration on resurrection as historical fact and eschatological certainty, Palm Sunday symbolizes the hope of the flock prepared to face Orthodoxy's greatest test: the Apocalypse.

Any ritual that reenacts the Entry into Jerusalem presents a complex of symbols, a model, that resonates in linear time and cyclical time.[14] The historical event is transformed into a pattern of cosmic order, identifiable through analogous events in the subsequent flow of history, and verifiable through cyclical repetition, the symbolic value of which serves to bond the members of a society together. In the terminology of Clifford Geertz, the ritual is both a "model of" and a "model for" social and psychological reality.[15] Performed on an annual basis, the Palm Sunday Ritual provided a model for reinforcing the spiritual commitment of the Russian Orthodox faithful to the salvation of mankind ordained by the First Coming of the Messiah and the Resurrection, a prefiguration of the Second Coming and the universal victory over death. The obvious success of the Palm Sunday

---

[13] Translation from the Greek by Mother Mary and Archimandrite Kallistos Ware, *The Lenten Triodion* (London and Boston, 1978), 476.

[14] Cf. views of geological time discussed in Stephen Jay Gould, *Time's Arrow, Time's Cycle: Myth and Metaphor in the Discovery of Geological Time* (Cambridge, Mass. and London, 1987).

[15] "Religion as a Cultural System," *Anthropological Approaches to the Study of Religion,* ed. M. Banton (London, 1966), reprinted in Clifford Geertz, *The Interpretation of Cultures: Selected Essays* (New York, 1973), 93.

Ritual in Moscow provides the clearest evidence that the ceremony made the historical and eschatological dimensions of the celebration a social reality, that is, had the transformative power to bring contemporary Moscow into contact with the Jerusalem of old and the New Jerusalem beyond time. Through the power of formalized recurrence, the ritual images of tsar and metropolitan were shaped by and in turn shaped the model of salvation in the minds of the Orthodox faithful.

Development of the Palm Sunday Ritual in Muscovy

The Palm Sunday Ritual was an established part of ceremonial life in Moscow by the middle of the sixteenth century. As such, it would not be expected to attract particular attention in Russian sources, and indeed, early Russian references to the Ritual are scant, three in all. Remarkably these sixteenth-century Russian accounts are limited to the Ritual as performed in Novgorod, not Moscow, and thus provide a complement to the foreign sources.

The first reference to the Novgorod Ritual is found in the "Tale of the White Cowl," a work attributed to the court of Archbishop Gennadius (1484–1504) in the late fifteenth century.[16] The epilogue to the "Tale" mentions a Palm Sunday celebration that included a procession from the Cathedral of the Holy Sophia to the Church of Holy Jerusalem (inside the Novgorod kremlin) led by Archbishop Gennadius, riding on the back of the foal of an ass. No secular official is described as holding the reins of the ass during the procession. Labunka suggests that this omission could have been accidental, that it is actually difficult to imagine an archbishop riding in such a procession without assistance.[17] It is likely that the equerry service was performed, if one assumes that the archbishop held the Gospels in one hand and a cross in the other.

The second reference is from 1548, the earliest *dated* performance of the Ritual. In the description of the service in the Novgorod kremlin, the governors (*namestniki*) of Novgorod, Princes Ivan Mikhailovich Shuiskii and Iurii Mikhailovich Bulgakov, lead the foal of an ass ridden by the archbishop from the Cathedral of Holy Sophia to the Church of the Entry into Jerusalem

---

[16] Labunka, "Legend," (see n. 9), 194ff. There is controversy over the dating of the "Tale," some assigning it to the 1490s, others to the middle of the sixteenth century, see Ia. S. Lur'e, *Ideologicheskaia bor'ba v russkoi publitsistike kontsa XV–nachala XVI veka* (Moscow and Leningrad, 1960), 231ff. If the latter position is correct, then the Ritual may very well have been introduced in Moscow and then ascribed a Novgorodian provenience to give it greater traditional authority. Be that as it may, I will present the traditional argument here with a Novgorodian source.

[17] Ibid., 240–241.

and back.[18] The archbishop presented both princes with icons on smooth gold, and processional silver cups worth five Muscovite rubles each. He hosted them at a banquet following the ceremony. There is no mention of other aspects of the Ritual known from Moscow: the tree, the disguised horse, the boys singing hosannas, the boys spreading garments or cloth before the procession.

The third reference is found in an archiepiscopal ordinary of Novgorod the Great and Pskov,[19] apparently compiled between 1550 and 1563 at the Volokolamsk Monastery, but based on commentary dating as far back as 1527. Golubtsov assumes that the ordinary reflects the liturgical practices of Novgorod in the 1540s.[20] After Matins and the Third Hour of the Sunday morning Palm Sunday service, the archbishop mounts the foal of an ass in front of Holy Sophia, and is led away by the two governors. A large willow prepared ahead of time is decorated with various fruits (*na vetvekh zh eia obesheno grozdie razno*) and transported in front of the archbishop in imitation (*v obraz*) of our Lord, Jesus Christ. The procession makes its way to the Church of the Entry into Jerusalem, where the archbishop dismounts. Following a brief service, he again mounts the foal of the ass and is led back by the governors to Holy Sophia, where he dismounts, blesses the governors with his cross and invites them to a meal in compensation for their services (*za trudy ikh esti zovet*). It should be noted, however, that the description of the Palm Sunday Ritual is found in a part of the ordinary written in as many as six hands with numerous interpolations and annotations, one dated as late as 1556.[21] The *entire* passage concerning the preparation and movement of a large willow tree hung with fruit in the Palm Sunday service is set apart by editor Golubtsov in a different typeface, indicative of a later interpolation, a fact not noted by Labunka in his analysis of this text.[22] The decorated tree may indeed be a Muscovite innovation.[23] Other Russian

---

[18] I. K. Kupriianov, "Otryvki iz Raskhodnykh knig Sofiiskogo doma za 1548-i god," *Izvestiia Imp. Arkheologicheskogo obshchestva* 3, [no. 1] (1861), col. 48.

[19] "Chin tserkovnyi arxiepiskopa Velikogo Novagoroda i Pskova," in A. P. Golubtsov, *Chinovnik Novgorodskogo Sofiiskogo sobora, ČOIDR*, 1899, bk. 2, pt. 1, 239–262. The Palm Sunday material is found on pp. 256–257.

[20] Ibid., ix–xiii. See Labunka, "Legend," (see n. 9), 231ff.

[21] Golubtsov, *Chinovnik Novgorodskogo Sofiiskogo sobora* (see n. 19), xii–xiii.

[22] "Legend," (see n. 9), 503.

[23] In favor of this interpretation is the fact that there are no specific expenditures noted for services rendered on the part of singers, people casting garments, carpenters, or fruit vendors in the 1548 expense records for the Palm Sunday Ritual at Holy Sophia. Chaldeans in the December Fiery Furnace play, in contrast, are listed as receiving eight altyns for boots and mittens, and two Moscow grivnas, apparently for their performance. See Kupriianov, "Otryvki," (see n. 18), cols. 34, 36.

descriptions of the Palm Sunday Ritual in Novgorod and Moscow are from the seventeenth century and add nothing of significance to our understanding of the origins of the Ritual.[24]

The evidence for the existence of the Palm Sunday Ritual in Novgorod by the late fifteenth century finds no counterpart for Moscow during the same period. In fact Labunka proposes concrete proof that the Ritual did not exist in Moscow before 1498.[25] An embroidered shroud belonging to Princess Elena, widowed daughter-in-law of Ivan III, apparently depicts the royal Palm Sunday ceremony in Moscow on 8 April of that year (plate 4). The procession shows Grand Prince Ivan III, his son Basil, his grandson Crown Prince Dmitrii, Princess Elena, and Metropolitan Simon. The ceremony proceeds on foot; there is no horse or ass in sight. Labunka follows the analysis of Shchepkina,[26] and supported by Svirin and Maiasova.[27] Grabar' agrees that the scene depicted reflects Russian reality but excludes a Palm Sunday procession as the likely subject because it is not the members of the court who hold the branches.[28] Thus the identification of the procession as a Palm Sunday ceremony remains open. It should be noted, however, that in the 1622 ceremonial book for Moscow's Cathedral of the Dormition a priest is described as carrying an image of the Mother of God with two sextons guarding it on either side.[29] Regardless of the status of the shroud, which would provide negative evidence at best, there is no earlier mention of the Palm Sunday Ritual in any of the foreign reports about Moscow before the Jenkinson description of 1558, including the extensive descriptions of Muscovite life provided by Herberstein on the basis of his trips to Russia in 1517 and 1526.[30]

To summarize the findings from Russian sources, we can state that as

---

[24] A. P. Golubtsov, *Chinovnik Novgorodskogo Sofiiskogo sobora* (see n. 19), 180–188; and idem., *Chinovnik Moskovskogo Uspenskogo sobora*, in *ČOIDR*, 1907, bk. 4, pt. 1, 102–108 (second version), 250–253 (third version).

[25] See "Legend," (see n. 9), 255–256 and n. 1.

[26] M. V. Shchepkina, *Izobrazhenie russkikh istoricheskikh lits v shit'e XV veka* (Moscow, 1954), 12–21.

[27] A. V. Svirin, *Drenerusskoe shit'e* (Moscow, 1963), 52–55; N. A. Maiasova, *Drevnerusskoe shit'e* (Moscow, 1971), 20, pl. 27.

[28] A. I. Grabar', "Zametka o metode ozhivleniia traditsii ikonopisi v russkoi zhivopisi XV–XVI vekov," *TODRL* 36 (1981), 291–294. Maiasova continues to support Shchepkina's identification of specific personages in the Muscovite court, but does not insist that the scene depicted is indeed a Palm Sunday procession, apparently agreeing with Grabar' that it simply shows the veneration of the Virgin Hodegetria icon: N. A. Maiasova, "Pamiatniki litsevogo shit'ia iz sobraniia Uspenskogo sobora," *Uspenskii sobor Moskovskogo kremlia*, ed. E. S. Smirnova (Moscow, 1985), 198–200.

[29] Golubtsov, *Chinovnik Moskovskogo Uspenskogo sobora*, (see n. 24), 105.

[30] Sigmund von Herberstein, *Rerum Moscoviticarum Commentarii* (Vienna, 1549, and subsequent Latin and German editions). Herberstein was not in Moscow itself for Palm Sunday on either occasion, however. The relevant dates for Palm Sunday were 5 April 1517, and 25 March

Plate 4. *Shroud of Princess Elena.* 1498. State Historical Museum, Moscow. Reproduced with permission. From N. A. Maiasova, *Drevnerusskoe shit'e* (Moscow, 1971), pl. 27. Center row, left side [left to right]: Crown Prince Dmitrii [wearing crown with nimbus, arms crossed], son of Elena; Basil, son of Ivan III; Grand Prince Ivan III [wearing crown with nimbus]. Center row, right side: Metropolitan Simon [pictured with nimbus]. Front row, left side: Princess Sophia Paleologue [fourth from left] followed by her two unmarried daughters Theodora and Eudocia, who flank Princess Elena.

compared to the Muscovite Ritual described by foreigners from 1558 on, the Palm Sunday Ritual in Novgorod was apparently less elaborate, at least until the middle of the sixteenth century. Aside from specific prayers and

---

1526; his stays in Moscow were 14 April –21 November 1517, and 26 April–11 November 1526. Given his interest in church customs, however, one might have expected a passing reference to unusual Palm Sunday practice.

songs associated with the holiday, it was limited to the Procession on the Ass between the Cathedral of Holy Sophia and the Church of the Entry into Jerusalem. The equerry service was provided by the governors of Novgorod.

The Origins of the Ritual

In light of the manuscript evidence, domestic and foreign, received opinion holds that the Palm Sunday Ritual in Russia originated in Novgorod in the late fifteenth century and was introduced in Moscow by Macarius sometime after 1542, when he left his post as archbishop of Novgorod to become metropolitan of Moscow.[31]

In his pioneering study of the equerry service (*Stratordienst*) Ostrogorsky allowed for the likelihood that the Palm Sunday reenactment ritual itself might have come to Novgorod from Jerusalem via the Greeks, but that the equerry service contained within the Novgorod version could not have come from the same source. Rituals in Jerusalem were noted for their faithfulness to the text and since Christ was without equerry in the Gospel account of the Entry, the Jerusalem Church would not have permitted the inclusion of such a person.[32] Likewise there is no accounting for the equerry service from Byzantine Palm Sunday rituals.[33] Furthermore, Ostrogorsky proposed that

---

[31] See Ostrogorsky, "Zum Stratordienst," (see n. 9), 195, 202. Labunka ("Legend," [see n. 9], 251ff.) correctly identifies Archbishop Gennadius of Novgorod as the initiator of the Palm Sunday Ritual and not Macarius, who simply brought knowledge of the basic ritual to Moscow when he took on the duties of metropolitan there. Gennadius's connection with the "Tale of the White Cowl" and the mention of the Palm Sunday Ritual with the Procession on the Ass in its epilogue substantiate Labunka's hypothesis.

[32] The Greeks had apparently reenacted Christ's Entry into Jerusalem in the Holy Land on Palm Sunday as far back as the early fifth century: a procession went from the Mount of Olives to the Church of the Anastasis within the Basilica of the Holy Sepulchre. The pilgrim Egeria states that "the bishop is led in the same manner as the Lord once was led," which some scholars have interpreted to mean riding on the back of an ass. Children sing hosannas and carry palm and olive branches. From the sixth through eighth centuries the Palm Sunday procession spread to the Nestorian church of Persia and to Western Europe. *Egeria: Diary of a Pilgrimage*, trans. and annot. George E. Gingras (New York and Ramsey, N.J., 1970), 103–105, 156 (n. 167), 234 (n. 359).

[33] In Constantinople itself, Palm Sunday was celebrated in separate ceremonies by the patriarch and the emperor. By the ninth or tenth century the patriarch participated in the Procession on the Ass from Hagia Sophia to the Church of the Forty Martyrs, then went *on foot* to the Forum of Constantine and back to Hagia Sophia. There is no mention of equerry service in the ceremonial. The emperor celebrated in ceremonies in and around the imperial palace, avoiding the patriarch and thus not diminishing his imperial prestige in the presence of the prelate when he enacted the role of Christ. On those occasions when Palm Sunday coincided with Annunciation Day and the emperor was obliged to be at the Church of the Forty Martyrs for services, he went to the church only *after* the patriarch had concluded the Procession on the Ass and distributed palms. The procession following was conducted in the prescribed manner with both patriarch and emperor walking on foot. See A. Dmitrievskii, "Khozhdenie patriarkha Konstantinopol'skogo na zhrebiati v nedeliu vaii v IX i X vekakh," *Sbornik statei v chest' aka-*

the source of the equerry service in the Novgorod Palm Sunday Ritual with the Procession on the Ass was the *Donation of Constantine*, the eighth-century western forgery in which Constantine the Great grants to Pope Sylvester primacy over the Christian Church in Rome and its environs. The *Donation* served as the basis for upholding the Church's authority in the continual struggle between the Western Church and secular officials. The *Donation* proper may be termed forgery 1. A later interpolation in the *Donation* notes that Constantine crowned Pope Sylvester with a white cowl, served as equerry for the pontiff by holding the horse's bridle, as a sign of deference to the first pope, Saint Peter, and ordered that all Peter's successors and they alone would wear the white cowl. The one-time equerry service and exclusive use of the white cowl is forgery 2. Specifically the passage that reads

> ... and in deference to the blessed Peter we [Constantine] held the bridle of his [Pope Sylvester's] horse, rendering to him the service of equerry ...

has been used since the eighth century in Western Europe to justify the symbolic respect and submission of secular to ecclesiastical authority shown through the performance of the equerry service. In the earliest documented case,[34] Pepin the Short, king of the Franks, held the reins of the horse mounted by Pope Stephen II at Ponthion in January 754.

Can the identification of the equerry service in the Novgorod Palm Sunday Ritual with the *Donation* as a gesture of royal submissiveness explain why the Ritual was introduced in the late fifteenth century? We know that this was a time when the Church of that city was developing ideological weapons to use against the Judaizer heresy and the growing encroachment of secular authority in matters of Church property.[35] In a city open to Western ideas and with a long antiprincely tradition, the Ritual might have emphasized the spiritual and even political preeminence of the archbishop over secular officialdom. Members of the circle around Gennadius were responsible for introducing a number of works that extolled the superiority of ecclesiastical authority, including original compositions inspired by the

---

demika Alekseiia Ivanovicha Sobolevskogo (Leningrad, 1928), 69–75, and Averil Cameron, "The Construction of Court Ritual: The Byzantine *Book of Ceremonies,* " in *Rituals of Royalty: Power and Ceremonial in Traditional Societies,* ed. David Cannadine and Simon Price (Cambridge, 1987), 116. The Procession on the Ass was eliminated by the time the emperor began to participate in the Palm Sunday Ritual together with the patriarch, probably during the fourteenth century. See Labunka, "Legend," (see n. 9), 225–226.

[34] Ostrogorsky, "Zum Stratordienst," (see n. 9), 187.

[35] Joseph L. Wieczynski, "Archbishop Gennadius and the West: The Impact of Catholic Ideas upon the Church of Novgorod," *Canadian–American Slavic Studies* 6, no. 3 (1972): 374ff.

Donation: the "Tale of the White Cowl" by Dmitrii the Small[36] and the "Brief Discourse against Those Who Encroach upon Things that are Holy" (1497) by the Croatian Dominican priest, Benjamin. The Palm Sunday Ritual, briefly described in the epilogue of Gerasimov's "Tale," was simply part of this larger arsenal. One must ask, however, whether the motivation for the Ritual's introduction should be limited to the religious-political issue of the secularization of Church property, especially since it was not the Muscovite grand prince, the proclaimed head of state, but the governors of Novgorod who performed the equerry service in the northern city.

Evidence from chronicles, ecclesiastical tracts, epistles, painting, and linguistic innovation indicates that Russia had far more pressing concerns at the end of the fifteenth century. As the bastion of independent Eastern Orthodoxy after the fall of Constantinople in 1453, Muscovy believed itself to be on the brink of a new age.[37] According to Byzantine apocalyptic thought, world history was destined to endure one cosmic week, seven millennia. At the onset of the Eighth Millennium Christ would return to earth in the Second Coming to sit at the Last Judgment. Following the General Resurrection of the Dead the righteous would be permitted to share life eternal in the New Jerusalem whereas the rest of mankind would be cast into the everlasting flames of Hell. Byzantine reckoning calculated the Creation as having occurred 5508 years before Christ; thus the Eighth Millennium would commence on 1 September 1492.

It was anxiety over the End Times that prompted Archbishop Gennadius to send Dmitri Trachaniotes to Western Europe to learn more about the scientific determination of the precise time of the Apocalypse. The Orthodox Church was so convinced that the world would end in the year 7000 that the paschal tables used to compute the date of Easter and correlated holidays provided calculations only up to the year 7000.[38]

During a period taken with apocalyptic thoughts, the message of Palm Sunday would have held out the greatest comfort, focused as it is on the General Resurrection at the Last Judgment. The neologism for Palm Sunday, "Willow Resurrection" (*Verbnoe Voskresenie*), emerged in the late fif-

---

[36] Most specialists assume Dmitrii the Small to be Dmitrii Gerasimov, despite the reference in some copies of the "Tale" to Dmitri the Translator or the Greek. For details, see Lur'e *Ideologicheskaia bor'ba* (see n. 16), 226–230, and "Legend" (see n. 9), 43–84.

[37] For an essentially anti-Byzantine view of Muscovite mythmaking in response to the decline of the Byzantine Empire, see George P. Majeska, "Russia's Perception of Byzantium after the Fall," *The Byzantine Legacy in Eastern Europe*, ed. Lowell Clucas (Boulder and New York, 1988), 19–31.

[38] "Drevnie russkie paskhalii na os'muiu tysiachu let ot sotvoreniia mira," *Pravoslavnyi Sobesednik*, 1860, no. 3:333–334; and "Legend" (see n. 9), 73–76.

teenth century, and generated a paschal "resurrection cycle," that underscored the timeless validity of the Resurrection of Christ (*Voskresenie Khristovo*) and the General Resurrection (*Obshchee Voskresenie*).[39]

The introduction of the Palm Sunday Ritual in its turn can be interpreted as part of an effort by Gennadius and the Novgorod Church to reassure the Orthodox faithful that the General Resurrection was attainable in the face of the imminent end of the world, despite the doubts cast by the Judaizer heresy. The attempt to elevate the spiritual role of the Church leadership at a time of terrifying crisis is probably also behind the introduction of the Procession on the Ass with the equerry service in the installation ceremony of the metropolitan at the end of the fifteenth century. When Simon was installed as the metropolitan of Moscow in 1495 by Grand Prince Ivan III, the Vologodsko-Permskaia Chronicle notes that "The colt of an ass under the metropolitan was led then by Mikhail Rusalka."[40] It is important to keep the apocalyptic as well as the historical meaning of the Palm Sunday Ritual in mind when considering the image of the tsar in its Muscovite instantiation.

Breaking the Code

Fleshed out with a few details from later sources, the Jenkinson account of the Ritual provides us with the earliest and most detailed description of the ceremony in Moscow. The arrangement of the participants in the Palm Sunday Ritual presents a hierarchy in microcosm of contemporary Muscovite society identified with high culture.[41] The *narod* in this sense is devoid of semiotic value and without representation. In the center—the focus of the procession—we find the tsar and the metropolitan, the respective heads of State and Church, flanked in front and in back by the Muscovite nobility and state officials, the power elite. Processing in front of the nobility is the clergy, responsible for sustaining the society spiritually; behind the nobility are the merchants, responsible for sustaining the society materially. The children, sons of the nobility and the priesthood, serve to focus attention on the major parts of the procession: boys standing in the tree and singing hosannas, boys casting their garments before the central entry as a mark of honor. The procession takes place before an audience of the tsar's own

---

[39] See Flier, "Sunday," (see n. 12), 141–145.
[40] *PSRL*, v. 26 (1959), 326. See Labunka, "Legend," (see n. 9), 266–273 for references. The fact that a secular official performs the equerry service in the installation ceremony makes it likely that the same service was performed in the earliest Novgorod version of the Palm Sunday Ritual.
[41] Cf. Crummey, "Court Spectacles," (see n. 9), 136.

harquebusiers (*strel'tsy*) and special invited guests, including foreign officials.

The tsar, walking on foot, pulls the metropolitan's disguised horse. Following the service conducted by the metropolitan in the state cathedral (Cathedral of the Dormition), the procession is formed and probably makes its way to the necropolis church (Cathedral of the Archangel Michael) and the palace church (Cathedral of the Annunciation) before returning to the Dormition for the end of the service. In the second version the procession spans the space between the Dormition inside the Kremlin and the Intercession in Red Square.

At the level of immediate performance the contrast between the central figures as regards position, mode of movement, and activity signals hierarchical inequality. The tsar is low (on the ground), walking, and pulling the reins of a horse; the metropolitan is high (mounted), riding, and embracing holy relics. Little wonder that the English viewed the Ritual as a direct reflection of inequality of dignity between emperor and prelate. In the Jenkinson interpretation inequality was a mark of submission of the tsar to the metropolitan's authority:

> The Metropolitane is next unto God, our Ladie and S. Nicholas accepted: for the Emperours majestie judgeth and affirmeth him to bee of higher dignitie then himselfe: for that saith he is Gods spirituall officer, and I the Emperour am his temporall officer, and therefore his majestie submitteth himselfe unto him in many things concerning religious matters, as in leading the Metropolitans horse upon Palme sunday, and giving him leave to sit on a chaire upon the 12. day [Epiphany], when the river Mosko was in blessing, and his majestie standing on the ice.[42]

The "submission hypothesis" is at the center of Ostrogorsky's discussion of the significance of the equerry service in Russia. Metropolitan Macarius's allusion to the example of Emperor Constantine, "Equal-to-the-Apostles," serving as groom to his spiritual father, Pope Sylvester, could not fail to impress upon the young, impulsive, and passionately devout Tsar Ivan the need to do the same.[43] Metropolitan Macarius cites the *Donation* in a reply to Tsar Ivan IV (thus after the coronation on 16 January 1547). He warns Ivan against expropriating Church lands and possessions, but in addition introduces his own touch to Constantine's statement to Sylvester by claiming that the emperor ordered that all of Peter's successors (prelates) were entitled to the equerry service as well.

---

[42] Hakluyt, *Principall Navigations,* (see n. 4), 343–344.
[43] "Zum Stratordienst," (see n. 9), 201.

We [Constantine] . . . holding the bridle of his horse (*brozdy konia ego*) with our own hands for the sake of the blessed Peter, have offered ourselves to him [Sylvester] in the dignity of equerry (*koniushskim sanom dakhomsia emu*). And we order this office and custom to be rendered always to all the prelates after him in their processions (*v poiazdekh svoikh*), in imitation of our empire.[44]

The introduction of continuous equerry service produced forgery 3, or "a forgery raised to the third power."[45] Ostrogorsky's view has received the recent support of two Russian medievalists, Robert Crummey and Paul Bushkovitch.

Crummey recognizes that the emphasis of the Muscovite Palm Sunday Ritual is on the tsar's humility before Christ as represented by the metropolitan, but suggests that "it is impossible to ignore the overtones of submission of the secular arm to the church."[46] Bushkovitch makes an even stronger claim, asserting that in the Palm Sunday Ritual "the tsar showed humility before a living person, the head of the Russian Church, not God or Christ."[47] The features of the tsar's performance just described stand counter to those we expect in other conventional situations. Only he and the metropolitan have thrones on which to sit during services in the state cathedral. During a royal audience, the tsar remains seated while those attending typically stand. If his courtiers sit, the level of their seats is below that of his throne.[48] Thus if inequality is signalled at the immediate level of performance by the tsar, then it is *purposeful* inequality, designed to enhance the image of the tsar. He performs a topos of humility as a *podvig*, a pious deed. In exchange for his labors, the metropolitan does not give him gifts, precious

---

[44] G. N. Moiseeva, "Starshaia redaktsiia 'Pisaniia' mitropolita Makariia Ivanu IV," *TODRL* 16 (1960): 471. The text here is reproduced from manuscript PS No. 7 from the end of the sixteenth century. That manuscript contains two texts: 1) an epistle [*pisanie*] from Metropolitan Macarius to Grand Prince Ivan, apparently written prior to 1547, and 2) Macarius' reply [*otvet*] and epistle to Tsar Ivan, written after 1547. The reference to the *Donation* occurs in the second, *contra* Labunka, who ascribes it to the first, apparently not realizing that two texts were copied into the same manuscript ("Legend," [see n. 9], 252, n. 1). Donald Ostrowski provides textological evidence to suggest that the epistle was actually derived from the reply, and that both were written between Ivan IV's coronation in 1547 and the convocation of the Stoglav Council in 1551: "A 'Fontological' Investigation of the Muscovite Church Council of 1503," unpublished doctoral dissertation (Pennsylvania State University, 1977), 127ff. These documents provide further evidence that the Palm Sunday Ritual was brought to Moscow by Macarius and introduced with elaborations after Ivan was crowned as tsar.

[45] Ernst H. Kantorowicz, "The 'King's Advent' and the Enigmatic Panels in the Doors of Santa Sabina," *Art Bulletin* 26, no. 4 (1944): 230.

[46] "Court Spectacles," (see n. 9), 134.

[47] "The Epiphany Ceremony of the Russian Court in the Sixteenth and Seventeenth Centuries," *RR* 49, no. 1 (1990), 3.

[48] Crummey, "Court Spectacles," (see n. 9), 136–138.

religious objects, as in the case of the Novgorod ceremony, but rubles, coin of the realm, venal money. Since a Russian tsar is not otherwise required to perform manual labor for monetary compensation, such an exchange renders him even more humble. The act may be construed as an instance of rendering unto Caesar the things which are Caesar's (Matt. 22:21), but it still has the effect of casting the emperor in the role of a lowly servant. That the most powerful person in Muscovy would so humble himself before his court and selected foreigners must have impressed all in attendance. And as a model for ritual humility, the tsar could look back past Emperor Constantine to Christ, who humbled himself before John the Forerunner by undergoing baptism (Matt. 3:13–17) and by entering Jerusalem on the back of an ass (Matt. 21:4–5) instead of a horse. Such a public display of spiritual devotion performed by the tsar every year would, in fact, manifest the second of two complementary images of the ideal ruler recently proposed as prototypical in Muscovite literary ideology: meekness and humility, as opposed to strength and power.[49] Possessed of both images in theory, the ideal tsar would be able to carry out his primary obligations: mediating between God's will and the action of his subjects, protecting the Orthodox faith as spiritual shepherd, and maintaining the established order throughout the realm.[50] The Palm Sunday Ritual provides a regulated context in which the tsar's topos of humility is to be performed. But it is a mistake to attribute to symbols in one context the same value they have in others. The tsar's humility is *not* directed towards the metropolitan as head of the Church, but towards the metropolitan as the representation of Christ. This is an important distinction reflected in the findings of the 1678 Synod, which conducted an inquiry into the Ritual. It concluded that the Palm Sunday Ritual should be continued in Moscow precisely because it glorified Christ through the tsar's humility and was thus pleasing and laudable:

> ... most of all, since our most pious autocrats deign to be in it, in order to show the Orthodox people the image of their humility and submission before Christ the Lord, for they have accepted a most humble custom, that when the patriarch has mounted the colt to commemorate the Lord's Entry into Jerusalem, they restrain their imperial haughtiness and hold fast to the reins of that ass's foal with their sceptre-beautiful hands and thus lead it right to the cathedral church to serve Christ the Lord: this act is indeed praiseworthy, for many are moved by so much humility on the part of the

---

[49] Daniel Rowland, "Did Muscovite Literary Ideology Place Limits on the Power of the Tsar (1540s-1660s)?" *RR* 49, no. 2 (1990): 135.
[50] Ibid., 132ff.

earthly Emperor before the Heavenly Emperor and having grasped from God the spirit of grief inside themselves, they descend to soul-sparing humility and from the bottom of their hearts they release a warm groan towards Christ the Lord, singing forth through reverent lips: "Hosanna in the highest, blessed is he who comes in the name of the Lord, King of Israel."[51]

If the equerry service is defined as "a ritual through which respect and submission are demonstrated by a person in a subordinate position vis-à-vis his superior by the act of leading (holding the reins of) the animal, mounted by the latter,"[52] then the Synod's statement about "humility on the part of the earthly Emperor before the Emperor of Heaven" makes it clear that the tsar humbles himself before Christ, not the metropolitan.

When the metropolitan represents himself, as in the installation ceremony, he is ordained in a solemn service during which he is presented with his ceremonial staff by the tsar. After the *mnogoletie* is said for him and the tsar, the metropolitan participates in the Procession on the Ass, first within the confines of the courtyard near Cathedral Square and later around the wall of the Kremlin to the Nicholas Gates, where he blesses the people and the city. In all cases, the equerry service is performed by grooms and boyars from the courts of the tsar or the metropolitan, never by the tsar himself.[53] If the instruction of the *Donation* were truly followed, the tsar would serve as equerry out of deference to Saint Peter in all such processions, as specifically stated in Macarius's reply cited above.

This distinction between humility before Christ and not before the metropolitan makes sense in the historical context as well. The church historian Golubinsky points out that from the time of Ivan III, the metropolitan was in fact a creature of the grand prince. It was the ruler *de facto* who determined the selection of the chief prelate and was instrumental in having him deposed, as in the case of Metropolitan Barlaam under Basil III, or even murdered, as in the case of Metropolitan Philip under Ivan IV.[54]

We do well to remember that Ostrogorsky's analysis proposes the merger of a religious ritual (Procession on the Ass) and a quasi-religious ritual (equerry service), the latter with significant *political* overtones. The Western examples of medieval kings and emperors performing the equerry service

---

[51] *ASob*, v. 4: *1645–1700*, no. 223, pp. 308–309.
[52] Labunka, "Legend," (see n. 9), 245.
[53] *PSRL*, v. 26 (1959), s.a. 1495, p. 326; *ASob* (see n. 51), v. 1: *1294–1598*, no. 184 (6 Feb. 1539), 160–161; no. 264 (20 Feb. 1564), 299–300.
[54] E. Golubinskii, *Istoriia russkoi tserkvi*, 2 vols. in 4 pts. and atlas (Moscow, 1901 [2d ed.], 1904 [2d ed.], 1900, 1910, 1911), v. 2, pt. 1, 648–649.

for the Pope are all associated with a strictly political intent, involving alliances with the Papacy; in the Russian Palm Sunday Ritual the equerry service is incorporated into a *religious* ritual, as Ostrogorsky himself notes,[55] and thus takes on a different significance. The importance of this contextual distinction is what brings us to the alternative analysis mentioned in the introduction.

Iconographic Analysis of the Ritual

What is especially intriguing about the Muscovite Palm Sunday Ritual is that its structure cannot be directly derived from the Gospel accounts of the historical Entry into Jerusalem. Two of the major elements are missing in the New Testament narrative and a third is much less prominent: there are no children and there is no equerry, no person leading Christ into Jerusalem. Furthermore, trees as the sources for branches to spread before Christ are mentioned in passing and fruit is nowhere to be found, odd in light of the apparently major role of the fruit-laden tree in the Ritual.

The inspiration for much of the Ritual is not to be found so much in the Scriptures as in the liturgy and especially in the visualization of the event in Orthodox iconography. Icons of the Entry (see plate 5) for the festival tier of the iconostasis typically depict Christ riding side-saddle on the ass, with children cutting off branches from a fruit-bearing tree, preparing to hail him as the victor. The dominant role of children in the depiction relies on the apocryphal Gospel of Nicodemus. It is children, and not the undifferentiated crowd or multitude, as in the Gospel account, who are typically described spreading garments in the path of Christ, an ancient symbol of an anointed king. The Palm Sunday Ritual in Moscow can be viewed as a dynamic manifestation of the Palm Sunday icon. As a living tableau, the participants become, according to the Byzantine doctrine of images, tangible representations of the intangible. The Ritual provides counterparts of all the roles in the icon—disciples, townspeople, boys in the tree, boys spreading garments in the path of the procession, and the fruit-laden tree itself. The disguised horse represents the ass; the metropolitan, the Savior.[56] In point of fact, the

---

[55] "Zum Stratordienst," (see n. 9), 202–203.

[56] In a letter to Aleksei Mikhailovich dated 30 March 1659, the estranged Patriarch Nikon wrote to complain about Metropolitan Pitirim taking his place in the Muscovite Palm Sunday Ritual, saying that it was terrifying for him as patriarch to represent (*izobrazhat'*) the person of Christ, i.e. to take on the image of God, to be a living icon. See V. M. Zhivov and B. A. Uspenskii, "Tsar' i Bog. Semioticheskie aspekty sakralizatsii monarkha v Rossii," in *Iazyki kul'tury i problemy perevodimosti*, ed. B. A. Uspenskii (Moscow, 1987), 110.

Plate 5. *Entry into Jerusalem*. Obverse of two-sided icon. Novgorod. Cathedral of Holy Sophia. Late fifteenth–early sixteenth c.

only major element in the ritual without a counterpart in the icon or the historical event behind it is the tsar himself. But by juxtaposing himself to the representations of the holy personages, the living tsar is himself provided with an aura of holiness. His singular status is thus enhanced by virtue of a shift of genres, from static icon to dynamic ritual. He is the touchstone of the present that functions to unite the past event with future promise.

The dual reference of Palm Sunday mentioned earlier determines multiple levels of reference for the symbols within the Ritual. Individually and collectively these symbols are capable of multiple meanings.[57] I turn now to the symbols that most directly represent the tsar's image and permit historical as well as eschatological reference. The equerry service provides an appropriate point of departure for the analysis.

The medieval conception of the equerry service described in the *Donation* is illustrated by the thirteenth-century fresco from the Chapel of Saint Sylvester in the Church of the Santissimi Quattro Coronati in Rome (see plate 6). A comparison of the equerry service from the Palm Sunday Ritual with the imagery of imperial submission from the fresco is illuminating. Note that Constantine pulls the Pope's horse by the bridle; the reins remain in the pontiff's hands. The bridle is associated with deference, the reins with authority and control.

It is no small matter that in the Muscovite Palm Sunday Ritual a nobleman performs the equerry service by holding the bridle of the ass. The reins that actually guide the ass are not in the hands of the metropolitan, but rather the tsar, crowned by God as his representative on earth. The moving force of the entire procession is given over to him. The symbolic effective reins of power—*brazdy pravleniia*—have been transferred from the hands of the iconographic Christ to his own. The ambivalence of this image—pulling and leading—would not have been lost on those observing the Ritual. In the famous "Moscow, Third Rome" letter of Monk Philotheus to Ivan's father, Grand Prince Basil III, the ruler of Muscovy is addressed as the Orthodox Christian emperor and lord, holder of the reins (*brozdoderzhateliu*) of all God's churches of the Holy Ecumenical Apostolic Church of the Most Pure Mother of God.[58] Peresvetov's imagery from the "Tale of Magmet-Saltan" is apt as well:

---

[57] See the discussion of the synthetic and analytic properties of ritual symbolism and its ambiguity in David I. Kertzer, *Ritual, Politics, and Power* (New Haven and London, 1988), 11.
[58] V. Malinin, *Starets Eleazarova monastyria Filofei i ego poslaniia. Istoriko-literaturnoe issledovanie* (Kiev, 1901), app. IX, 49–50.

And it is impossible for an emperor to be without awe (*bez grozy*); like a horse under an emperor without a bridle (*bez uzdy*), so is an empire without awe.[59]

The equerry service is therefore ambiguous, uniting within the same symbolic framework the complementary images of the ideal tsar: the acts of pulling and leading are identified with humility and strength. The first two antiphons from the Palm Sunday liturgy cite versicles from Psalms 114 and 115 (115 and 116 in Western reckoning) that illuminate the tsar's humble purpose, modelled after that of King David:

> I am filled with love, for the Lord will hear the voice of my supplication.... I will walk acceptably before the Lord in the land of the living. I believed, and therefore have I spoken: but I was deeply humiliated. What shall I render unto the Lord, for all His benefits unto me? I will take the cup of salvation, and I will call upon the Name of the Lord. I will pay my vows unto the Lord in the presence of all His people.[60]

In time present, the combination of humility and active leadership communicated by the tsar's role in the Palm Sunday Ritual evokes comparison of the "earthy Emperor" with the "Heavenly Emperor," the humble Messiah come to take possession of the flock. One of the common metaphors for Ivan in the apologetic literature and chronicles of his time is that of shepherd, leader of the flock. In this role, Ivan conflated the images of emperor and priest, the secular and the spiritual shepherd. Certainly the comments of Papal legate Possevino in 1581-1582 bear out such intentions on Ivan's part:

> ... each generation of Muscovites is accustomed from childhood to think and speak so highly of the Prince that its members often answer a question by saying: "Only God and Our Great Lord (i.e., the Prince) know this. Our Great Lord knows everything. He can solve all our problems and difficulties with a single word. There is no religion whose ritual and dogma he does not know. All that we have during our entire life we possess through the mercy of the Great Lord." The Prince takes the greatest pains to encourage this view. He wishes to be considered High Priest as well as Emperor, and in the splendour of his attire, his courtiers and his other appurtenances he rivals the Pope and surpasses other kings.[61]

---

[59] *Sochineniia I. Peresvetova*, comp. and annot. A. A. Zimin, ed. D. S. Likhachev (Moscow and Leningrad, 1956), 153.

[60] *The Lenten Triodion* (see n. 13), 502-503.

[61] *The Moscovia of Antonio Possevino, S.J.*, trans. and ed. Hugh F. Graham. UCIS Series in Russian and East European Studies, no. 1 (Pittsburgh, 1977), 47.

Plate 6. *Entrance of Pope Sylvester into Rome* [Emperor Constantine leading the pope's horse]. Fresco. Oratory of St. Sylvester in the Church of the SS. Quattro Coronati, Rome. 1246. From Guglielmo Matthiae, *Pittura romana del Medioevo*, 2d ed., 2 vols. (Rome, 1988), v. 2: *Secoli XI–XIV*, pl. 132. Reproduced with permission.

The image of the tsar as priestly shepherd is marked by a curious detail in the Ritual that has never been given proper attention by scholars. In the seventeenth-century accounts and engravings of the Ritual, the tsar does not pull the reins alone; he is supported under both arms by two of his highest noblemen who flank him as he moves in procession (see plate 7). If we view the Procession on the Ass in more general terms, apart from its place in the Palm Sunday Ritual per se, we are able to understand the full implications of this detail.

By the late fifteenth century the Procession on the Ass became a standard part of the installation ceremony for the Russian metropolitan. It was an overt sign of the connection between these newly installed shepherds and the great first priest or pontiff (*Velikii Pervosviashchennik*) Jesus Christ in his victorious Entry into Jerusalem; but not the only sign. After the celebration of the liturgy during the installation service (apparently used as far back as Hilarion's installation in 1051), the candidate is flanked on both sides by an archbishop and another senior priest or archdeacon. They take him under the arms and

Plate 7. *The Palm Sunday Ritual in Moscow,* 23 March 1662. Detail of plate 3.

lift him up to his throne, all the while singing "Ispolla eti despota" 'May you live many years, O Lord.' This act—performed three times—is a overt sign of his attaining the office of prelate.[62] In the course of certain major ceremonies, such as the ritual Blessing of the Waters on 6 January, the ritual of installation as shepherd is recalled when the metropolitan is led around in like manner. This ritual flanking is an act so definitive in its significance that its use by the tsar is indicative of Ivan's intention to be perceived as the leader of his flock, spiritual as well as secular.

Since the later accounts reproduce so many of the details of the sixteenth-century Ritual in Moscow, the flanking of the tsar may be an original feature. It is also possible, however, that the flanking was introduced in the seventeenth century to emphasize the tsar's role as shepherd of the people. Be that as it may, the image in the present of Tsar Ivan IV as humble shepherd leading the way for Christ to enter Jerusalem, for the Orthodox faithful to achieve salvation, elicits immediate eschatological and historical connections.

---

[62] Nikol'skii, *O sluzhbakh* (see n. 1), 3–5.

The iconography of the Christian Entry into Jerusalem derives from Roman imperial imagery, specifically, the representation of the emperor's triumphant departure (*profectio*) or arrival (*adventus*) into a city. Kantorowicz has shown quite convincingly that the Entry of Christ can be viewed in two ways—as a historical event, where the representation alludes to specific historical circumstances—or as an abstracted, eschatological event, where the representation alludes to the messianic significance of the Entry.[63] In the latter case, the imagery of the mounted Roman emperor led by a winged Victory is transformed into the King of the Jews led by an angel, a precursor mentioned in both the Old and New Testament:

> Exodus 23:20. Behold, I send an Angel before thee, to keep thee in the way, and to bring thee into the place which I have prepared.
>
> Mark 1:2-3. As it is written in the prophets, Behold, I send my messenger before thy face, which shall prepare the way before thee.

In Christian doctrine, this harbinger of the coming of Lord is John the Baptist, the Orthodox John the Forerunner. The liturgical representation of his role is clear, for example, in the Great Vespers service of the Synaxis of Saint John:

> As the lover of the Spirit, the swallow that brings divine tidings of grace, O Forerunner, thou hast clearly made known to mankind the dispensation of the King, who shone forth in brightness from a pure Virgin unto the restoration of men. Thou dost banish the dominion of dark and evil ways, and guidest towards eternal life the hearts of those baptized in repentance, O blessed prophet inspired by God.[64]

Although the historical *adventus* represented by Palm Sunday can be distinguished from the eschatological *adventus* represented by the Second Coming, Kantorowicz notes that occasionally one concept would supersede or even replace the other in medieval thinking. He cites the Muscovite Palm Sunday Ritual as the unique example in which the two images are blended.[65] The reenactment of the Entry presents the historical image; the tsar pulling the ass at the end of a long rein presents the eschatological image. We can flesh out Kantorowicz's observation by noting that in the latter case the tsar can be identified as the harbinger of the Lord, John the Forerunner, who happens to be his own patron saint. Crucial here is that the eschatological image

---

[63] "The 'King's Advent'" (see n. 45), 221ff.
[64] Translation from the Greek by Mother Mary and Archimandrite Kallistos Ware, *The Festal Menaion*, intro. Georges Florovsky (London, 1969), 391–392.
[65] "The 'King's Advent'" (see n. 45), 229.

suspends the facts of history (John the Forerunner was killed before the historical Entry into Jerusalem occurred) to focus on the dynamic tension between the humble precursor and Christ at the Second Coming. For Moscow, which increasingly saw itself as the New Jerusalem, the apocalyptic connotations of the Ritual were a reminder that the Last Judgment might come at any time. The Ritual provided a model of a humble and powerful ruler prepared to lead the Orthodox faithful to salvation at the end of history as well as within it.

In addition to the resonances within the troubled present and the promised future, the image of the tsar also harkened back to the glorious past as a prefiguration of glory in the New Jerusalem. By extending the Procession on the Ass out of the Kremlin onto Red Square to the Church of the Intercession, Ivan was able to manipulate the connection between the eschatological and the historical.

The Cathedral of the Intercession (see plate 8) was built by Ivan to commemorate the momentous victory of Moscow over the Kazan' Tatars in 1552. In the context of an annual Church feast that celebrates a triumphant entry into the holy city of Jerusalem, Ivan's procession to the Jerusalem Chapel of a cathedral dedicated to his victory over the Kazan' infidels recalled that in real life, he too was a victor. He had entered a city of unbelievers—Kazan'—in triumph. And he returned to Moscow, the New Jerusalem, as a victor. According to the Nikon Chronicle, as he approached Moscow following the victory, he was greeted outside the city by the metropolitan, other church dignitaries, and his court as one of the great heroes of Orthodoxy. Following a speech by Metropolitan Macarius, in which the tsar was compared to Constantine the Great, Alexander Nevskii, and Dmitrii Donskoi, the entire entourage fell on their knees before him, shedding tears of joy and gratitude for his victory and safe return. Ivan then removed his military garb, donned his imperial garments, including the holy regalia of Monomakh, and walked *on foot* into Moscow to a tumultuous outpouring of popular exaltation and joy.[66] By walking in a procession from the Cathedral of the Dormition, where he was crowned by God as tsar, to the Jerusalem Chapel of the Intercession, which represented his triumph over Kazan', Ivan was able to commemorate his own conquest, his own Christian victory, his own stake on immortality. The historical and eschatological dimensions of Palm Sunday permitted him to make this commemoration an annual celebration coincident with a movable feast.

[66] *PSRL*, v. 13 (1965), 225–227.

Plate 8. Barma and Postnik. *Church of the Intercession on the Moat.* Northwest elevation. 1555–1561. The Chapel of the Entry into Jerusalem is at the head of the gallery staircase in the foreground.

The specific connections of the tsar with the victory over Kazan' would not have been available to Ivan's successors. Nonetheless, the unique status and charisma of the tsar and the metropolitan/patriarch in Muscovy would always impart to the Palm Sunday Ritual in Moscow an elevated, mystical significance found nowhere else. The proliferation of the Ritual in other dioceses in the mid-seventeenth century prompted the Synod of 1678 to abolish its performance everywhere except the capital, in recognition of the spiritual superiority of the Muscovite Ritual.[67]

> That this ritual . . . for the glory of Christ our Lord and the reverence of [our] most devout Crownbearers ought to be performed only in the capital city of Moscow itself in the presence of the Scepterbearer by the Patriarch himself and not by other Prelates, even with the patriarchy vacant; for it is scarcely fitting that an act to which the Patriarch alone is entitled (*soizvoliaemoe*) should be performed by a lower-ranking Prelate. In yet other cities of the entire Great-Russian State, let not a single Prelate dare to have an ass prepared for procession on it to commemorate the Entry of our Lord into the city of Jerusalem, since neither the Tsar is present, nor does the typikon order it to be done, nor do we find a precedent (model) for that in the piety of the ages (*ni obraza tomu vekov drevnikh vo blagochestii obretaem*).[68]

By the end of the century the iconographic view of the ceremony had given way to a secular one, undoubtedly due in part to the pretensions of Nikon regarding the relative authority of tsar and patriarch. Peter the Great abolished the Ritual in 1697.[69]

Conclusions

The Palm Sunday Ritual and the Epiphany Ritual (Blessing of the Waters) were the most noteworthy major public religious ceremonies in Moscow involving the heads of Church and State in the sixteenth and seventeenth centuries. They share the feature of imperial humility, and for that reason both have been viewed as rituals of imperial *submission*, either to the Church

---

[67] I disagree with Savva, who assumes that the Synod in effect limited the ceremony to Moscow as a way of raising the status of the patriarch (V. Savva, *Moskovskie tsari i vizantiiskie vasilevsy. K voprosu o vliianii Vizantii na obrazovanie idei tsarskoi vlasti moskovskikh gosudarei.* [Kharkov, 1901], 173-174). The role of Christ was limited to the patriarch in Moscow (although the exiled Nikon was replaced by Metropolitan Pitirim, as noted earlier), but the absence of the tsar is given as one of the primary reasons why no prelate should dare to perform the Procession on the Ass outside of Moscow. See Zhivov and Uspenskii, "Tsar' i Bog" (see n. 56), 111.

[68] *ASob* (see n. 51), v. 4, 309.

[69] Nikol'skii, *O sluzhbakh* (see n. 1), 53; Zhivov and Uspenskii, "Tsar' i Bog," (see n. 56), 112-115.

as an institution or to its leader, the metropolitan/patriarch. In the present analysis of the Palm Sunday Ritual, I have argued that the submission hypothesis relies too heavily on the level of immediate performance and ignores the more significant symbolic levels elicited by the Ritual itself as a religious ceremony. Regardless of one's views of the actual person of the tsar—unrestrained autocrat or corporate manager—the image of a submissive tsar, acting out a *subordinate* position twice a year with the court and invited foreign dignitaries in attendance would have served no one's purpose. It was precisely the image of imperial humility that guaranteed a special place for both rituals in the Muscovite calendar.

The Palm Sunday Ritual was unique among cultural artifacts that alluded directly or indirectly to the Apocalypse and the Second Coming. On a recurrent basis one week before the celebration of Christ's Resurrection, the model of the End Times was brought to life in the center of the capital by the most important figures of the realm. As the central participant who stood outside the event depicted, the tsar was able to honor Christ and at the same time emphasize his own role as the shepherd of a flock facing an uncertain apocalyptic future, all the while recalling his heroic Christian accomplishments in the recent past. Palm Sunday gave him an annual opportunity to remind his subjects that the Muscovite tsar, not the deposed Byzantine emperor, would bear the reins of power and, in humble imitation of Christ's earthly ministry, lead Orthodox Christianity to its final destiny.

NOTES ON CONTRIBUTORS

Paul A. Bushkovitch is Associate Professor of History at Yale University. His works include *The Merchants of Moscow, 1580-1650* (1980) and *Religion and Society in Russia: The Sixteenth and Seventeenth Centuries* (1992).

Daniel E. Collins is Assistant Professor of Slavic Languages and Literatures at Ohio State University. He has published articles and reviews on Slavic philology and is currently completing a monograph on the pragmatics of represented speech in Early Russian.

James Cracraft is Professor of History at the University of Illinois at Chicago. He is the author of *The Church Reform of Peter the Great* (1971) and *The Petrine Revolution in Russian Architecture* (1988).

Michael S. Flier is Oleksandr Potebnja Professor of Ukrainian Philology at Harvard University. He is the author of *Aspects of Nominal Determination in Old Church Slavic* (1974) and the co-editor (with Henrik Birnbaum) of *Medieval Russian Culture* (1984). His research interests include medieval East Slavic culture and Slavic linguistics.

Norman W. Ingham is Professor of Slavic Languages and Literatures at the University of Chicago. He is the author of *E. T. A. Hoffmann's Reception in Russia* (1974) and has done extensive research in early Slavic civilization with special emphasis on the cultural ties between Old Rus' and Bohemia.

Boris M. Kloss is Senior Researcher in the Institute of Russian History of the Russian Academy of Sciences, Moscow. His works include *Nikonovskij svod i russkie letopisi XVI-XVII vekov* (1980).

Nancy S. Kollmann is Professor of History at Stanford University. She is the author of *Kinship and Politics: The Making of the Muscovite Political System, 1345–1547* (1987).

Jakov S. Luria is Senior Researcher in the Institute of Russian Literature of the Russian Academy of Sciences, St. Petersburg. He is the author of *Ideologičeskaja bor'ba v russkoj publicistike konca XV–načala XVI veka* (1960), *Obščerusskie letopisi XIV-XV vv.* (1976), and *Russkie sovremenniki Vozroždenija. Knigopisec Efrosin, d'ak Kuricyn* (1988).

Eduard Mühle is head of the Central and Eastern European Department for the Conference of Rectors and Presidents of German Universities and Higher Educational Institutions in Bonn, and a specialist in medieval East Slavic archaeology and history. His works include *Die städtischen Handelszentren der nordwestlichen Ruś* (1991).

Hugh M. Olmsted is Slavic Specialist, Research Services, at the Harvard College Library. His fields of specialization include Russian archaeography and the works of Maksim Grek.

Richard Pope is Professor of Slavic Languages and Literatures at York University near Toronto. He is the author of *The Literary History of the Kievan Caves Patericon up to 1500* (1970) and co-editor (with Daniel Armstrong and C. H. van Schooneveld) of *The Old Church Slavonic Translation of the Ἀνδρῶν ἁγίων Βίβλος* in the edition of Nikolaas van Wijk (1975).

Daniel Rowland is Associate Professor of History at the University of Kentucky. He is the author of *Mannerism—Style and Mood: An Anatomy of Four Works and Three Art Forms* (1964). His fields of specialization include Russian political thought and culture of the sixteenth and seventeenth centuries.

Olga Strakhov holds the equivalent of a C.Phil. degree from Moscow State University. She has published articles and reviews on East Slavic philology and is currently writing a book-length study on the Greek philological tradition in Russia in the late-seventeenth–early-eighteenth centuries.

William R. Veder holds the Chair of Slavic Philology at the University of Amsterdam. His works include *The Scaliger Paterikon* (1976) and, together with Anatolij A. Turilov, *The Edificatory Prose of Kievan Rus'* (1994).

PARTICIPANTS IN THE FIRST SUMMER WORKSHOP ON MEDIEVAL EAST SLAVIC CULTURE

UCLA, 2–7 JUNE 1990

Henrik Birnbaum (UCLA)
Paul A. Bushkovitch (Yale)
Daniel E. Collins (Ohio State)
James Cracraft (Illinois at Chicago)
Robert O. Crummey (UC, Davis)
Michael S. Flier (Harvard)
Christian Hannick (Trier)
Paul Hollingsworth (Falls Church, Va.)
Norman W. Ingham (Chicago)
Edward L. Keenan (Harvard)
Michael Khodarkovsky (Chicago)
Valerie Kivelson (Michigan)
Boris M. Kloss (Moscow)
Nancy S. Kollmann (Stanford)

Gail Lenhoff (UCLA)
Jakov S. Luria (St. Petersburg)
Robert Mathiesen (Brown)
Georg Michels (Harvard)
Eduard Mühle (Bonn)
Hugh M. Olmsted (Harvard)
Donald Ostrowski (Harvard)
Richard Pope (York, Toronto)
Daniel Rowland (Kentucky)
Nancy Ševčenko (Cambridge, Mass.)
Olga Strakhov (Cambridge, Mass.)
Nina Ulff-Møller (Copenhagen)
William R. Veder (Amsterdam)
Daniel C. Waugh (Washington)

NAME INDEX

Abelard, Peter 20
Abraham 104, 188, 196, 197
Adašev, Aleksej 163
Afanasij, monk 38
Afanasij (Jaroslav-Afanasij)
  Vladimirovič, Prince 68, 69n
Agapetus, Archdeacon 36, 36n, 37n,
  38n, 39, 39n, 41, 42, 42n, 167n
Aksak, Temir 72
Aleksandr Nevskij 138, 139n, 141,
  141n, 142, 142n, 156, 156b, 174n,
  189, 191, 192, 193, 196, 239
Aleksandr Svirskij 37, 137, 137n, 144,
  157
Alexander II, Tsar 164n, 170n
Aleksej Mixajlovič, Tsar 43, 95, 171n,
  195n, 232n
Aleksij, Hegumen 37, 38
Aleksij, the Miracleworker, Metro-
  politan 69, 69n, 94n, 95n, 96, 96n,
  97, 97n, 98, 98n, 102, 102n, 103,
  103n, 104, 104n, 105, 105n, 167n,
  179
Alexius, Metropolitan, see Aleksij,
  Metropolitan
Anastasija, Princess (wife of Prince
  Jurij Dmitrievič) 60
Anastasija, Princess (wife of Prince
  Konstantin Dmitrievič) 60
Anastasija Romanovna, Tsaritsa 163,
  163n, 173
Andrej (military saint), see Andrew
  Stratelatos, Saint
Andrej-Afanasij, Metropolitan 138n
Andrej Dmitrievič, Grand Prince 68,
  69n, 147
Andrej Rostovskij, Prince 69
Andrej Starickij, Prince 43
Andrew Stratelatos, Saint 189
Andronicus II, Emperor 67, 68
Anna, debtor 86
Anna Ivanovna (daughter of Ivan IV),
  Princess 171n, 174
Anthony of Egypt, Saint 136n

Antiochus Monachus 22, 24, 103n
Antonij Rimljanin 138, 138n, 142, 144,
  145
Antonius IV, Patriarch 68, 69n
Arsenij, Bishop 72
Arsenius, see Arsenij
Asgut 82, 82n
Avraamij of Smolensk, see Avraamij
  Smolenskij
Avraamij Smolenskij 138, 138n, 139n,
  141
Axmulov 67, 67n

Barlaam, Metropolitan, see Varlaam,
  Metropolitan
Barma 240
Barrabas 105
Basil, Saint, see Vasilij Blažennyj
Basil III, see Vasilij III, Grand Prince
Basmanov, Aleksej 40
Batu (Batyj), Khan 52
Behr, Martin, see Bussov, Konrad
Benjamin, priest 226
Berengar 20
Bojan 82, 82n
Boreckaja, Marfa 54
Boreckij, Isak 54
Boris, Saint 15, 173, 187, 188, 189,
  191, 193, 197, 198n, 205
Buchau, Daniel von, Prince 215, 215n
Bulgakov, Jurij Mixajlovič, Prince,
  Governor 220
Bussov, Konrad 213n, 216n

Callistus, Patriarch 67, 68
Cervantes 10
Collins, Samuel 215n
Constantine the Great, Emperor 187,
  191, 225, 228, 229, 230, 234, 236, 239
Cornelius, see Kornilij
Cyprian, Metropolitan, see Kiprian,
  Metropolitan
Cyril of White Lake (Beloozero), see
  Kirill Belozerskij, Hegumen

Cyril of Turov, see Kirill Turovskij, Bishop
Čeljadnina, Agrafena 172

Daniel, prophet 186, 187, 188, 196
Daniil of Perejaslavl', see Daniil Perejaslavskij
Daniil Perejaslavskij 138, 141, 141n, 144, 144n, 145, 145n
Daniil Zatočnik 26
Danešinica 83
Dan'ša 81, 81n
Dante 10
David, King 39, 187, 188, 190, 196, 197, 235
Demetrius of Thessalonica, Saint 189
Denisov, Andrej 119
Dimitrij, see Dmitrij
Dmitrij (military saint), see Demetrius of Thessalonica, Saint
Dmitrij the Greek 226n
Dmitrij the Small, see Gerasimov, Dmitrij
Dmitrij the Translator 226n
Dmitrij Ivanovič (grandson of Ivan III), Prince 222, 223
Dmitrij Ivanovič (son of Ivan IV), Prince 174
Dmitrij Ivanovič Donskoj, Grand Prince 52, 65, 68, 68n, 69, 69n, 71, 72, 152, 152n, 153, 154, 156, 187, 239
Dmitrij Konstantinovič, Grand Prince 71
Dmitrij Mixajlovič, Grand Prince 68
Dionisij, Metropolitan 34n
Dionisij, icon-painter 193
Dionisij, monk 70
Dobromysl 82, 82n
Dobrovit 82, 82n
Dobrožir 82, 82n
Dorotheus, Patriarch 68, 69n
Dovmont 138, 139n, 141, 141n, 146, 146n
Drozd 82, 82n
Družina-Osor'in, Kalistrat 141n
Dumin, Iona, Archbishop 113, 113n, 115, 118, 118n, 121, 122, 141, 141n, 142

Edigej 51, 57, 61

Edward I, King 185
Efrem, monk 139n
Egeria 224n
Elena, Princess 222, 223
Epifanij Premudryj 58, 59, 59n, 60, 61, 62, 63, 64, 65, 66, 67, 68, 69, 70, 71, 72, 137, 137n, 140n, 144n, 145n, 146, 146n
Epifanij Slavineckij 94, 94n, 95, 95n, 96, 97, 100, 101, 102, 103n, 106
Epiphanius of Cyprus, Saint 61, 62
Epiphanius the Wise, see Epifanij Premudryj
Ermak 193, 198, 208
Ermogen, Patriarch 33
Eudocia, see Evdokija
Evaristos the Studite 136n
Evdokija (daughter of Ivan III), Princess 223
Evdokija Ivanovna (daughter of Ivan IV), Princess 171n
Evfimij Čudovskij 94n, 96, 97, 98, 98n, 99, 100,101, 102, 103n
Evfimij Novgorodskij 156, 156n
Evfrosin of Pskov, Hegumen 137, 137n, 147
Evfrosinija of Polock, see Evfrosinija Polockaja
Evfrosinija Polockaja 141, 141n
Evstafij, priest 38

Fedor, debtor 86, 86n
Fedor Černyj (Rostislavič) Jaroslavskij 154, 154n, 155, 155n, 156
Fedor Ivanovič (son of Ivan IV), Tsar 171n, 194
Fedor of Jaroslavl', see Fedor Černyj (Rostislavič) Jaroslavskij
Feodora (daughter of Ivan III), Princess 223
Feodosij, Archbishop 38
Feodosij, Archimandrite 33, 40
Feodosij, icon-painter 193, 193n
Feodosij Pečerskij, Saint 12, 13, 14, 136, 137, 137n, 139, 139n, 142n, 143, 143n, 144, 145, 157
Feognost, Metropolitan 68
Ferapont 173
Fevronija, Saint 177
Filipp, Metropolitan 32, 32n, 33, 33n, 34, 34n, 35, 35n, 36, 36n, 37, 37n,

38, 38n, 39, 39n, 40, 40n, 41, 41n,
42, 42n, 43, 44, 44n, 45, 45n, 46,
46n, 231
Filofej, monk 31, 31n, 234, 234n
Firsov, Gerasim 33n, 44n, 45n, 46n
Fletcher, Giles 215n
Fotij, Metropolitan 52, 59, 72

Gennadij, Archbishop 220, 224n, 225, 225n, 226
Gennadius, Archbishop, see Gennadij, Archbishop
George, Saint 189, 193
Gerasim, Metropolitan 53
Gerasimov, Dmitrij 226, 226n,
Gerasimus, metropolitan's emissary 67
German, Archbishop 38
Gerontij, Metropolitan 157, 157n
Gideon 188, 194, 196, 212
Gleb, Saint 15, 173, 187, 188, 189, 191, 193, 197, 198n, 205
Gleb Jur'evič, Prince 150
Godunov, Boris Fedorovič, Tsar 34n, 113, 195
Gregory of Nazianzus, the Theologian, Saint 21, 103n
Gundarov, Andrej 213n

Hakluyt, Richard 215n, 216n, 228n
Herberstein, Sigmund von 222, 222n
Hesychius of Jerusalem 22, 24
Hezekiah, King 188, 196, 203
Hilarion, see Ilarion, Metropolitan
Homer 10

Igor' Jaroslavič 151, 152n
Il'ja (Elias), cellarer 64
Ilarion, Metropolitan 16, 19, 236
Innokentij, Hegumen 139, 139n, 141, 142, 147, 148, 157, 158
Ioann Novgorodskij 138, 139n, 146
Ioann of Novgorod, see Ioann Novgorodskij
Ioann Zlatoust, see John Chrysostom, Saint
Ioasaf, Patriarch 142n, 167n, 170n, 171n, 177n
Iona, Metropolitan 52, 53, 53n, 156
Iona, monk 37
Iona Novgorodskij, Archbishop 137, 137n, 147

Iona of Novgorod, see Iona Novgorodskij
Iosif of Volokolamsk, see Iosif Volockij, Hegumen
Iosif Volockij, Hegumen 137, 137n, 144, 147, 169, 195, 195n
Iov, Patriarch 113
Irodion, Hegumen 137n, 144, 144n
Isaiah, see Isaja, hieromonk
Isaja, hieromonk 144, 144n
Isak, monk 65
Isidor, Metropolitan 53, 53n
Ivan, debtor 83
Ivan Ivanovič, Prince (son of Ivan III) 157, 157n
Ivan Ivanovič, Prince (son of Ivan IV) 171n
Ivan Vasil'evič, Prince (son of Vasilij II) 167n
Ivan Vladimirovič, Prince 68, 69n
Ivan Jaroslavskij, Prince 69, 69n
Ivan of Yaroslavl', see Ivan Jaroslavskij, Prince
Ivan I (Ivan Danilovich), Kalita, Grand Prince 68, 69, 151n
Ivan II (Ivan Ivanovič), Grand Prince 154n
Ivan III (Ivan Vasil'evič), Grand Prince 31n, 53, 54, 55, 55n, 56, 154, 154n, 157, 157n, 166, 166n, 167, 170, 176, 222, 223, 227, 231
Ivan IV (Ivan Vasil'evič), the Terrible (Groznyj), Tsar 34, 35, 36, 36n, 37, 37n, 38, 39, 39n, 40, 40n, 41, 41n, 42, 43, 44, 45, 154n, 163, 164, 166, 167n, 171, 171n, 172, 173, 174, 175, 176,177, 178, 179, 185, 186, 187, 189, 194, 194n, 196n, 197, 215, 218, 218n, 228, 229n, 231, 234, 235, 237, 239, 241
Ivirit, Dionisij 101
Izjaslav Jaroslavič, Grand Prince 151, 152n

Jakov, Hegumen 41, 41n, 45n
Jareševic 83
Jaroslav Vladimirovič, Mudryj, Grand Prince 151, 193
Jaroškov 82, 82n
Jenkinson, Anthony 214, 215, 215n, 216n, 222

Jeremias, Patriarch 34n
John Chrysostom, Saint 94n, 95n, 96, 96n, 100, 101n, 102, 102n, 103, 103n, 104, 104n, 105, 105n, 107n, 132
John Climacus, Saint 23
John the Baptist, Saint, see John the Forerunner, Saint
John the Forerunner, Saint 230, 238, 239
John the Evangelist, Saint 39, 99, 100, 101n, 103, 103n, 104, 104n, 105, 105n, 108n
John the Theologian, see John the Evangelist, Saint
John V, Emperor 68, 68n
Joseph 194
Joseph Volockij, see Iosif Volockij
Joshua 188, 192, 193, 194, 196, 197, 201, 202, 206, 207, 210
Jurij, creditor 85n, 86
Jurij Dmitrievic (Galickij), Prince, Grand Prince 51, 52, 60, 64, 68, 69n
Jurij Vasil'evič, son of Grand Prince Vasilij I 68, 69n
Jurij Vasil'evič, Prince 37n

Kiprian, Metropolitan 59, 64, 68, 69n
Kirik, monk 84
Kirill, monk, friend of Epifanij Premudryj 61
Kirill Belozerskij, Hegumen 50, 140, 141, 142, 144, 147, 156, 168, 173, 175
Kirill of Beloozero, see Kirill Belozerskij, Hegumen
Kirill Turovskij, Bishop 13, 13n, 16
Klimjata 86, 86n
Kolyčev, Fëdor, see Filipp, Metropolitan
Kolyčev, Grigorij Ivanovič 40n
Kolyčev, Mixail Dmitrievič 33
Kolyčev-Xromoj, Mixail Ivanovič 41, 41n
Kolyčev, Stefan 37, 37n
Kolyčev, Varvara 37
Konstantin Dmitrievič, Prince 60, 68, 69n
Kornilij, Hegumen 173
Kornilij (Kornelij), Metropolitan 138n
Kosnjatin 86, 86n

Kotošixin, Grigorij 171n
Kruse, Elert 34, 34n, 35n, 36, 37n
Ksenja, Princess 60
Kubenskij, I. I., Prince 172
Kurbskij, Andrej, Prince 39n, 40n, 43, 44, 44n, 101

Lazarus 219
Leo, Emperor 187
Leontii, Hegumen 64
Leontii, hieromonk 144, 144n
Leontius, see Leontii, Hegumen
Luke, the Evangelist, Saint 99, 100, 102, 103, 103n

Macarius, see Makarij, Metropolitan
Magmet-Saltan 234
Makarij, Archbishop, Metropolitan 35, 38, 144, 144n, 167n, 178, 188, 190, 194, 197, 224, 228, 229n, 231, 239
Maksim Grek xiv, 30, 96, 96n, 100, 100n, 101, 101n, 102, 104, 104n, 106, 107, 107n, 108, 108n, 109, 109n, 110, 110n, 111, 111n, 112, 113, 113n, 118, 118n, 119n, 121, 121n, 122, 122n, 125, 125n, 128, 128n, 129, 129n, 131, 132
Mamaj 51, 68, 68n, 69, 69n
Manuel II, Paleologus, Emperor 68, 69n
Marija, Dowager, Grand Princess 157
Marija Ivanovna (daughter of Ivan IV), Princess 171n
Mark, the Evangelist, Saint 96n, 98, 99, 100, 238
Mark, Patriarch 68, 69n
Martirij of Zelenaja Pustynja 138, 138n, 141, 145
Mary of Egypt, Saint 62
Mat[v]ej 85n, 86
Mat[v]ejka 84, 85, 85n
Matthew, the Apostle, Saint 37, 94n, 95n, 99, 100, 101, 102, 102n, 103n, 108n, 230
Medvedev, Sil'vestr 94n
Methodius, Saint 27
Meyerberg, Augustin, Baron 217, 218
Michael, Archangel 167n, 184, 185n, 186, 187, 188, 189, 190, 191, 191n, 192, 192n, 193, 194, 195, 196, 197,

198, 201, 202, 203, 206, 207, 208, 211, 212, 216, 228
Mixail, Prince 157
Mixail Aleksandrovič (Tverskoj), Grand Prince 69, 69n, 72, 152, 156, 157
Mixail Klopskij 138, 138n, 142, 142n, 143, 156, 156n
Mixail Olel'kovič, Prince 54, 55
Mixail Rusalka 227
Molière 10
Moses 104, 104n, 194, 196, 197, 211
Mstislav Izjaslavič, Prince 150
Mstislav Vasil'kovič, Prince 149, 150

Negorad 82, 82n
Nesdič 82, 82n
Nestor, monk 12, 14, 137n, 139n
Nežek Prožnevič 82, 82n
Nicholas, Saint 172, 228, 231
Nicholas the Elder, Saint 41
Nicodemus 232
Nifont Novgorodskij 141, 141n
Nifont of Novgorod, see Nifont Novgorodskij
Nikanor, Saint 40
Nikita, Bishop 138n
Nikodim, hieromonk 144, 144n
Nikola of Zaraisk, see Nikola Zaraiskij
Nikola Zaraiskij 171, 175
Nikolaj, see Nicholas, Saint
Nikon, Patriarch 29, 32, 34, 43, 45, 46, 48, 49, 50, 51, 106, 157, 166, 167n, 174n, 179, 179n, 232n, 239, 241, 241n
Nikon of Radonež, see Nikon Radonežskij
Nikon Radonežskij 99n, 137n, 140n, 146n
Nilus, Patriarch 68, 69n
Nilus of Salonika 98
Nustuj 81, 81n

Obnorskij, Pavel 173
Olearius, Adam 215n, 217, 218
Oleg Rjazanskij, Prince 65, 65n, 69, 69n
Oleg of Rjazan', see Oleg Rjazanskij, Prince
Olgerd, Prince 70
Olisej 82, 82n
Olisej Grečin, priest 89, 90
Osokin, Ioannikij 128

Osor'ina, Julianija 141, 141n, 156
Ostromir, Posadnik 103n
Ozbjak 68

Pachomius the Serb, see Paxomij Logofet
Pafnutij, Bishop 38, 40
Pafnutij Borovskij, monk 139, 139n, 140n, 141, 141n, 142, 148, 148n, 157, 157n, 158, 169
Pafnutij of Borovsk, see Pafnutij Borovskij, monk
Paisij, Hegumen 40
Paleologue, Sophia (Zoë), see Sophia Paleologue, Grand Princess
Pantoleon, deacon 191n
Parmen, Saint 40
Paul, Metropolitan 95
Paul, metropolitan's emissary 67
Paxomij Logofet 59, 137n, 138n, 139n, 140, 140n, 141, 141n, 144n, 146, 146n, 147n, 156n
Paxomij Serb, see Paxomij Logofet
Penkov, I. D., Prince 172
Pepin the Short, King 225
Peresvetov, Ivan 167n, 234, 235n
Peter, debtor 81, 81n
Peter, the Apostle, Saint 225, 228, 229, 231
Peter of Murom, Saint, see Petr Muromskij, Saint
Peter, Archbishop, Metropolitan 68, 167n
Petr Muromskij, Saint 177
Peter I, the Great, Emperor xvi, xix, 19, 20, 241
Petr Dmitrievič, Prince 65, 68, 69n
Petrovskij, Ivan, Archimandrite 70
Philip, Metropolitan, see Filipp, Metropolitan
Philotheus, monk, see Filofej, monk
Philotheus (Kokkinos), Patriarch 68, 68n
Photius, Metropolitan, see Fotij, Metropolitan
Pimen of the Kievan Caves, see Pimen Pečerskij
Pimen Pečerskij 156
Pimin, Archbishop 38, 39, 40, 45n
Pitirim, Metropolitan, Patriarch 95, 232n, 241n

Platon, Metropolitan 97
Pogoščani 82, 82n
Porrée, Gilbert de la 20
Possevino, Antonio 215n, 235, 235n
Postnik 240
Proxor, Saint 40
Prus 84, 85, 85n

Quintillian 136n

Rjurik, Prince 57
Roland 198
Rožnet 81, 81n
Rublev, Andrej 9

Samuel, King 188
Sanin, Iosif, see Iosif Volockij,
    Hegumen
Sanin, Vassian, Archbishop 140, 140n,
    141, 142, 157, 157n
Savonarola 118n, 129n
Savva Černyj, Bishop 137n
Savvatij, monk 37
Selivan, monk 100, 101, 101n, 108n
Semen Olel'kovič, Prince 54
Sennacherib, King 188, 192
Sergej, see Sergij
Sergij Aleksandrovič, Grand Prince
    187n
Sergij of Radonež, see Sergij
    Radonežskij
Sergij Radonežskij, Saint, Hegumen 31,
    51, 58, 59, 60, 62, 63, 64, 64n, 65,
    65n, 66, 66n, 67, 69, 70, 71, 121,
    121n, 137, 137n, 140n, 141n, 144,
    144n, 146, 146n, 167, 169, 170,
    171, 171n, 172, 173, 174, 175, 187n
Sergius, see Sergij
Shakespeare 10
Shemjaka, Dmitrij, Grand Prince 51,
    52, 53, 55
Sil'vestr, priest 163
Simeon, Tsar 21, 24
Simeon Ivanovič, Grand Prince 151n
Simeon Polockij 94n
Simeon Vladimirovič, Prince 68, 69n
Simon, Metropolitan 222, 223
Sirom 82, 82n
Skuratov, Maljuta 39, 41
Sofija, Grand Princess, see Sophia
    Paleologue, Grand Princess

Solomon, King 187, 188, 197
Sophia Paleologue, Grand Princess 53,
    157, 167, 223
Spiridon, Archbishop 191
Spirok 84, 85, 85n
Staden, Heinrich von 34, 34n, 215,
    215n
Stefan, monk of the Kievan Caves
    Monastery 137n, 143, 143n
Stefan Permskij, Saint, Bishop 58, 59,
    59n, 63, 68, 69, 70, 71, 145, 145n
Stephen of Perm', Saint, Bishop, see
    Stefan Permskij, Saint, Bishop
Stephen II, Pope 225
Steuco, Agostino 180n
Stojan 81, 81n
Svjatopolk, Prince 193
Svjatoslav Jaroslavič, Prince 21, 151,
    152n
Sylvester, Pope, Saint 225, 228, 229,
    234, 236
Sylvester, priest, see Sil'vestr, priest
Šelonin, Sergej 33, 46n
Šujskij, Ivan, boyar 172
Šujskij, Ivan Mixajlovič, Prince,
    Governor 220
Šujskij, Petr, Prince 119n
Šujskij, V. V., Prince 172

Tamerlane 69, 69n
Taube, Johann 34, 34n, 35n, 36, 37n
Telepnev-Obolenskij, I. F., Prince 172
Temir Kutlui, see Tamerlane
Temkin-Rostovskij, Vasilij, Prince 40,
    40n
Theodora, see Feodora
Theodore Stratelatos, Saint 189
Theodosius, see Feodosij Pečerskij,
    Saint
Theognost, Metropolitan, see
    Feognost, Metropolitan
Theophanes the Greek 61
Therapontus, see Ferapont
Toxtamyš, Khan 69, 69n, 72
Trachaniotes, Dmitrij 226
Trivolis, Michael, see Maksim Grek
Turpin, Archbishop 198
Tušueviv 83

Ušakov, Simon 194n, 195

Varlaam, Metropolitan 231
Varlaam of Xutyn', see Varlaam Xutynskij
Varlaam Xutynskij 138, 138n, 157, 157n
Vasilij Davidovič 155, 155n
Vasilij Blažennyj 166, 216
Vasilij Grjaznoj 39
Vasilij Jur'evič (nephew of Ivan IV), Prince 171n
Vasilij I (Vasilij Dmitrievič), Grand Prince 51, 57, 68, 69n, 153n, 154, 154n
Vasilij II, the Blind (Temnyj), Grand Prince 51, 52, 52n, 54, 167, 167n, 176
Vasilij III (Vasilij Ivanovič), Grand Prince 31, 37, 38, 42, 44, 167, 170, 171, 193, 222, 223, 231, 234
Vasilij-Varlaam, priest 137n, 141, 141n, 142, 156n
Vasilij Vladimirovič, Prince 68, 69n
Vasilisa, Princess 67, 70
Vassian, Archbishop 55, 56
Virgil 10
Viskovatyj, Ivan 185, 194, 194n
Vitovt Kestutievič, Grand Prince 68, 69n
Vjačeslav Jaroslavič, Prince 151, 152n
Vladimir Andreevič, Prince 63, 64n, 68, 69n

Vladimir Andreevič of Starica, see Vladimir Andreevič Starickij, Prince
Vladimir Andreevič Starickij, Prince 174, 175
Vladimir Monomax, Grand Prince 150, 191n, 194, 239
Vladimir Svjatoslavič, Saint, Grand Prince 146, 147n, 187, 189, 193, 197, 205
Vlot'ko 81, 81n
Vojeslav 86, 86n
Volodimir Vasil'kovič, Prince 149, 150
Vsevolod Jaroslavič, Prince 151, 152
Vysockij, Anafasij, monk 64

Warenne, Earl of 185

Xarlampij, Hegumen 147
Xomun 82, 82n
Xripan 82, 82n

Zavid 82, 82n
Zlatoust, see John Chrysostom, Saint
Zobninovskij, Dionisij, Archimandrite 119, 125, 129, 130
Zosima, monk 37
Zosima Soloveckij 54
Žirovit 81, 81n
Žitobud 82, 82n
Životek 82, 82n

Compositor: Berkeley Slavic Specialties
Text: 10/13 Monotype Times New Roman
Display: Monotype Times New Roman

www.ingramcontent.com/pod-product-compliance
Lightning Source LLC
Chambersburg PA
CBHW021659230426
43668CB00008B/665